FEEDING GROUND

LANG ✦ LAPINSKI ✦ MANGUN

ARCHAIA ENTERTAINMENT LLC
WWW.ARCHAIA.COM

FEEDING GROUND™

created and story by

SWIFTY LANG
script

MICHAEL LAPINSKI
art/colors

CHRIS MANGUN
production design/letters

translation by
NATHALIA RUIZ MURRAY

edited by
PAUL MORRISSEY

production design
SCOTT NEWMAN

cover art/book design
MICHAEL LAPINSKI

ARCHAIA™
NEW STORIES. NEW WORLDS.

Published by **Archaia**

Archaia Entertainment LLC
1680 Vine Street, Suite 912
Los Angeles, California, 90028, USA
www.archaia.com

FEEDING GROUND English Edition Hardcover. September 2011. FIRST PRINTING

10 9 8 7 6 5 4 3 2 1

ISBN: 1-936393-02-6
ISBN 13: 978-1-936393-02-2

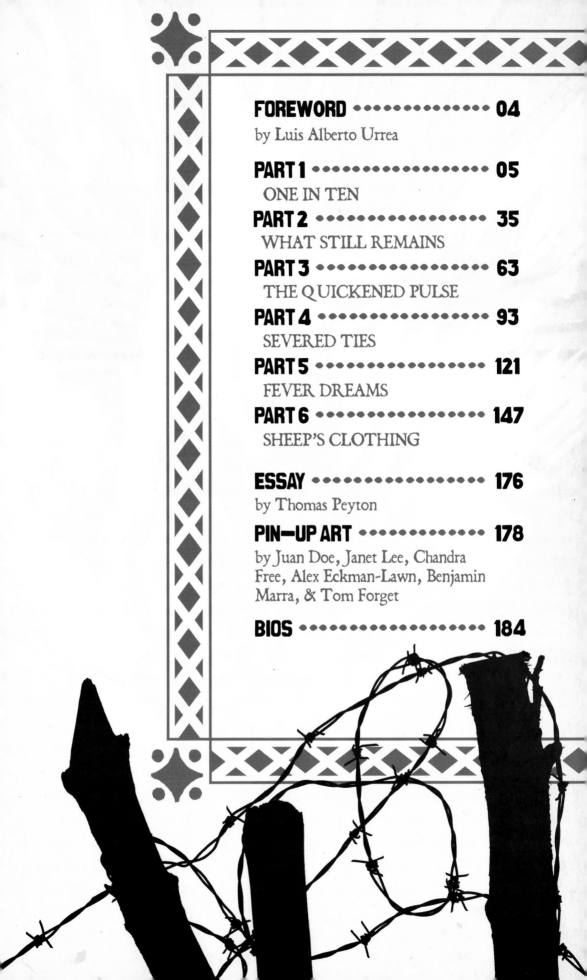

FEEDING GROUNDS
❧OF THE ELDER GODS❧

BY LUIS ALBERTO URREA

As a writer, I am repeatedly confronted with the same question: What are the most Influential books in your life? I always want to answer: Armadillo Comix #2 by Jim Franklin. You see, I came to writing through drawing. As much as my dad hated it, Batman and Hawkman fueled visions that later remained in my prose; unspeakable visions, spoken. I'd love to see how many of us in the writing trade owe our "cinematic" styles to early comics and graphic novels.

As huge as the craft has become, comic books retain enough outsider, underground cachet to tackle subjects many of us wouldn't dare touch -- not in polite company, not at Tea Party rallies. One shouldn't approach such vile, filthy subject matter as the worth of a human life, the dignity of a human soul, or the value of, as Bob Dylan once sang, "these children that you spit on." I'm talkin' to you, Mr. Politician.

And, here is a series of books that leaps deep into the brilliant heart of darkness: the damned (in every sense) and glorious border. The place I write about. The place where I was born.

Swifty Lang and I share an interest in the exquisite horror and beauty of the wastelands through which the undocu-mented wanderers must struggle. It is a formidable region of unforgiving landscape and gods who rule with little mercy. In my book, THE DEVIL'S HIGHWAY, I stated that we are all aliens in this landscape, what I call "Desolation." For fans of the occult, this comes from The Book of Enoch. Yeah, the lands wherein the fallen Watchers and their earth spawn, The Nephilim, are chained beneath the burning desert mountains. They wait to return for their revenge.

How stunned and delighted was I when these amazing comics arrived in my mailbox. As all great graphic novels do, these books create a literary work of searing poetry and awe. The art allows us to see things we might not be able to—or

want to—imagine for ourselves. That my work has had even a little to do with the genesis of this epic is as cool as it gets. I laugh out loud in appreciation when I see the smugglers (Coyotes) and The Devil's Highway itself, the sly gangsters come alive, as if they had jumped out of my book. But I don't laugh because it's funny. No. I'm whistling past the graveyard, amigos. This shit's scary.

What Feeding Ground has envisioned and what Lang, Lapinski and Mangun have captured, is the eldritch nature of this new myth. The darkness at the heart of the sun-baked killing fields. There is something...other about it. There is something from our deep nightmares lurking there. Yes, there is a relentless toll of suffering and death to go with the realistic adventure and thrills and violent action. That is a given—every border-book ever written deals with it. However, Border Patrol agents know, DEA agents know, the medicine people of those canyons and dunes know that something...other...lurks.

I'm trying to capture this Lovecraftian feeling in my own work. Yeah, a little pissed that Swifty et al have done it first, and done it so well. This sensation is what the philosophers call "the sublime" in art. It is beauty, but it is also terror. It's a higher horror: a sense of the eternal, the dark, the overwhelming. This epic is so addictive that it will lure you into a deep redrock canyon where the worst dream awaits. It's so bad; it's so pretty. It's a festival of wonder that shows you the true awe of awful death.

Luis Alberto Urrea
Chicago, 2011

LUIS ALBERTO URREA *is the award-winning novelist and non-fiction author of such work as ACROSS THE WIRE: LIFE AND HARD TIMES ON THE MEXICAN BORDER and THE DEVIL'S HIGHWAY, finalist for the 2005 Pulitzer Prize for general nonfiction.*

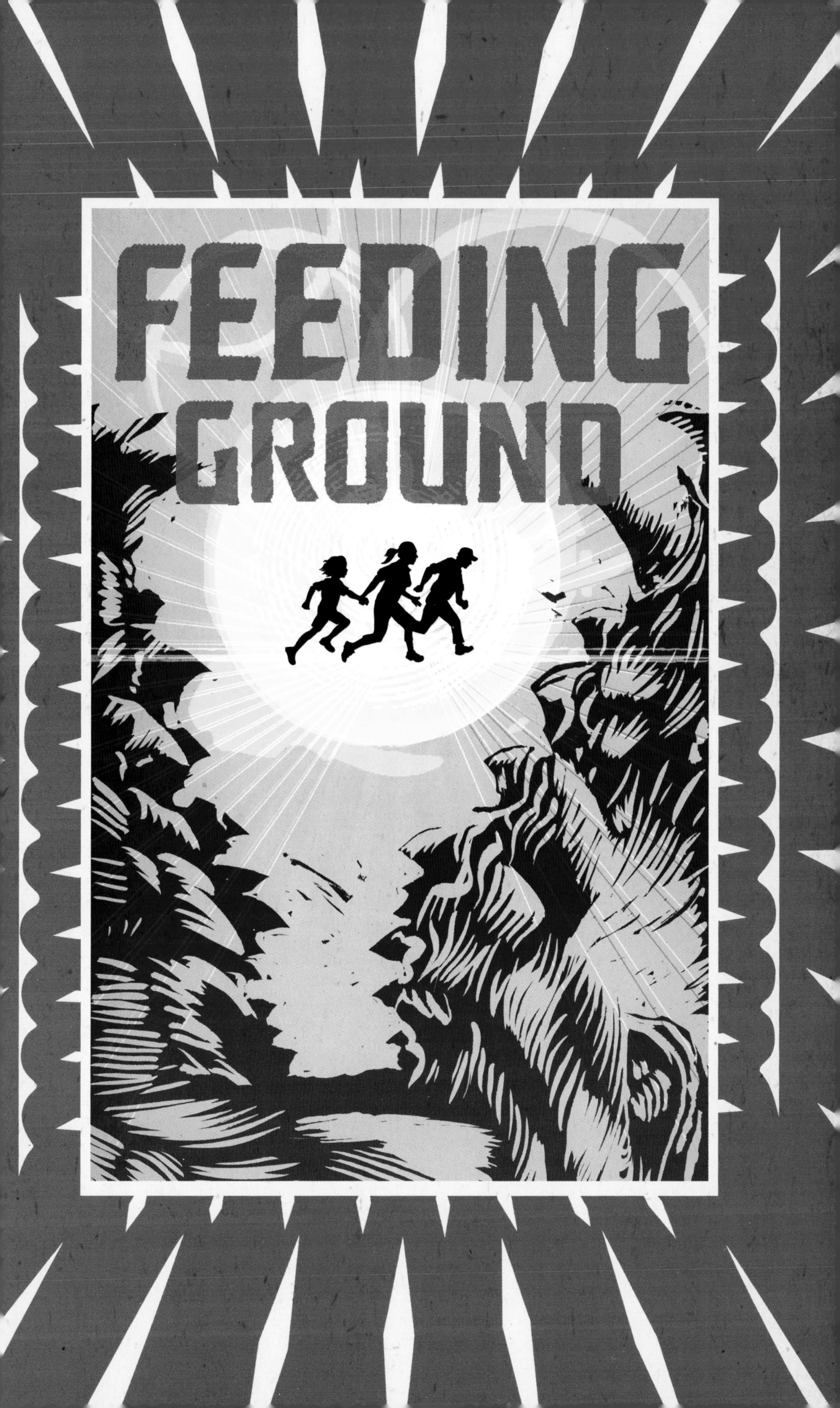
FEEDING
GROUND

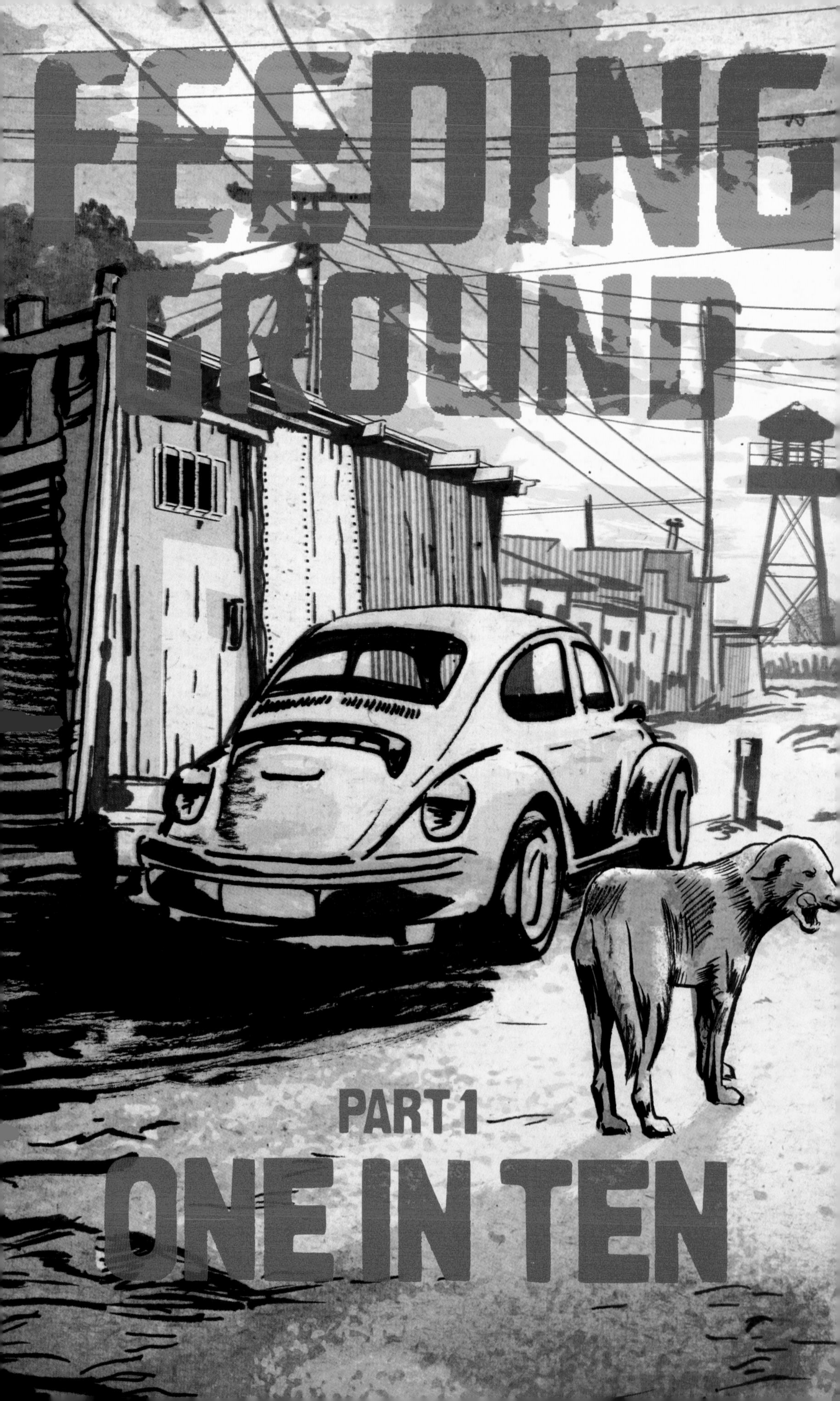
FEEDING
GROUND
PART 1
ONE IN TEN

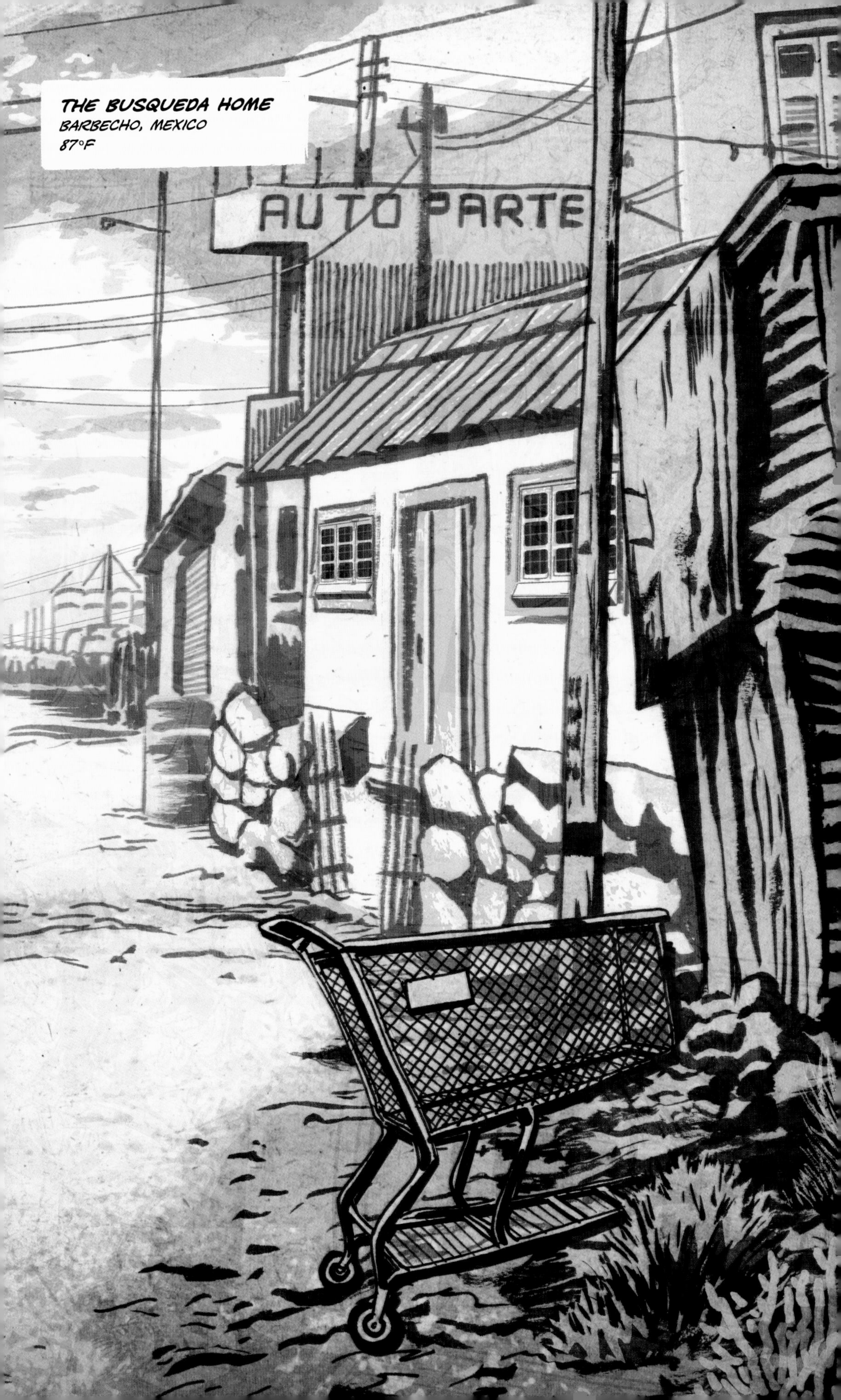
THE BUSQUEDA HOME
BARBECHO, MEXICO
87°F
AUTO PARTE

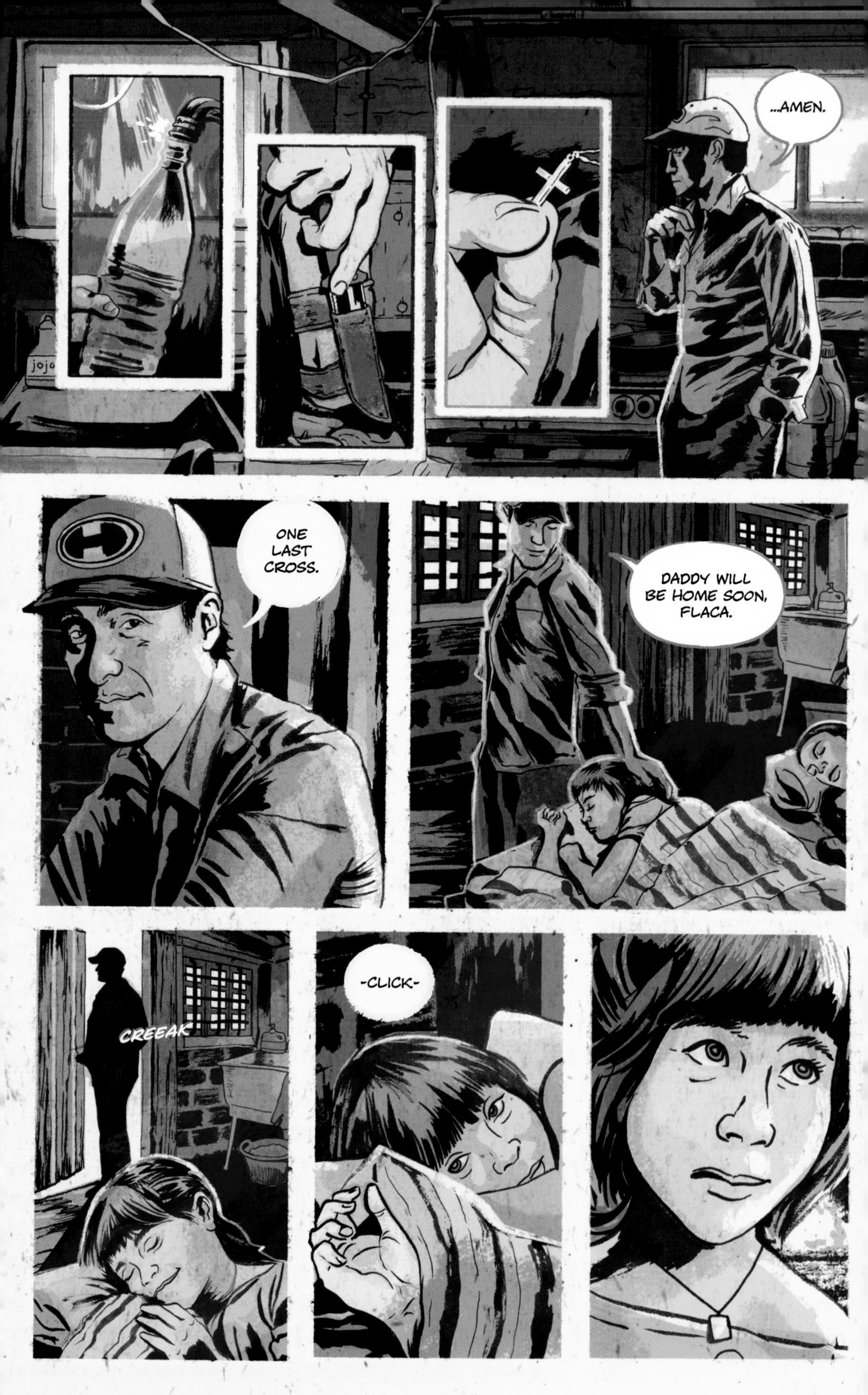
jojo
...AMEN.
ONE LAST CROSS.
DADDY WILL BE HOME SOON, FLACA.
CREEAK
-CLICK-

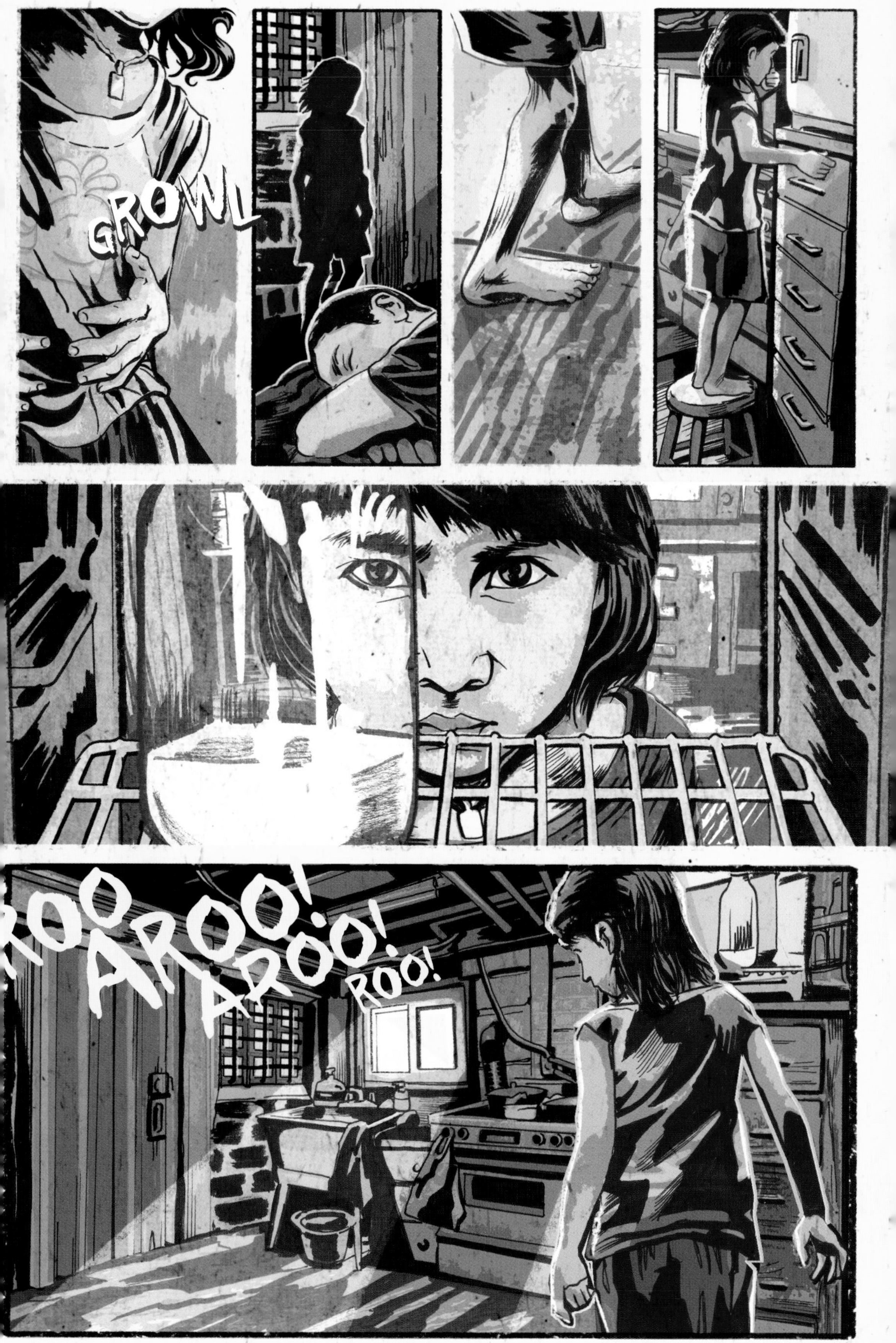
GROWL
ROO
AROO!
AROO!
ROO!

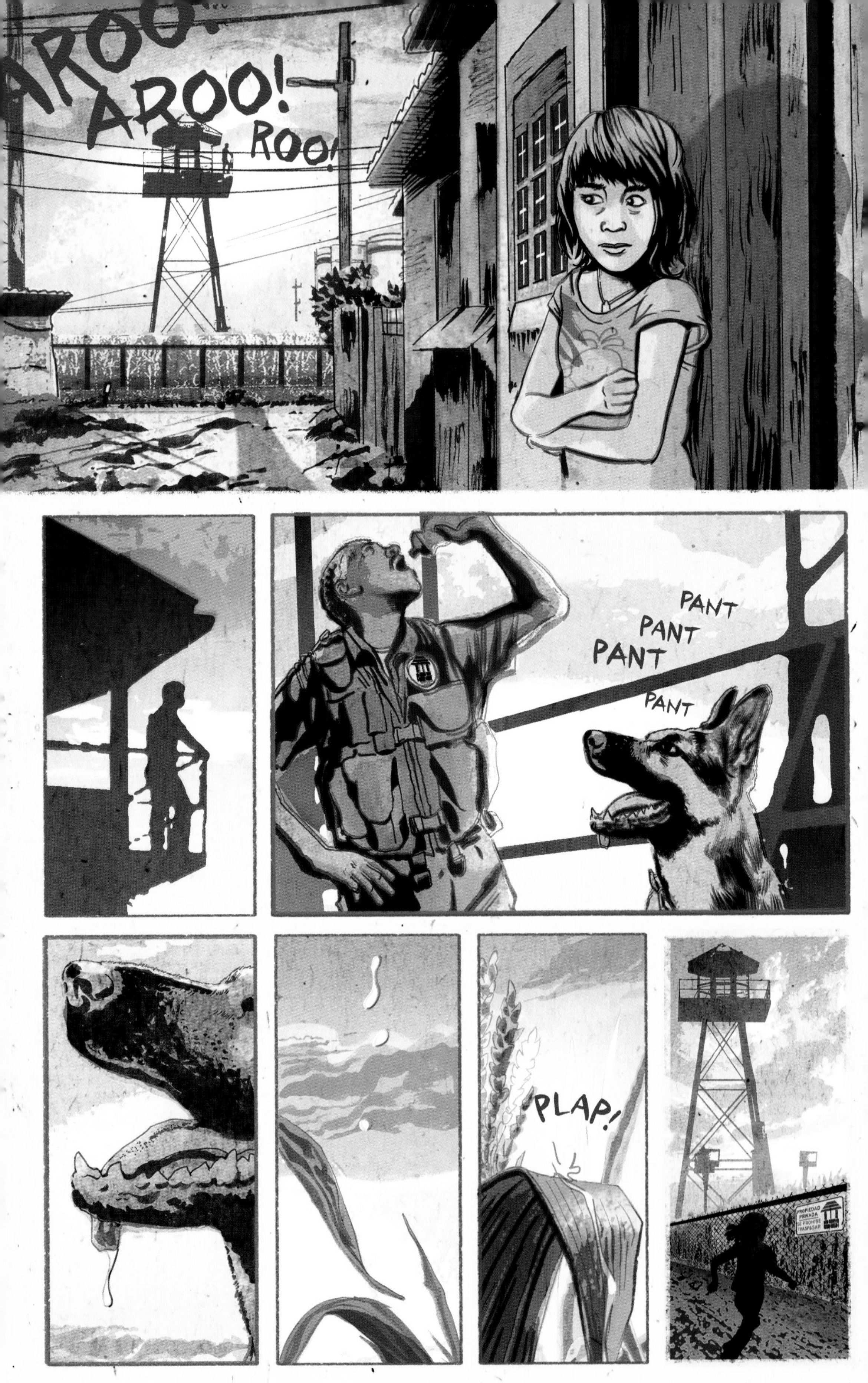
AROO!
AROO!
ROO!
PANT
PANT
PANT
PANT
PLAP!
PROPIEDAD PRIVADA SE PROHIBE TRASPASAR

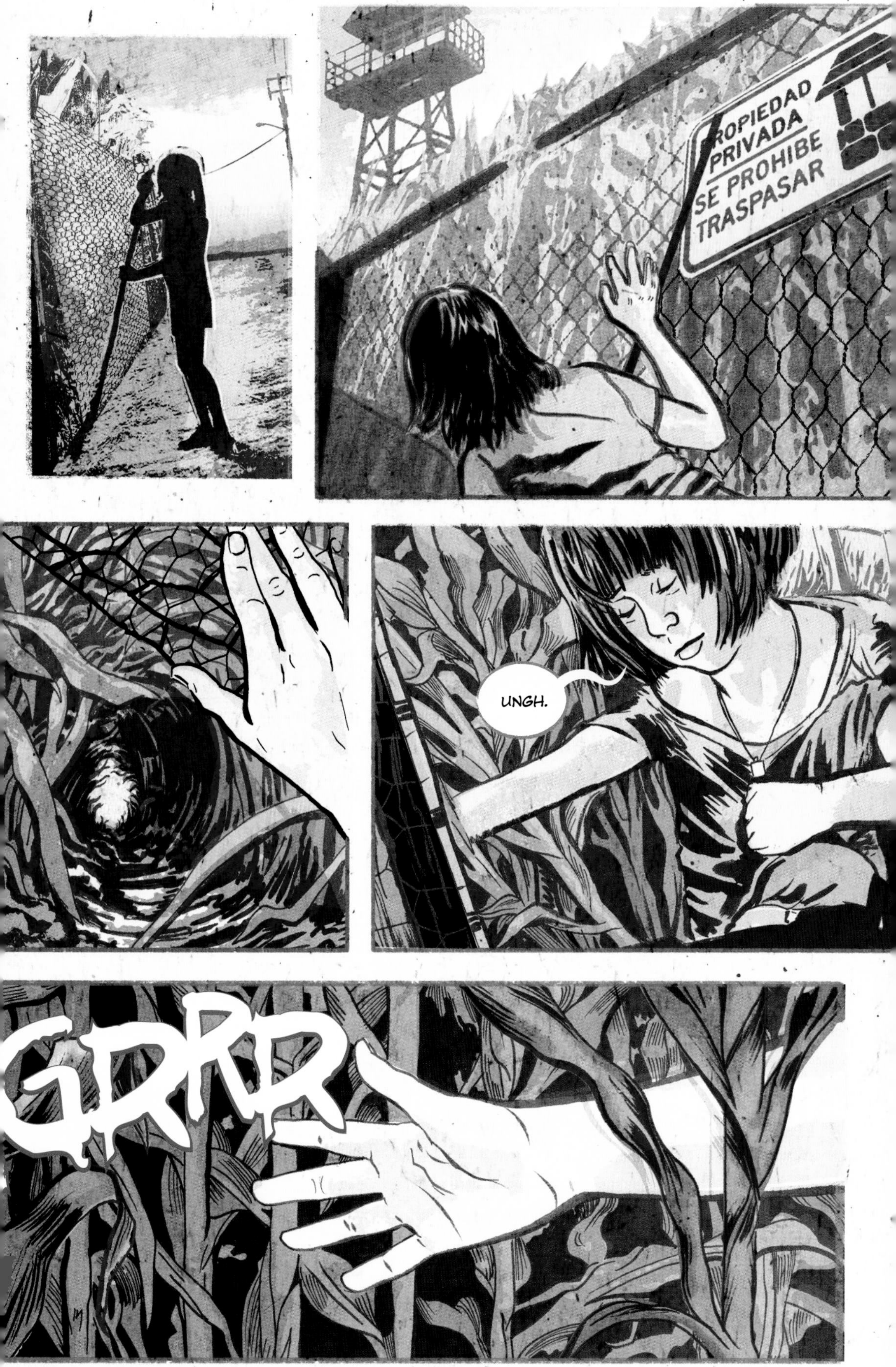
PROPIEDAD
PRIVADA
SE PROHIBE
TRASPASAR
UNGH.
GRRR

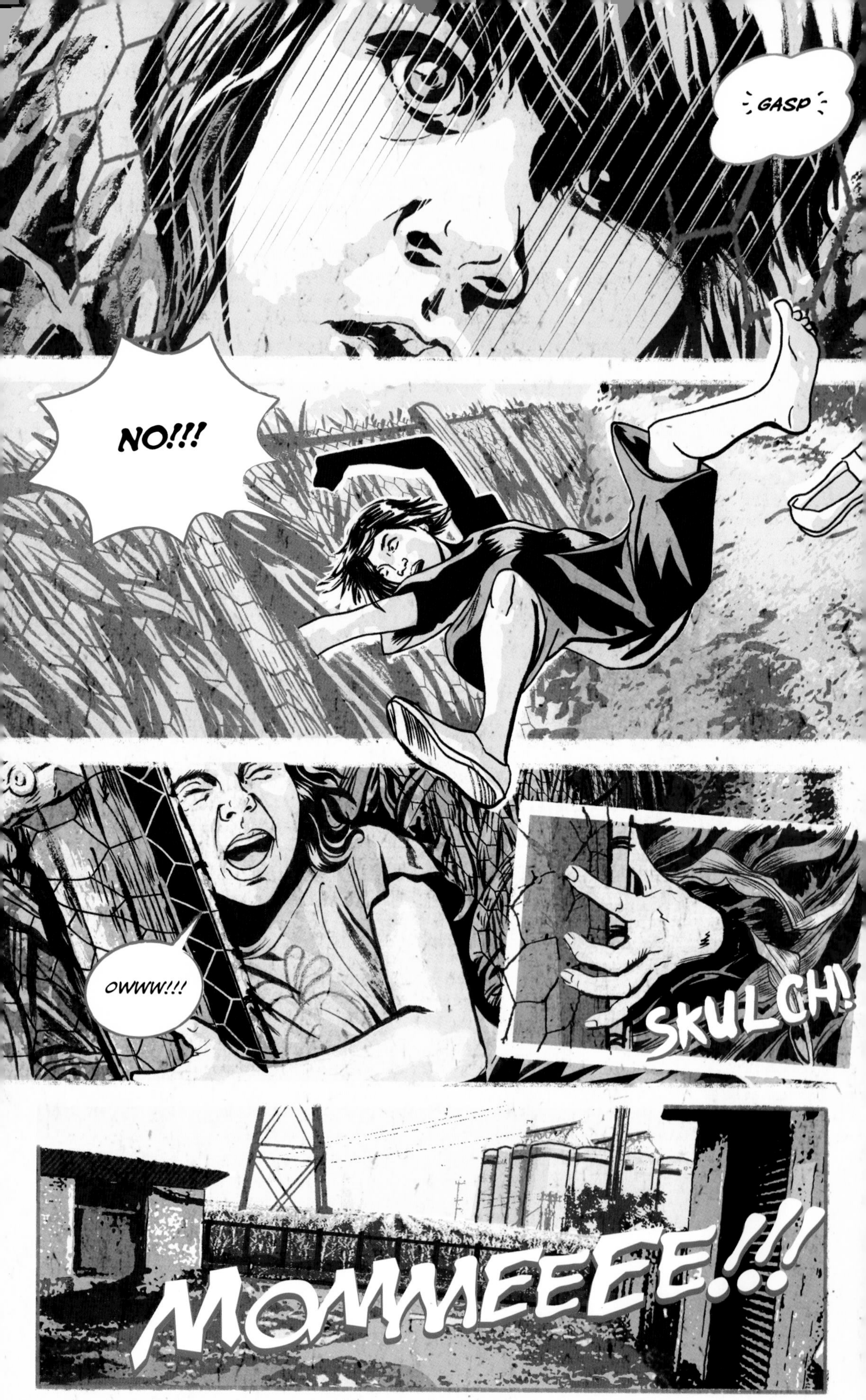
GASP
NO!!!
OWWW!!!
SKULCH!
MOMMEEEE!!!

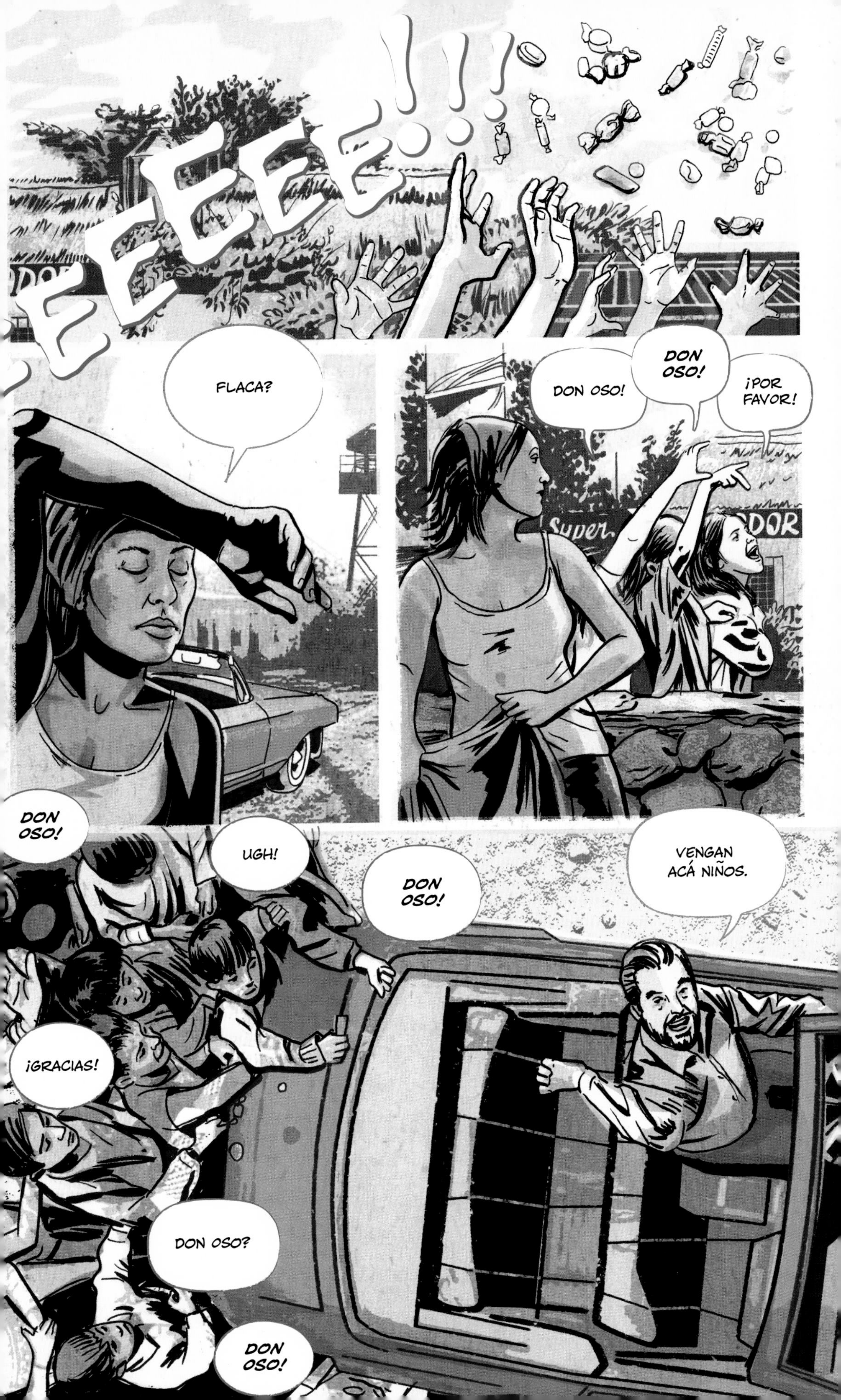
EEEEEE!!!
FLACA?
DON OSO!
DON OSO!
¡POR FAVOR!
DON OSO!
UGH!
DON OSO!
VENGAN ACÁ NIÑOS.
¡GRACIAS!
DON OSO?
DON OSO!

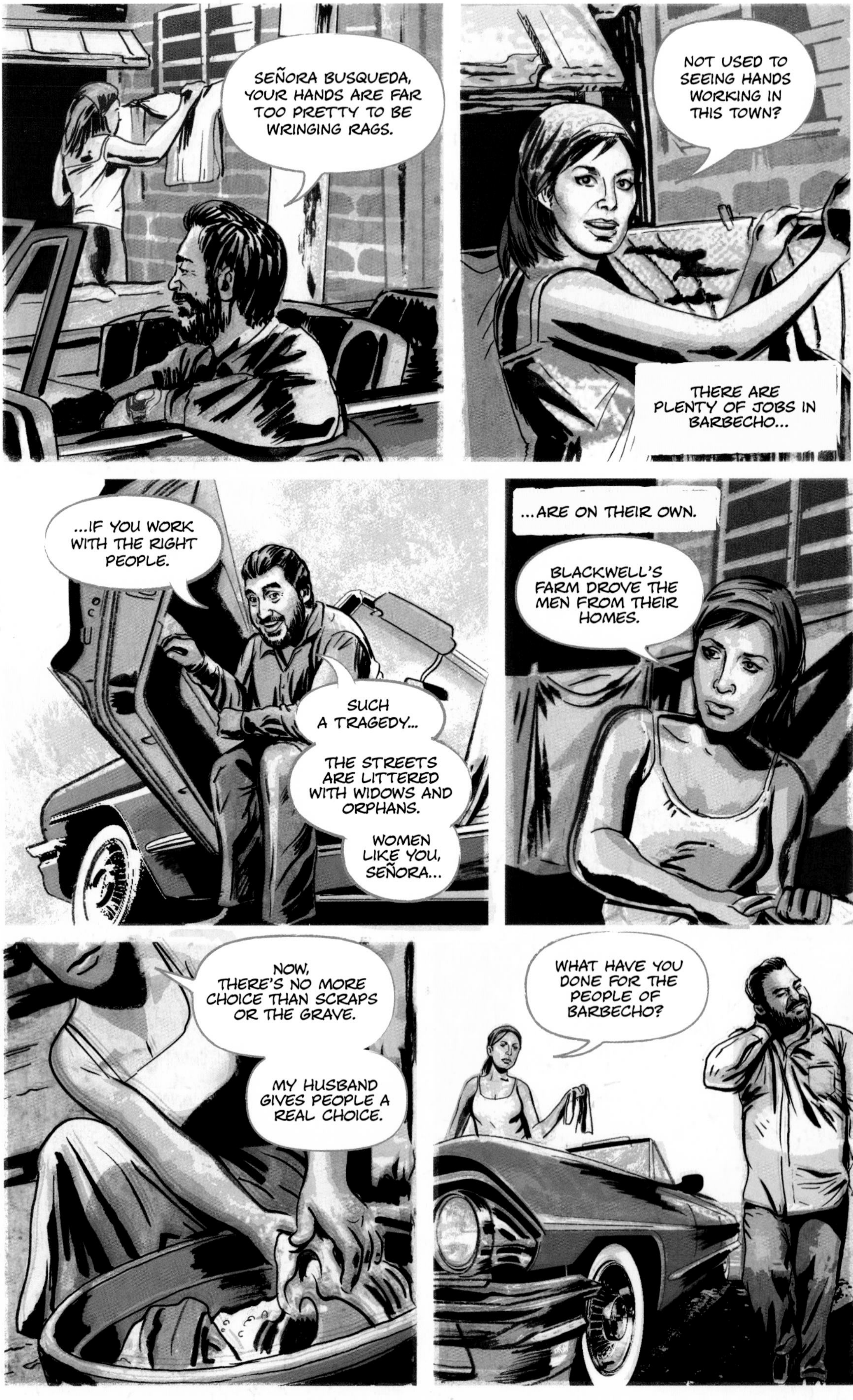
SEÑORA BUSQUEDA, YOUR HANDS ARE FAR TOO PRETTY TO BE WRINGING RAGS.
NOT USED TO SEEING HANDS WORKING IN THIS TOWN?
THERE ARE PLENTY OF JOBS IN BARBECHO...
...IF YOU WORK WITH THE RIGHT PEOPLE.
SUCH A TRAGEDY...
THE STREETS ARE LITTERED WITH WIDOWS AND ORPHANS.
WOMEN LIKE YOU, SEÑORA...
...ARE ON THEIR OWN.
BLACKWELL'S FARM DROVE THE MEN FROM THEIR HOMES.
NOW, THERE'S NO MORE CHOICE THAN SCRAPS OR THE GRAVE.
MY HUSBAND GIVES PEOPLE A REAL CHOICE.
WHAT HAVE YOU DONE FOR THE PEOPLE OF BARBECHO?

SEÑORA BUSQUEDA.

THE NIÑOS KNOW I'M GENEROUS.

VERY, VERY GENEROUS.

IT'S A SHAME YOU CAN'T RECOGNIZE AN OPPORTUNITY.

I CAN PROVIDE ANYTHING YOU NEED.

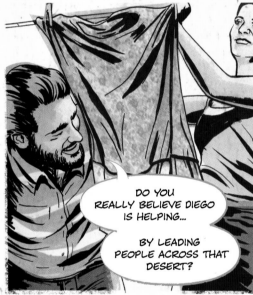

DO YOU REALLY BELIEVE DIEGO IS HELPING...

BY LEADING PEOPLE ACROSS THAT DESERT?

YOUR HUSBAND IS SELLING A DREAM.

AND INTEGRITY DOES NOT PAY FOR FOOD.

I'M NOT SUCH A MONSTER, SEÑORA...

TAKE YOUR GENEROSITY SOMEWHERE ELSE.

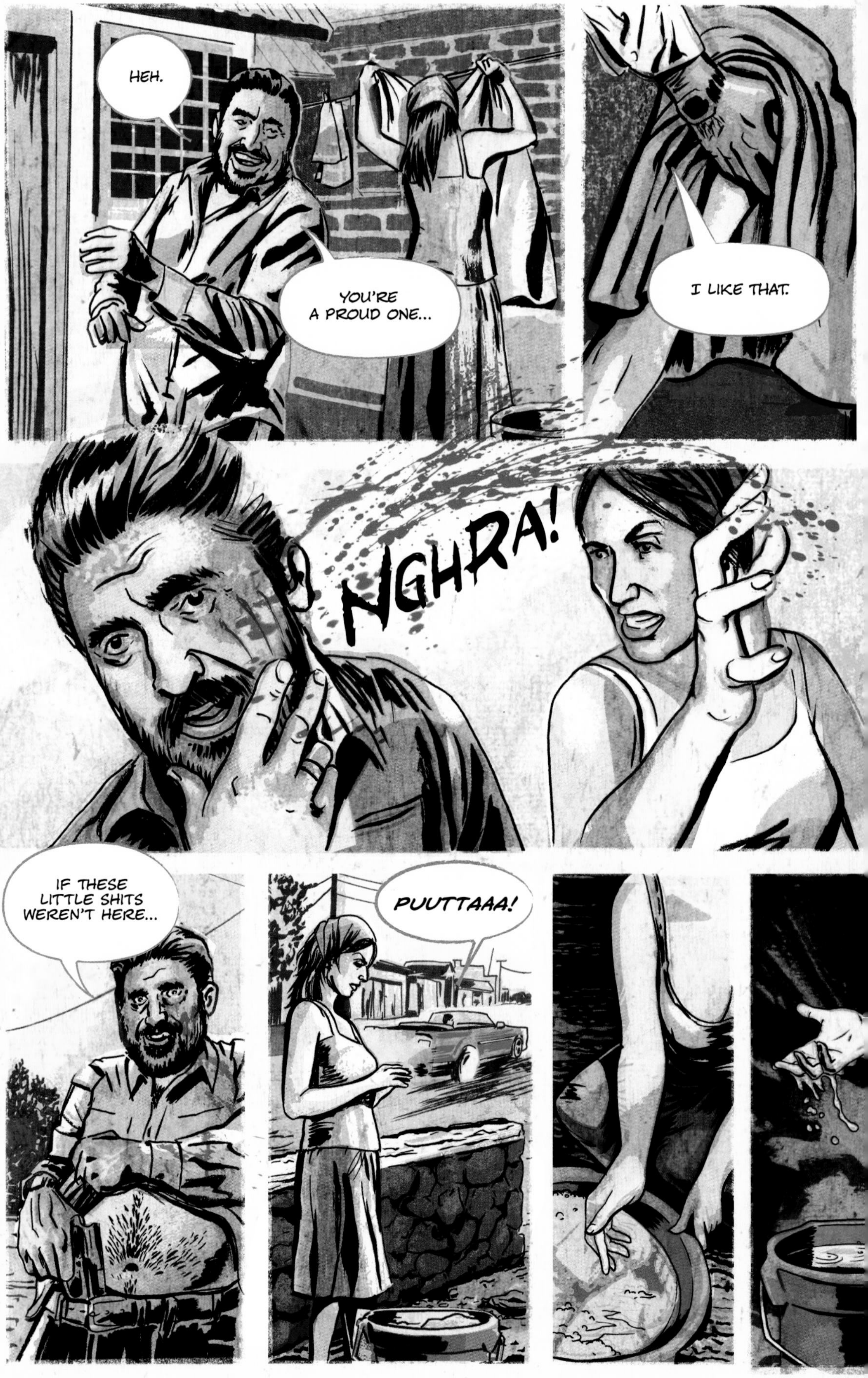
HEH.
YOU'RE A PROUD ONE...
I LIKE THAT.
NGHRA!
IF THESE LITTLE SHITS WEREN'T HERE...
PUUTTAAA!

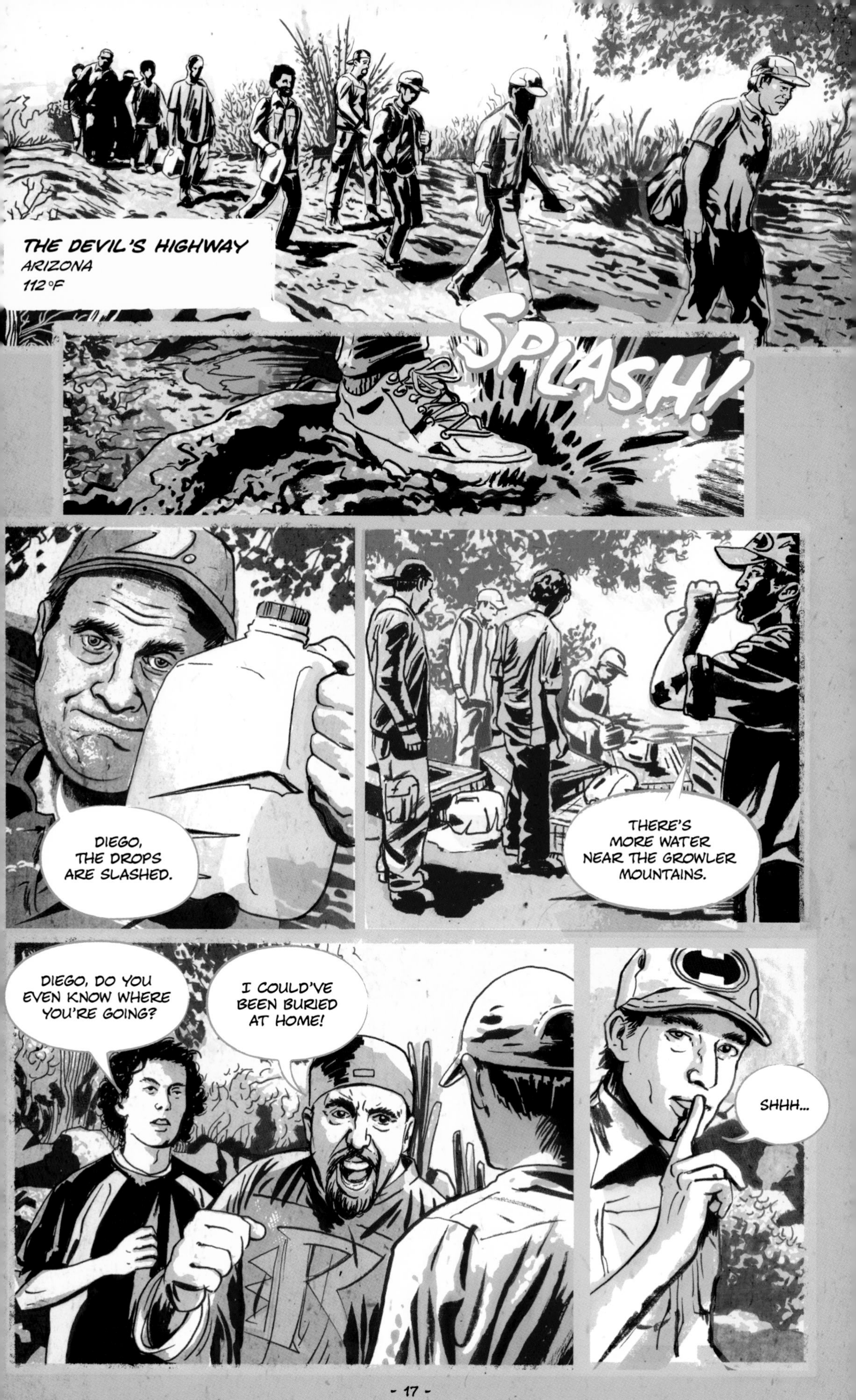

THE DEVIL'S HIGHWAY
ARIZONA
112°F
SPLASH!
DIEGO, THE DROPS ARE SLASHED.
THERE'S MORE WATER NEAR THE GROWLER MOUNTAINS.
DIEGO, DO YOU EVEN KNOW WHERE YOU'RE GOING?
I COULD'VE BEEN BURIED AT HOME!
SHHH...

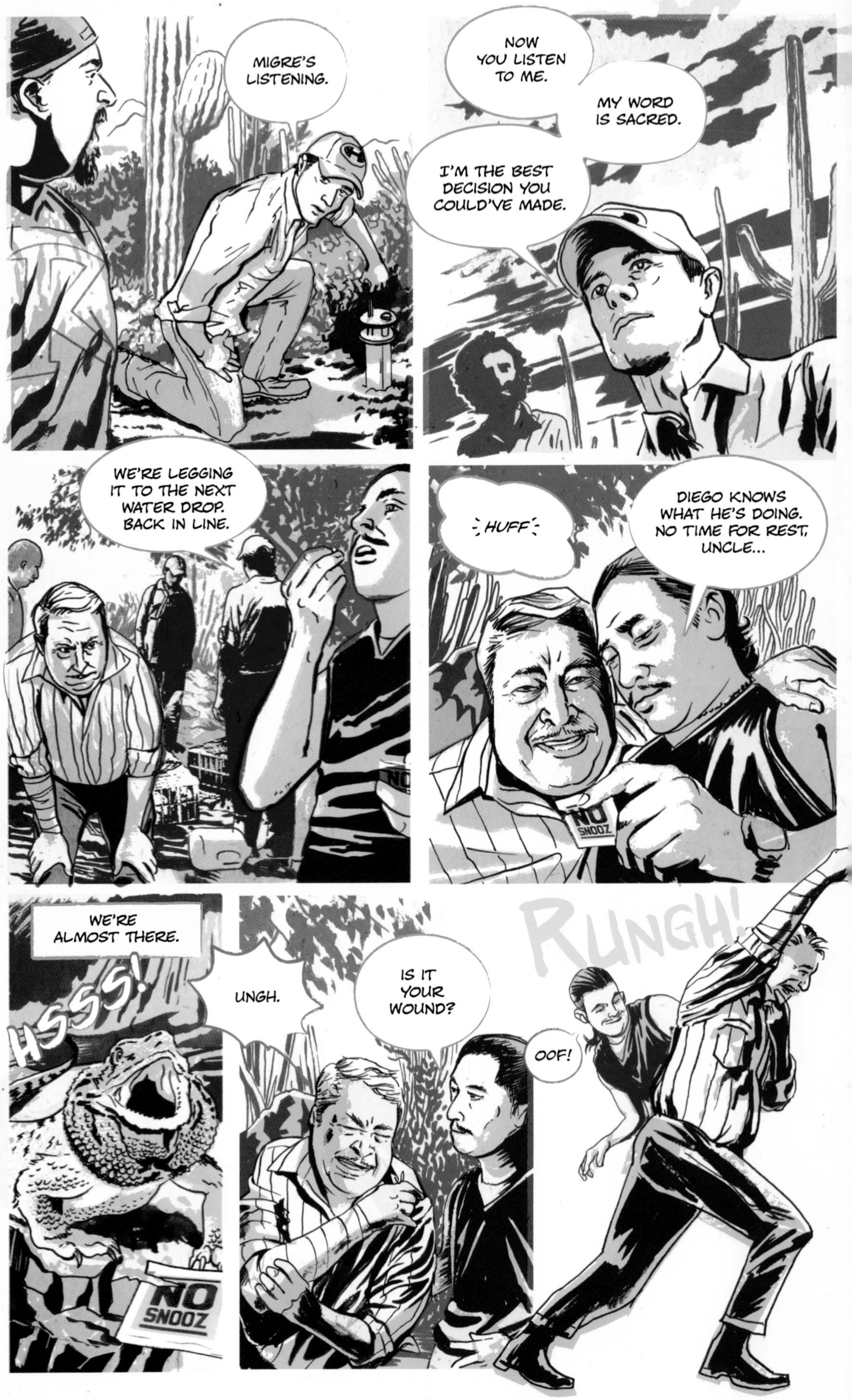
MIGRE'S LISTENING.
NOW YOU LISTEN TO ME.
MY WORD IS SACRED.
I'M THE BEST DECISION YOU COULD'VE MADE.
WE'RE LEGGING IT TO THE NEXT WATER DROP. BACK IN LINE.
NO SNOOZ
HUFF
DIEGO KNOWS WHAT HE'S DOING. NO TIME FOR REST, UNCLE...
NO SNOOZ
WE'RE ALMOST THERE.
HSSSS!
UNGH.
NO SNOOZ
IS IT YOUR WOUND?
RUNGH!
OOF!

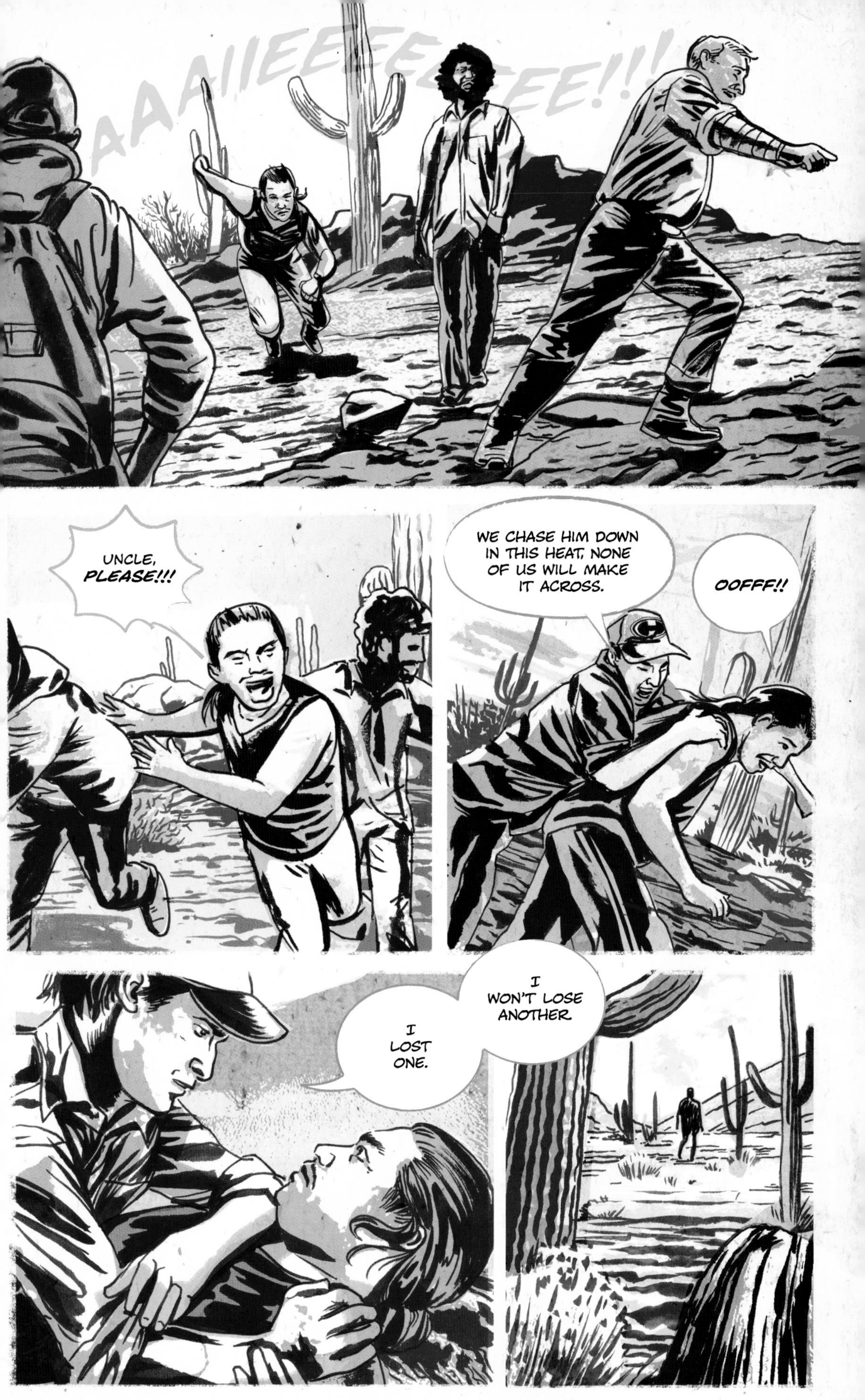
AAAIIEEEEEEEEE!!!
UNCLE, PLEASE!!!
WE CHASE HIM DOWN IN THIS HEAT, NONE OF US WILL MAKE IT ACROSS.
OOFFF!!
I LOST ONE.
I WON'T LOSE ANOTHER

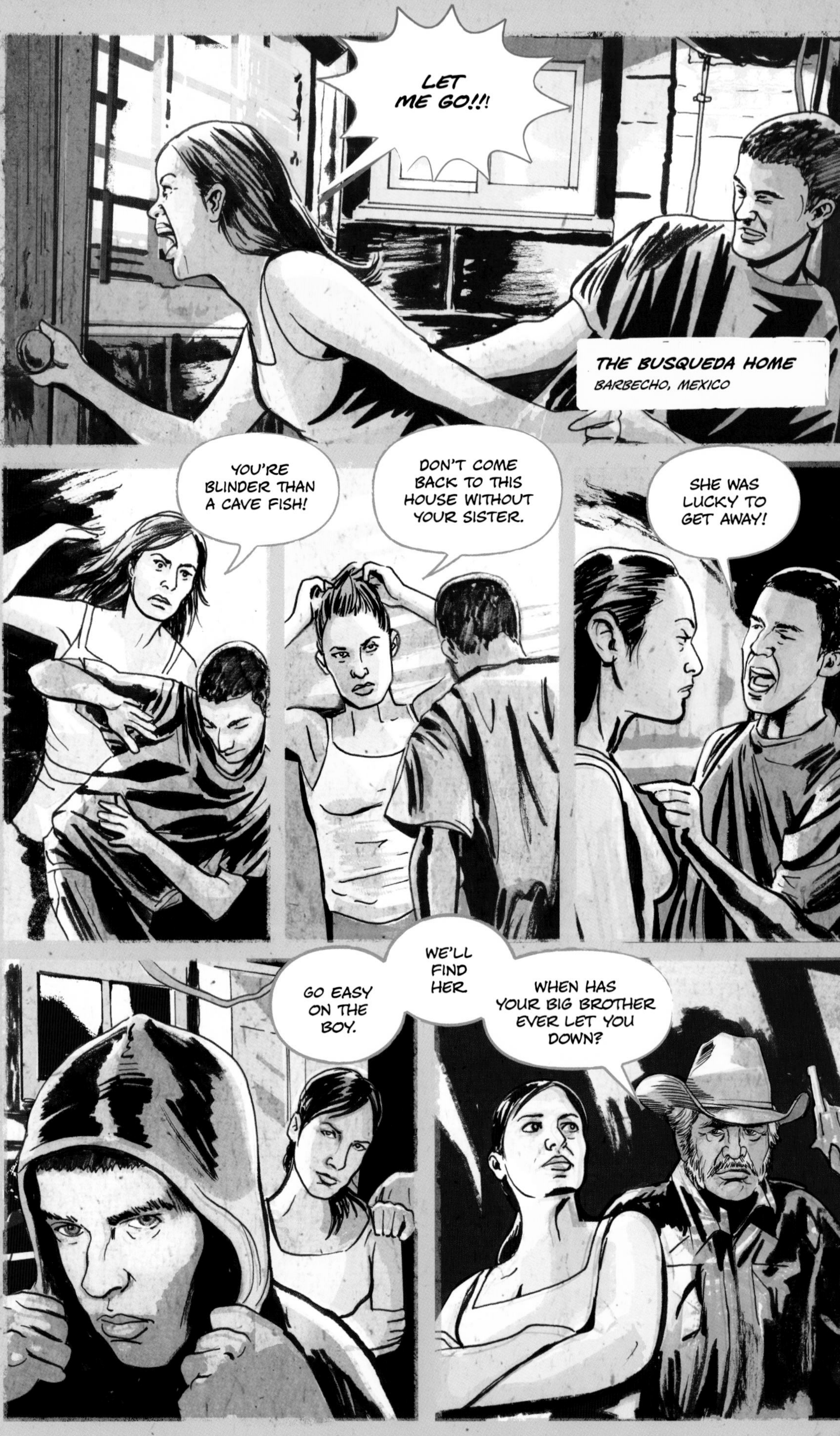
LET ME GO!!!
THE BUSQUEDA HOME
BARBECHO, MEXICO
YOU'RE BLINDER THAN A CAVE FISH!
DON'T COME BACK TO THIS HOUSE WITHOUT YOUR SISTER.
SHE WAS LUCKY TO GET AWAY!
GO EASY ON THE BOY.
WE'LL FIND HER.
WHEN HAS YOUR BIG BROTHER EVER LET YOU DOWN?

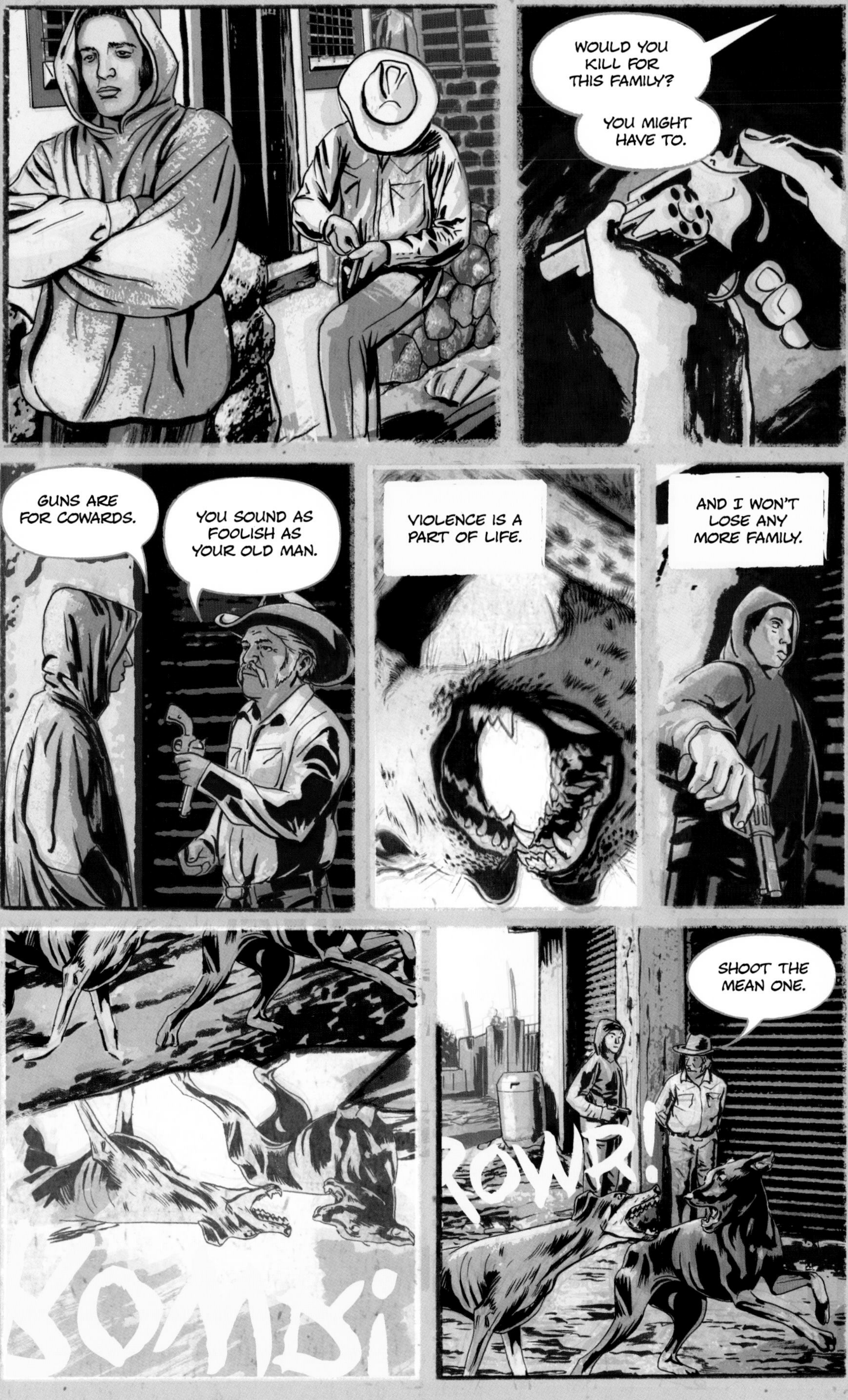
WOULD YOU KILL FOR THIS FAMILY?
YOU MIGHT HAVE TO.
GUNS ARE FOR COWARDS.
YOU SOUND AS FOOLISH AS YOUR OLD MAN.
VIOLENCE IS A PART OF LIFE.
AND I WON'T LOSE ANY MORE FAMILY.
SHOOT THE MEAN ONE.

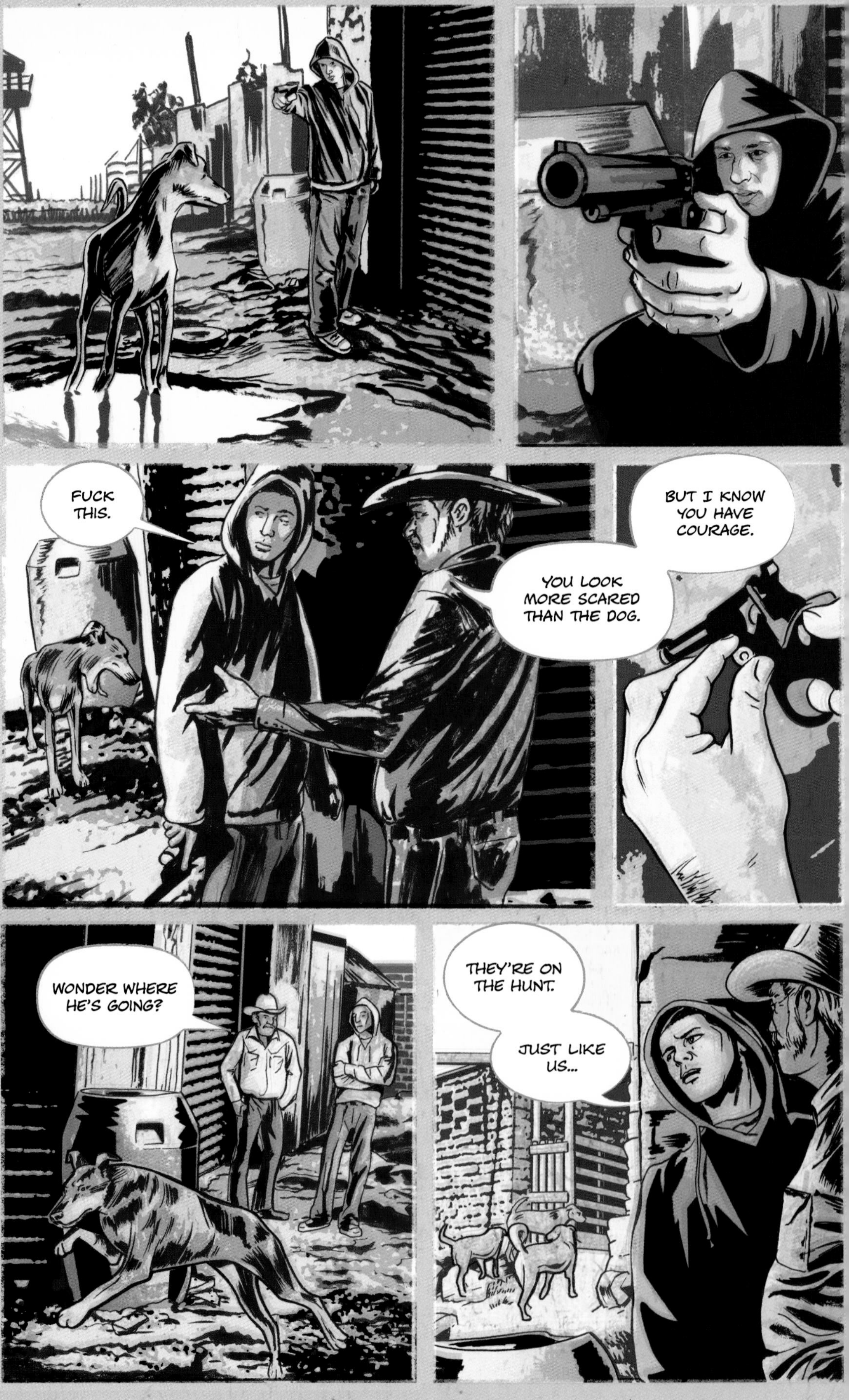
FUCK THIS.
YOU LOOK MORE SCARED THAN THE DOG.
BUT I KNOW YOU HAVE COURAGE.
WONDER WHERE HE'S GOING?
THEY'RE ON THE HUNT.
JUST LIKE US...

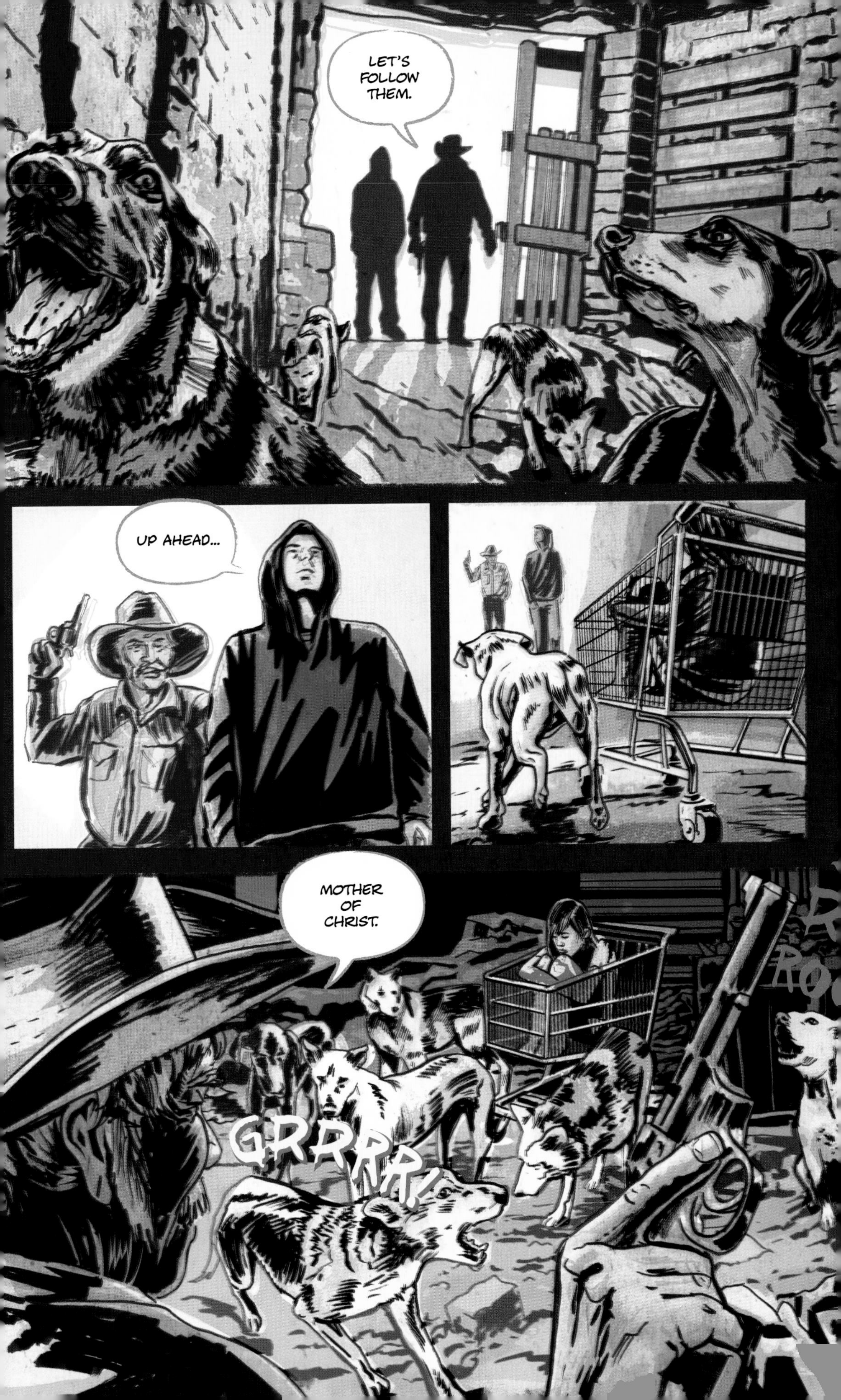
LET'S FOLLOW THEM.
UP AHEAD...
MOTHER OF CHRIST.
GRRRR!

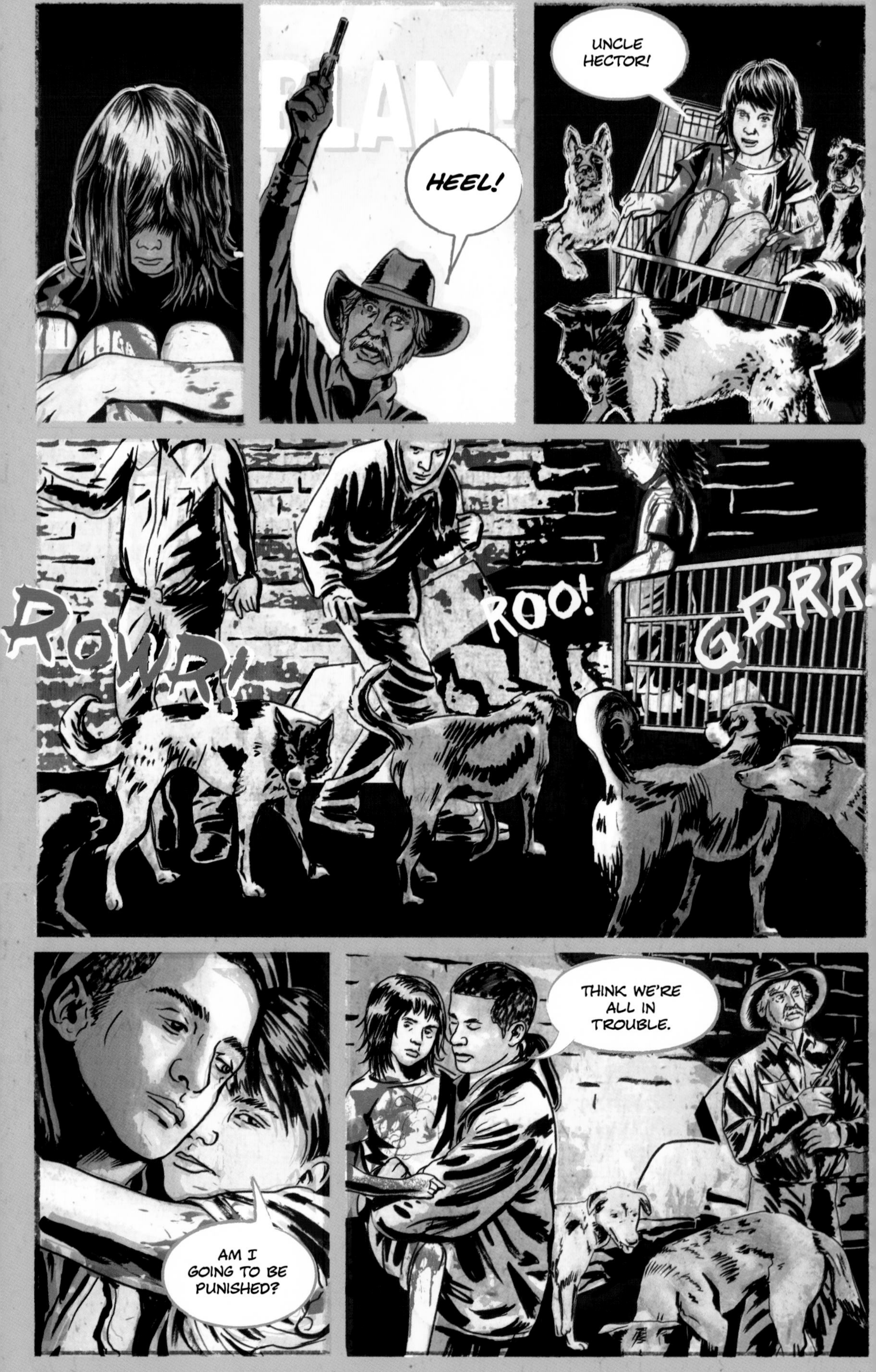
BLAM!
HEEL!
UNCLE HECTOR!
ROWR!
ROO!
GRRR!
AM I GOING TO BE PUNISHED?
THINK WE'RE ALL IN TROUBLE.

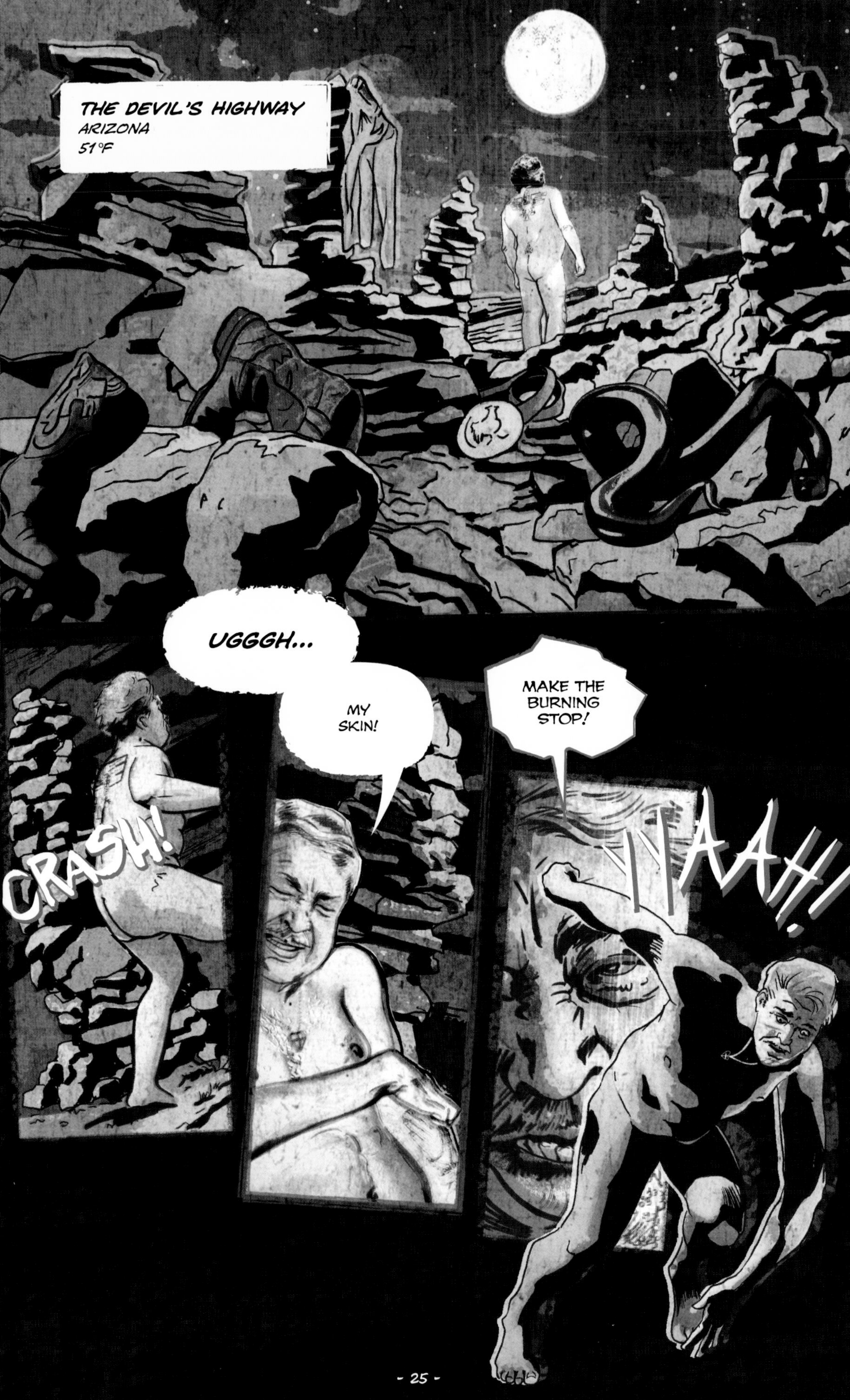
THE DEVIL'S HIGHWAY
ARIZONA
51°F
UGGGH...
CRASH!
MY SKIN!
MAKE THE BURNING STOP!
YYAAH!!

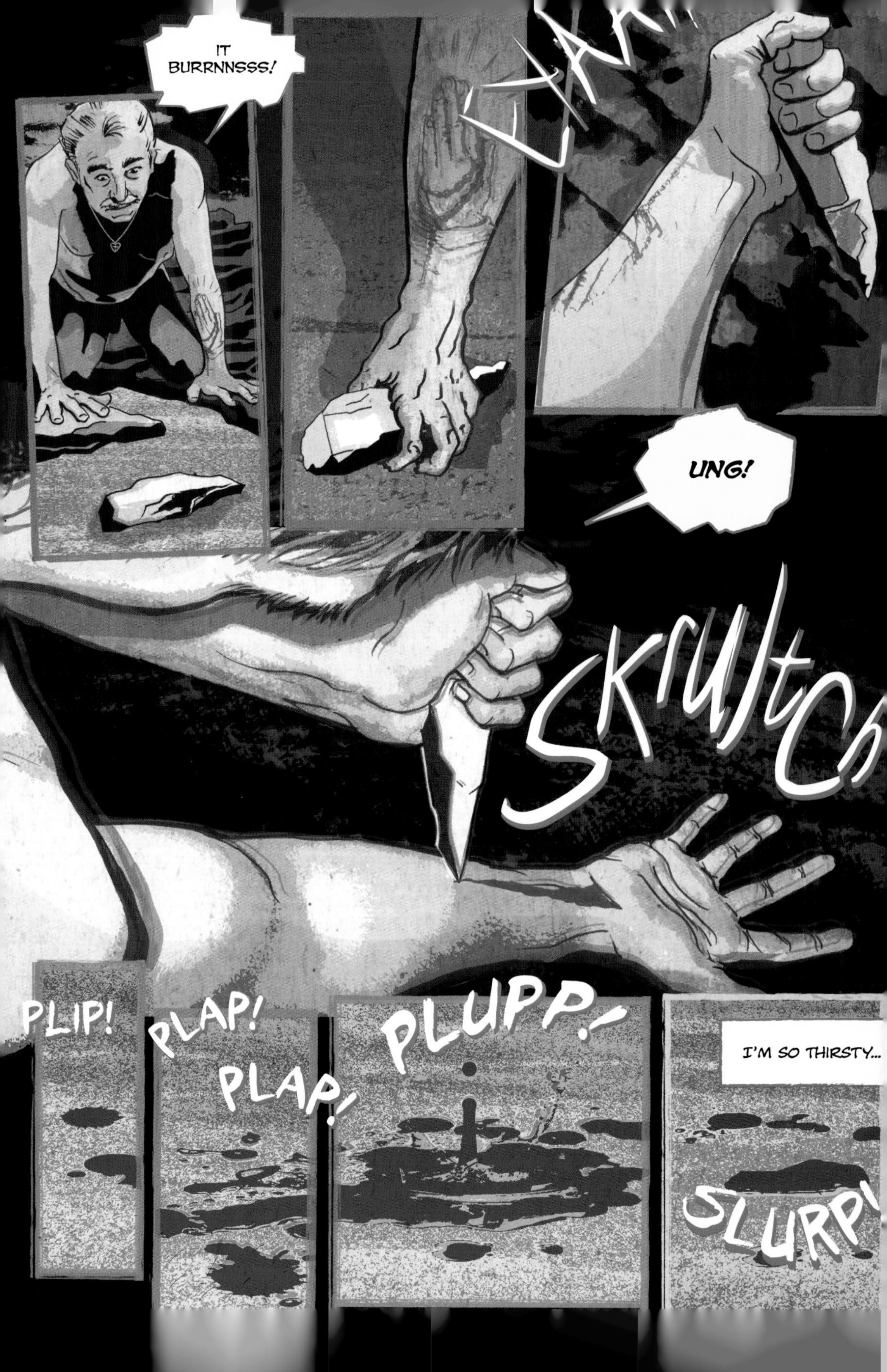
IT BURRNNSSS!
UNG!
PLIP!
PLAP!
PLAP!
PLUPP!
I'M SO THIRSTY...
SLURP!

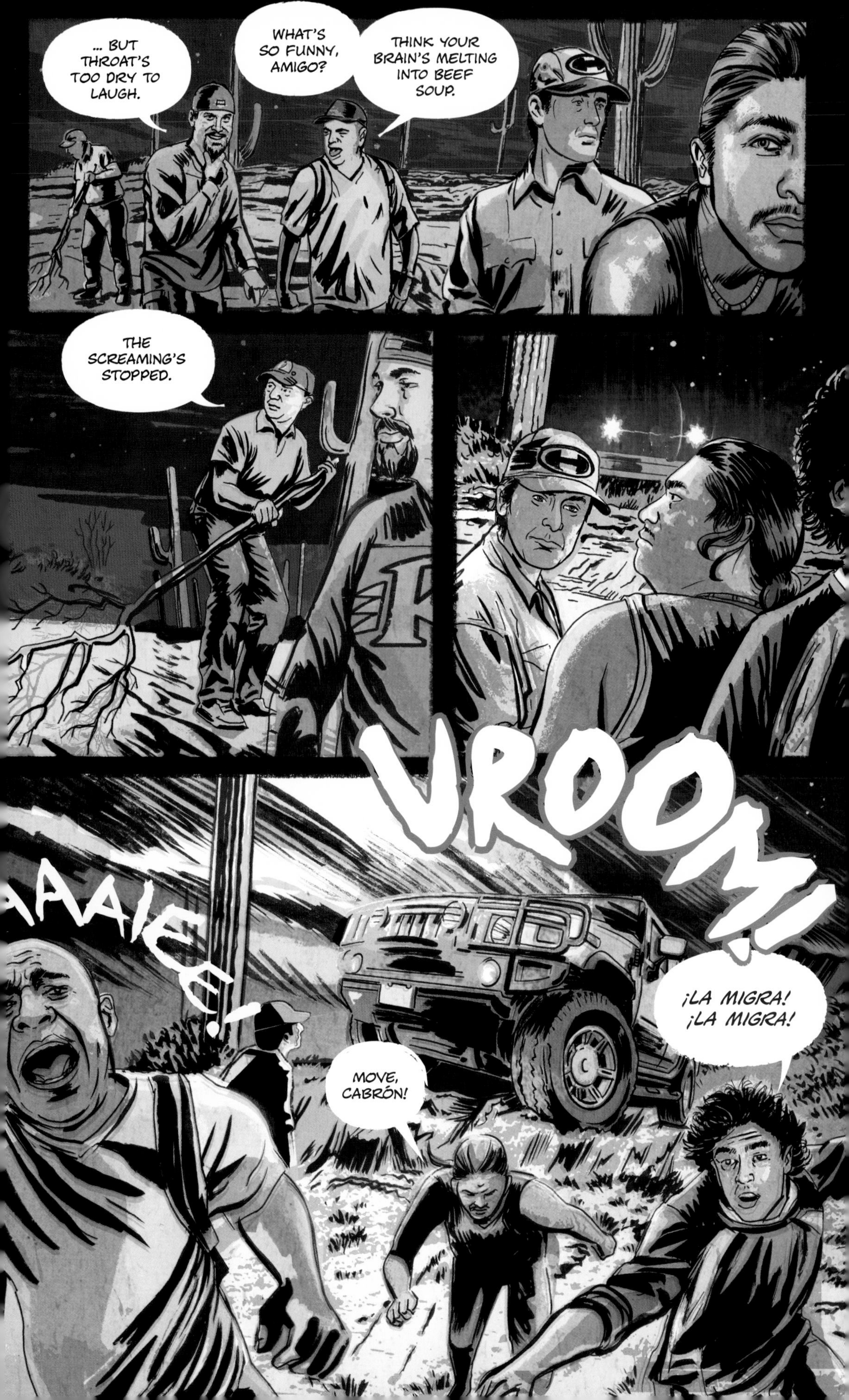

... BUT THROAT'S TOO DRY TO LAUGH.
WHAT'S SO FUNNY, AMIGO?
THINK YOUR BRAIN'S MELTING INTO BEEF SOUP.
THE SCREAMING'S STOPPED.
VROOM!
AAAIEE!
¡LA MIGRA! ¡LA MIGRA!
MOVE, CABRÓN!

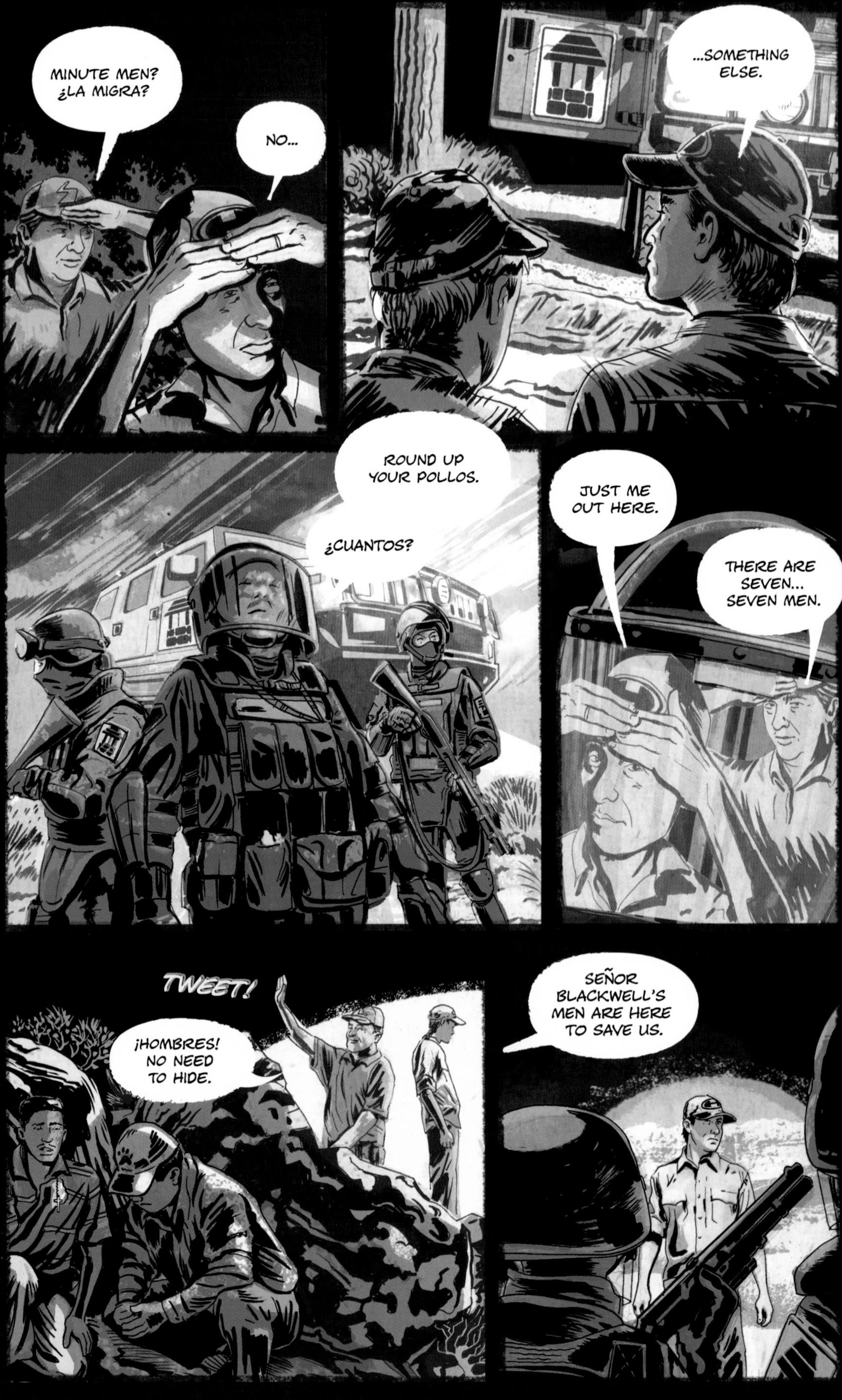
MINUTE MEN? ¿LA MIGRA?
NO...
...SOMETHING ELSE.
ROUND UP YOUR POLLOS.
¿CUANTOS?
JUST ME OUT HERE.
THERE ARE SEVEN... SEVEN MEN.
TWEET!
¡HOMBRES! NO NEED TO HIDE.
SEÑOR BLACKWELL'S MEN ARE HERE TO SAVE US.

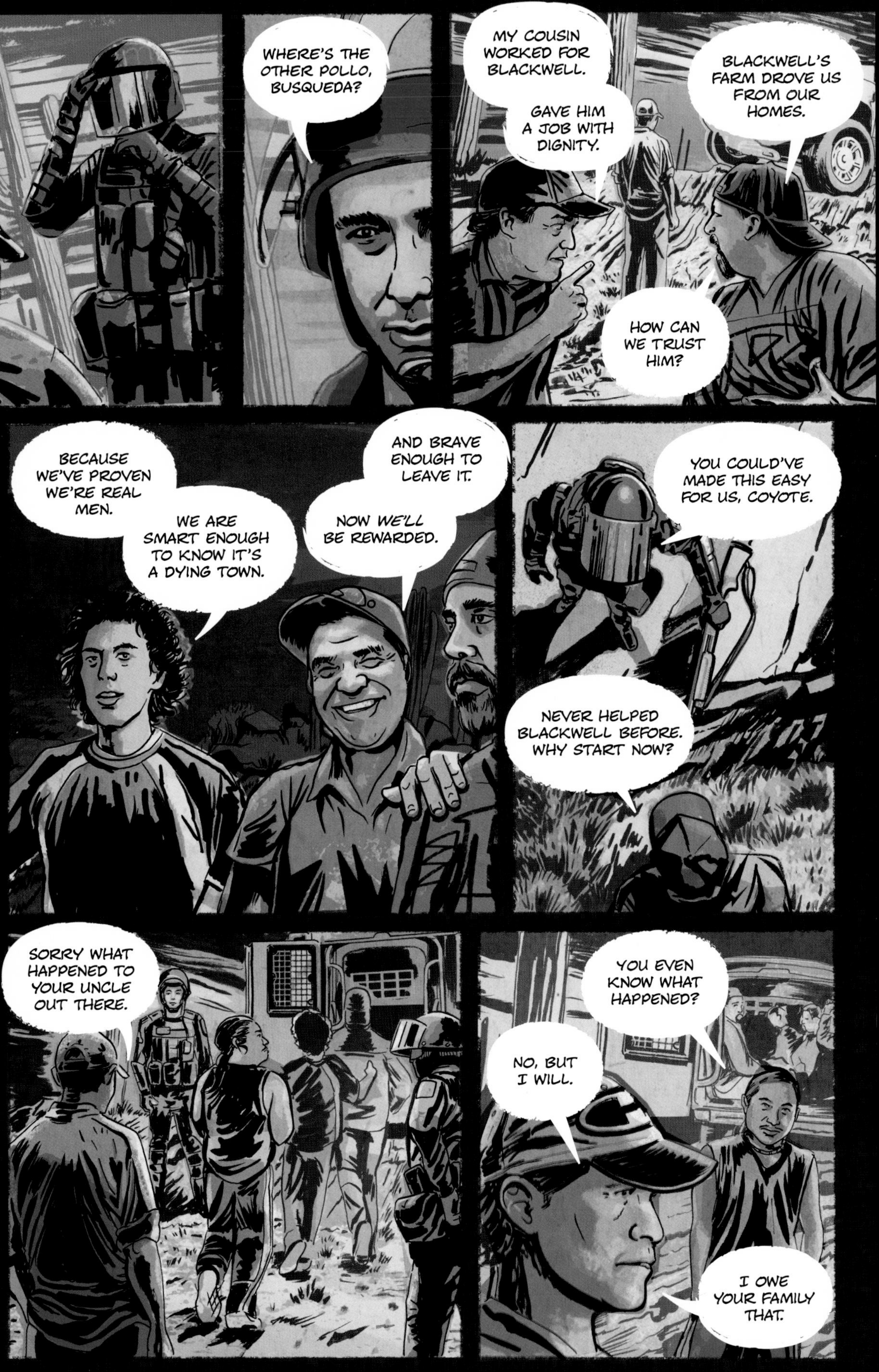
WHERE'S THE OTHER POLLO, BUSQUEDA?
MY COUSIN WORKED FOR BLACKWELL.
GAVE HIM A JOB WITH DIGNITY.
BLACKWELL'S FARM DROVE US FROM OUR HOMES.
HOW CAN WE TRUST HIM?
BECAUSE WE'VE PROVEN WE'RE REAL MEN.
WE ARE SMART ENOUGH TO KNOW IT'S A DYING TOWN.
AND BRAVE ENOUGH TO LEAVE IT.
NOW WE'LL BE REWARDED.
YOU COULD'VE MADE THIS EASY FOR US, COYOTE.
NEVER HELPED BLACKWELL BEFORE. WHY START NOW?
SORRY WHAT HAPPENED TO YOUR UNCLE OUT THERE.
YOU EVEN KNOW WHAT HAPPENED?
NO, BUT I WILL.
I OWE YOUR FAMILY THAT.

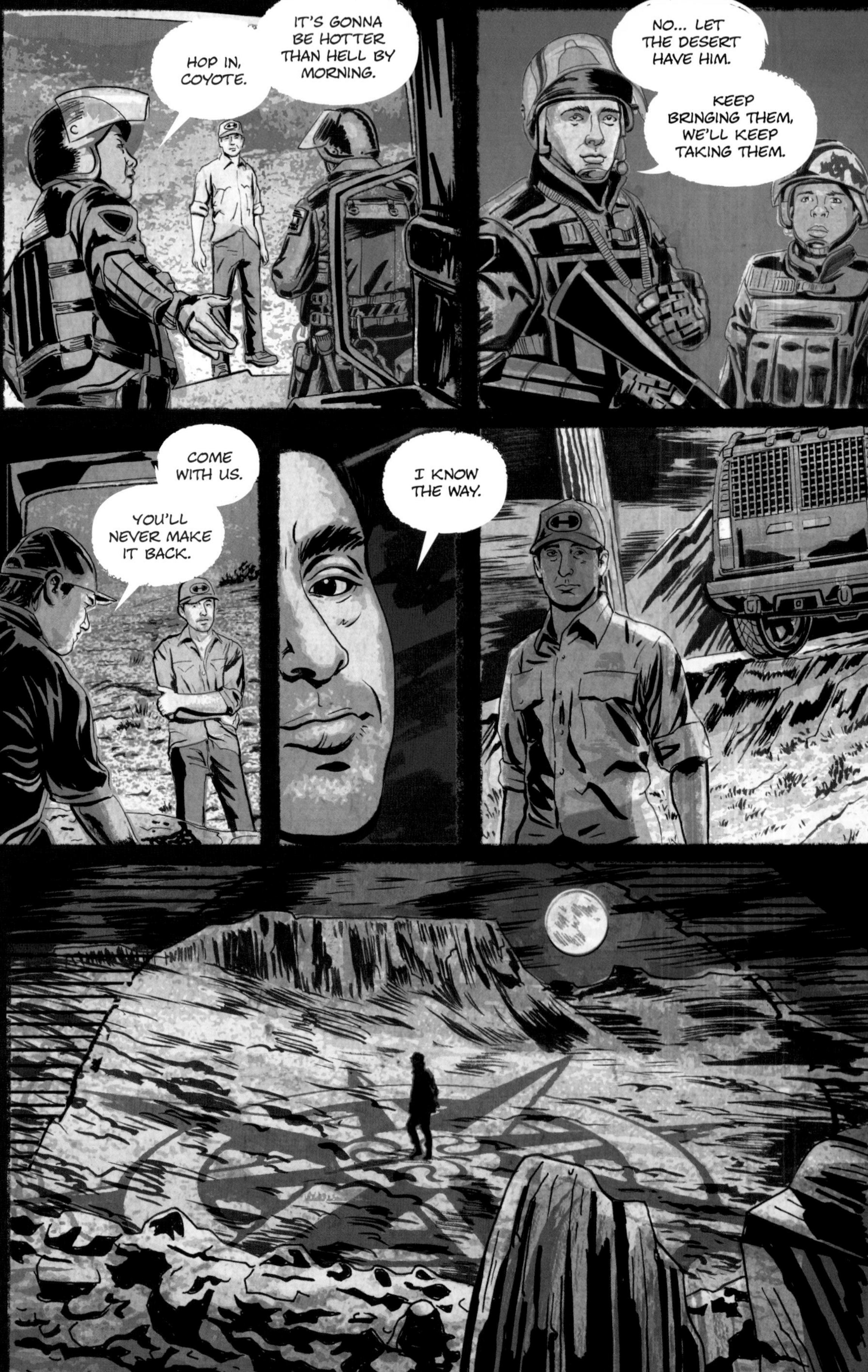
HOP IN, COYOTE.
IT'S GONNA BE HOTTER THAN HELL BY MORNING.
NO... LET THE DESERT HAVE HIM.
KEEP BRINGING THEM, WE'LL KEEP TAKING THEM.
COME WITH US.
YOU'LL NEVER MAKE IT BACK.
I KNOW THE WAY.

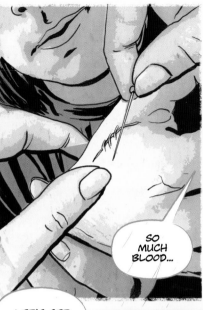

SO MUCH BLOOD...

...FOR SUCH A LITTLE SCRATCH, FLAQUITA.

THE BUSQUEDA HOME
BARBECHO, MEXICO

LET'S GET YOU CHANGED.

WE'RE GOING TO PLAY AT SABINA'S HOUSE.

DON'T WORRY. SHE'S GOT ANOTHER ARM.

ALWAYS THE CLOWN.

GO PACK. WE'RE LEAVING.

WE HAVE TO STAY.

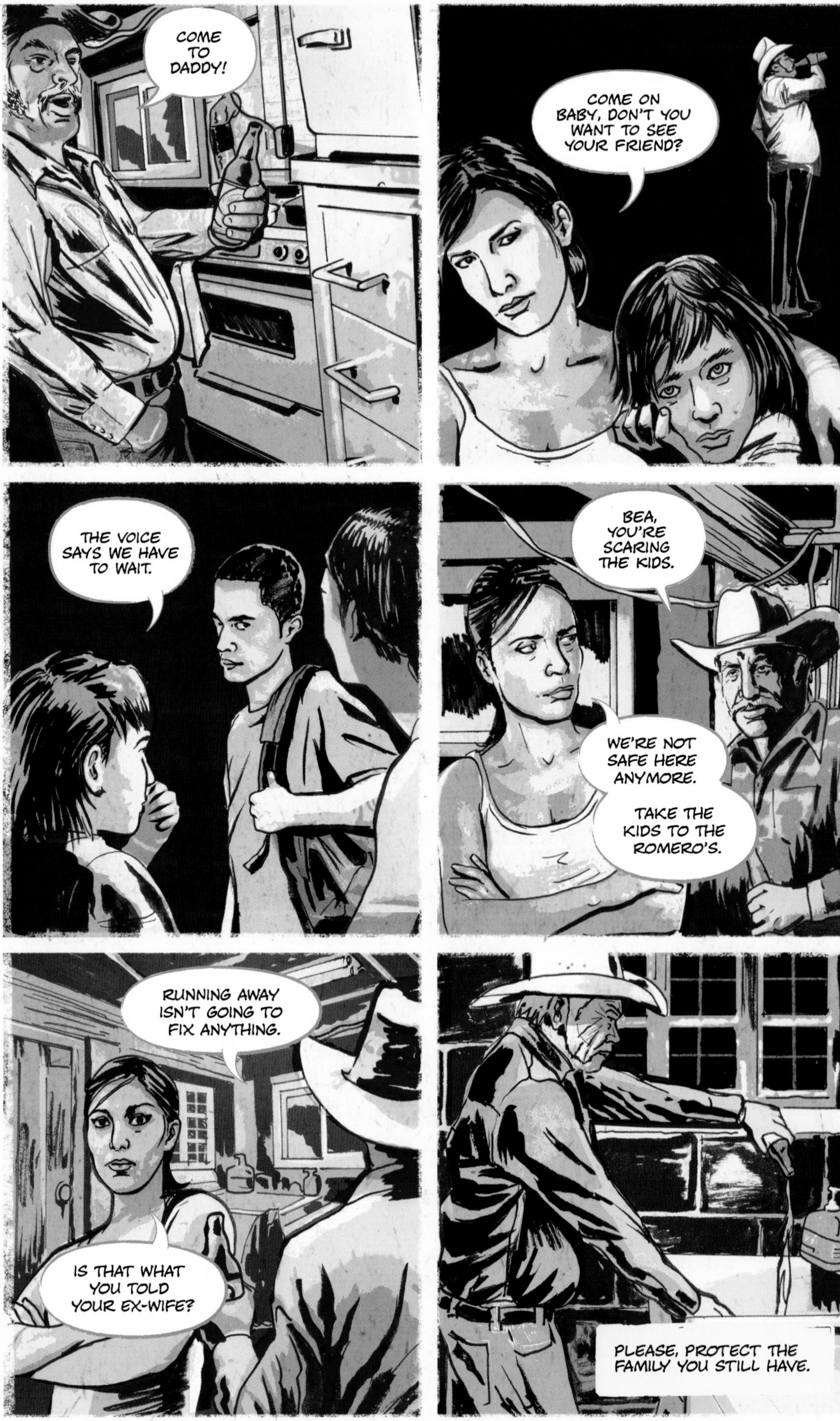
COME TO DADDY!
COME ON BABY, DON'T YOU WANT TO SEE YOUR FRIEND?
THE VOICE SAYS WE HAVE TO WAIT.
BEA, YOU'RE SCARING THE KIDS.
WE'RE NOT SAFE HERE ANYMORE.
TAKE THE KIDS TO THE ROMERO'S.
RUNNING AWAY ISN'T GOING TO FIX ANYTHING.
IS THAT WHAT YOU TOLD YOUR EX-WIFE?
PLEASE, PROTECT THE FAMILY YOU STILL HAVE.

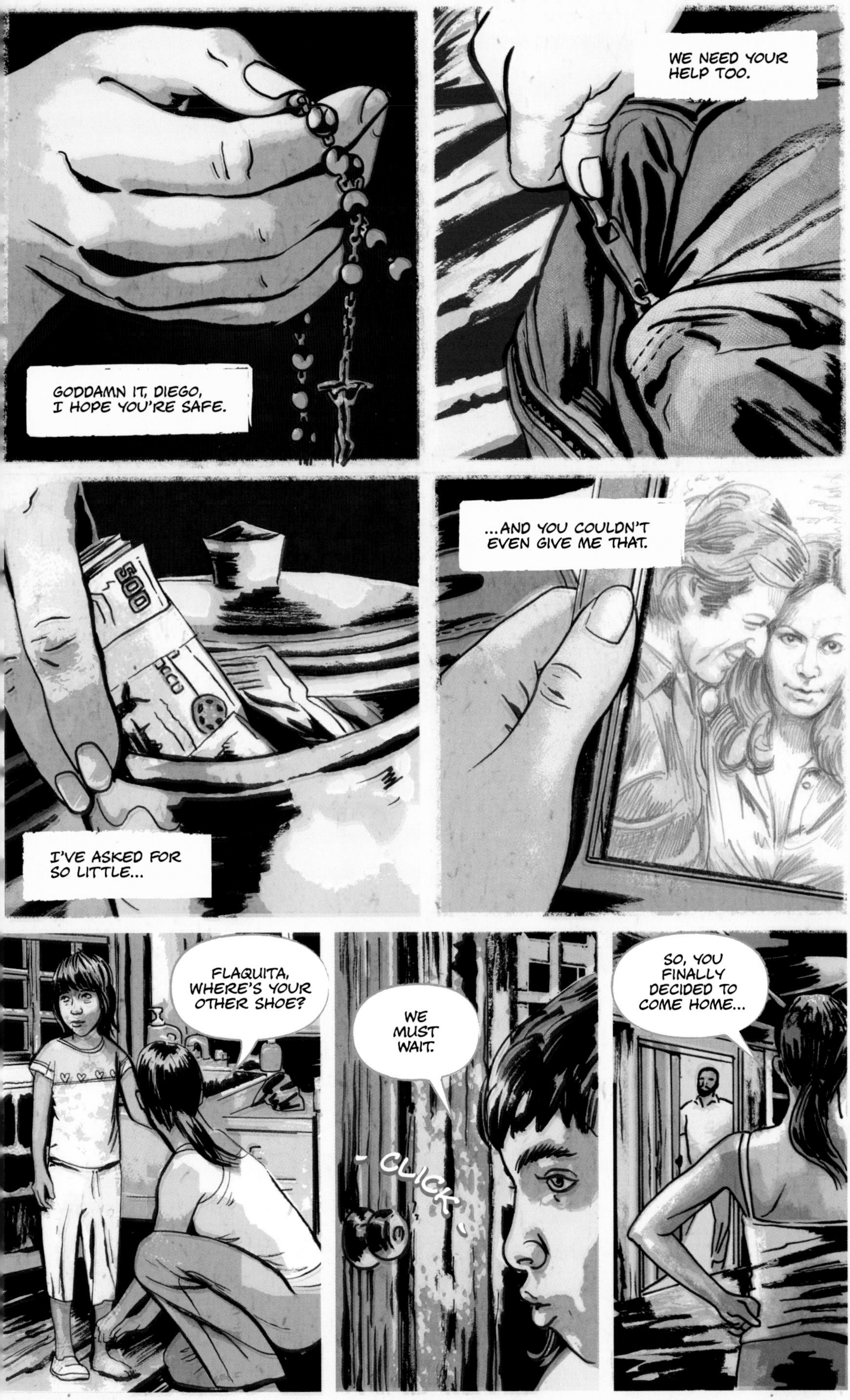
GODDAMN IT, DIEGO, I HOPE YOU'RE SAFE.
WE NEED YOUR HELP TOO.
I'VE ASKED FOR SO LITTLE...
...AND YOU COULDN'T EVEN GIVE ME THAT.
FLAQUITA, WHERE'S YOUR OTHER SHOE?
WE MUST WAIT.
- CLICK -
SO, YOU FINALLY DECIDED TO COME HOME...

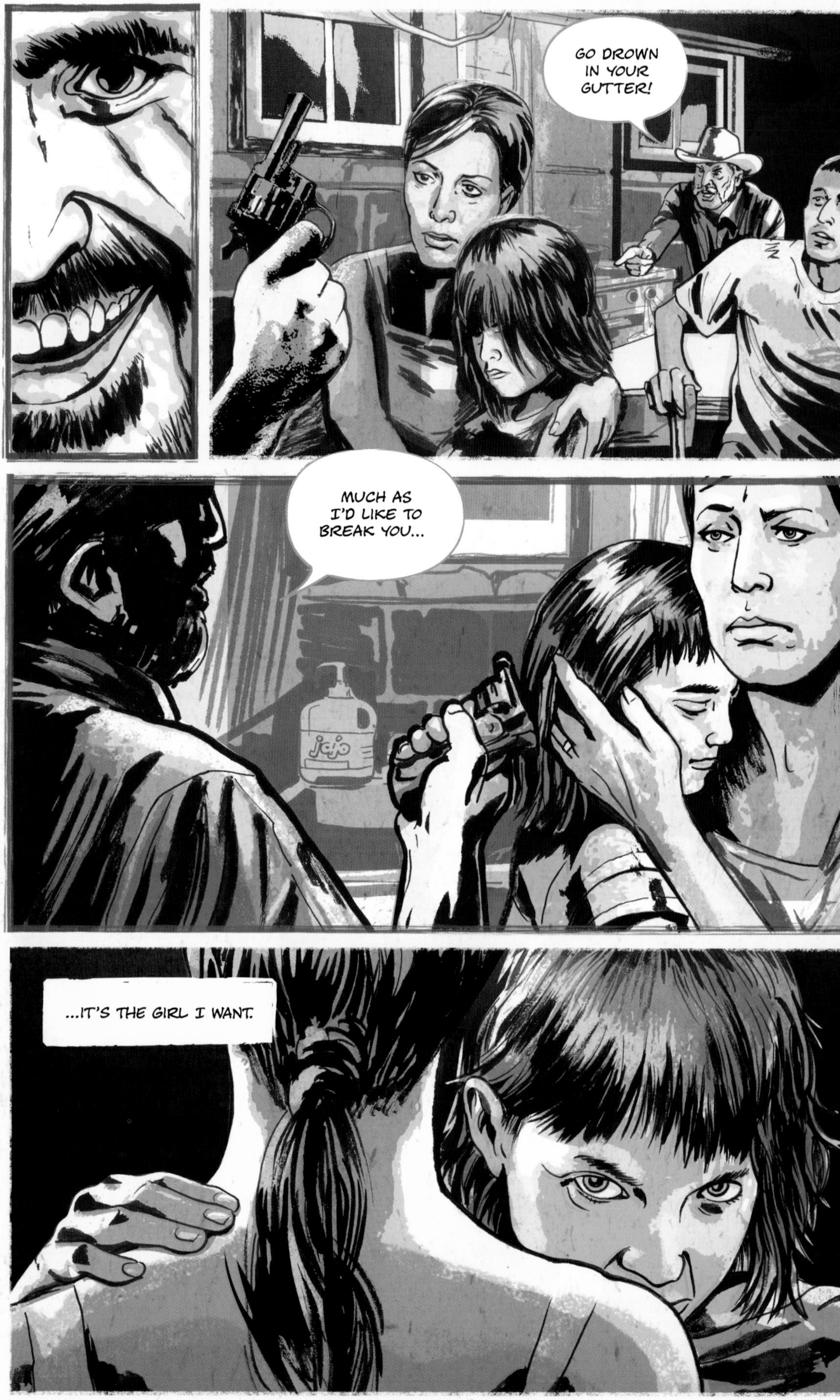
GO DROWN IN YOUR GUTTER!
MUCH AS I'D LIKE TO BREAK YOU...
...IT'S THE GIRL I WANT.
jojo

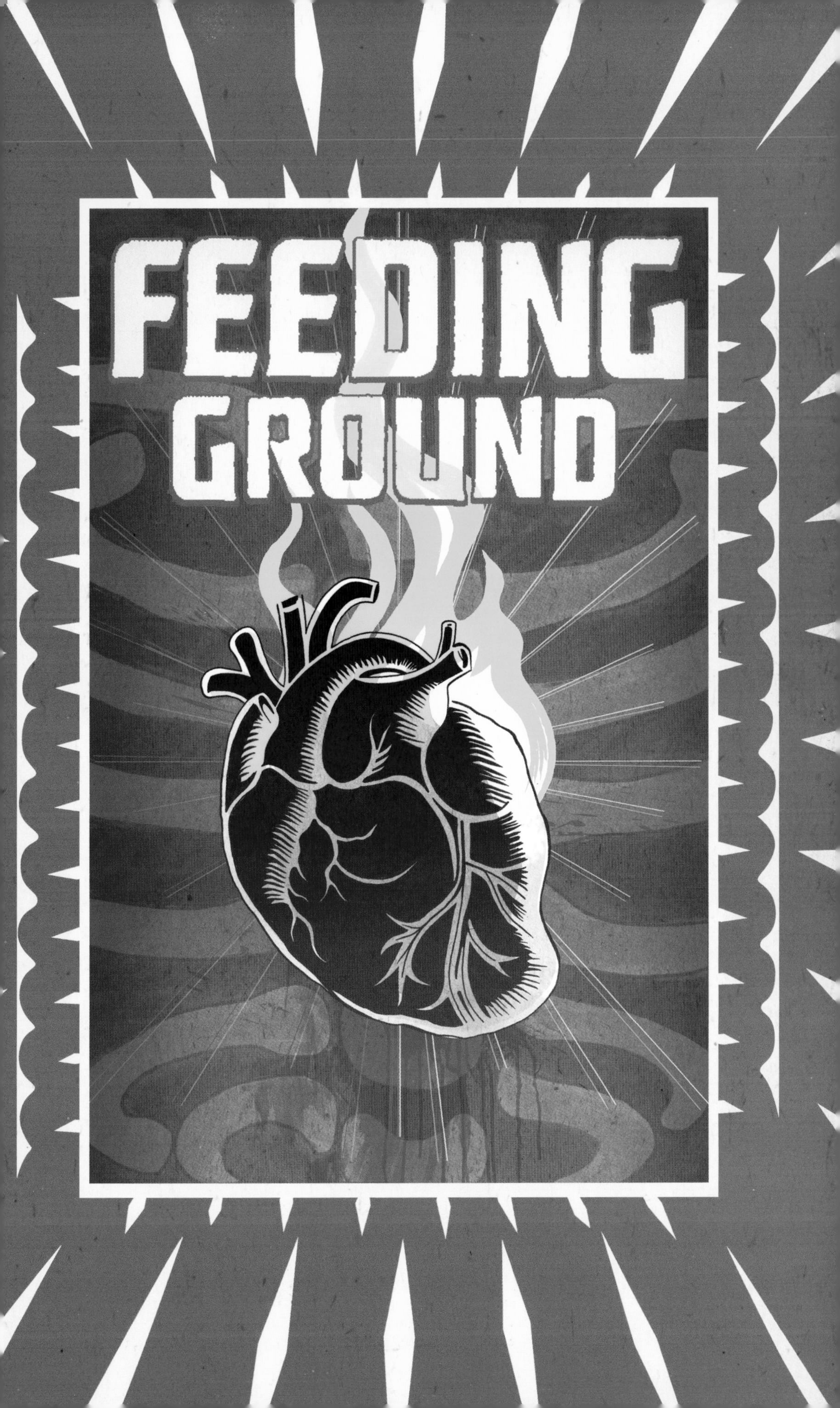
FEEDING
GROUND

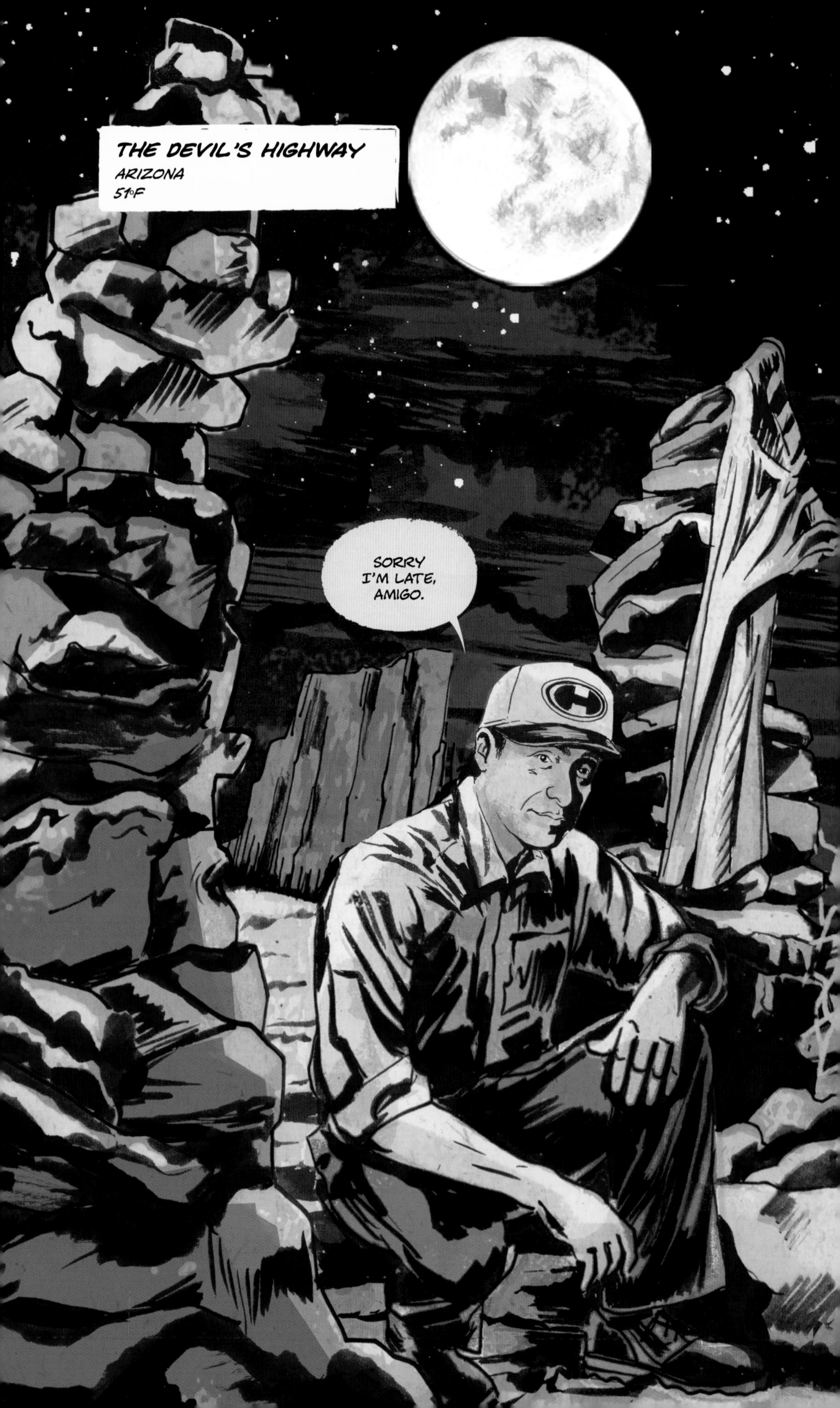
THE DEVIL'S HIGHWAY
ARIZONA
51°F
SORRY I'M LATE, AMIGO.

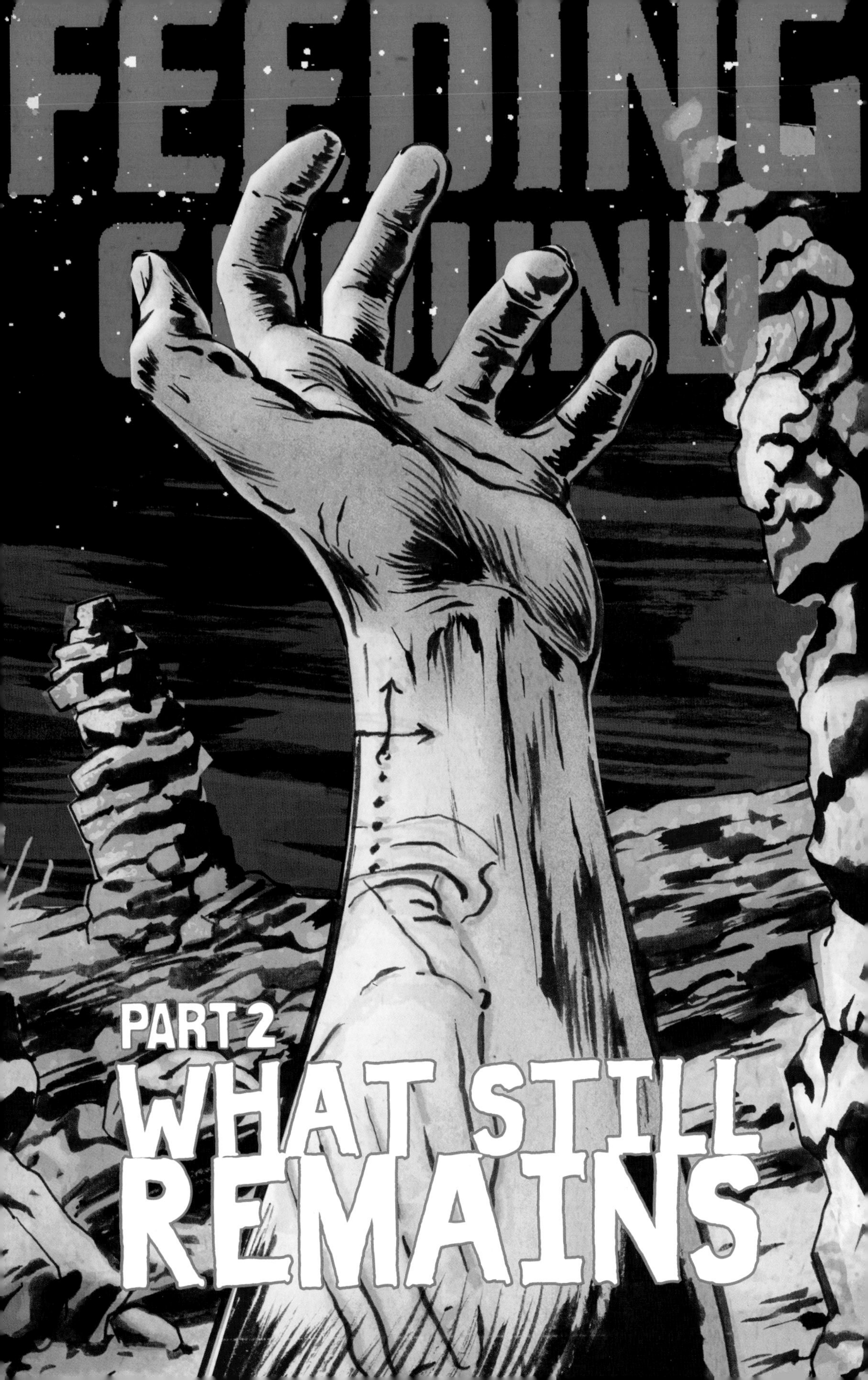
FEEDING
PART 2
WHAT STILL
REMAINS

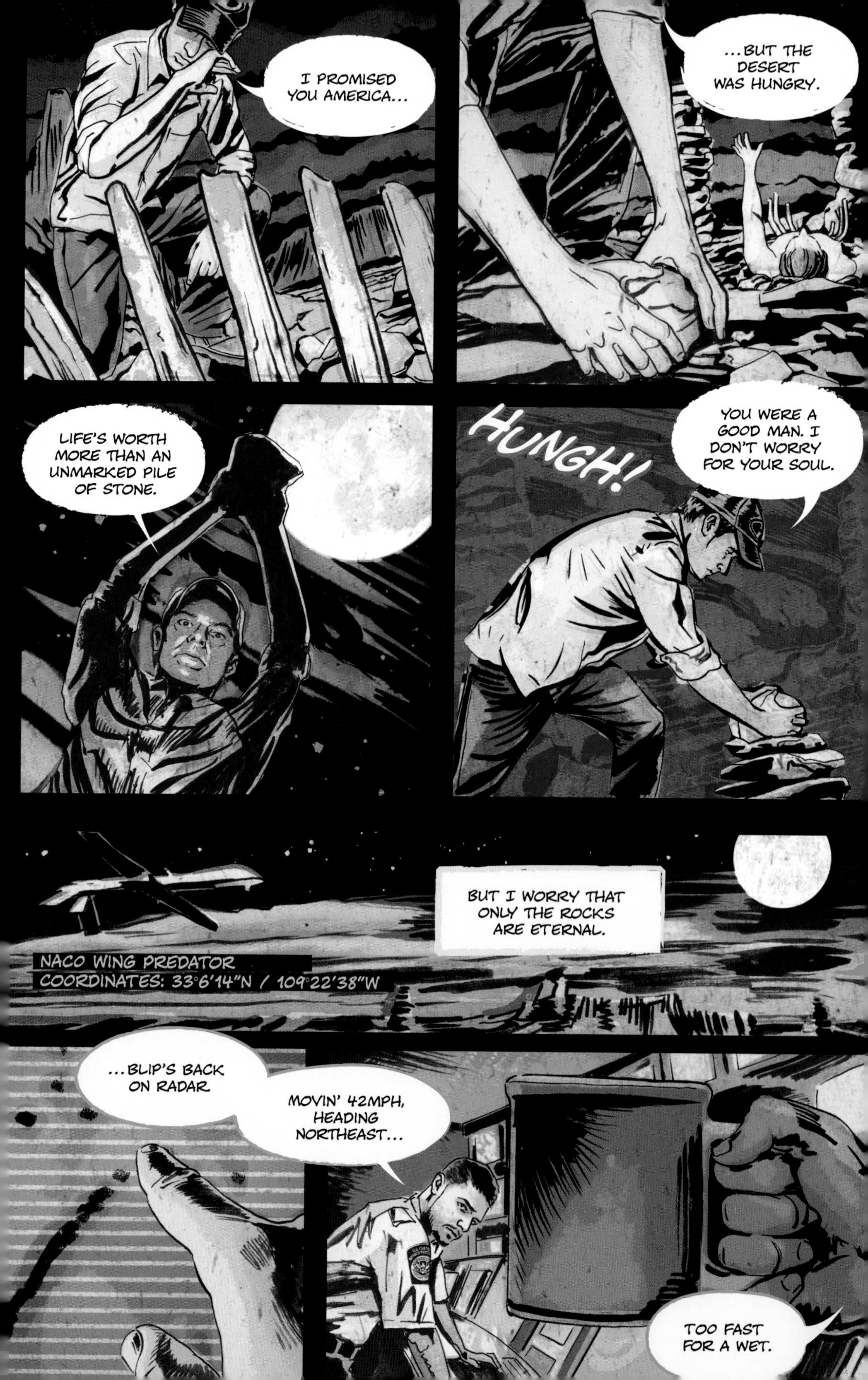
I PROMISED YOU AMERICA...
...BUT THE DESERT WAS HUNGRY.
LIFE'S WORTH MORE THAN AN UNMARKED PILE OF STONE.
HUNGH!
YOU WERE A GOOD MAN. I DON'T WORRY FOR YOUR SOUL.
BUT I WORRY THAT ONLY THE ROCKS ARE ETERNAL.
NACO WING PREDATOR
COORDINATES: 33°6'14"N / 109°22'38"W
...BLIP'S BACK ON RADAR.
MOVIN' 42MPH, HEADING NORTHEAST...
TOO FAST FOR A WET.

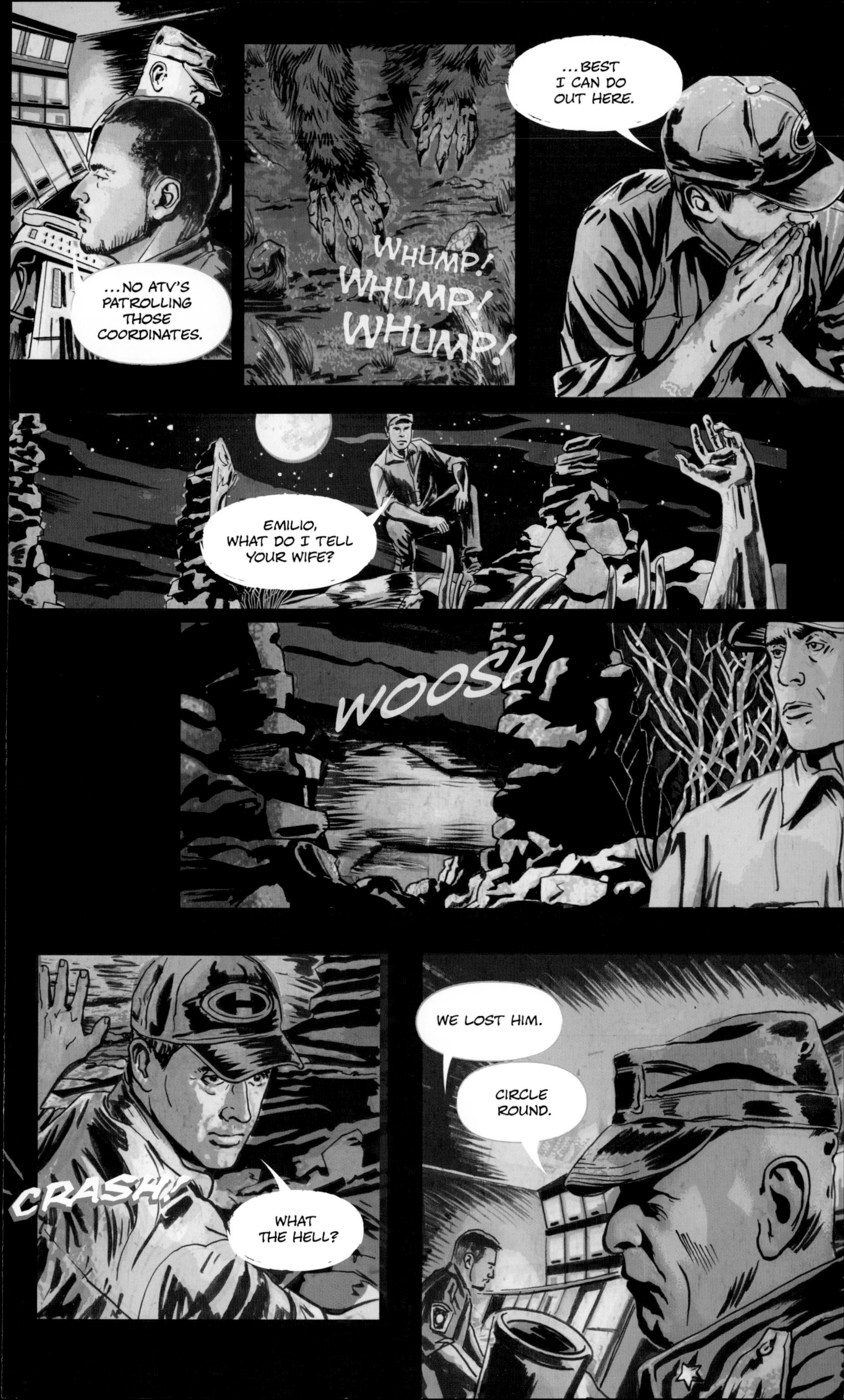
...NO ATV'S PATROLLING THOSE COORDINATES.
WHUMP! WHUMP! WHUMP!
...BEST I CAN DO OUT HERE.
EMILIO, WHAT DO I TELL YOUR WIFE?
WOOSH
CRASH!
WHAT THE HELL?
WE LOST HIM.
CIRCLE ROUND.

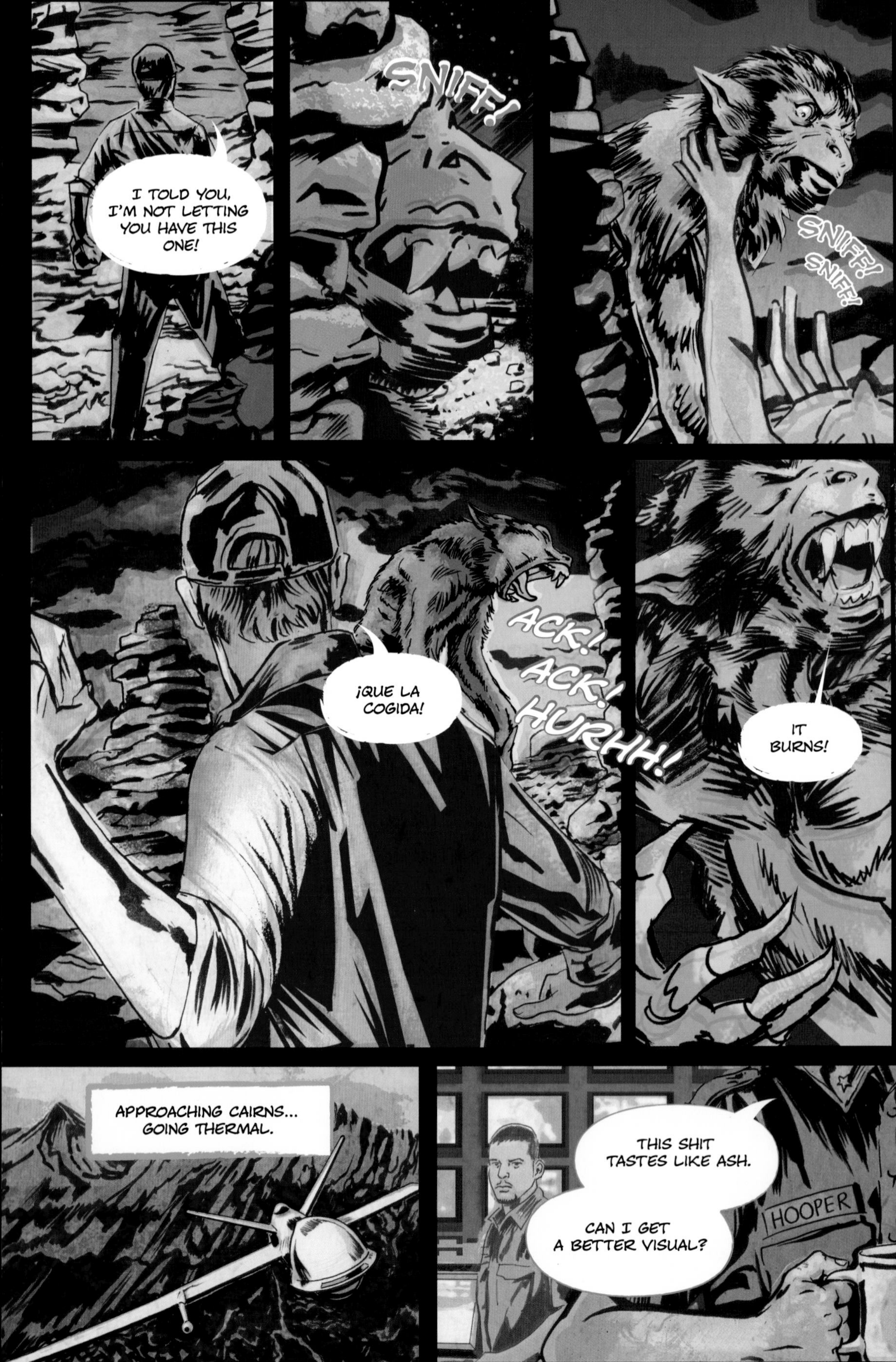
I TOLD YOU, I'M NOT LETTING YOU HAVE THIS ONE!
SNIFF!
SNIFF!
SNIFF!
¡QUE LA COGIDA!
ACK! ACK! HURHH!
IT BURNS!
APPROACHING CAIRNS... GOING THERMAL.
THIS SHIT TASTES LIKE ASH.
CAN I GET A BETTER VISUAL?
HOOPER

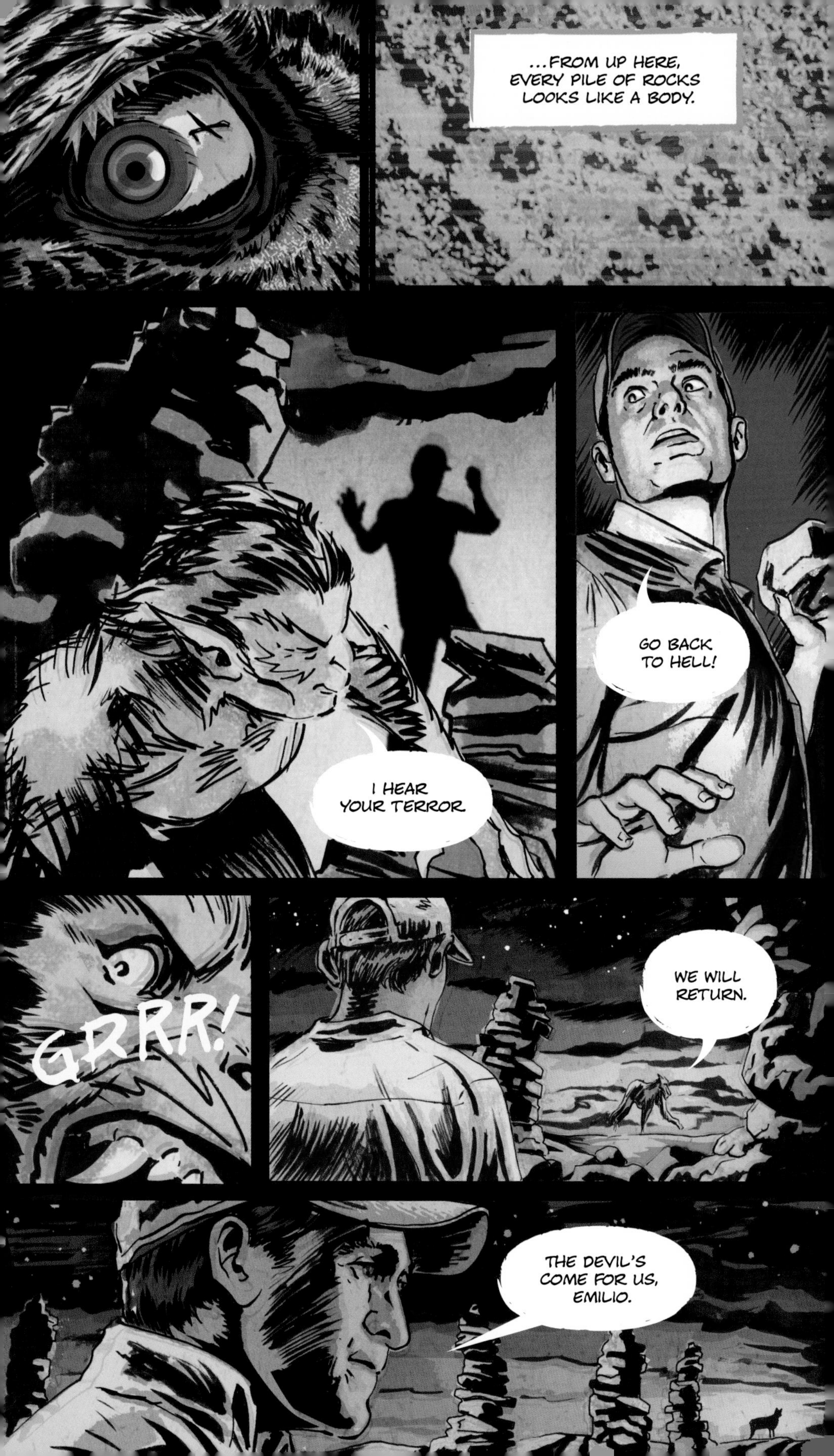
...FROM UP HERE, EVERY PILE OF ROCKS LOOKS LIKE A BODY.
I HEAR YOUR TERROR
GO BACK TO HELL!
GRRR!
WE WILL RETURN.
THE DEVIL'S COME FOR US, EMILIO.

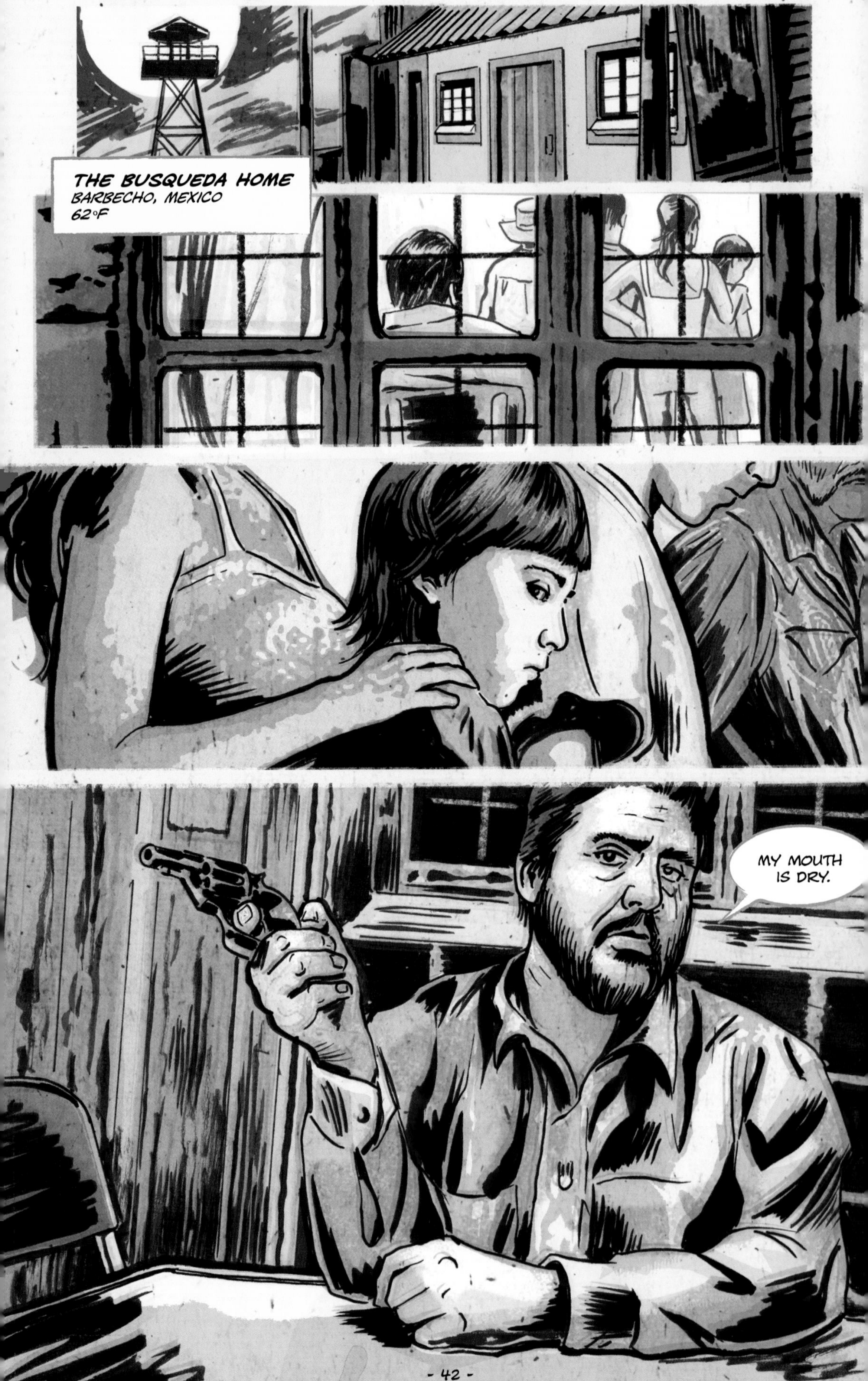
THE BUSQUEDA HOME
BARBECHO, MEXICO
62°F
MY MOUTH IS DRY.

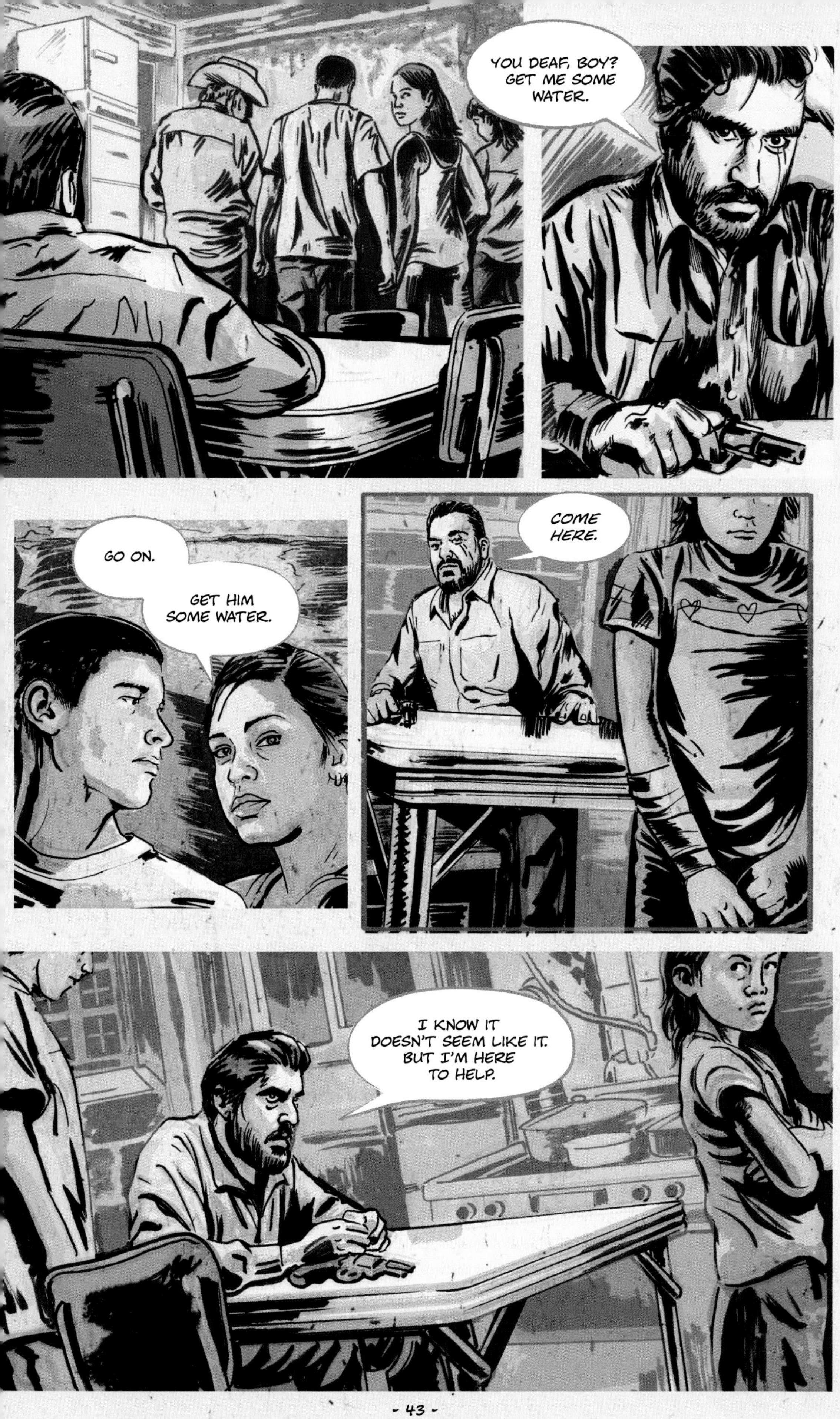
YOU DEAF, BOY? GET ME SOME WATER.
GO ON.
GET HIM SOME WATER.
COME HERE.
I KNOW IT DOESN'T SEEM LIKE IT. BUT I'M HERE TO HELP.

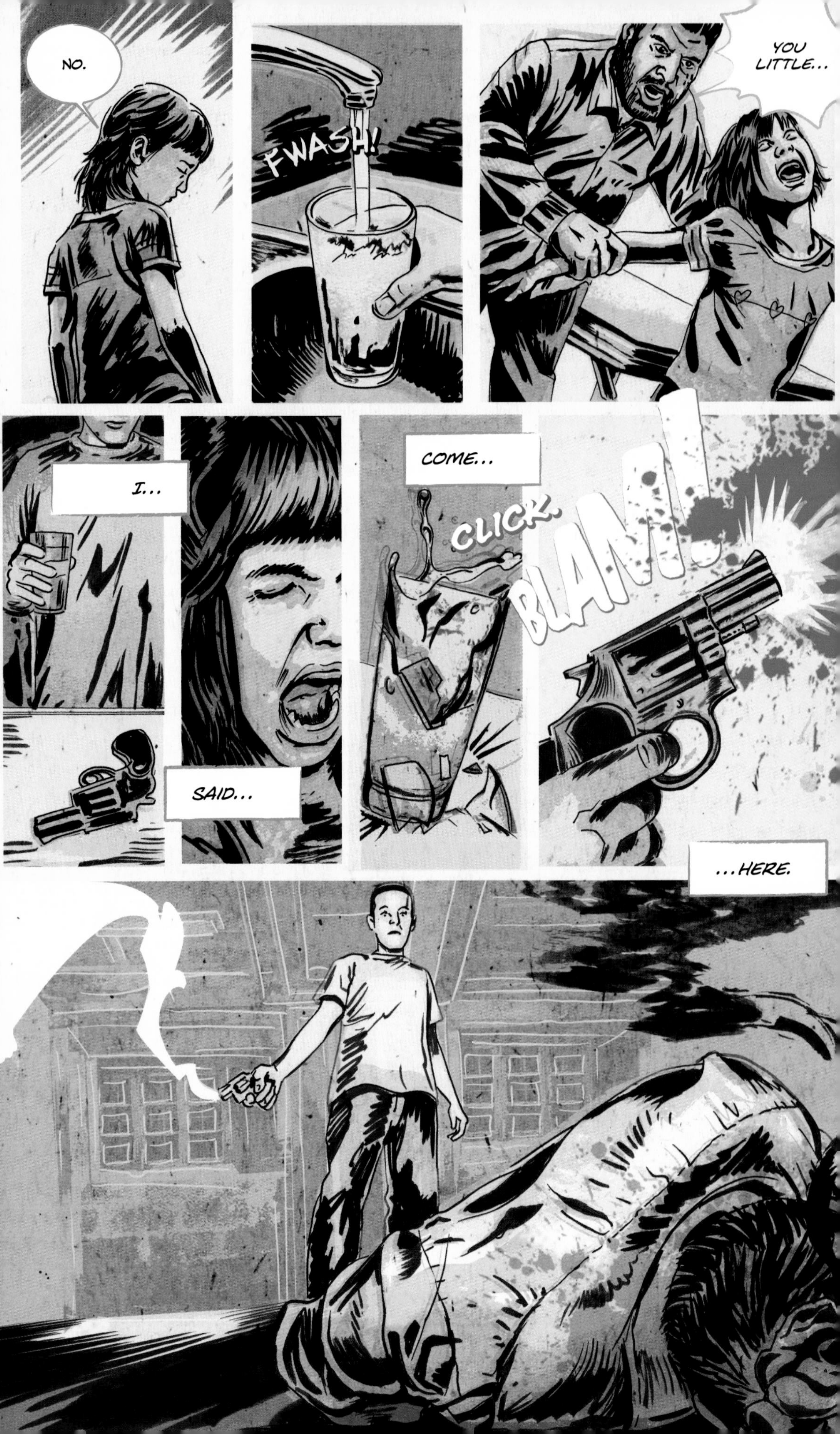

NO.
FWASH!
YOU LITTLE...
I...
SAID...
COME...
CLICK.
BLAM!
...HERE.

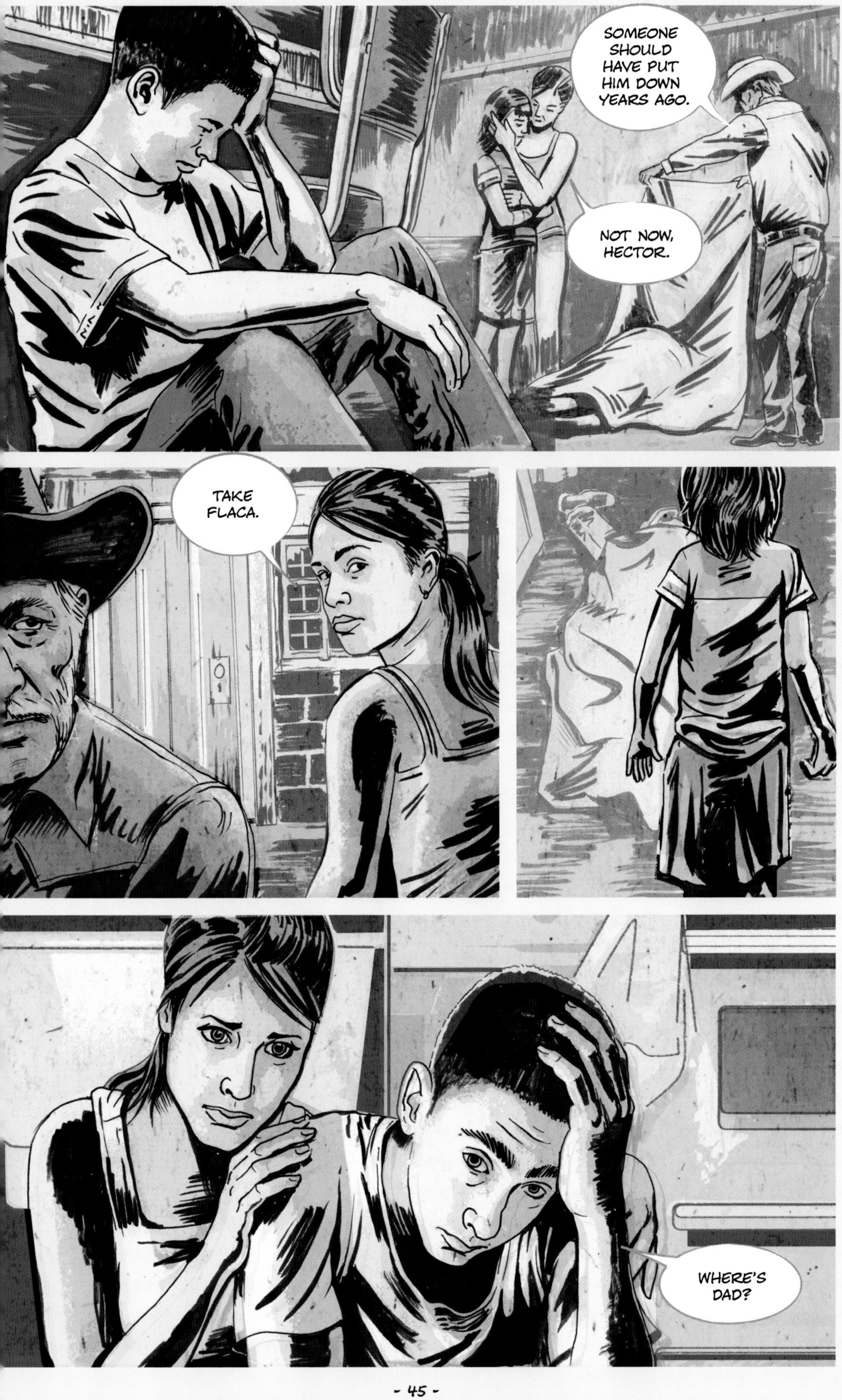
SOMEONE SHOULD HAVE PUT HIM DOWN YEARS AGO.
NOT NOW, HECTOR.
TAKE FLACA.
WHERE'S DAD?

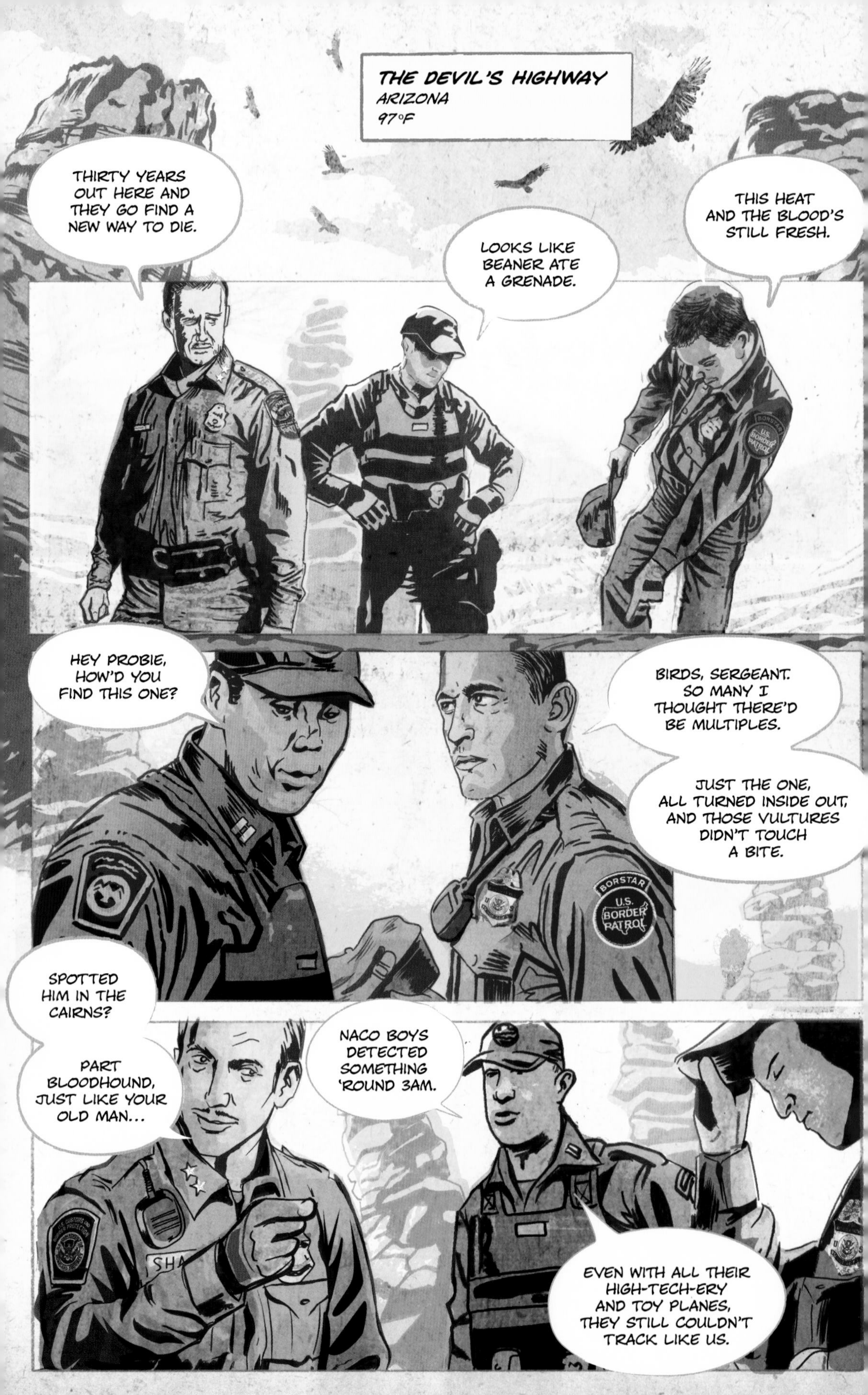
THE DEVIL'S HIGHWAY
ARIZONA
97°F
THIRTY YEARS OUT HERE AND THEY GO FIND A NEW WAY TO DIE.
LOOKS LIKE BEANER ATE A GRENADE.
THIS HEAT AND THE BLOOD'S STILL FRESH.
HEY PROBIE, HOW'D YOU FIND THIS ONE?
BIRDS, SERGEANT. SO MANY I THOUGHT THERE'D BE MULTIPLES.
JUST THE ONE, ALL TURNED INSIDE OUT, AND THOSE VULTURES DIDN'T TOUCH A BITE.
SPOTTED HIM IN THE CAIRNS?
PART BLOODHOUND, JUST LIKE YOUR OLD MAN...
NACO BOYS DETECTED SOMETHING 'ROUND 3AM.
EVEN WITH ALL THEIR HIGH-TECH-ERY AND TOY PLANES, THEY STILL COULDN'T TRACK LIKE US.

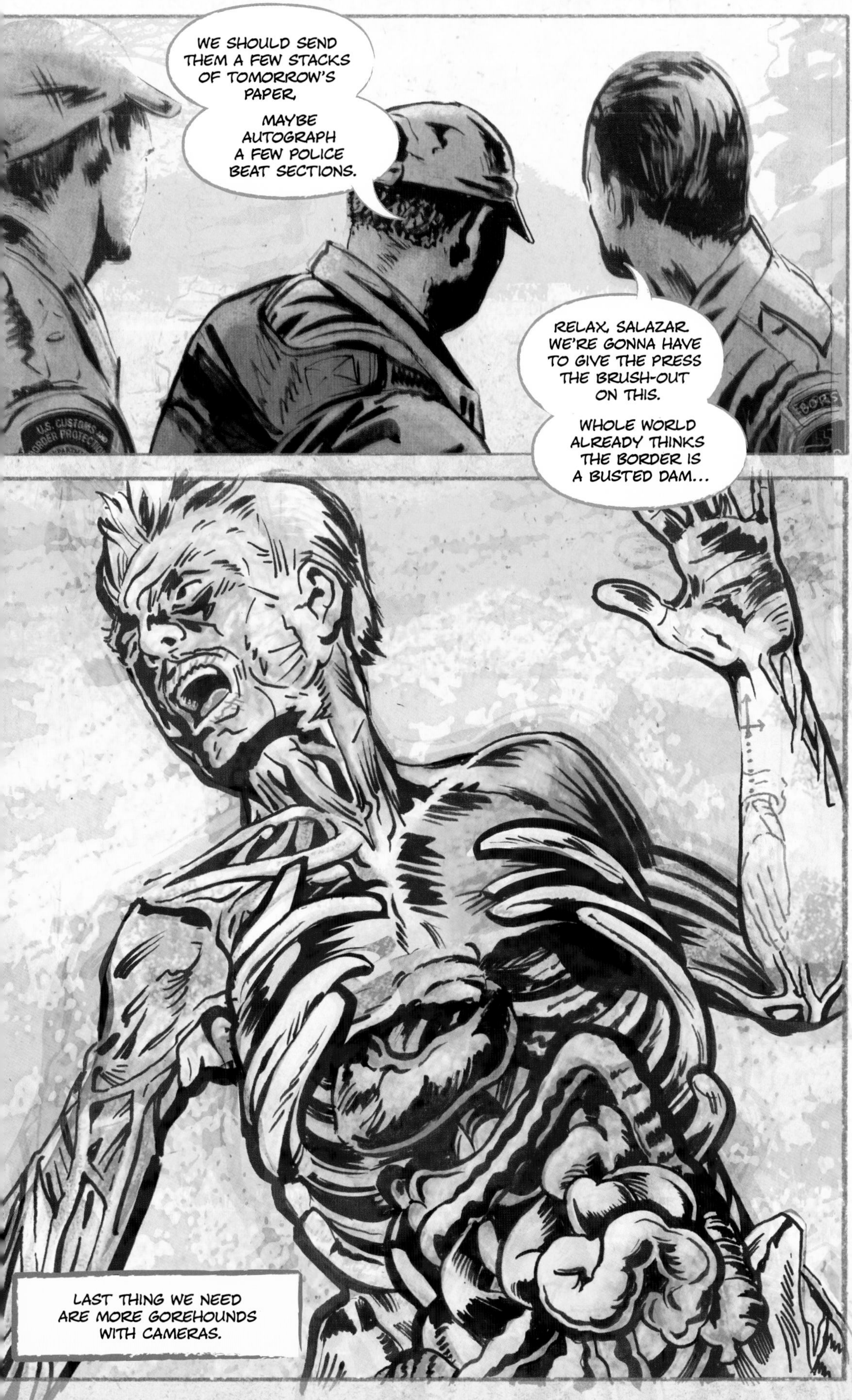
WE SHOULD SEND THEM A FEW STACKS OF TOMORROW'S PAPER.
MAYBE AUTOGRAPH A FEW POLICE BEAT SECTIONS.
RELAX, SALAZAR. WE'RE GONNA HAVE TO GIVE THE PRESS THE BRUSH-OUT ON THIS.
WHOLE WORLD ALREADY THINKS THE BORDER IS A BUSTED DAM...
LAST THING WE NEED ARE MORE GOREHOUNDS WITH CAMERAS.

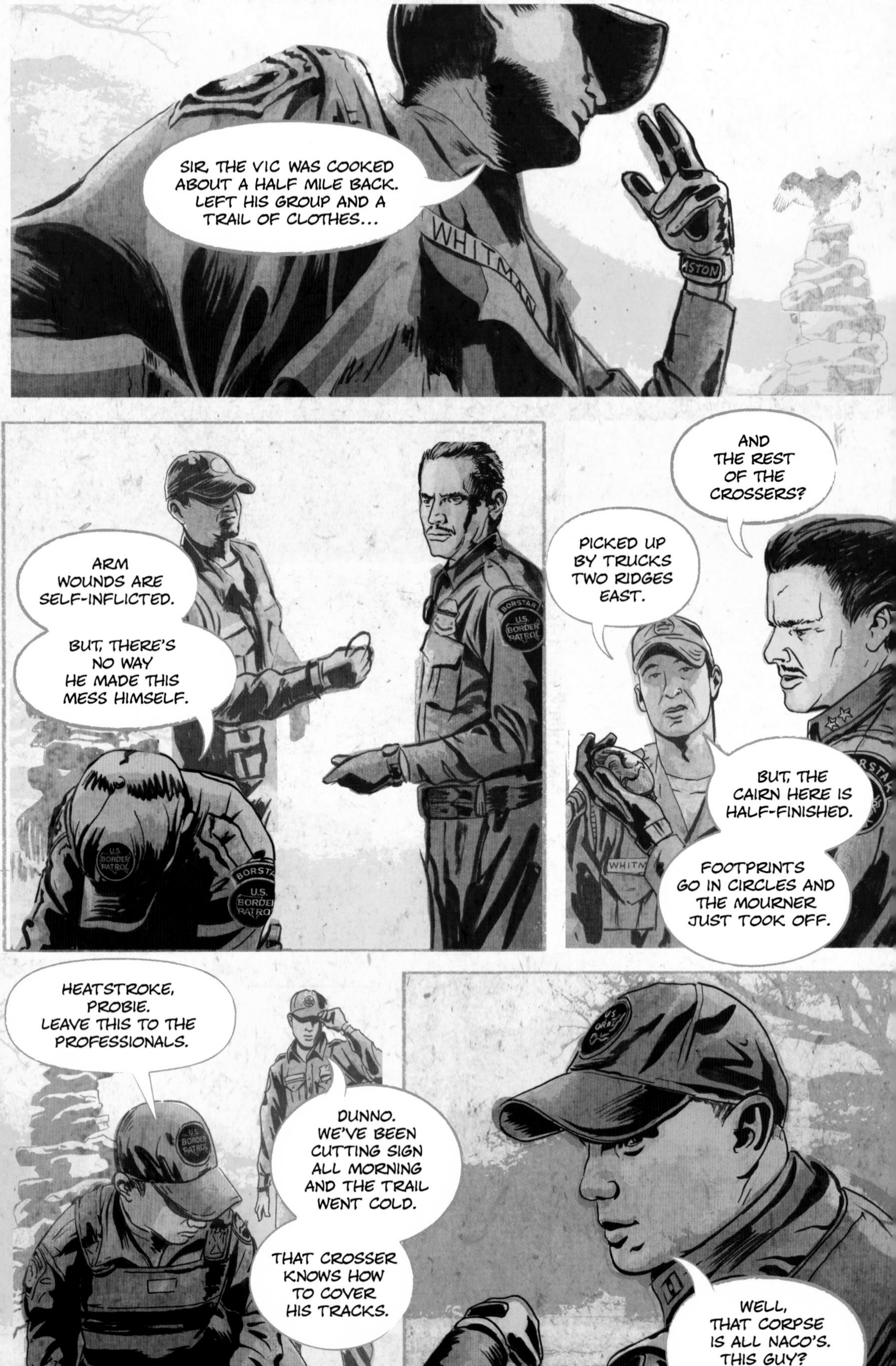

SIR, THE VIC WAS COOKED ABOUT A HALF MILE BACK. LEFT HIS GROUP AND A TRAIL OF CLOTHES...
WHITMAN
ARM WOUNDS ARE SELF-INFLICTED.
BUT, THERE'S NO WAY HE MADE THIS MESS HIMSELF.
AND THE REST OF THE CROSSERS?
PICKED UP BY TRUCKS TWO RIDGES EAST.
BUT, THE CAIRN HERE IS HALF-FINISHED.
FOOTPRINTS GO IN CIRCLES AND THE MOURNER JUST TOOK OFF.
HEATSTROKE, PROBIE. LEAVE THIS TO THE PROFESSIONALS.
DUNNO. WE'VE BEEN CUTTING SIGN ALL MORNING AND THE TRAIL WENT COLD.
THAT CROSSER KNOWS HOW TO COVER HIS TRACKS.
WELL, THAT CORPSE IS ALL NACO'S. THIS GUY? YOU FOUND HIM, YOU BAG HIM.

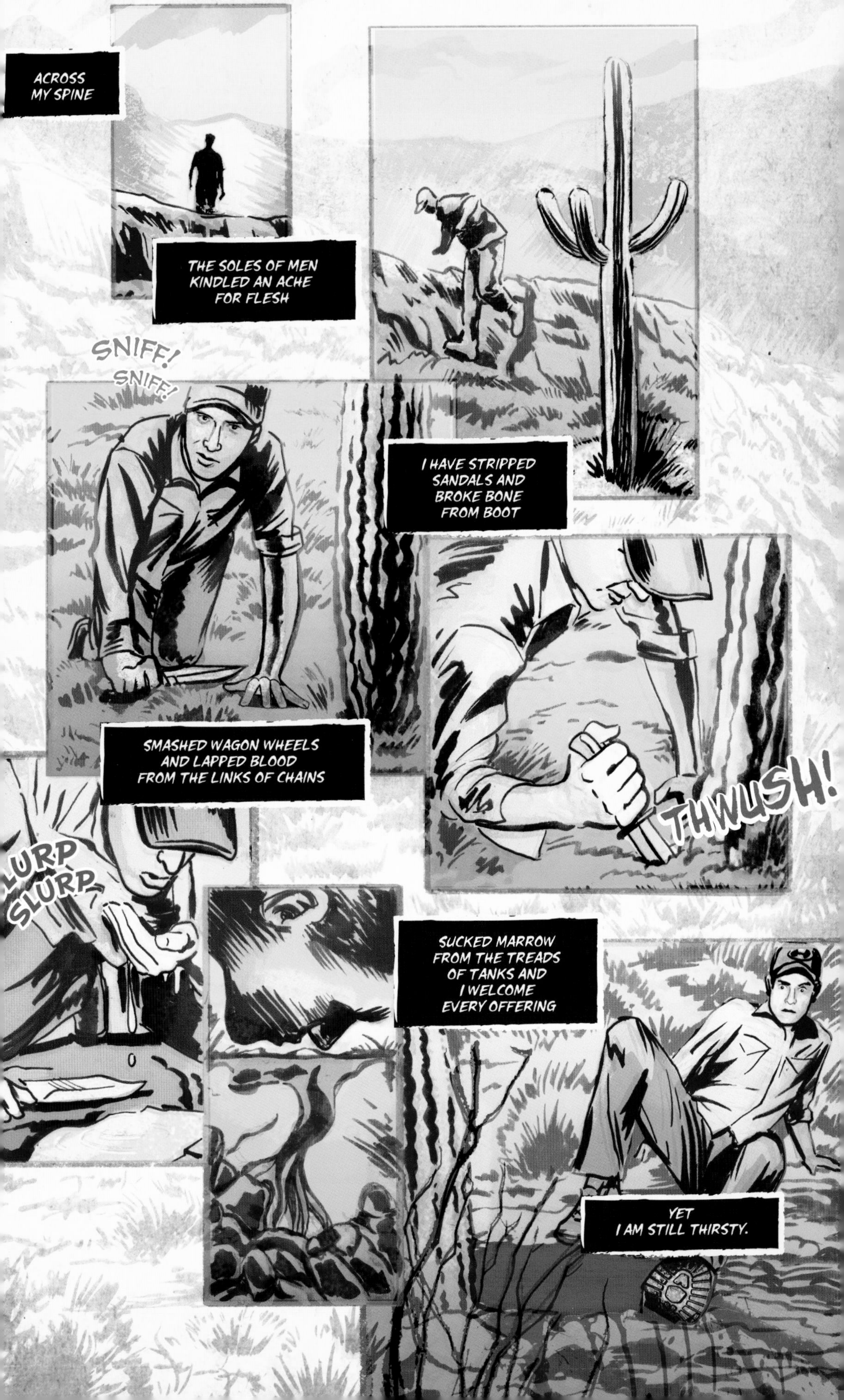
ACROSS MY SPINE
THE SOLES OF MEN KINDLED AN ACHE FOR FLESH
SNIFF! SNIFF!
I HAVE STRIPPED SANDALS AND BROKE BONE FROM BOOT
SMASHED WAGON WHEELS AND LAPPED BLOOD FROM THE LINKS OF CHAINS
THWUSH!
LURP SLURP
SUCKED MARROW FROM THE TREADS OF TANKS AND I WELCOME EVERY OFFERING
YET I AM STILL THIRSTY.

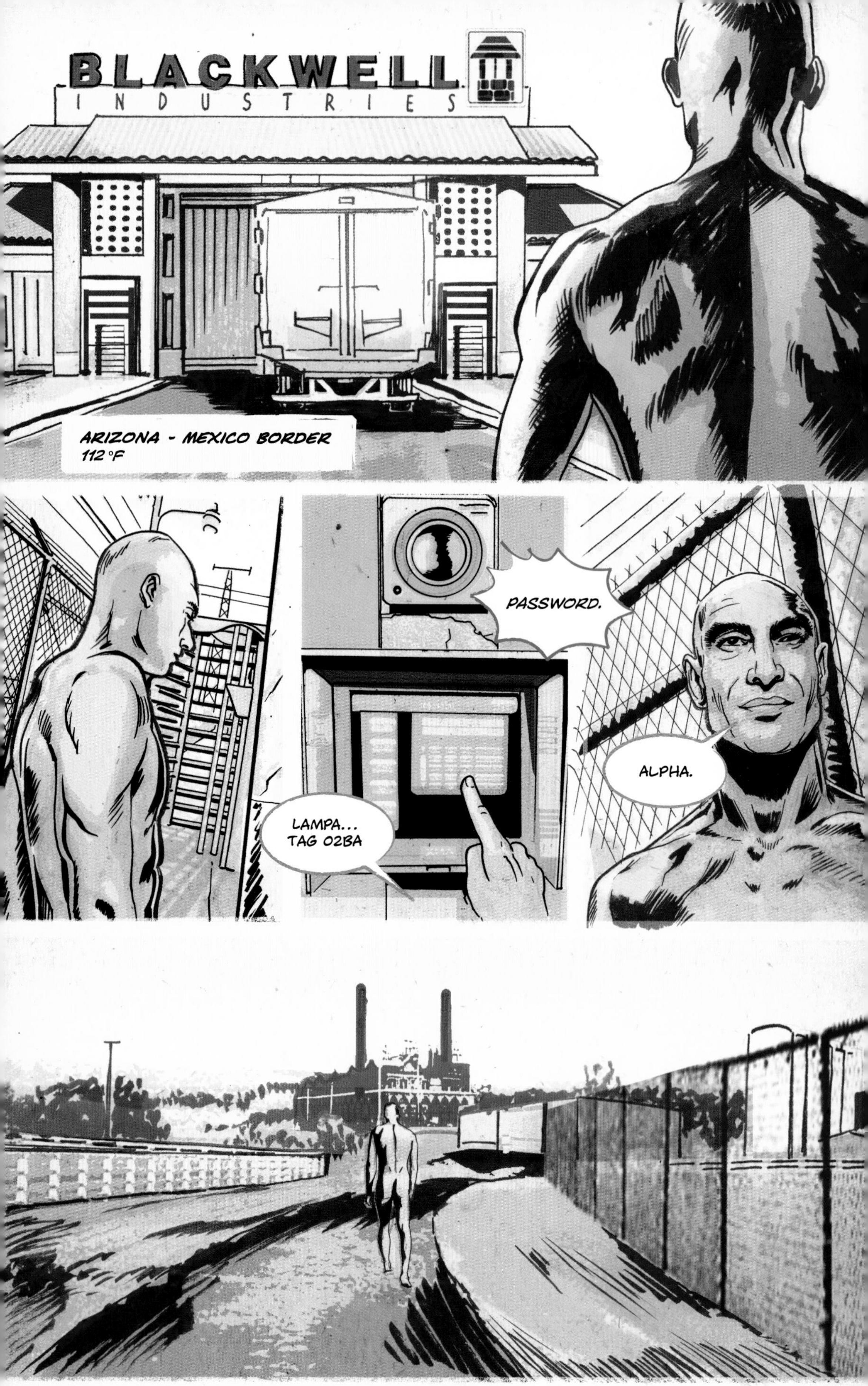
BLACKWELL
INDUSTRIES
ARIZONA - MEXICO BORDER
112 °F
PASSWORD.
LAMPA...
TAG O2BA
ALPHA.

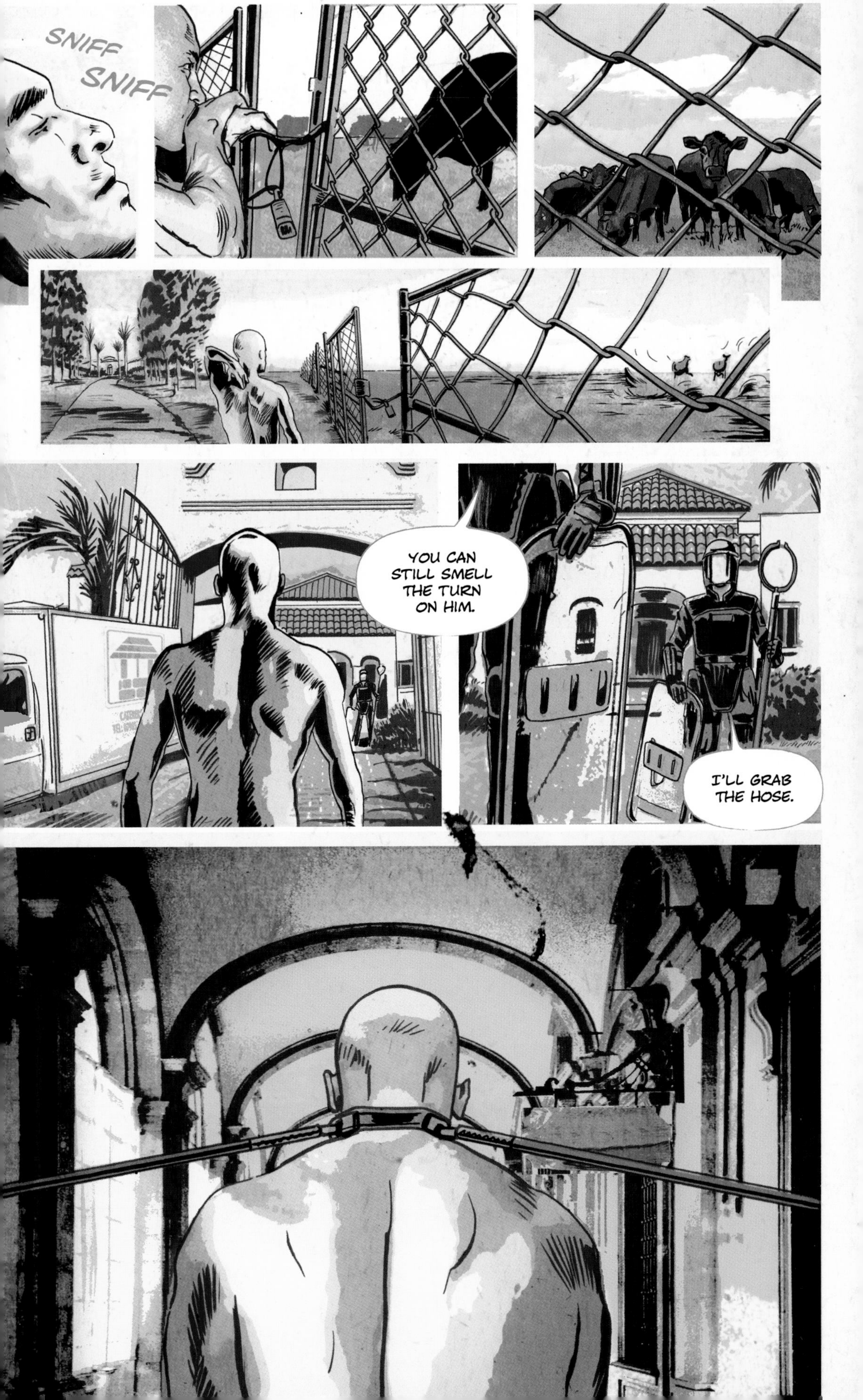
SNIFF
SNIFF
YOU CAN STILL SMELL THE TURN ON HIM.
I'LL GRAB THE HOSE.

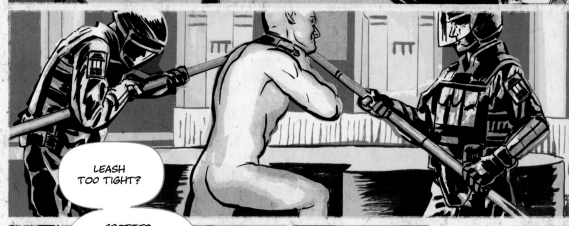

LEASH TOO TIGHT?

SPOTTED BY A MAN?! I EXPECT MORE COMPETENCE FROM AN ALPHA.

I SMELLED THE ROT IN THE WIND.

FAILURE IS INEXCUSABLE. YOU'RE A DISGRACE TO MY LINEAGE.

DR FLEISCHER, PLEASE FETCH THAT... MONSTROSITY.

ALL I ASKED WAS TO RETRIEVE THAT ABOMINATION.

IT'LL BE A PLEASURE TO EXAMINE THE SPECIMEN

THE BODY WAS SICK. IT OVERWHELMED MY SENSES. I COULDN'T...

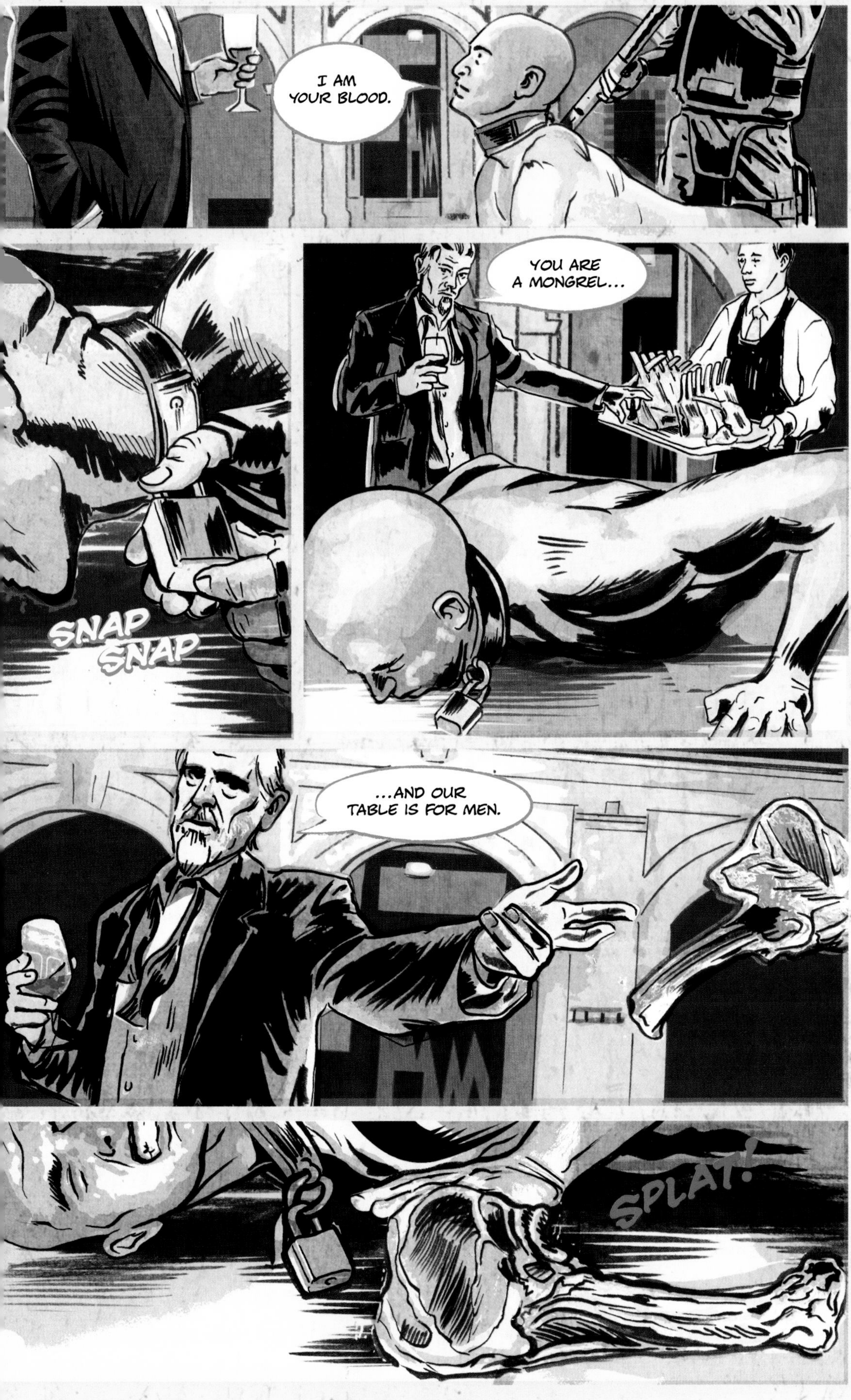
I AM YOUR BLOOD.
YOU ARE A MONGREL...
SNAP SNAP
...AND OUR TABLE IS FOR MEN.
SPLAT!

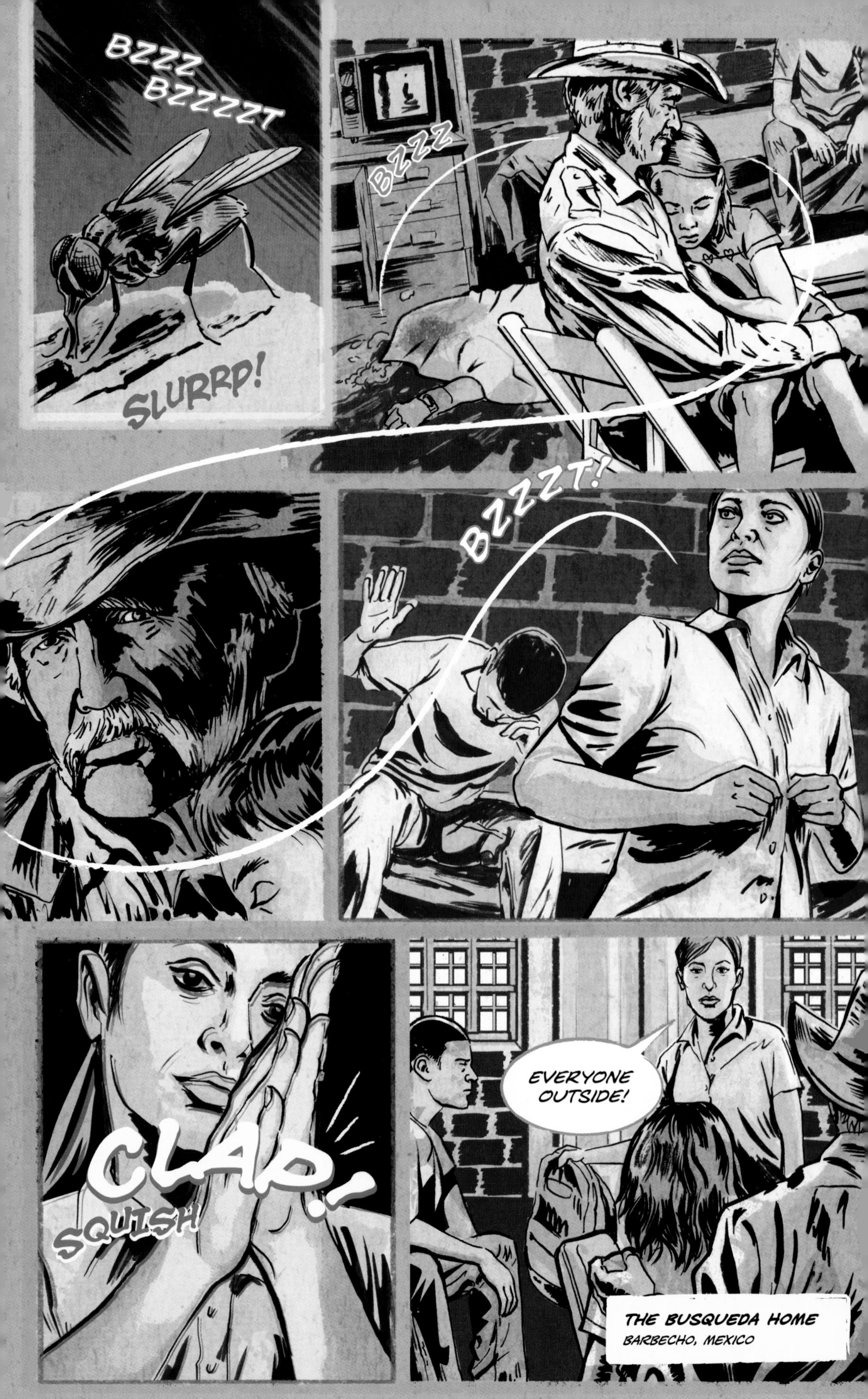
BZZZ
BZZZZZT
SLURRP!
BZZZ
BZZZZT!
CLAP!
SQUISH
EVERYONE OUTSIDE!
THE BUSQUEDA HOME
BARBECHO, MEXICO

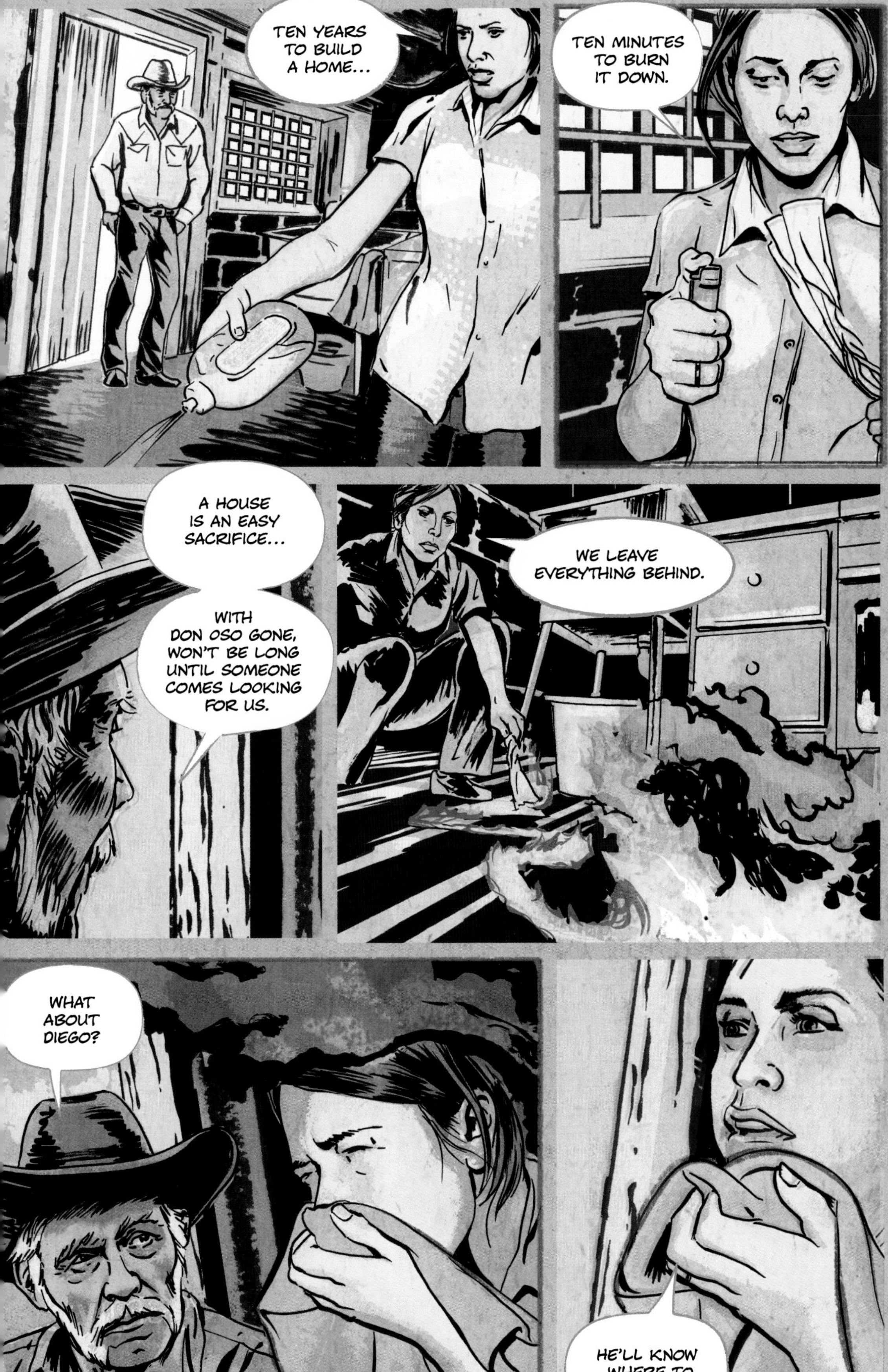
TEN YEARS TO BUILD A HOME...
TEN MINUTES TO BURN IT DOWN.
A HOUSE IS AN EASY SACRIFICE...
WITH DON OSO GONE, WON'T BE LONG UNTIL SOMEONE COMES LOOKING FOR US.
WE LEAVE EVERYTHING BEHIND.
WHAT ABOUT DIEGO?
HE'LL KNOW WHERE TO FIND US.

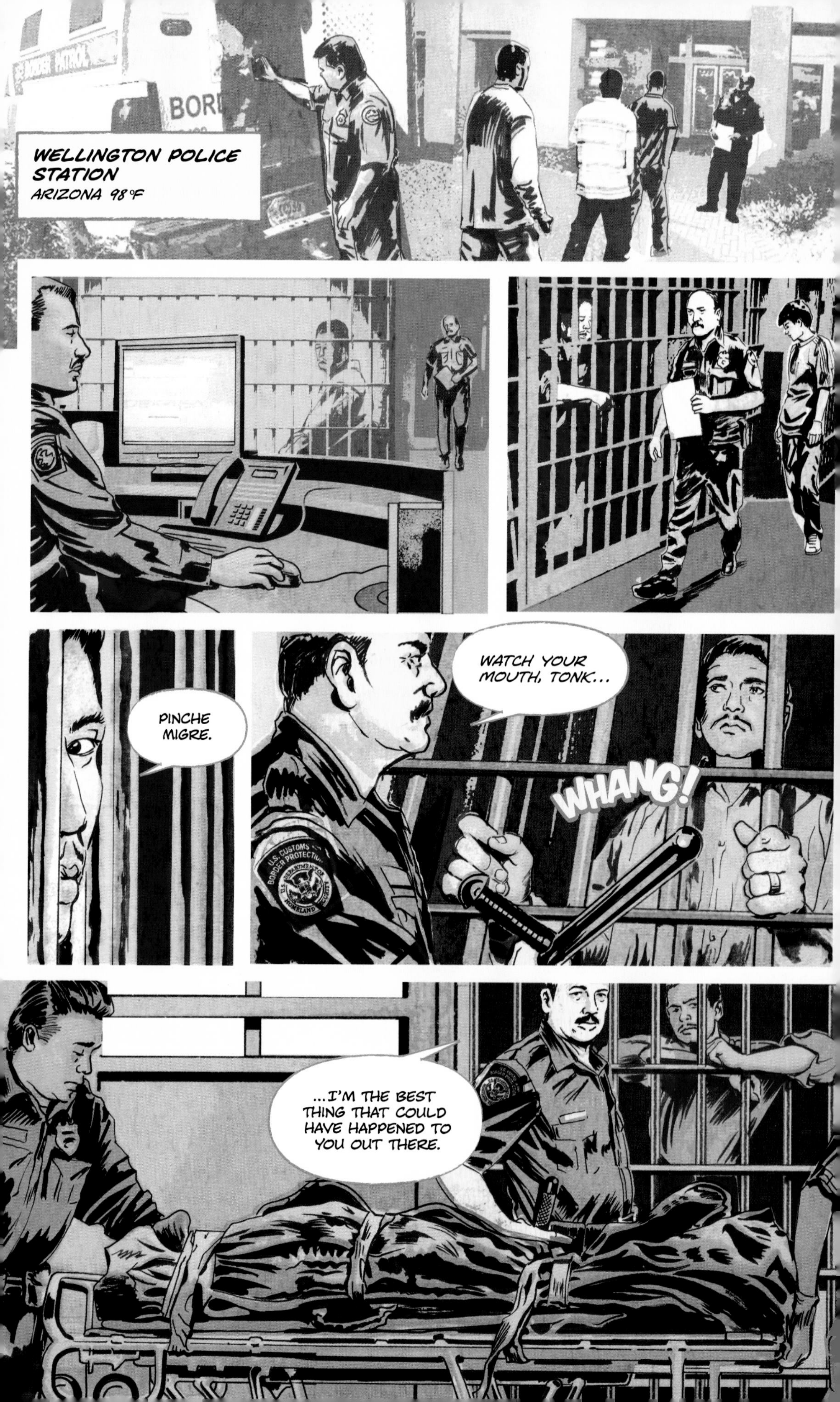
WELLINGTON POLICE STATION
ARIZONA 98°F
BORDER PATROL
PINCHE MIGRE.
WATCH YOUR MOUTH, TONK...
WHANG!
...I'M THE BEST THING THAT COULD HAVE HAPPENED TO YOU OUT THERE.

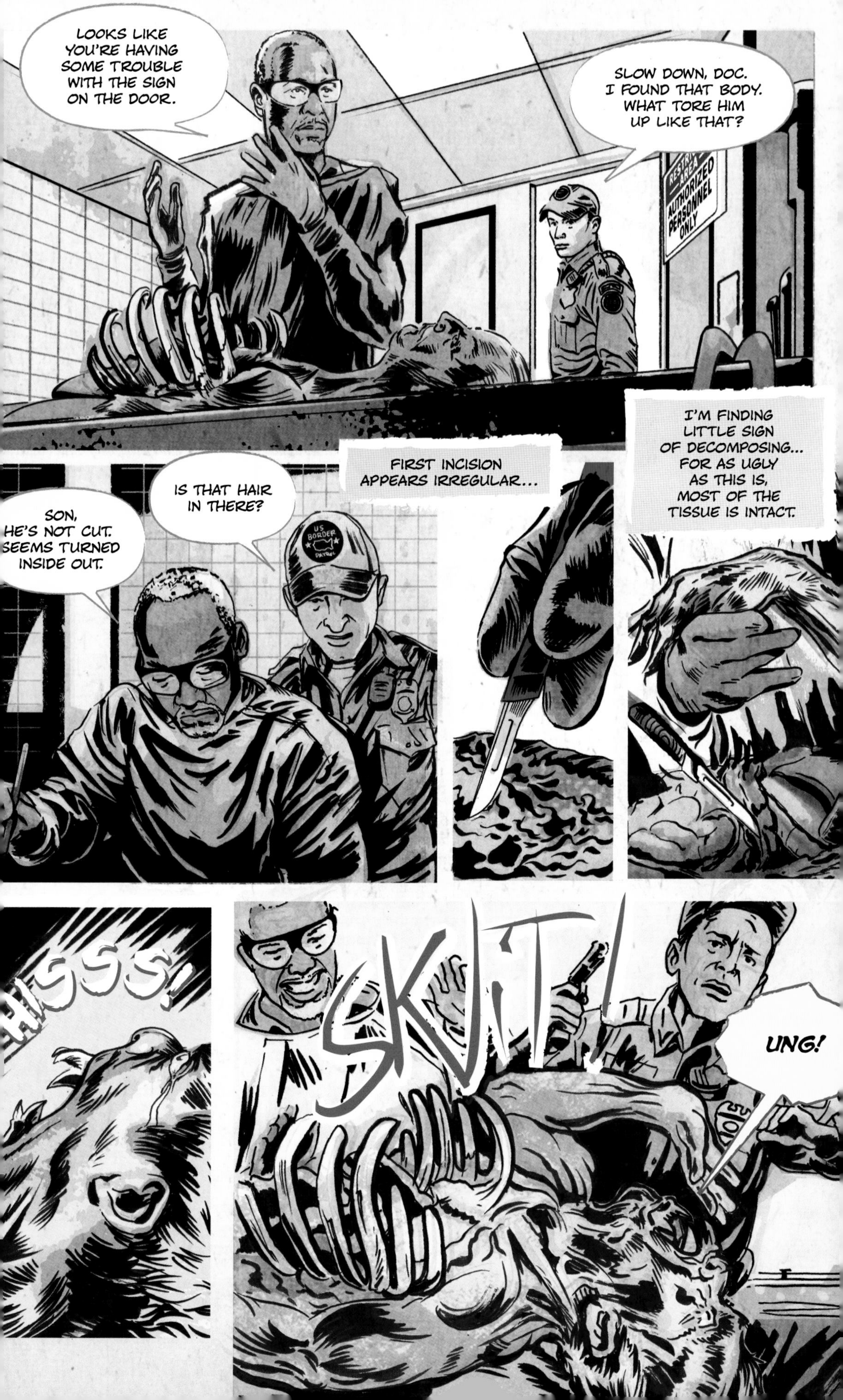
LOOKS LIKE YOU'RE HAVING SOME TROUBLE WITH THE SIGN ON THE DOOR.
SLOW DOWN, DOC. I FOUND THAT BODY. WHAT TORE HIM UP LIKE THAT?
RESTRICTED AREA AUTHORIZED PERSONNEL ONLY
SON, HE'S NOT CUT. SEEMS TURNED INSIDE OUT.
IS THAT HAIR IN THERE?
US BORDER PATROL
FIRST INCISION APPEARS IRREGULAR...
I'M FINDING LITTLE SIGN OF DECOMPOSING... FOR AS UGLY AS THIS IS, MOST OF THE TISSUE IS INTACT.
HISSS!
SKLIT!
UNG!

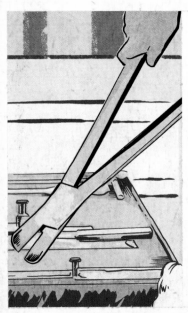

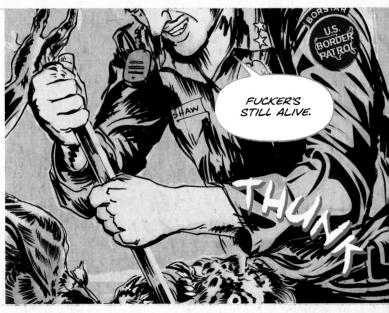

BORSTAR
U.S. BORDER PATROL
SHAW
FUCKER'S STILL ALIVE.
THUNK
KRAKT!
BORSTAR
U.S. BORDER PATROL
THIS ROOM IS LOCKED DOWN!

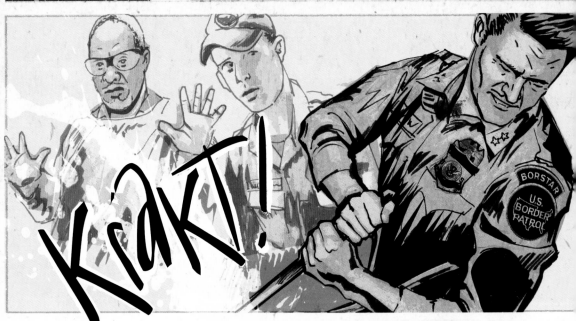

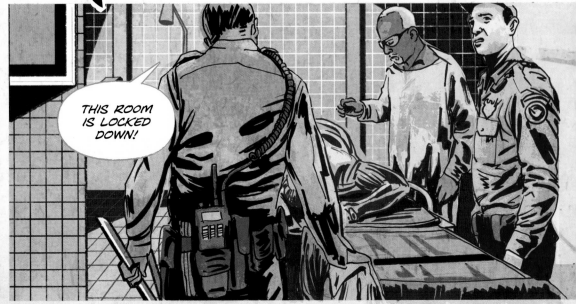

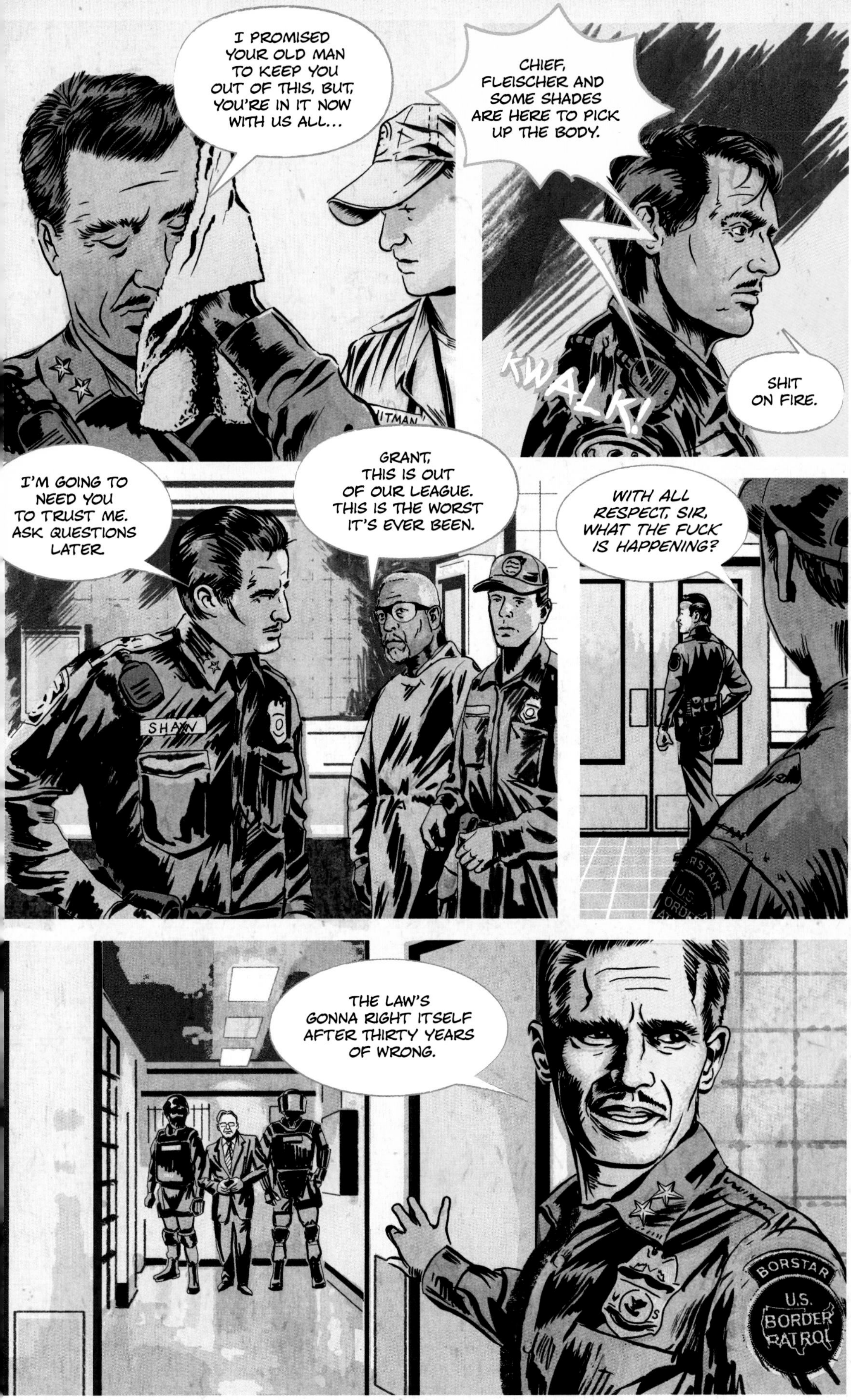
I PROMISED YOUR OLD MAN TO KEEP YOU OUT OF THIS, BUT, YOU'RE IN IT NOW WITH US ALL...
CHIEF, FLEISCHER AND SOME SHADES ARE HERE TO PICK UP THE BODY.
KWALK!
SHIT ON FIRE.
I'M GOING TO NEED YOU TO TRUST ME. ASK QUESTIONS LATER
GRANT, THIS IS OUT OF OUR LEAGUE. THIS IS THE WORST IT'S EVER BEEN.
SHAW
WITH ALL RESPECT, SIR, WHAT THE FUCK IS HAPPENING?
THE LAW'S GONNA RIGHT ITSELF AFTER THIRTY YEARS OF WRONG.
BORSTAR
U.S. BORDER PATROL

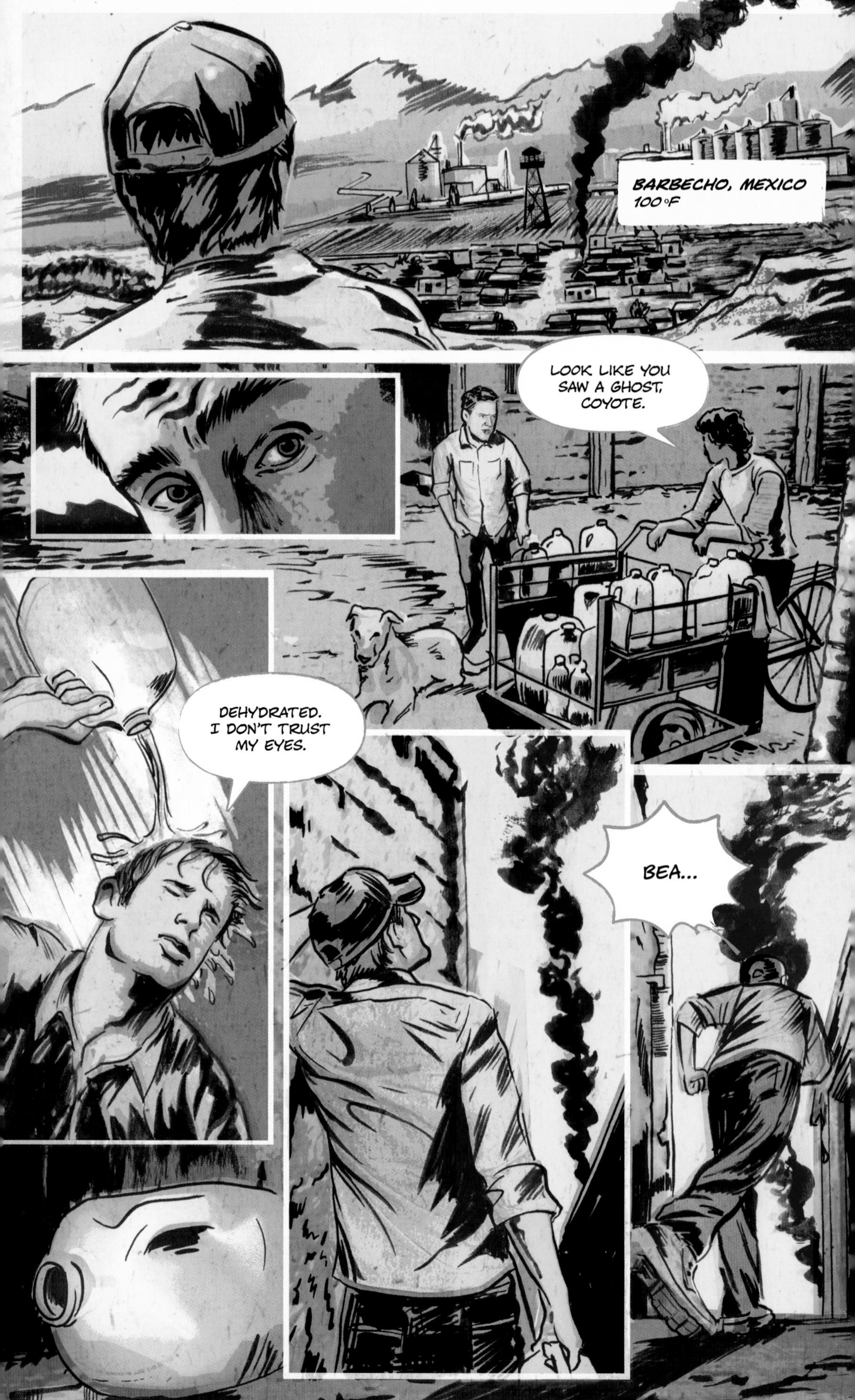

BARBECHO, MEXICO
100°F
LOOK LIKE YOU SAW A GHOST, COYOTE.
DEHYDRATED. I DON'T TRUST MY EYES.
BEA...

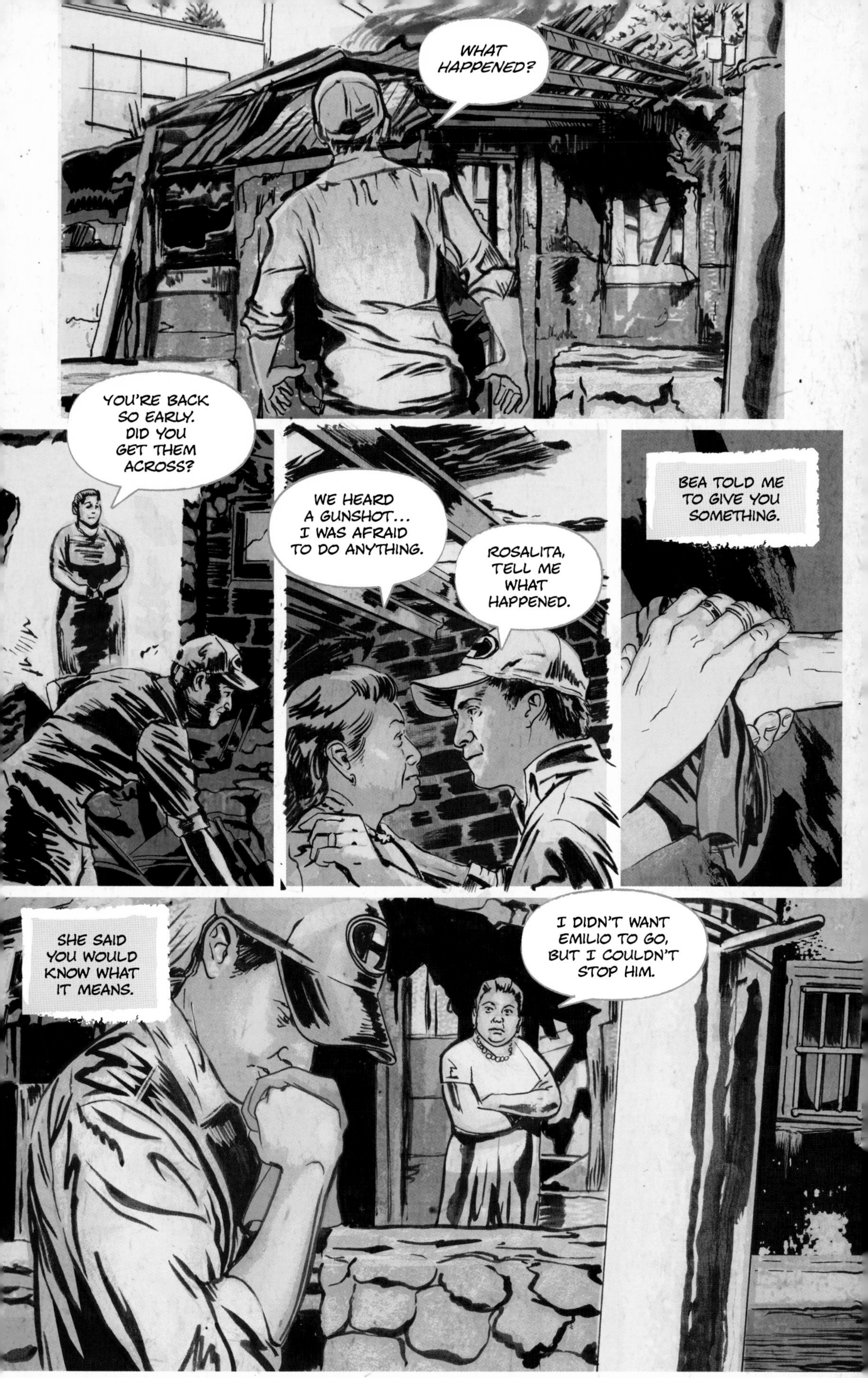
WHAT HAPPENED?
YOU'RE BACK SO EARLY. DID YOU GET THEM ACROSS?
WE HEARD A GUNSHOT... I WAS AFRAID TO DO ANYTHING.
ROSALITA, TELL ME WHAT HAPPENED.
BEA TOLD ME TO GIVE YOU SOMETHING.
SHE SAID YOU WOULD KNOW WHAT IT MEANS.
I DIDN'T WANT EMILIO TO GO, BUT I COULDN'T STOP HIM.

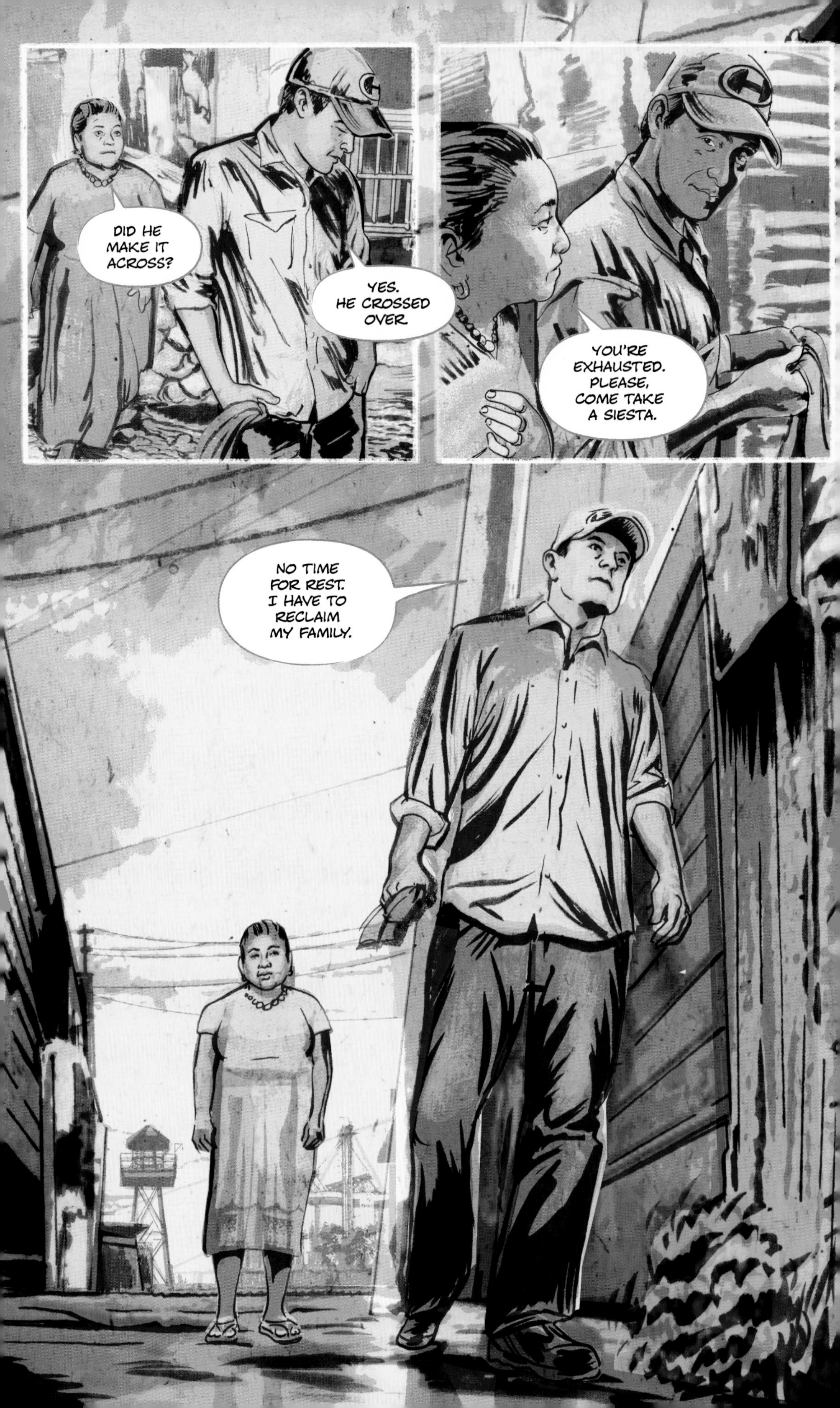
DID HE MAKE IT ACROSS?
YES. HE CROSSED OVER
YOU'RE EXHAUSTED. PLEASE, COME TAKE A SIESTA.
NO TIME FOR REST. I HAVE TO RECLAIM MY FAMILY.

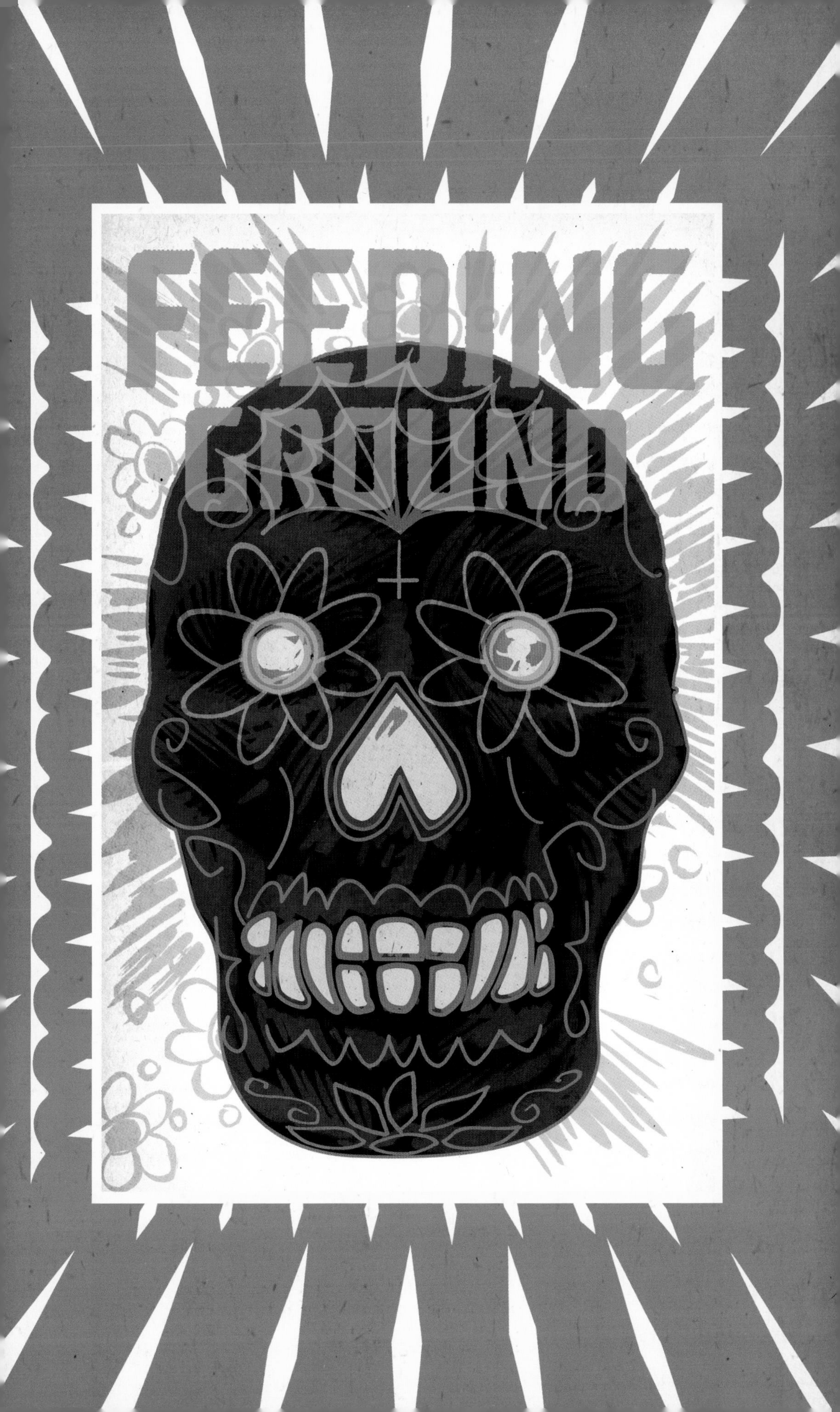
FEEDING
GROUND

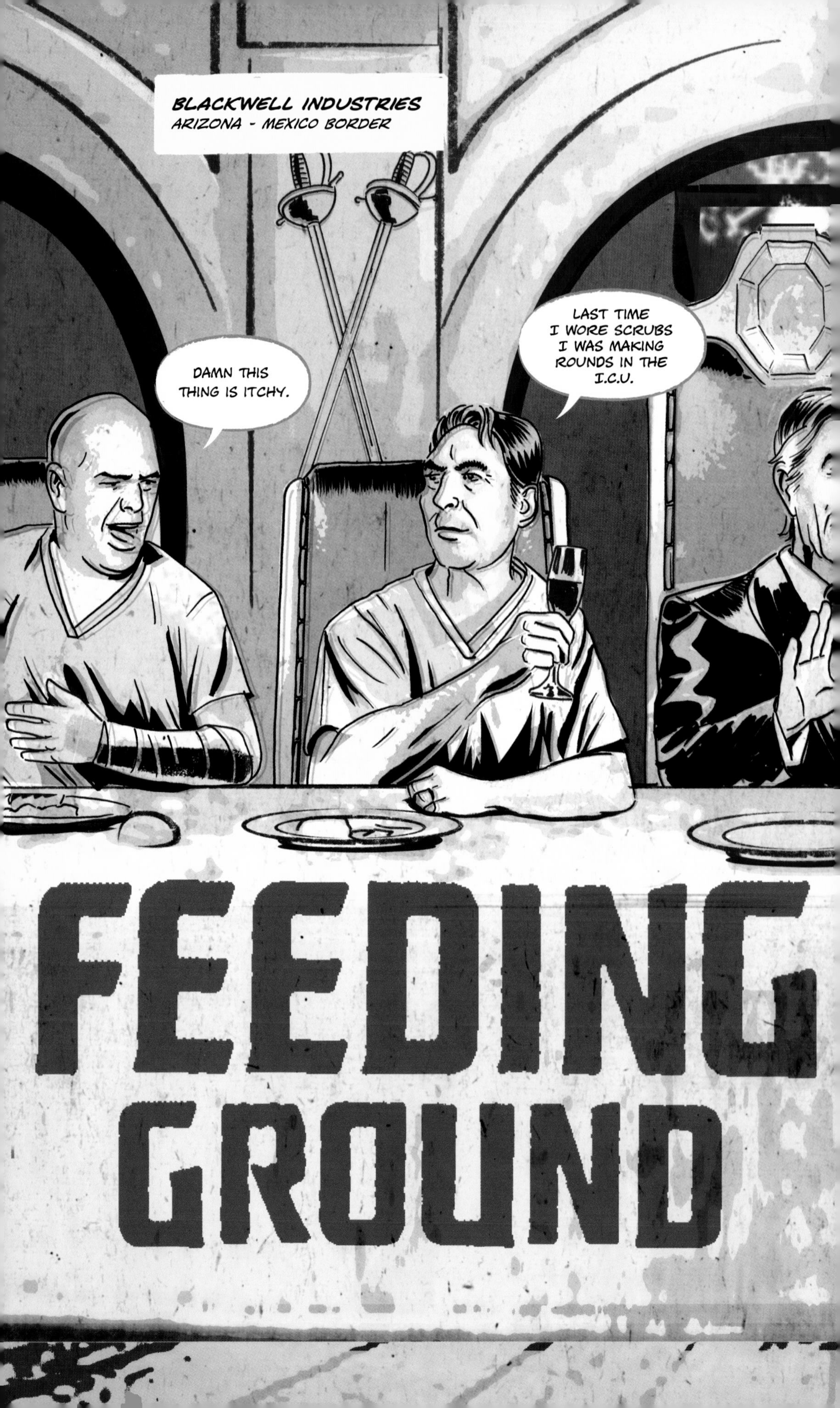
BLACKWELL INDUSTRIES
ARIZONA - MEXICO BORDER
DAMN THIS THING IS ITCHY.
LAST TIME I WORE SCRUBS I WAS MAKING ROUNDS IN THE I.C.U.
FEEDING GROUND

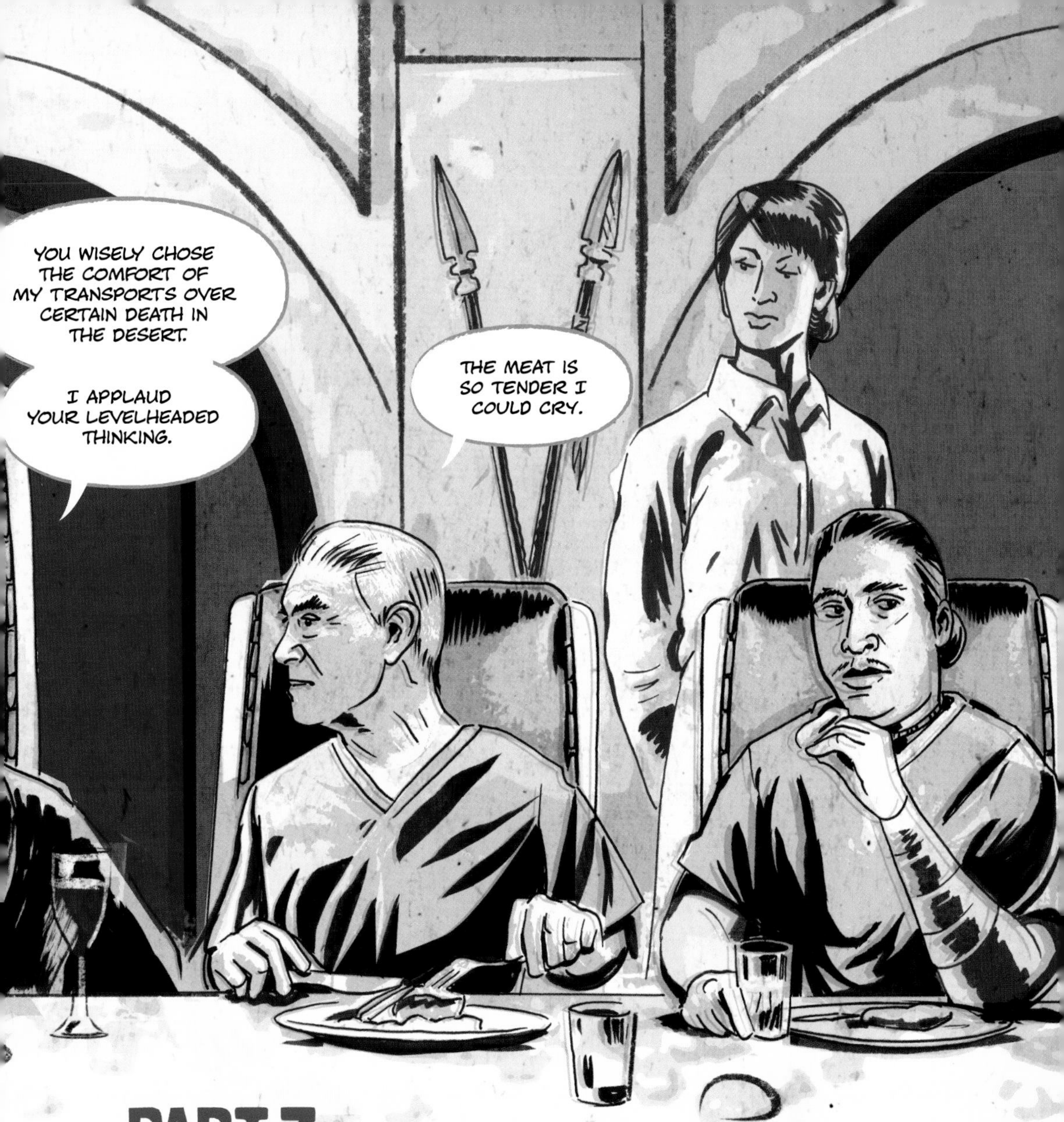
YOU WISELY CHOSE THE COMFORT OF MY TRANSPORTS OVER CERTAIN DEATH IN THE DESERT.
I APPLAUD YOUR LEVELHEADED THINKING.
THE MEAT IS SO TENDER I COULD CRY.

PART 3

THE QUICKENED PULSE

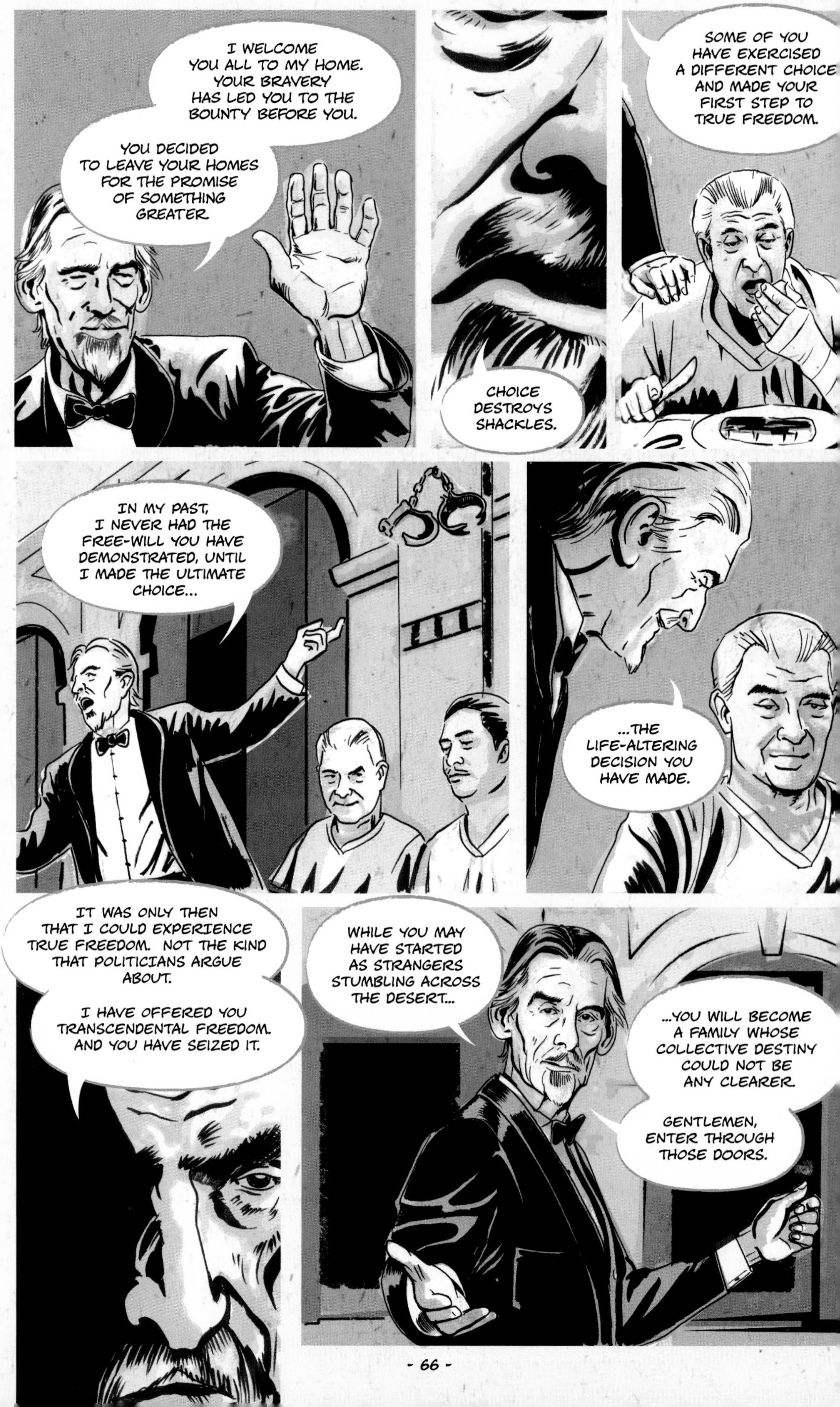
I WELCOME YOU ALL TO MY HOME. YOUR BRAVERY HAS LED YOU TO THE BOUNTY BEFORE YOU.
YOU DECIDED TO LEAVE YOUR HOMES FOR THE PROMISE OF SOMETHING GREATER
CHOICE DESTROYS SHACKLES.
SOME OF YOU HAVE EXERCISED A DIFFERENT CHOICE AND MADE YOUR FIRST STEP TO TRUE FREEDOM.
IN MY PAST, I NEVER HAD THE FREE-WILL YOU HAVE DEMONSTRATED, UNTIL I MADE THE ULTIMATE CHOICE...
...THE LIFE-ALTERING DECISION YOU HAVE MADE.
IT WAS ONLY THEN THAT I COULD EXPERIENCE TRUE FREEDOM. NOT THE KIND THAT POLITICIANS ARGUE ABOUT.
I HAVE OFFERED YOU TRANSCENDENTAL FREEDOM. AND YOU HAVE SEIZED IT.
WHILE YOU MAY HAVE STARTED AS STRANGERS STUMBLING ACROSS THE DESERT...
...YOU WILL BECOME A FAMILY WHOSE COLLECTIVE DESTINY COULD NOT BE ANY CLEARER.
GENTLEMEN, ENTER THROUGH THOSE DOORS.

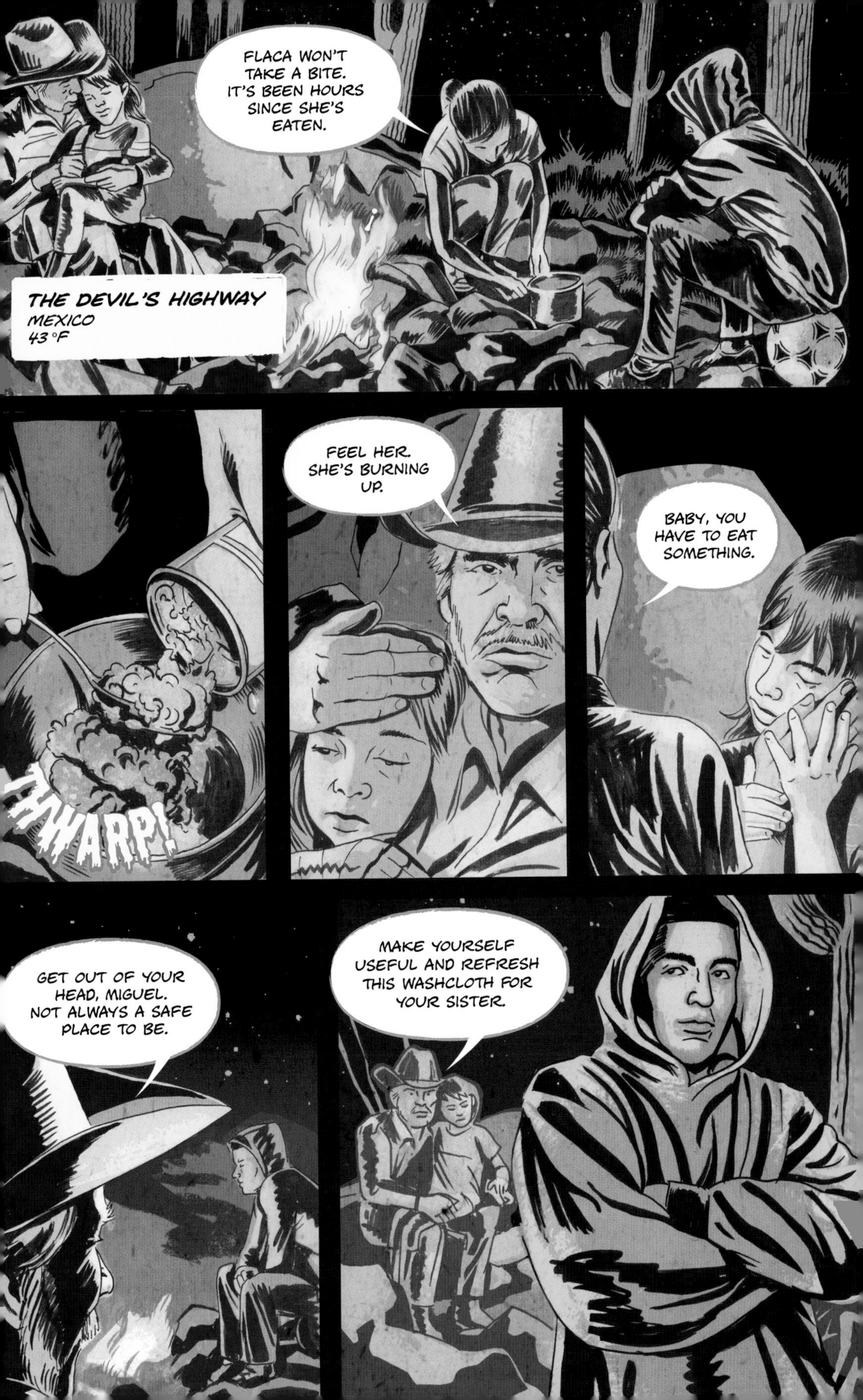
FLACA WON'T TAKE A BITE. IT'S BEEN HOURS SINCE SHE'S EATEN.
THE DEVIL'S HIGHWAY
MEXICO
43 °F
THWARP!
FEEL HER. SHE'S BURNING UP.
BABY, YOU HAVE TO EAT SOMETHING.
GET OUT OF YOUR HEAD, MIGUEL. NOT ALWAYS A SAFE PLACE TO BE.
MAKE YOURSELF USEFUL AND REFRESH THIS WASHCLOTH FOR YOUR SISTER.

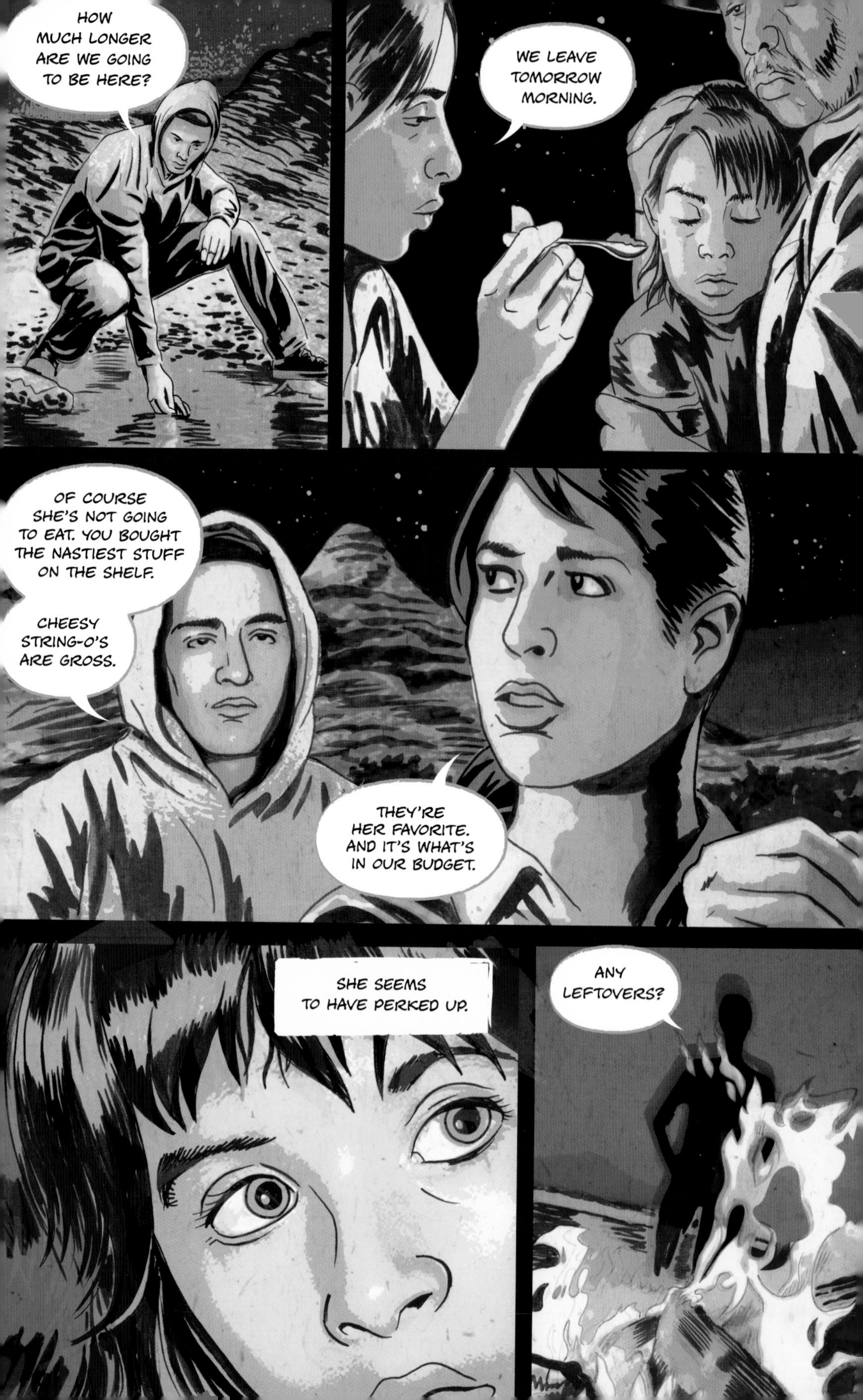
HOW MUCH LONGER ARE WE GOING TO BE HERE?
WE LEAVE TOMORROW MORNING.
OF COURSE SHE'S NOT GOING TO EAT. YOU BOUGHT THE NASTIEST STUFF ON THE SHELF.
CHEESY STRING-O'S ARE GROSS.
THEY'RE HER FAVORITE. AND IT'S WHAT'S IN OUR BUDGET.
SHE SEEMS TO HAVE PERKED UP.
ANY LEFTOVERS?

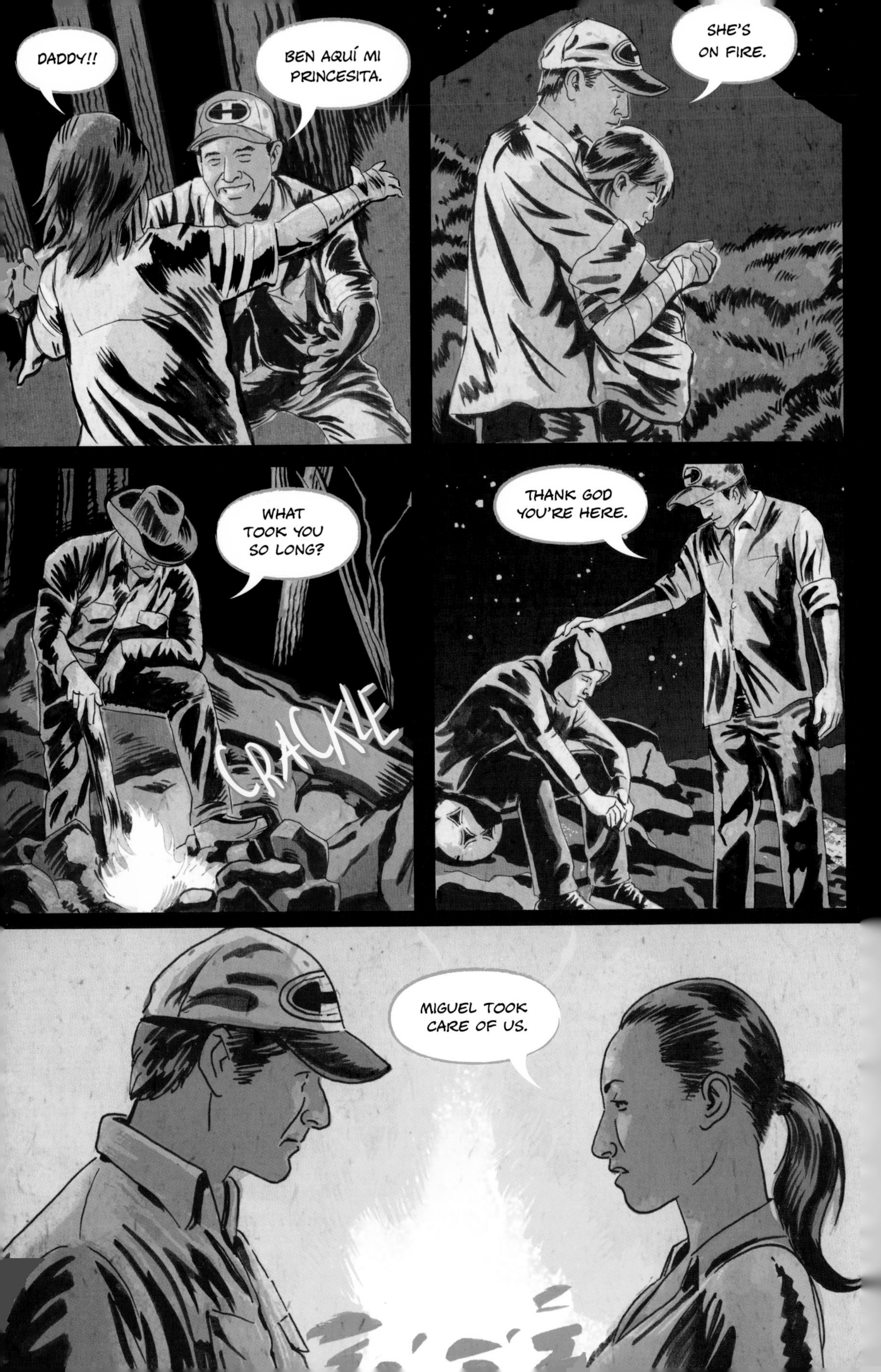
DADDY!!
BEN AQUÍ MI PRINCESITA.
SHE'S ON FIRE.
WHAT TOOK YOU SO LONG?
CRACKLE
THANK GOD YOU'RE HERE.
MIGUEL TOOK CARE OF US.

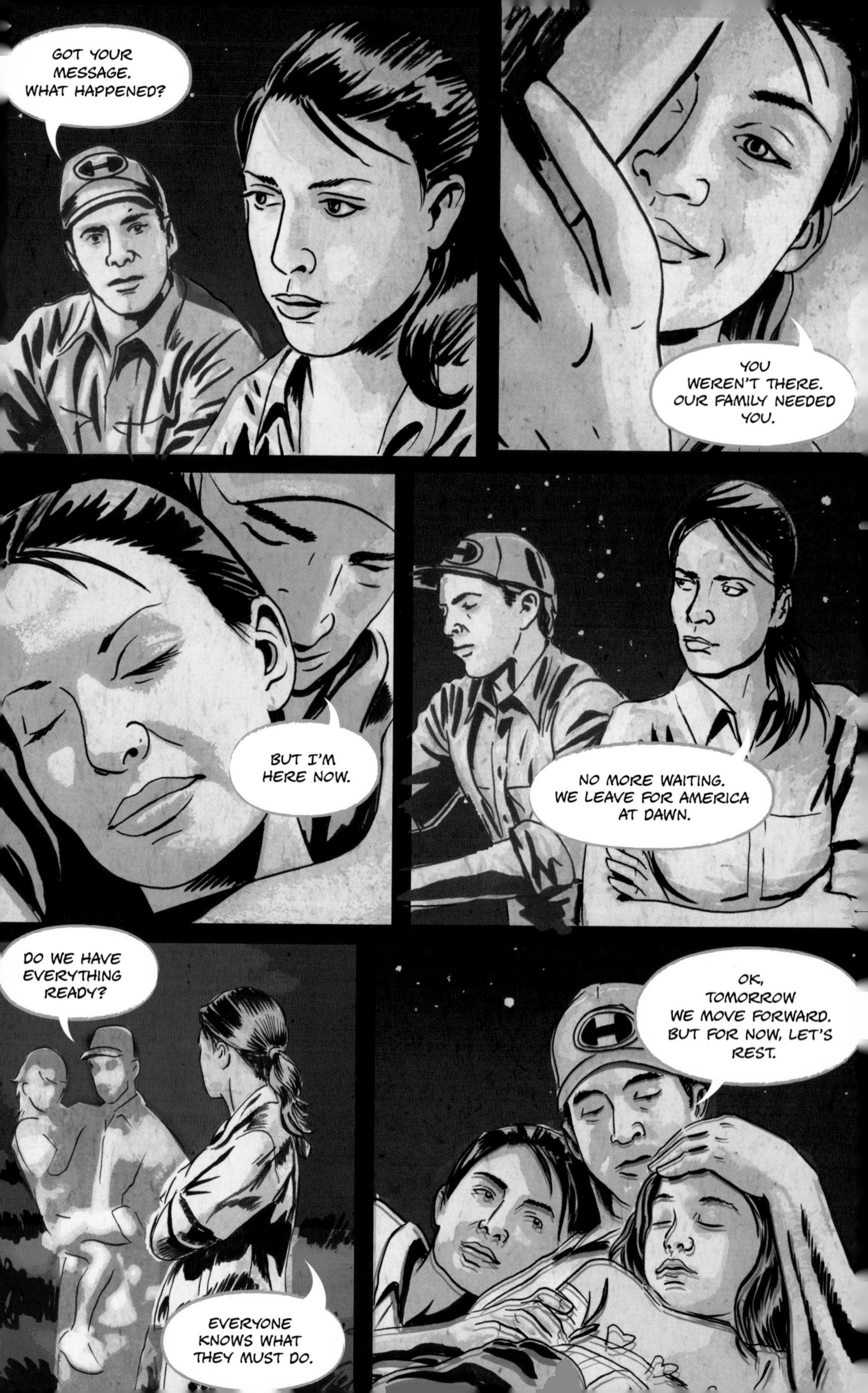
GOT YOUR MESSAGE. WHAT HAPPENED?
YOU WEREN'T THERE. OUR FAMILY NEEDED YOU.
BUT I'M HERE NOW.
NO MORE WAITING. WE LEAVE FOR AMERICA AT DAWN.
DO WE HAVE EVERYTHING READY?
EVERYONE KNOWS WHAT THEY MUST DO.
OK, TOMORROW WE MOVE FORWARD. BUT FOR NOW, LET'S REST.

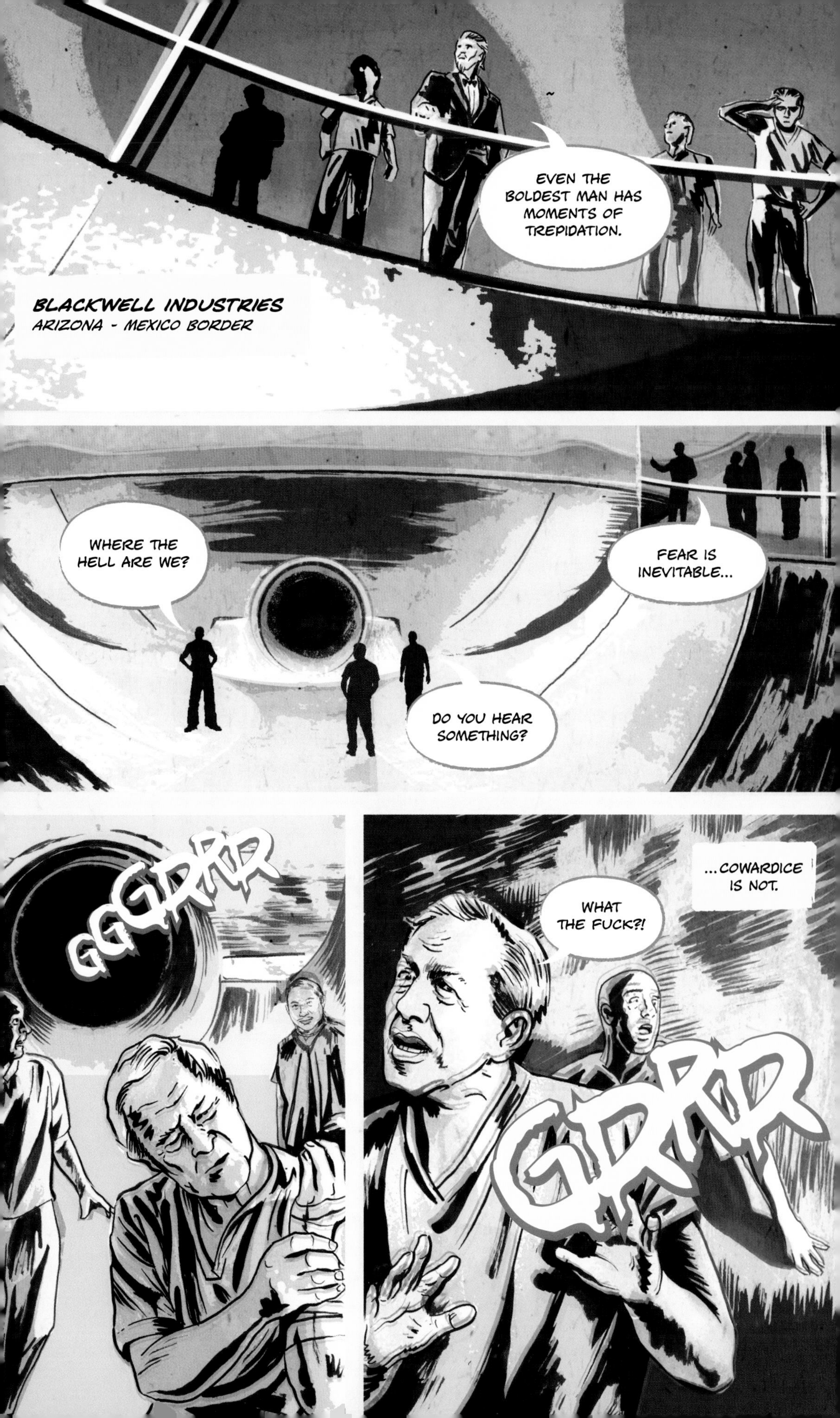

BLACKWELL INDUSTRIES
ARIZONA - MEXICO BORDER
EVEN THE BOLDEST MAN HAS MOMENTS OF TREPIDATION.
WHERE THE HELL ARE WE?
FEAR IS INEVITABLE...
DO YOU HEAR SOMETHING?
GGGDRDR
...COWARDICE IS NOT.
WHAT THE FUCK?!
GDRDR

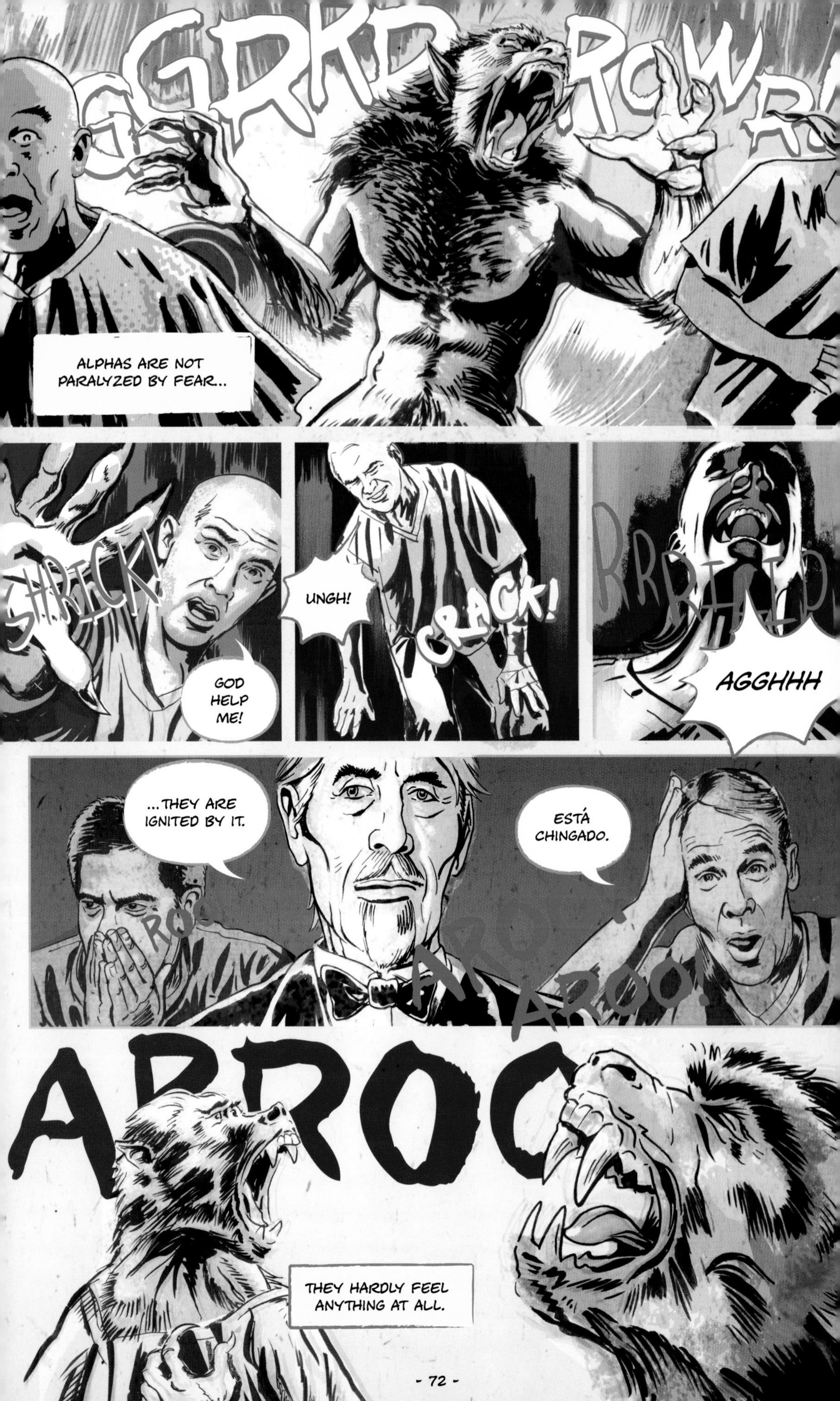
GRRR
ROWR
ALPHAS ARE NOT PARALYZED BY FEAR...
SHRICK!
GOD HELP ME!
UNGH!
CRACK!
RRRIIID
AGGHHH
...THEY ARE IGNITED BY IT.
ESTÁ CHINGADO.
ROO
AROO!
AROO!
AROO
THEY HARDLY FEEL ANYTHING AT ALL.

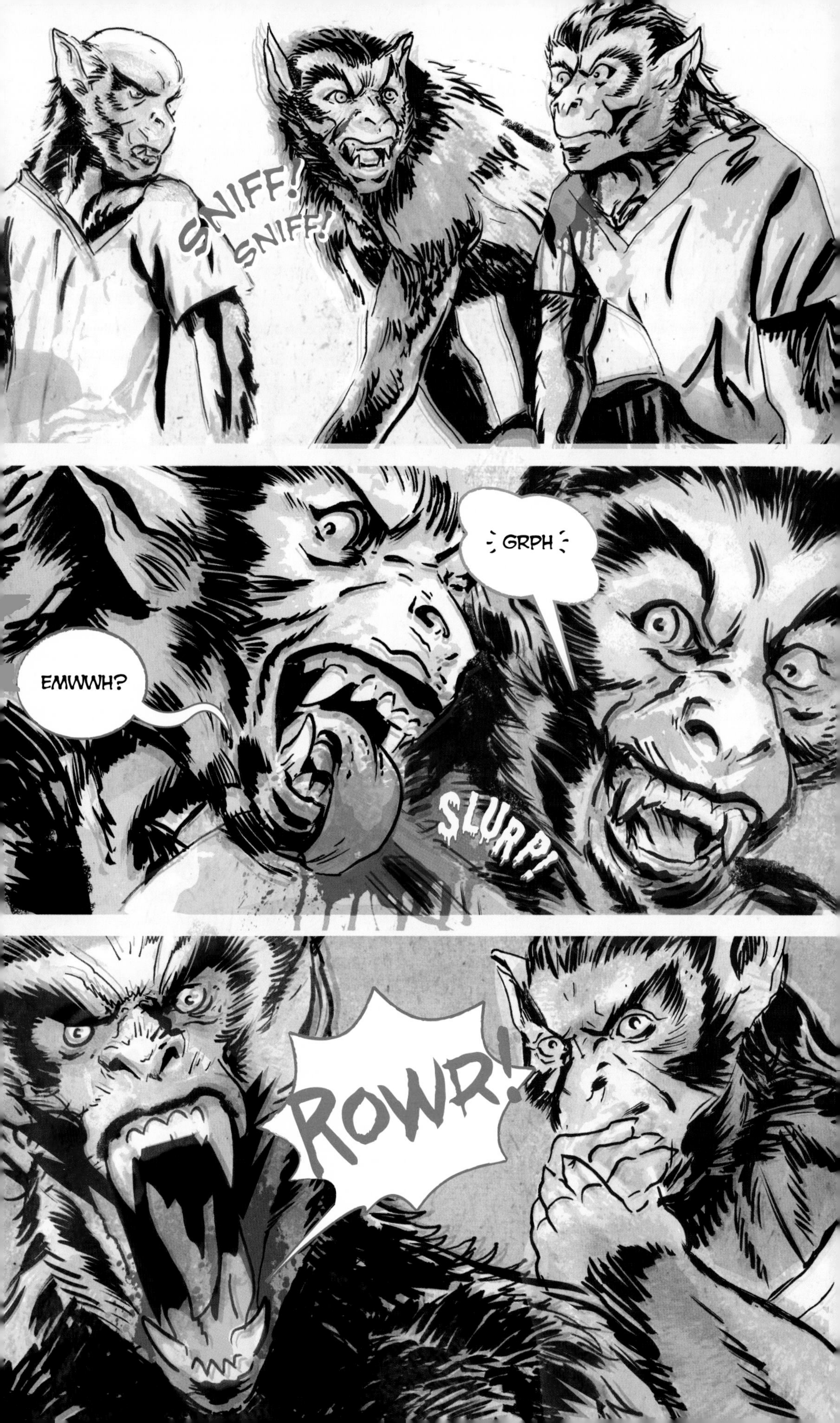
SNIFF!
SNIFF!
GRPH
EMWWH?
SLURP!
ROWR!

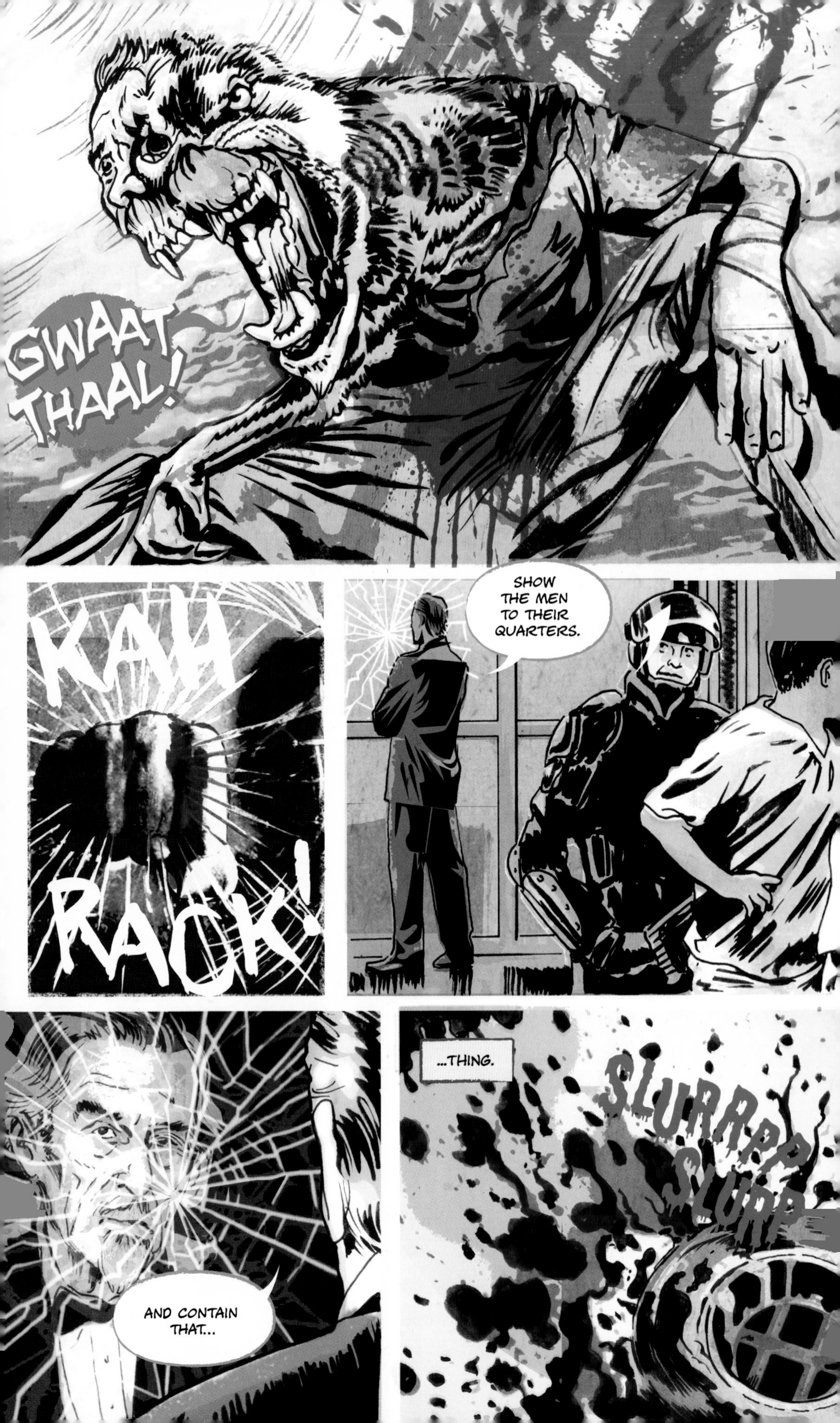
GWAAT THAAL!
KAH RACK!
SHOW THE MEN TO THEIR QUARTERS.
AND CONTAIN THAT...
...THING.
SLURRPP SLURP

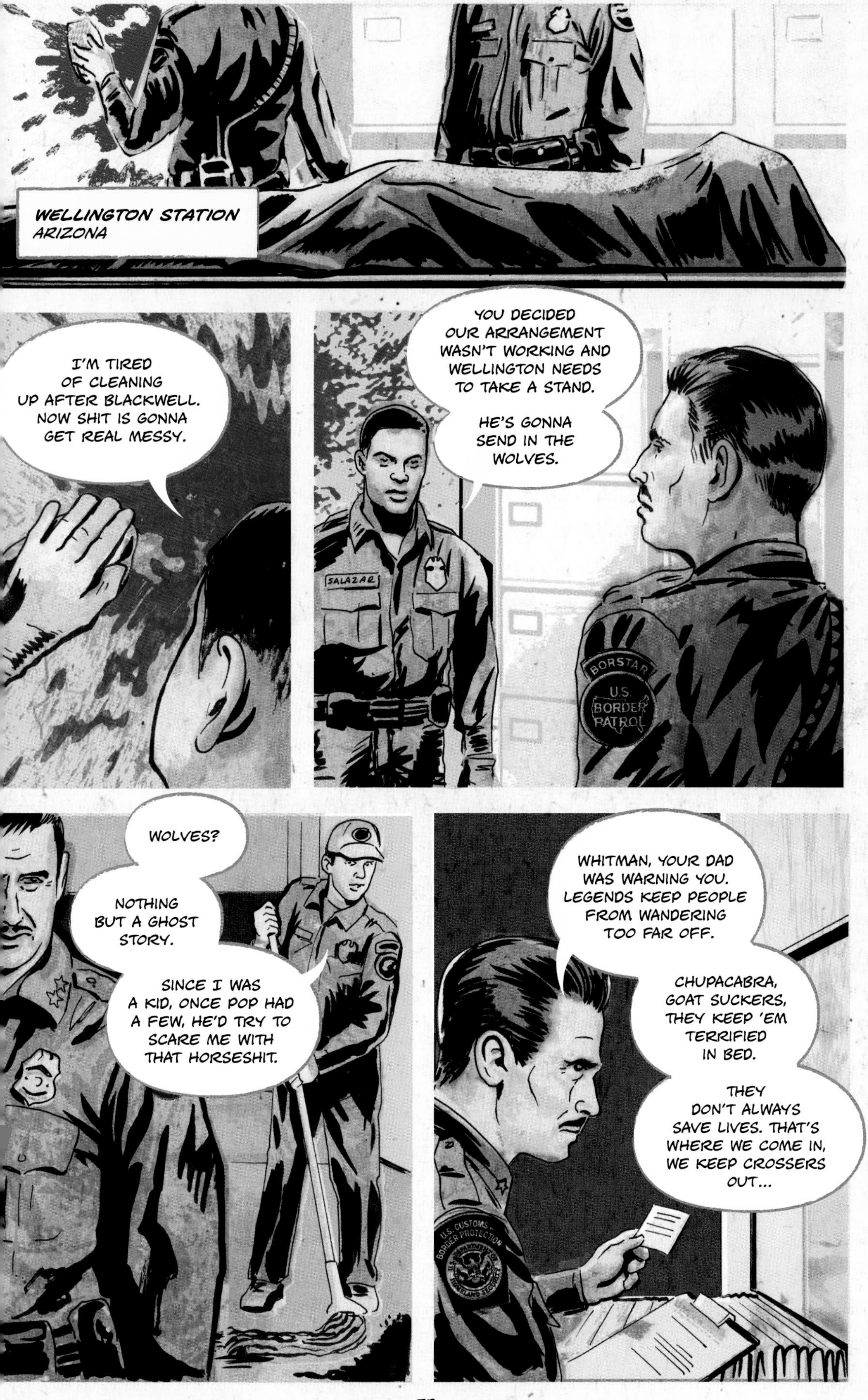
WELLINGTON STATION ARIZONA
I'M TIRED OF CLEANING UP AFTER BLACKWELL. NOW SHIT IS GONNA GET REAL MESSY.
YOU DECIDED OUR ARRANGEMENT WASN'T WORKING AND WELLINGTON NEEDS TO TAKE A STAND.
HE'S GONNA SEND IN THE WOLVES.
SALAZAR
BORSTAR
U.S. BORDER PATROL
WOLVES?
NOTHING BUT A GHOST STORY.
SINCE I WAS A KID, ONCE POP HAD A FEW, HE'D TRY TO SCARE ME WITH THAT HORSESHIT.
WHITMAN, YOUR DAD WAS WARNING YOU. LEGENDS KEEP PEOPLE FROM WANDERING TOO FAR OFF.
CHUPACABRA, GOAT SUCKERS, THEY KEEP 'EM TERRIFIED IN BED.
THEY DON'T ALWAYS SAVE LIVES. THAT'S WHERE WE COME IN, WE KEEP CROSSERS OUT...
U.S. CUSTOMS BORDER PROTECTION

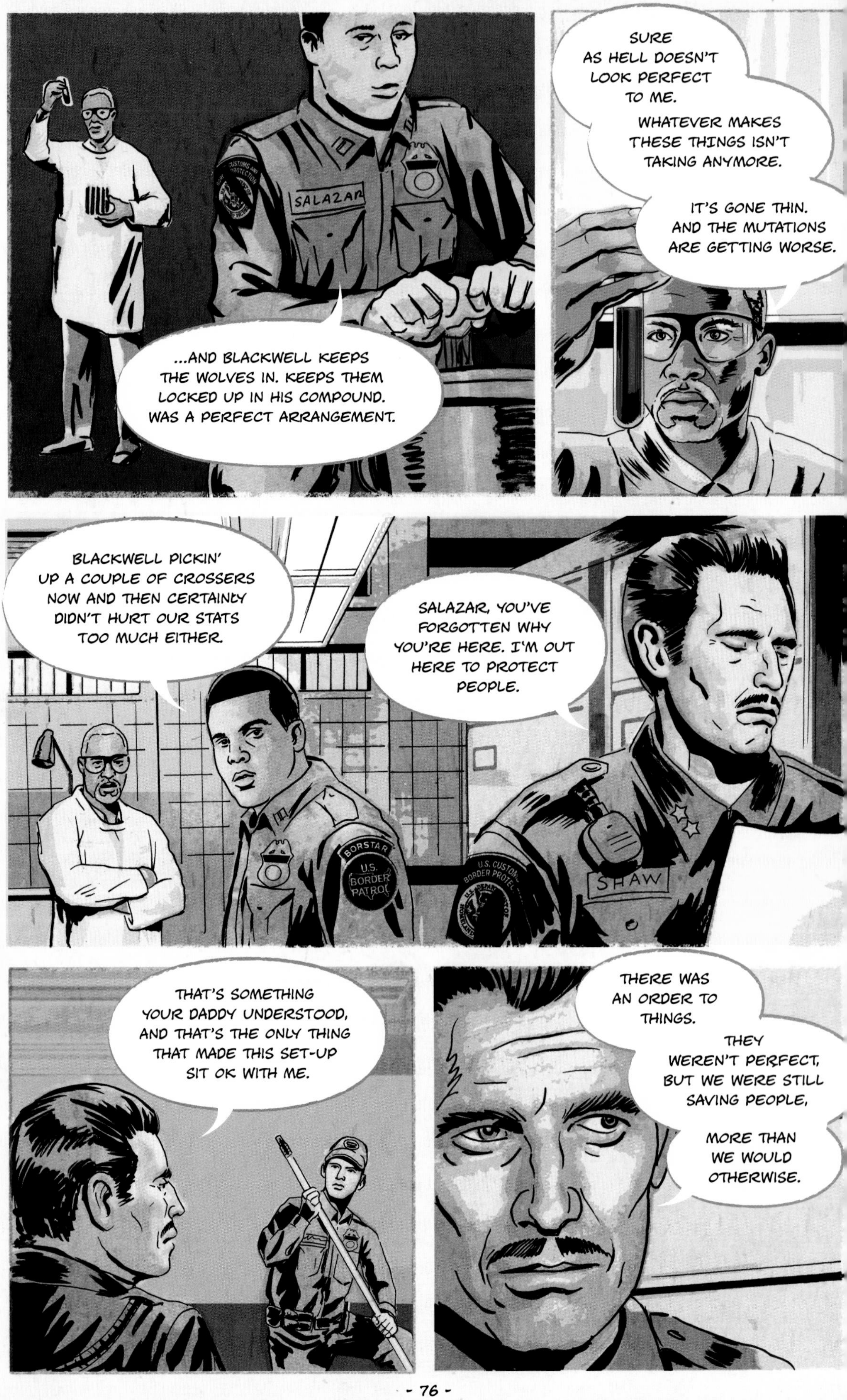

...AND BLACKWELL KEEPS THE WOLVES IN. KEEPS THEM LOCKED UP IN HIS COMPOUND. WAS A PERFECT ARRANGEMENT.
SALAZAR
SURE AS HELL DOESN'T LOOK PERFECT TO ME.
WHATEVER MAKES THESE THINGS ISN'T TAKING ANYMORE.
IT'S GONE THIN. AND THE MUTATIONS ARE GETTING WORSE.
BLACKWELL PICKIN' UP A COUPLE OF CROSSERS NOW AND THEN CERTAINLY DIDN'T HURT OUR STATS TOO MUCH EITHER.
SALAZAR, YOU'VE FORGOTTEN WHY YOU'RE HERE. I'M OUT HERE TO PROTECT PEOPLE.
BORSTAR
U.S. BORDER PATROL
SHAW
THAT'S SOMETHING YOUR DADDY UNDERSTOOD, AND THAT'S THE ONLY THING THAT MADE THIS SET-UP SIT OK WITH ME.
THERE WAS AN ORDER TO THINGS.
THEY WEREN'T PERFECT, BUT WE WERE STILL SAVING PEOPLE,
MORE THAN WE WOULD OTHERWISE.

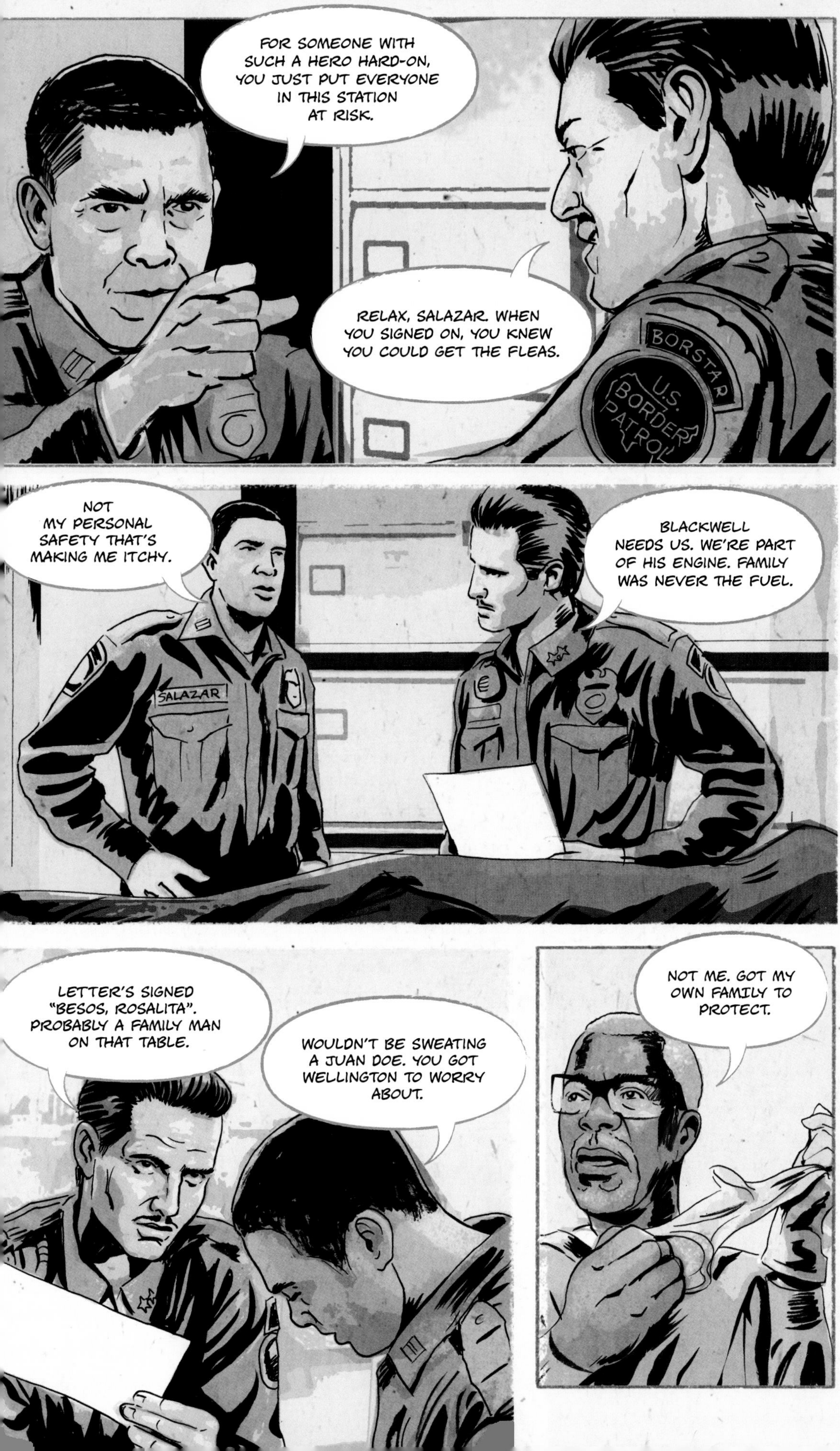

FOR SOMEONE WITH SUCH A HERO HARD-ON, YOU JUST PUT EVERYONE IN THIS STATION AT RISK.
RELAX, SALAZAR. WHEN YOU SIGNED ON, YOU KNEW YOU COULD GET THE FLEAS.
BORSTAR
U.S. BORDER PATROL
NOT MY PERSONAL SAFETY THAT'S MAKING ME ITCHY.
BLACKWELL NEEDS US. WE'RE PART OF HIS ENGINE. FAMILY WAS NEVER THE FUEL.
SALAZAR
LETTER'S SIGNED "BESOS, ROSALITA". PROBABLY A FAMILY MAN ON THAT TABLE.
WOULDN'T BE SWEATING A JUAN DOE. YOU GOT WELLINGTON TO WORRY ABOUT.
NOT ME. GOT MY OWN FAMILY TO PROTECT.

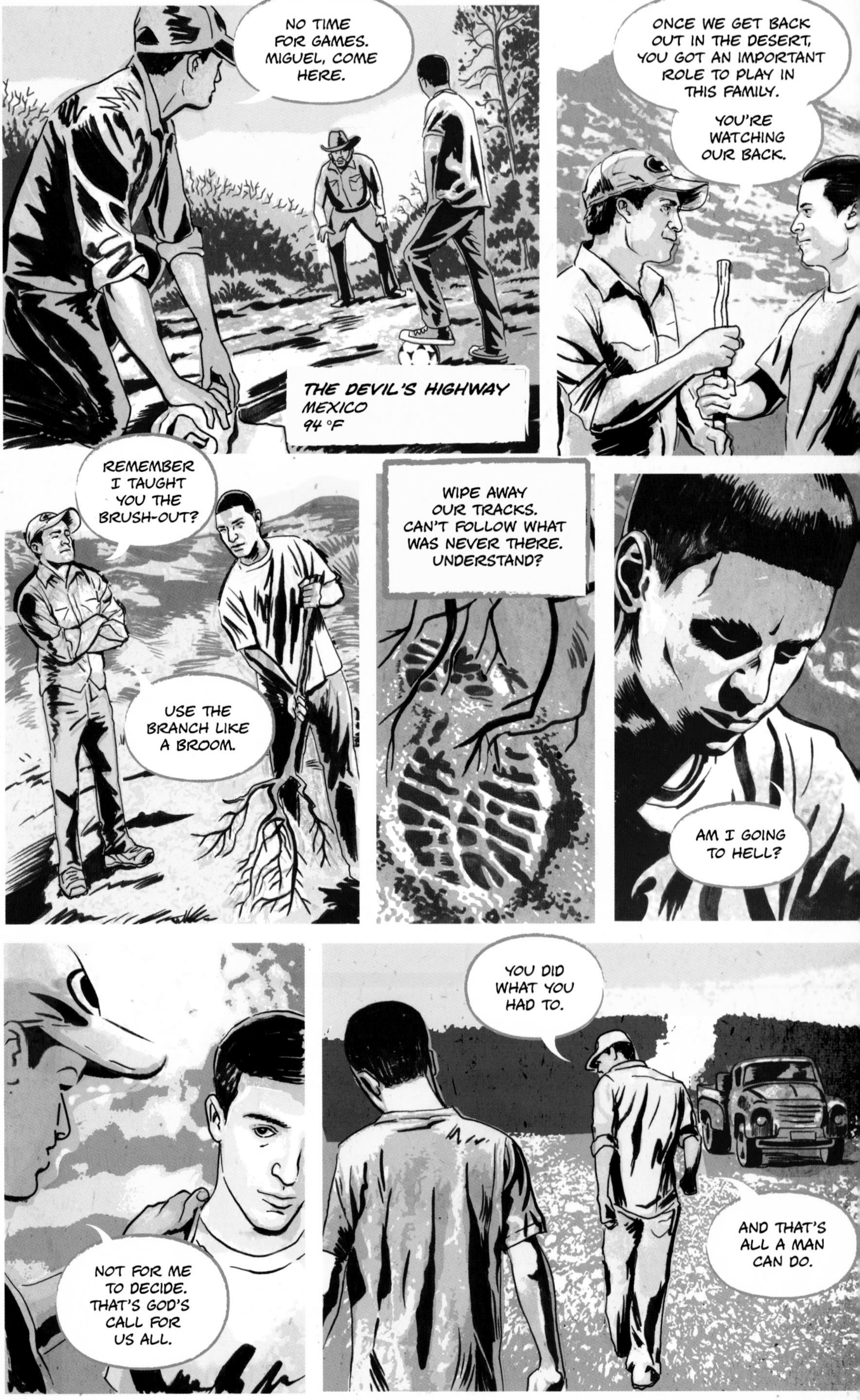
NO TIME FOR GAMES. MIGUEL, COME HERE.
THE DEVIL'S HIGHWAY MEXICO 94 °F
ONCE WE GET BACK OUT IN THE DESERT, YOU GOT AN IMPORTANT ROLE TO PLAY IN THIS FAMILY.
YOU'RE WATCHING OUR BACK.
REMEMBER I TAUGHT YOU THE BRUSH-OUT?
USE THE BRANCH LIKE A BROOM.
WIPE AWAY OUR TRACKS. CAN'T FOLLOW WHAT WAS NEVER THERE. UNDERSTAND?
AM I GOING TO HELL?
NOT FOR ME TO DECIDE. THAT'S GOD'S CALL FOR US ALL.
YOU DID WHAT YOU HAD TO.
AND THAT'S ALL A MAN CAN DO.

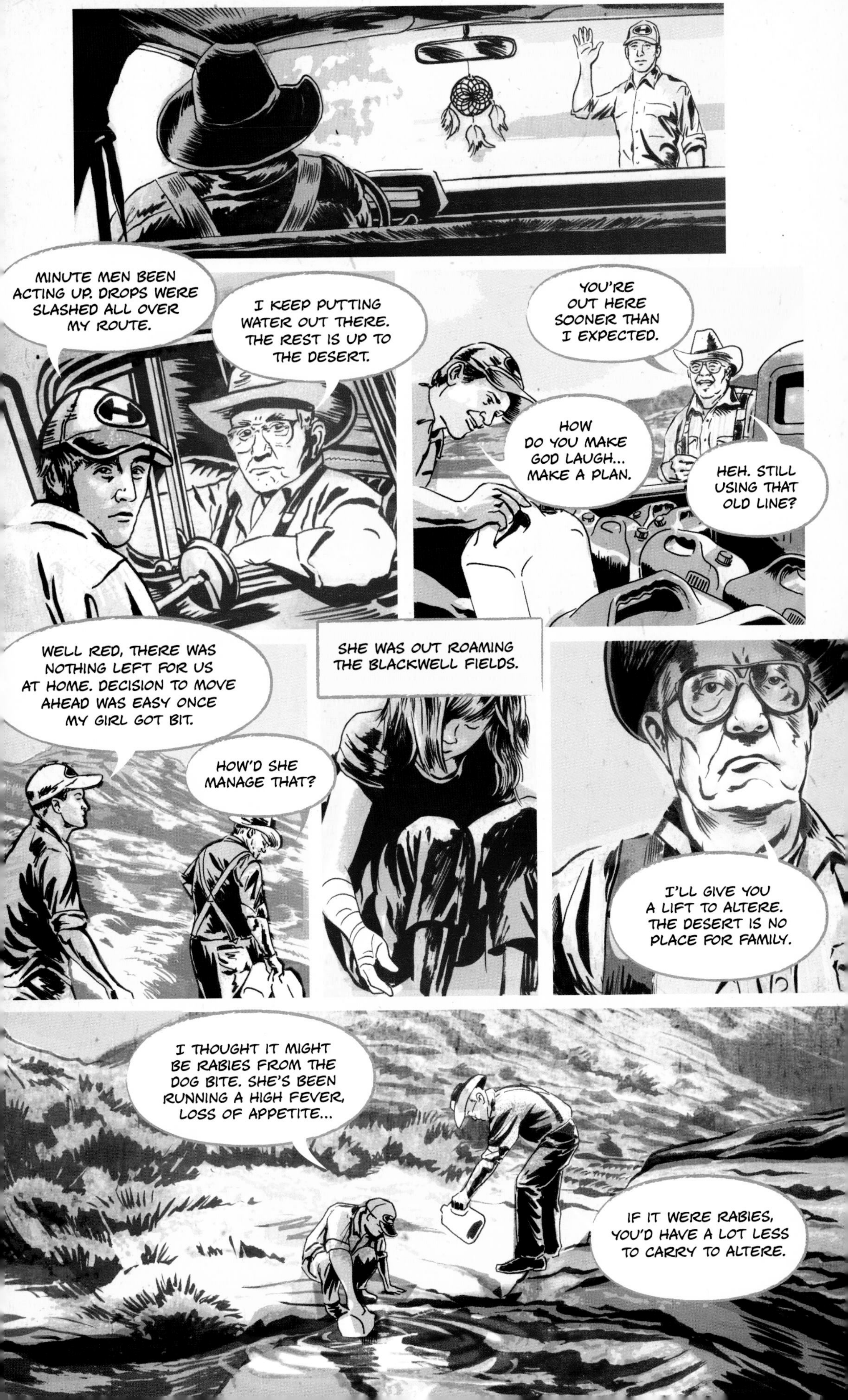
MINUTE MEN BEEN ACTING UP. DROPS WERE SLASHED ALL OVER MY ROUTE.
I KEEP PUTTING WATER OUT THERE. THE REST IS UP TO THE DESERT.
YOU'RE OUT HERE SOONER THAN I EXPECTED.
HOW DO YOU MAKE GOD LAUGH... MAKE A PLAN.
HEH. STILL USING THAT OLD LINE?
WELL RED, THERE WAS NOTHING LEFT FOR US AT HOME. DECISION TO MOVE AHEAD WAS EASY ONCE MY GIRL GOT BIT.
HOW'D SHE MANAGE THAT?
SHE WAS OUT ROAMING THE BLACKWELL FIELDS.
I'LL GIVE YOU A LIFT TO ALTERE. THE DESERT IS NO PLACE FOR FAMILY.
I THOUGHT IT MIGHT BE RABIES FROM THE DOG BITE. SHE'S BEEN RUNNING A HIGH FEVER, LOSS OF APPETITE...
IF IT WERE RABIES, YOU'D HAVE A LOT LESS TO CARRY TO ALTERE.

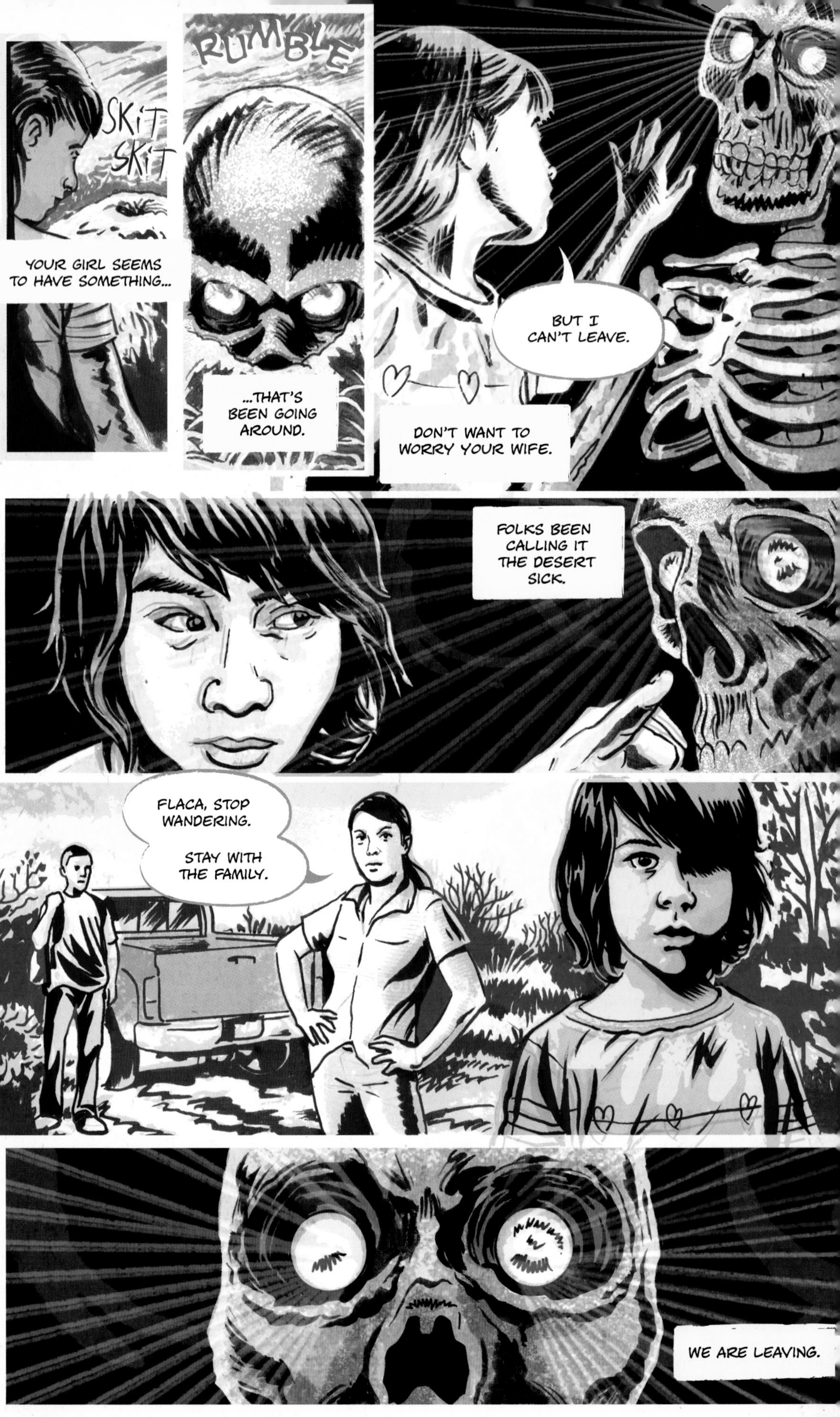
SKIT SKIT
YOUR GIRL SEEMS TO HAVE SOMETHING...
RUMBLE
...THAT'S BEEN GOING AROUND.
BUT I CAN'T LEAVE.
DON'T WANT TO WORRY YOUR WIFE.
FOLKS BEEN CALLING IT THE DESERT SICK.
FLACA, STOP WANDERING.
STAY WITH THE FAMILY.
WE ARE LEAVING.

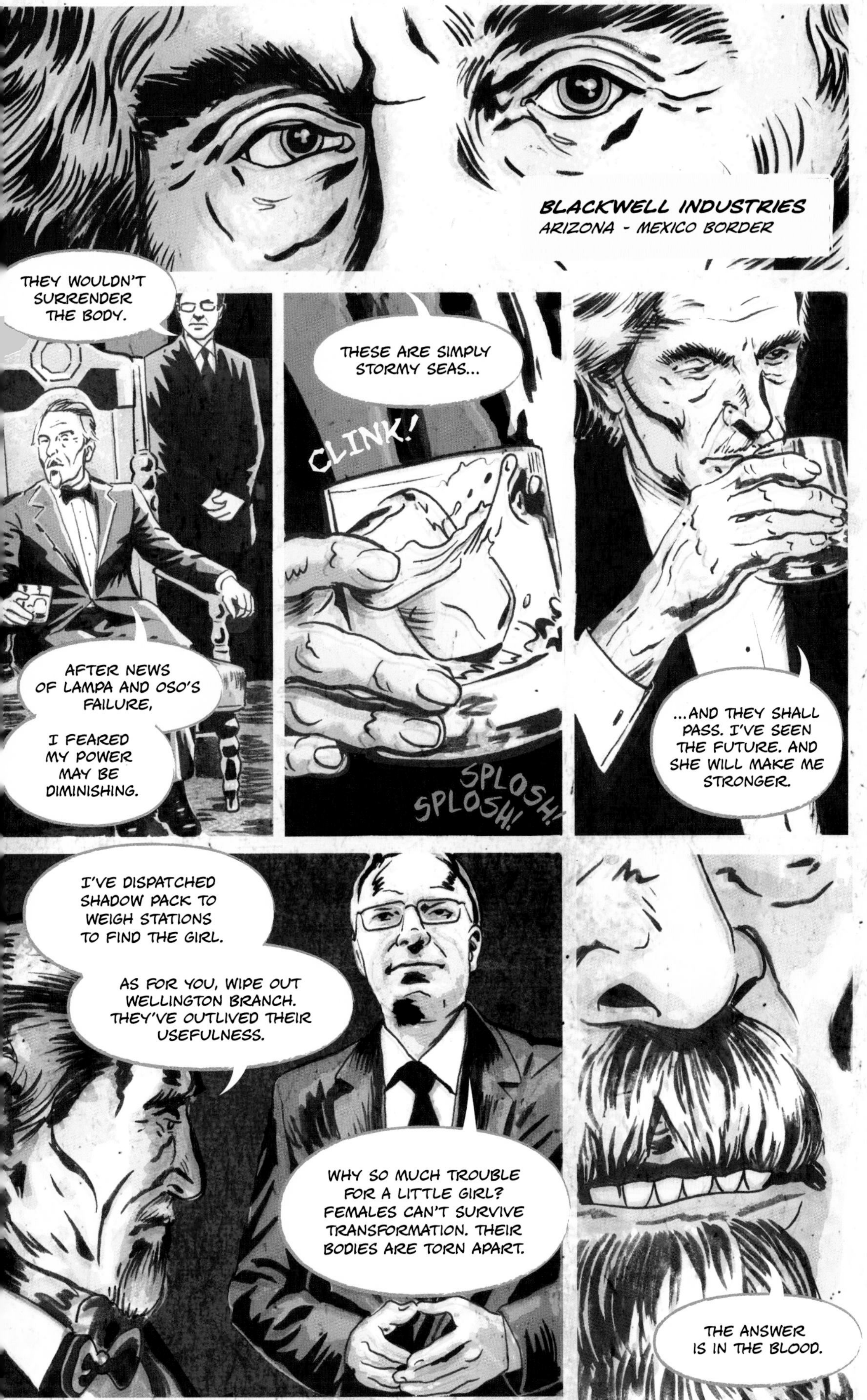
BLACKWELL INDUSTRIES
ARIZONA - MEXICO BORDER
THEY WOULDN'T SURRENDER THE BODY.
AFTER NEWS OF LAMPA AND OSO'S FAILURE,
I FEARED MY POWER MAY BE DIMINISHING.
THESE ARE SIMPLY STORMY SEAS...
CLINK!
SPLOSH! SPLOSH!
...AND THEY SHALL PASS. I'VE SEEN THE FUTURE. AND SHE WILL MAKE ME STRONGER.
I'VE DISPATCHED SHADOW PACK TO WEIGH STATIONS TO FIND THE GIRL.
AS FOR YOU, WIPE OUT WELLINGTON BRANCH. THEY'VE OUTLIVED THEIR USEFULNESS.
WHY SO MUCH TROUBLE FOR A LITTLE GIRL? FEMALES CAN'T SURVIVE TRANSFORMATION. THEIR BODIES ARE TORN APART.
THE ANSWER IS IN THE BLOOD.

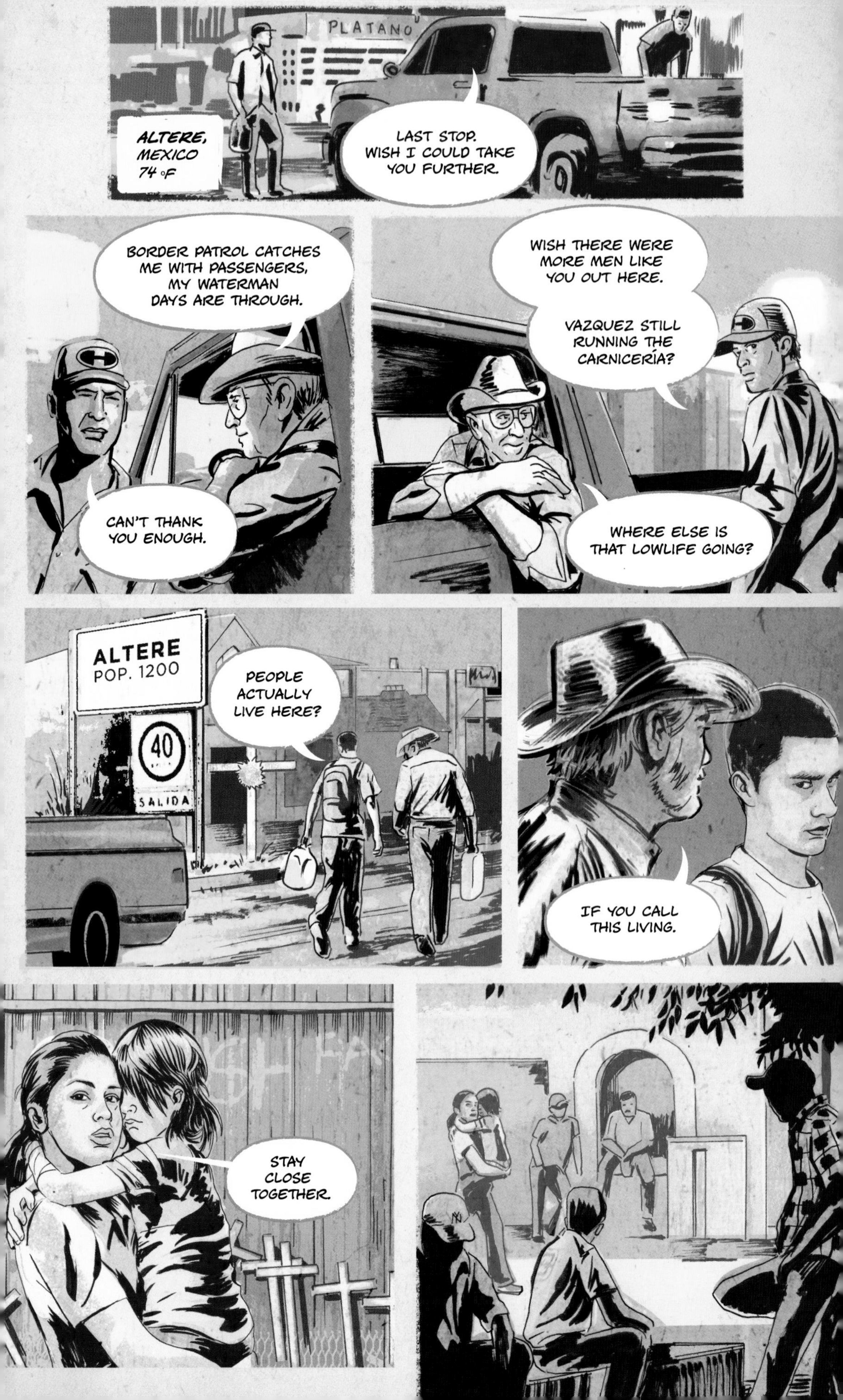
PLATANO
ALTERE, MEXICO 74 °F
LAST STOP. WISH I COULD TAKE YOU FURTHER.
BORDER PATROL CATCHES ME WITH PASSENGERS, MY WATERMAN DAYS ARE THROUGH.
CAN'T THANK YOU ENOUGH.
WISH THERE WERE MORE MEN LIKE YOU OUT HERE.
VAZQUEZ STILL RUNNING THE CARNICERÍA?
WHERE ELSE IS THAT LOWLIFE GOING?
ALTERE POP. 1200
40
SALIDA
PEOPLE ACTUALLY LIVE HERE?
IF YOU CALL THIS LIVING.
STAY CLOSE TOGETHER.

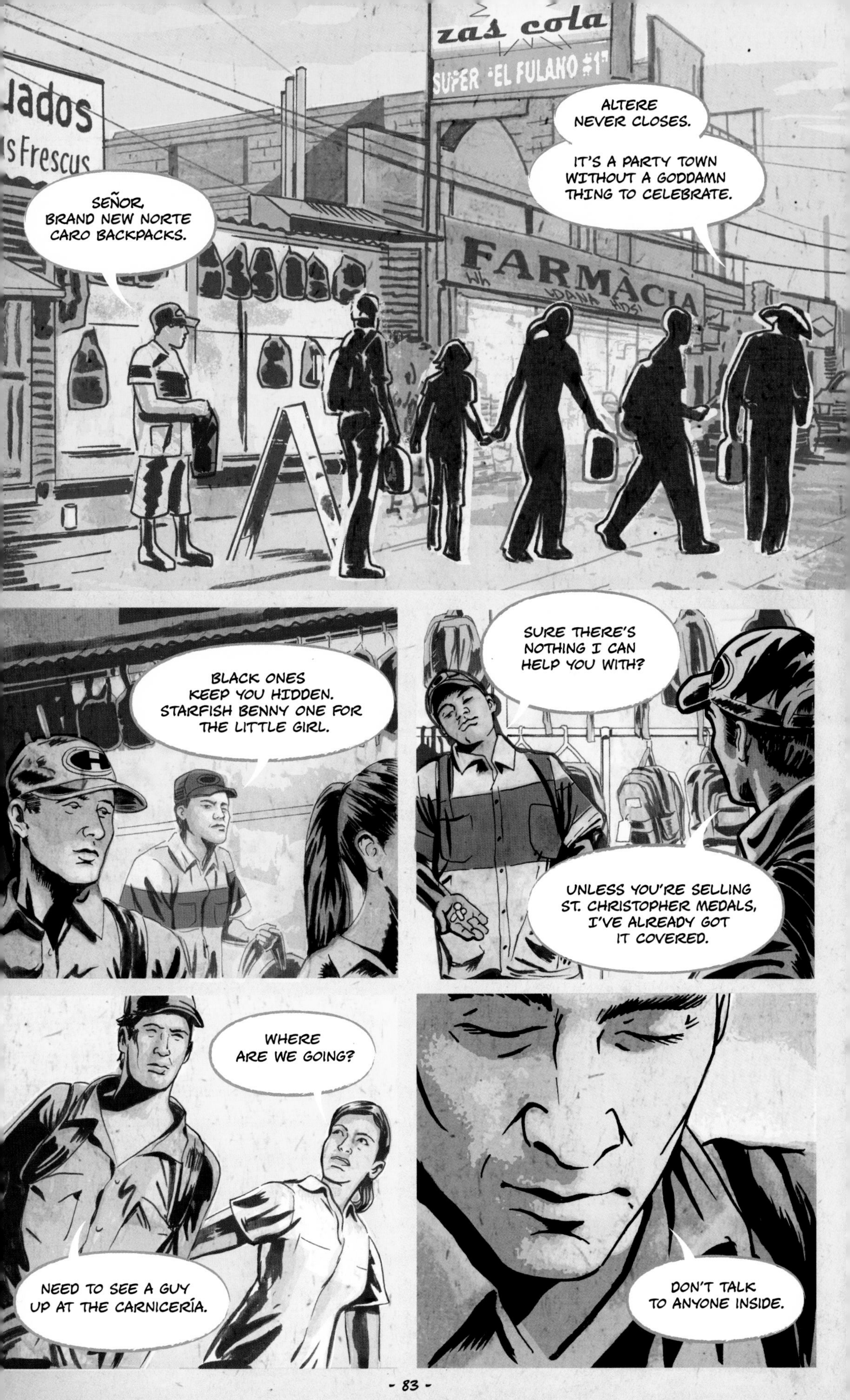
zas cola
SUPER "EL FULANO #1"
FARMÀCIA
SEÑOR, BRAND NEW NORTE CARO BACKPACKS.
ALTERE NEVER CLOSES.
IT'S A PARTY TOWN WITHOUT A GODDAMN THING TO CELEBRATE.
BLACK ONES KEEP YOU HIDDEN. STARFISH BENNY ONE FOR THE LITTLE GIRL.
SURE THERE'S NOTHING I CAN HELP YOU WITH?
UNLESS YOU'RE SELLING ST. CHRISTOPHER MEDALS, I'VE ALREADY GOT IT COVERED.
WHERE ARE WE GOING?
NEED TO SEE A GUY UP AT THE CARNICERÍA.
DON'T TALK TO ANYONE INSIDE.

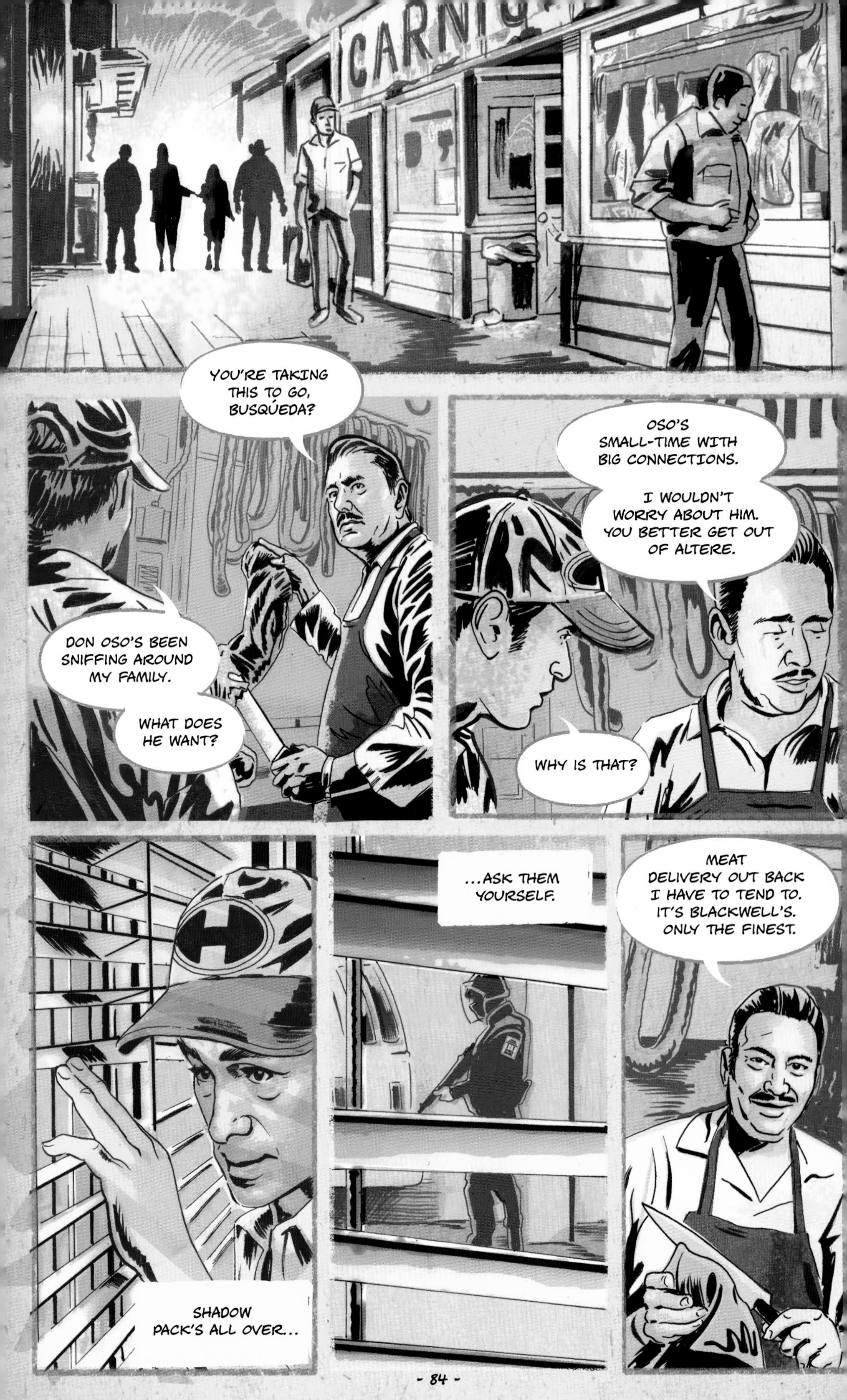
CARNIC
YOU'RE TAKING THIS TO GO, BUSQÚEDA?
DON OSO'S BEEN SNIFFING AROUND MY FAMILY.
WHAT DOES HE WANT?
OSO'S SMALL-TIME WITH BIG CONNECTIONS.
I WOULDN'T WORRY ABOUT HIM. YOU BETTER GET OUT OF ALTERE.
WHY IS THAT?
SHADOW PACK'S ALL OVER...
...ASK THEM YOURSELF.
MEAT DELIVERY OUT BACK I HAVE TO TEND TO. IT'S BLACKWELL'S. ONLY THE FINEST.

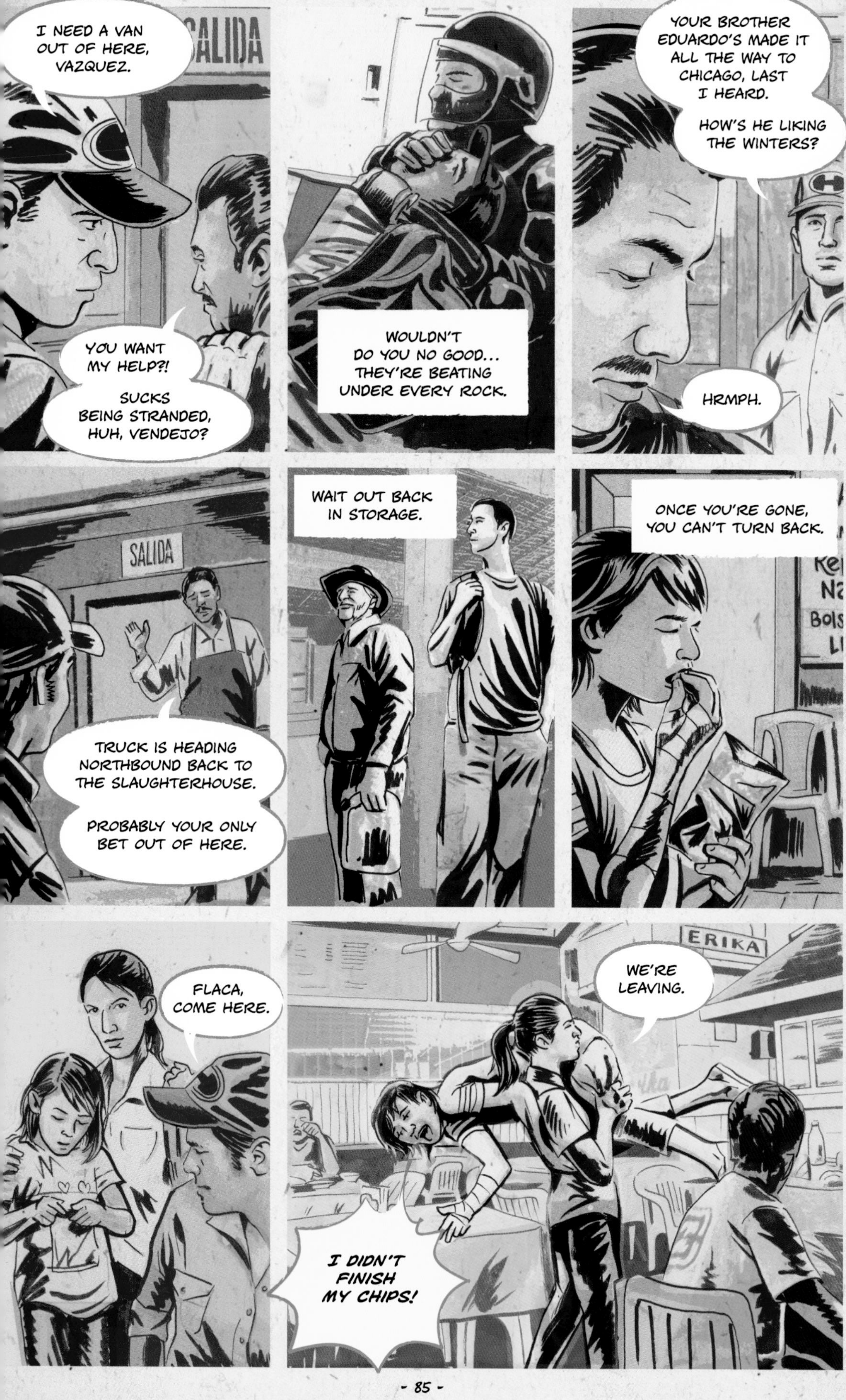
I NEED A VAN OUT OF HERE, VAZQUEZ.
SALIDA
YOU WANT MY HELP?!
SUCKS BEING STRANDED, HUH, VENDEJO?
WOULDN'T DO YOU NO GOOD... THEY'RE BEATING UNDER EVERY ROCK.
YOUR BROTHER EDUARDO'S MADE IT ALL THE WAY TO CHICAGO, LAST I HEARD.
HOW'S HE LIKING THE WINTERS?
HRMPH.
SALIDA
TRUCK IS HEADING NORTHBOUND BACK TO THE SLAUGHTERHOUSE.
PROBABLY YOUR ONLY BET OUT OF HERE.
WAIT OUT BACK IN STORAGE.
ONCE YOU'RE GONE, YOU CAN'T TURN BACK.
FLACA, COME HERE.
ERIKA
WE'RE LEAVING.
I DIDN'T FINISH MY CHIPS!

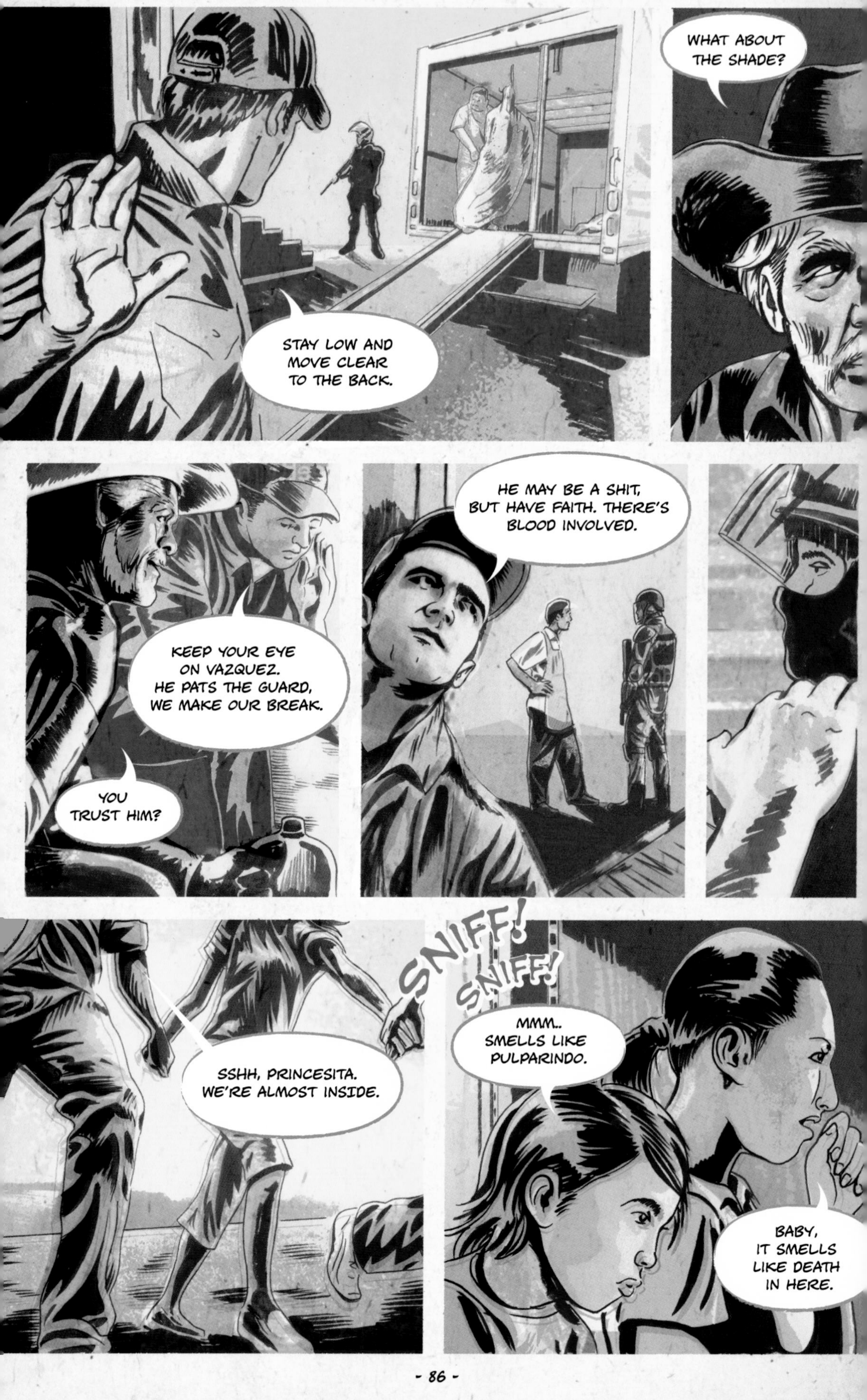
STAY LOW AND MOVE CLEAR TO THE BACK.
WHAT ABOUT THE SHADE?
KEEP YOUR EYE ON VAZQUEZ. HE PATS THE GUARD, WE MAKE OUR BREAK.
YOU TRUST HIM?
HE MAY BE A SHIT, BUT HAVE FAITH. THERE'S BLOOD INVOLVED.
SSHH, PRINCESITA. WE'RE ALMOST INSIDE.
SNIFF! SNIFF!
MMM.. SMELLS LIKE PULPARINDO.
BABY, IT SMELLS LIKE DEATH IN HERE.

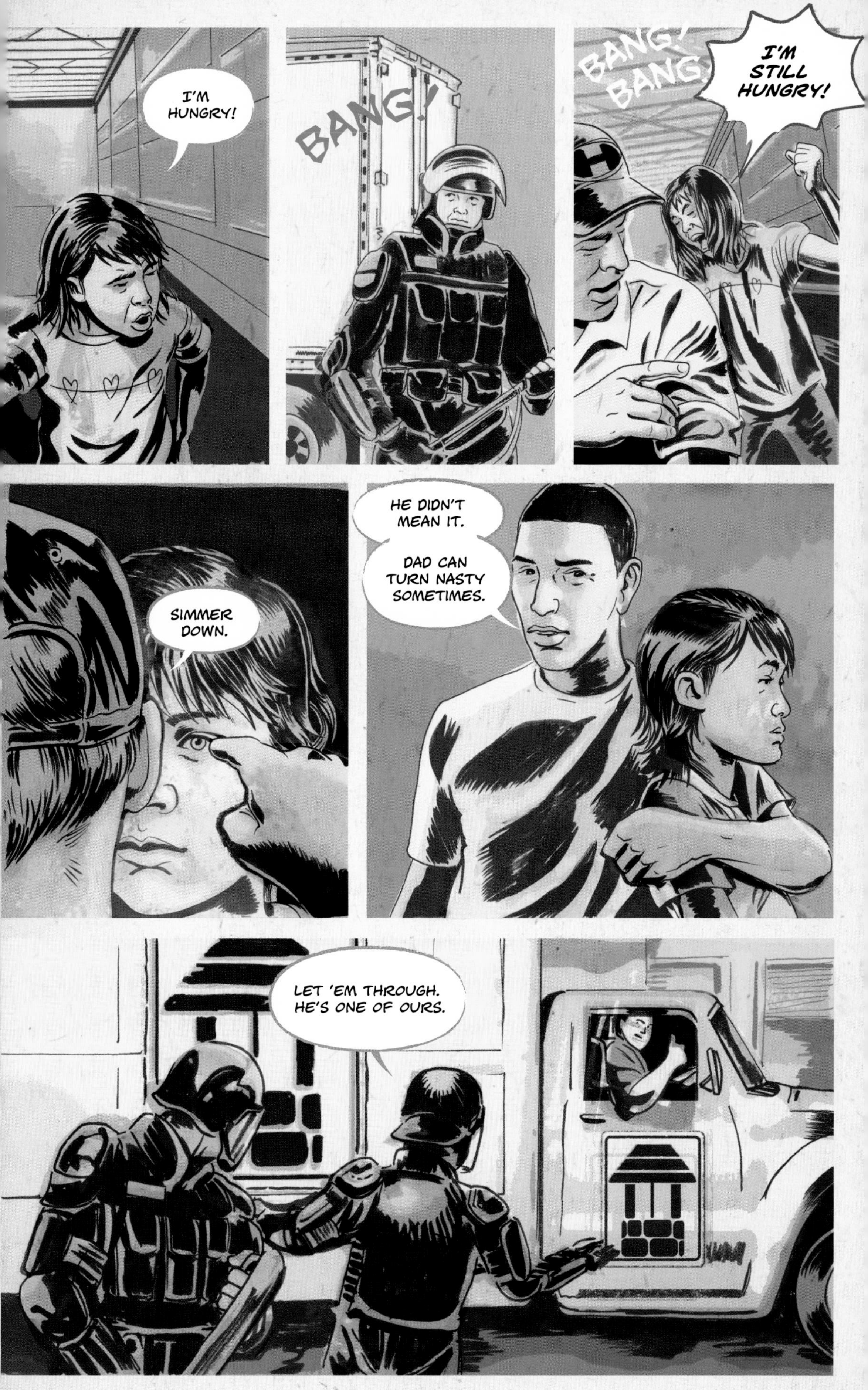
I'M HUNGRY!
BANG!
BANG! BANG!
I'M STILL HUNGRY!
SIMMER DOWN.
HE DIDN'T MEAN IT.
DAD CAN TURN NASTY SOMETIMES.
LET 'EM THROUGH. HE'S ONE OF OURS.

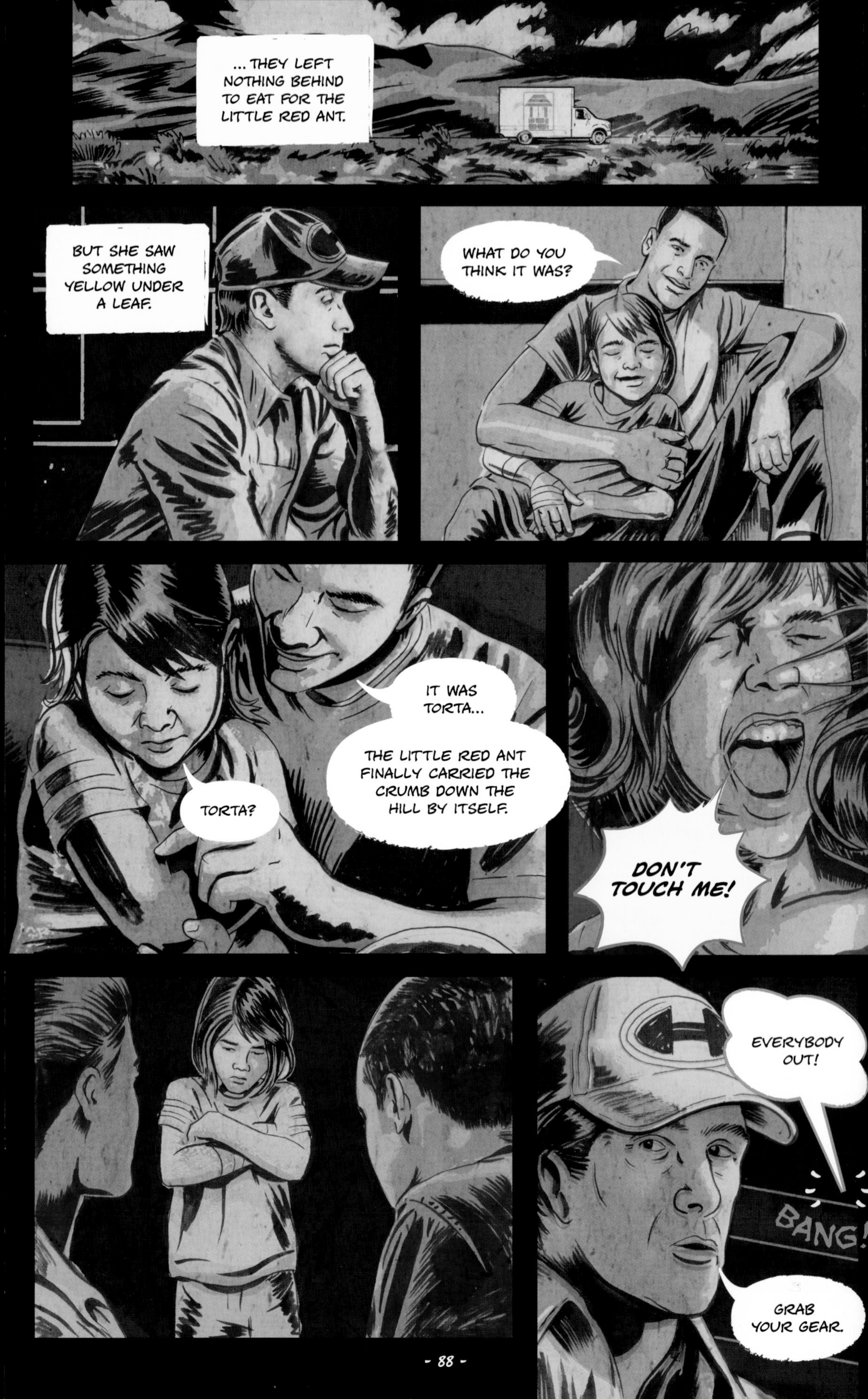
... THEY LEFT NOTHING BEHIND TO EAT FOR THE LITTLE RED ANT.
BUT SHE SAW SOMETHING YELLOW UNDER A LEAF.
WHAT DO YOU THINK IT WAS?
IT WAS TORTA...
TORTA?
THE LITTLE RED ANT FINALLY CARRIED THE CRUMB DOWN THE HILL BY ITSELF.
DON'T TOUCH ME!
EVERYBODY OUT!
BANG!
GRAB YOUR GEAR.

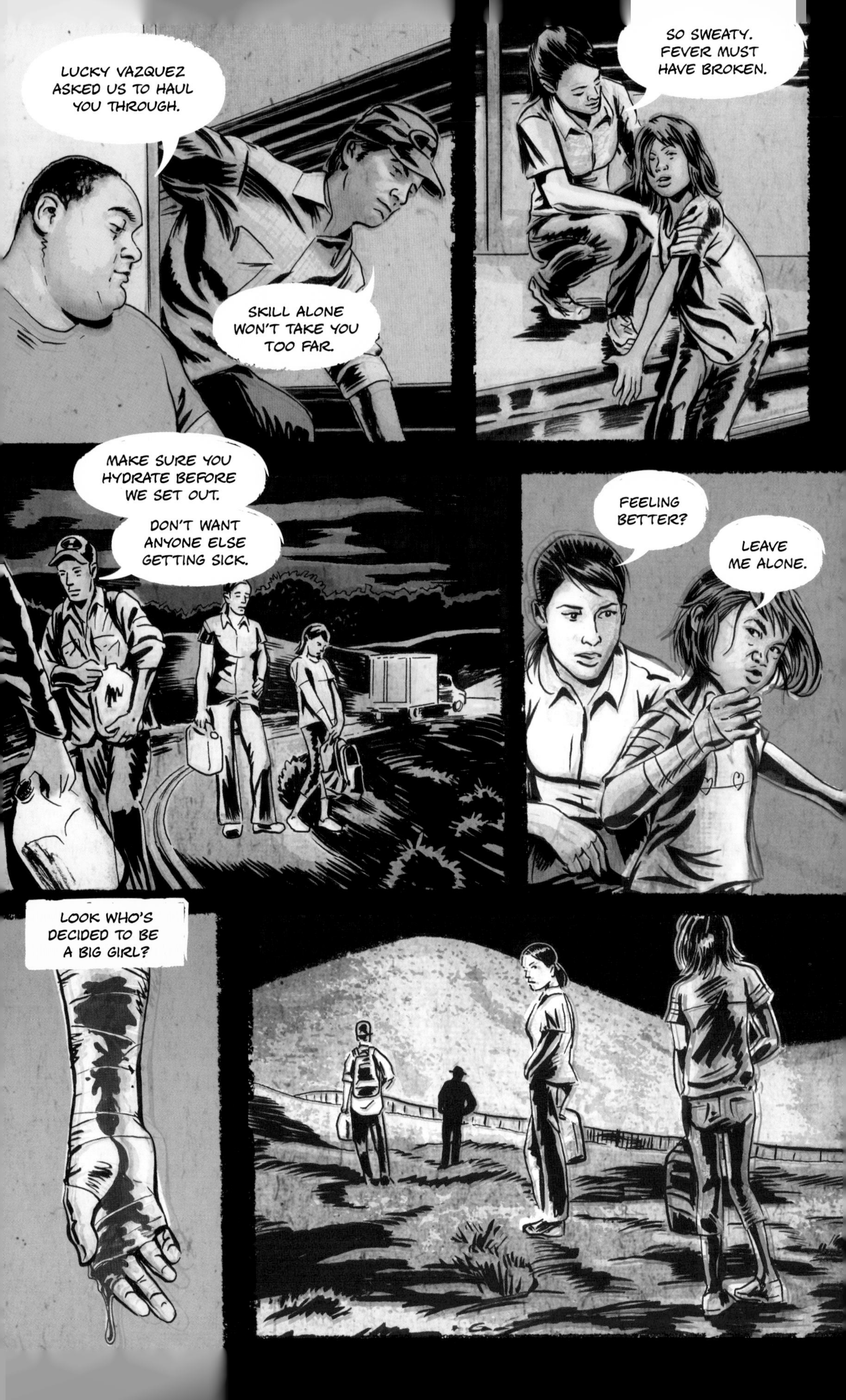
LUCKY VAZQUEZ ASKED US TO HAUL YOU THROUGH.
SKILL ALONE WON'T TAKE YOU TOO FAR.
SO SWEATY. FEVER MUST HAVE BROKEN.
MAKE SURE YOU HYDRATE BEFORE WE SET OUT.
DON'T WANT ANYONE ELSE GETTING SICK.
FEELING BETTER?
LEAVE ME ALONE.
LOOK WHO'S DECIDED TO BE A BIG GIRL?

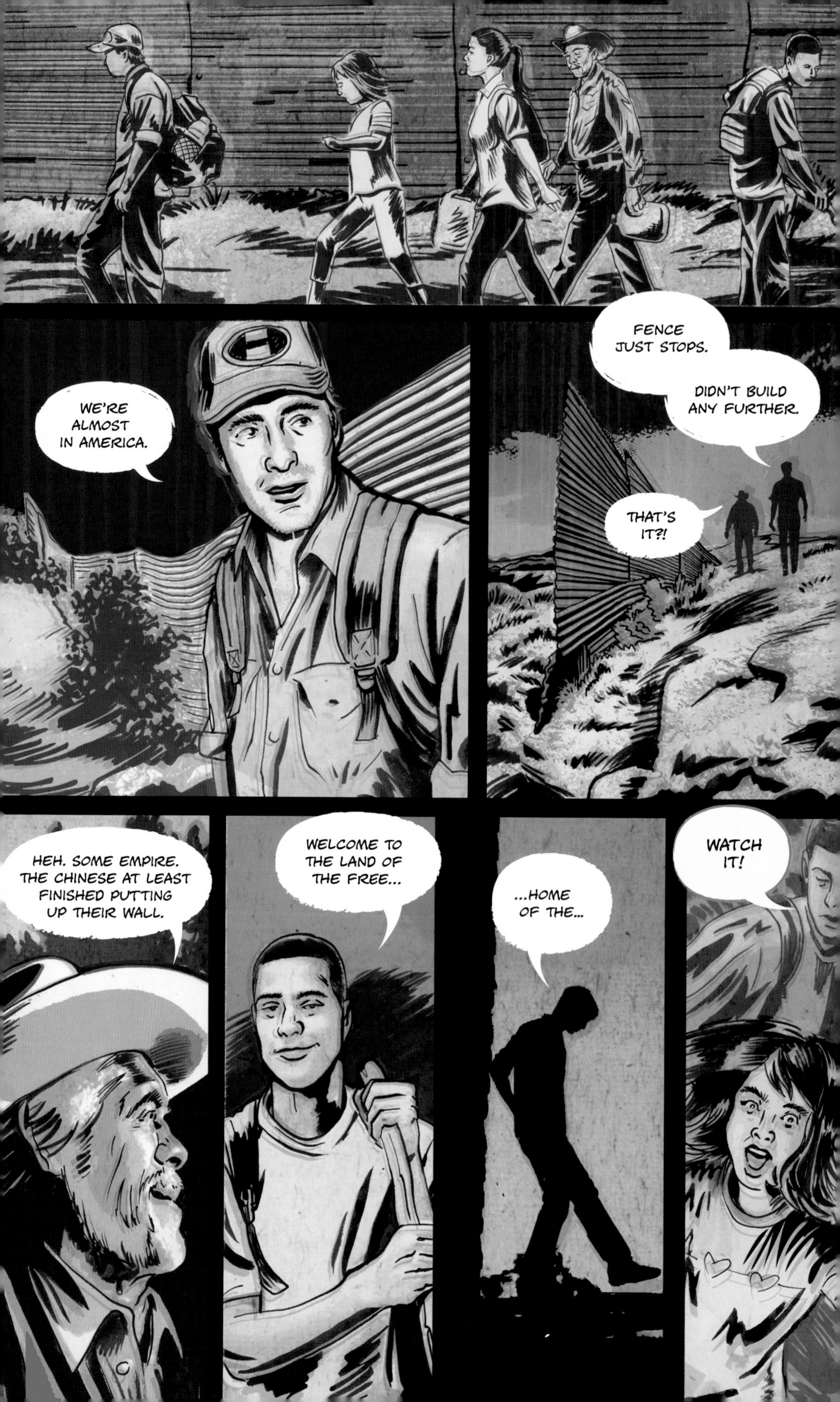
WE'RE ALMOST IN AMERICA.
FENCE JUST STOPS.
DIDN'T BUILD ANY FURTHER.
THAT'S IT?!
HEH. SOME EMPIRE. THE CHINESE AT LEAST FINISHED PUTTING UP THEIR WALL.
WELCOME TO THE LAND OF THE FREE...
...HOME OF THE...
WATCH IT!

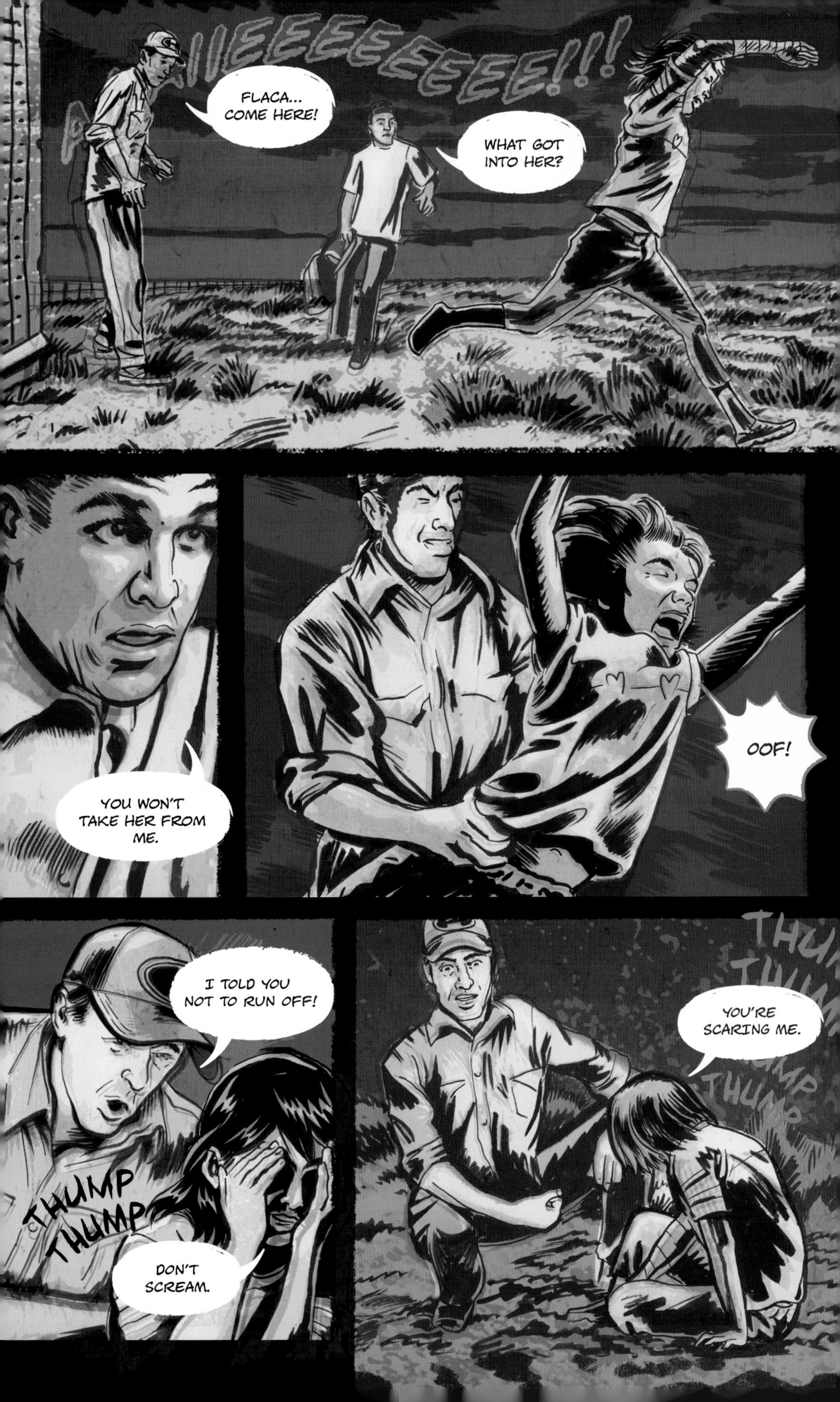
AAIIEEEEEEEEEEE!!!
FLACA... COME HERE!
WHAT GOT INTO HER?
YOU WON'T TAKE HER FROM ME.
OOF!
I TOLD YOU NOT TO RUN OFF!
THUMP THUMP
DON'T SCREAM.
YOU'RE SCARING ME.
THUMP THUMP THUMP THUMP

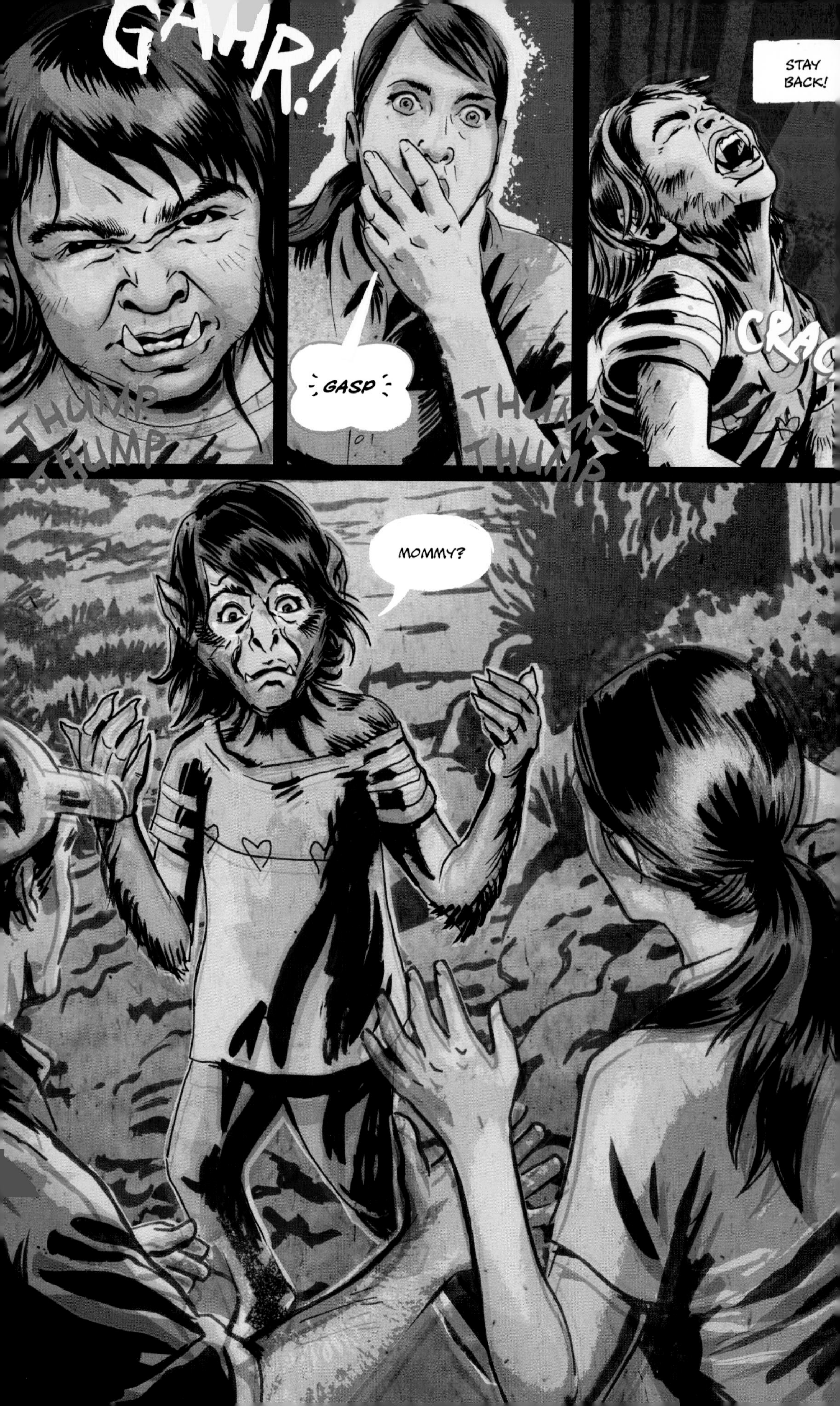
GAHR!
GASP
THUMP THUMP
THUMP THUMP
STAY BACK!
CRAC
MOMMY?

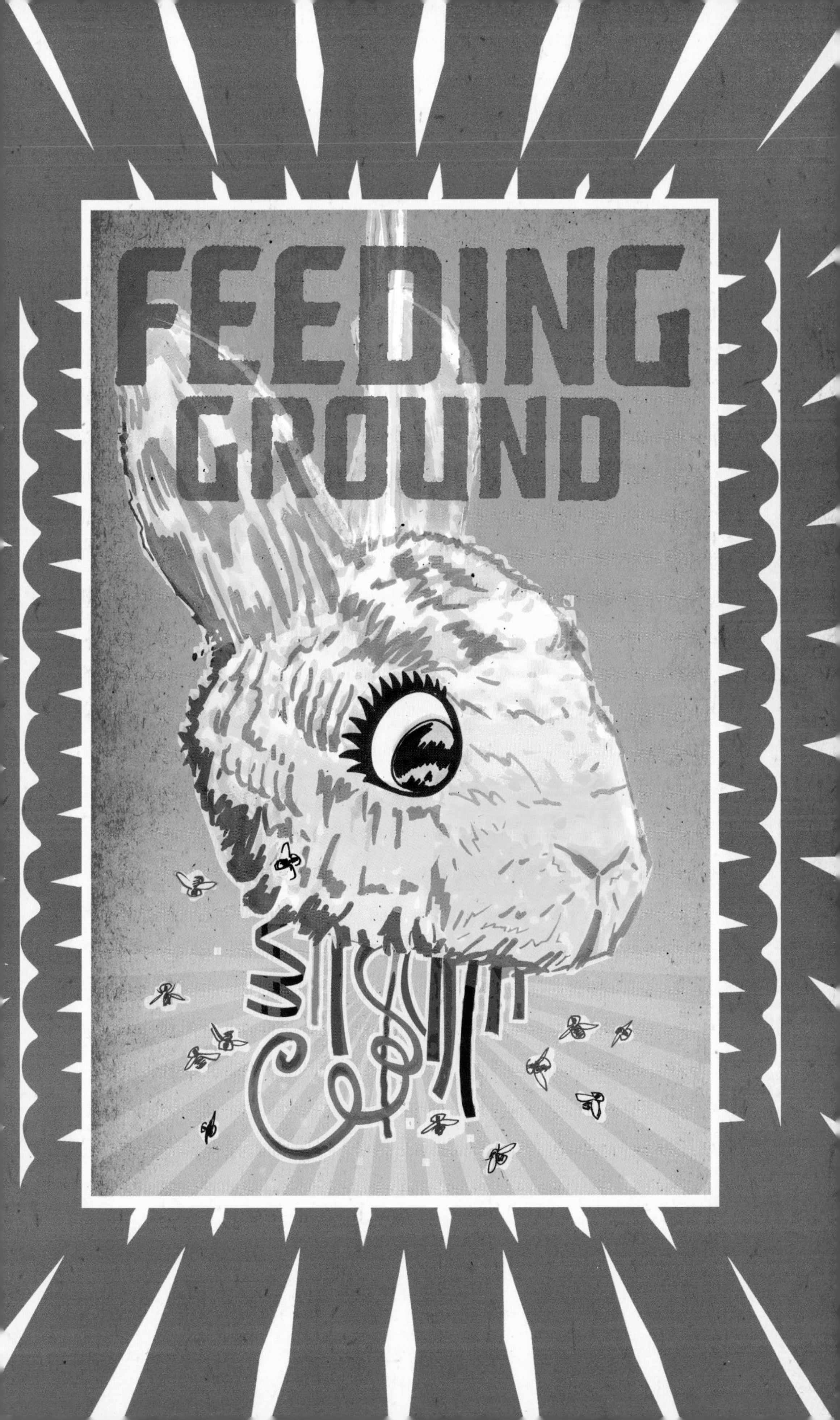
FEEDING
GROUND

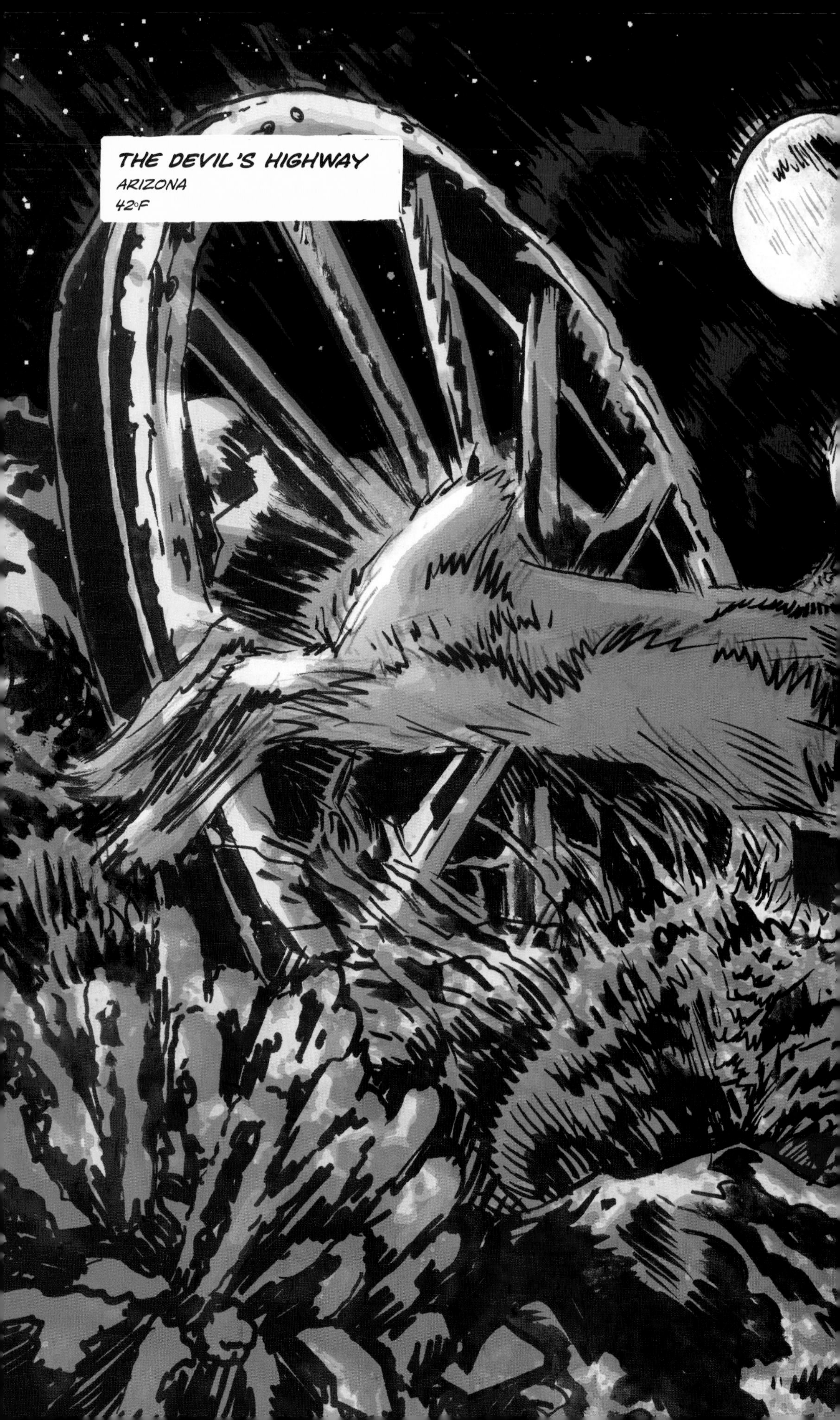
THE DEVIL'S HIGHWAY
ARIZONA
42°F

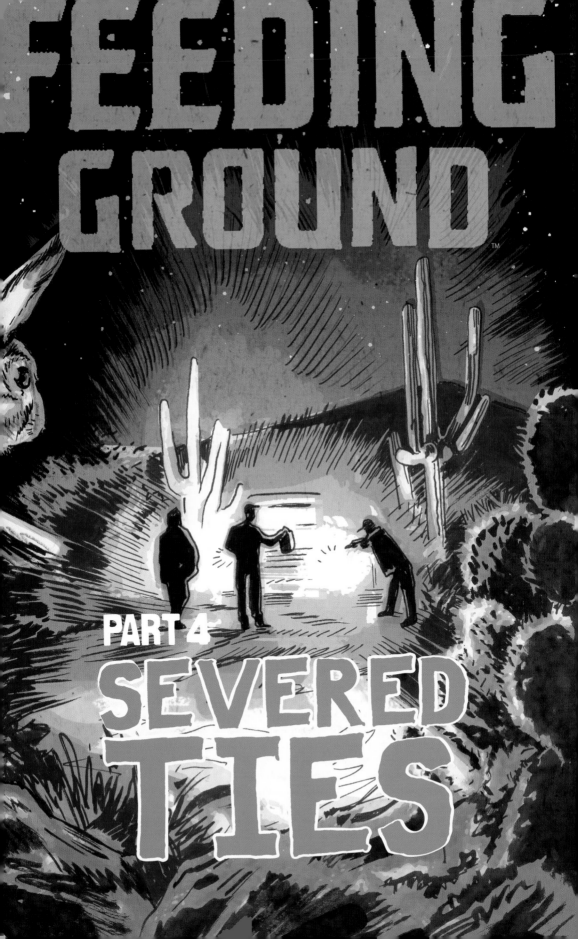

FEEDING GROUND

PART 4
SEVERED TIES

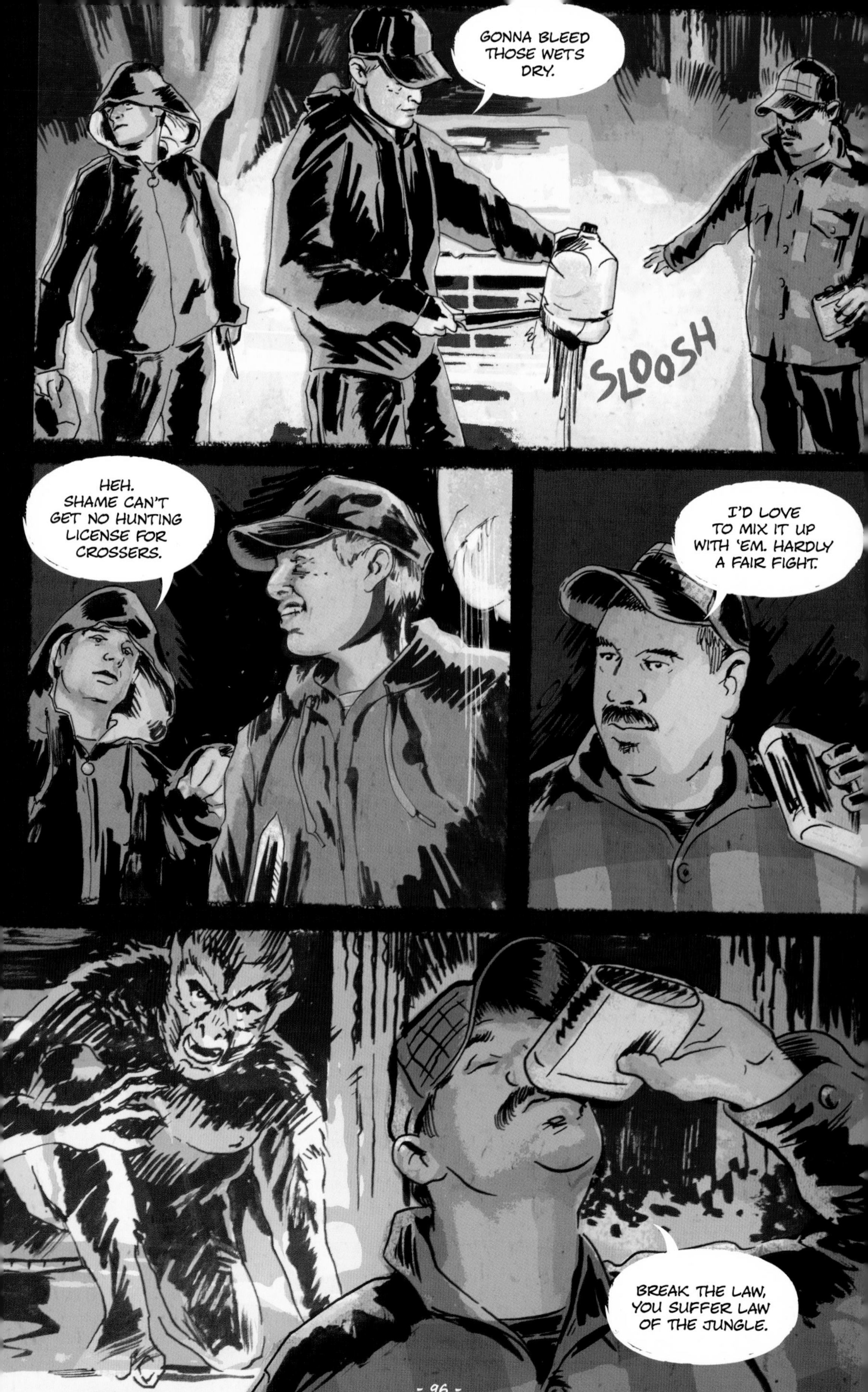
GONNA BLEED THOSE WETS DRY.
SLOOSH
HEH. SHAME CAN'T GET NO HUNTING LICENSE FOR CROSSERS.
I'D LOVE TO MIX IT UP WITH 'EM. HARDLY A FAIR FIGHT.
BREAK THE LAW, YOU SUFFER LAW OF THE JUNGLE.

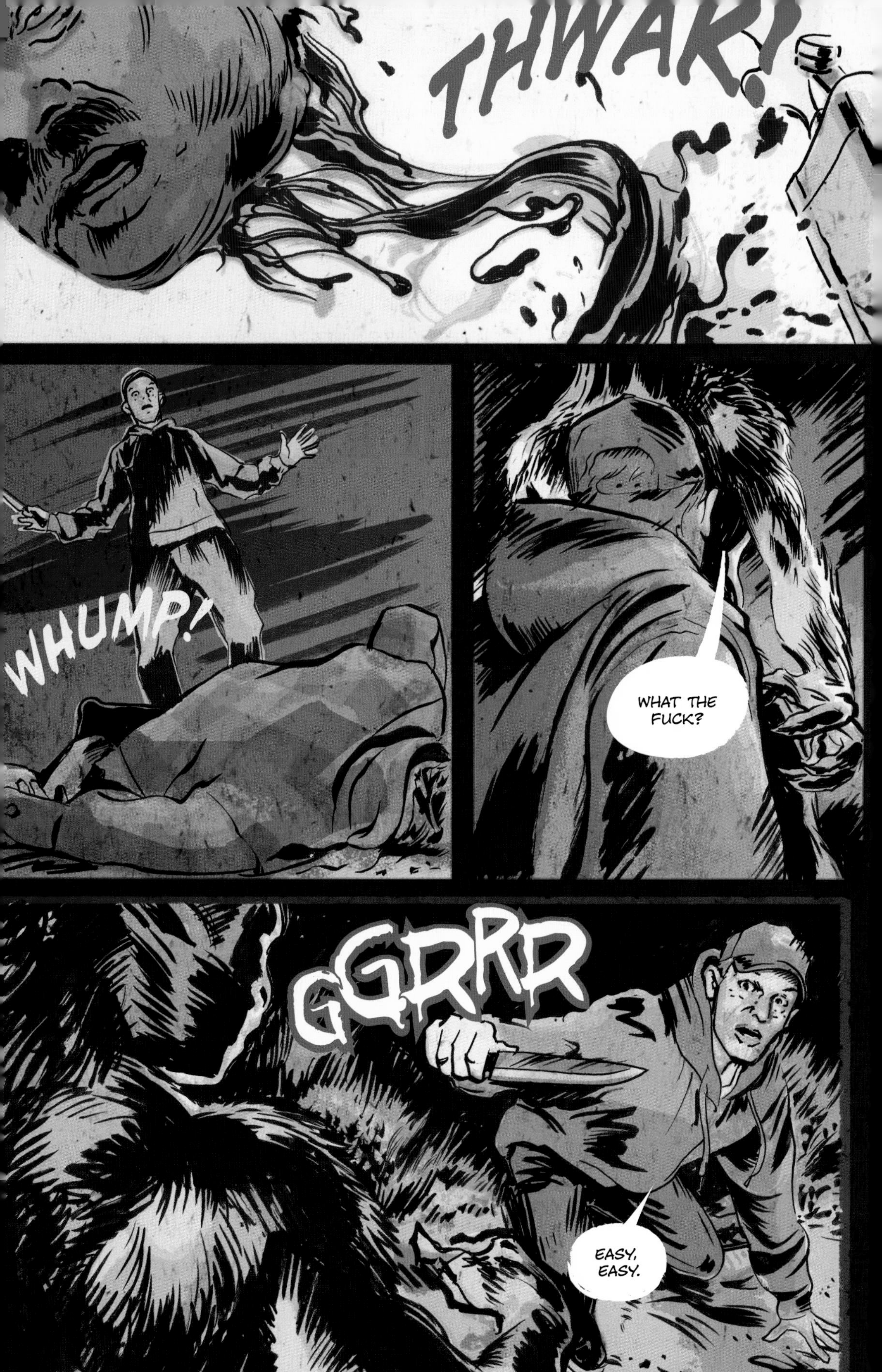
THWAK!
WHUMP!
WHAT THE FUCK?
GGRRR
EASY, EASY.

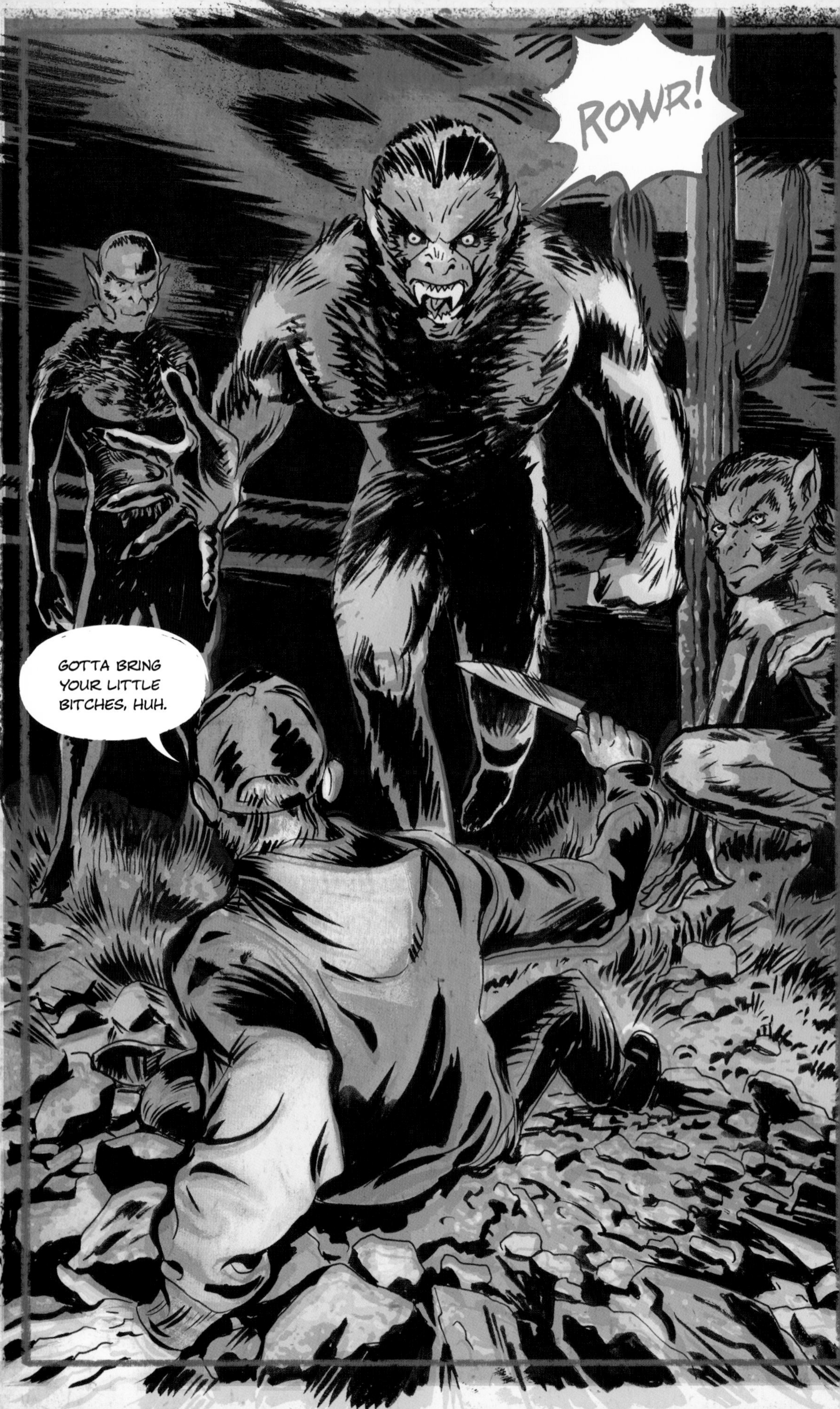
ROWR!
GOTTA BRING YOUR LITTLE BITCHES, HUH.

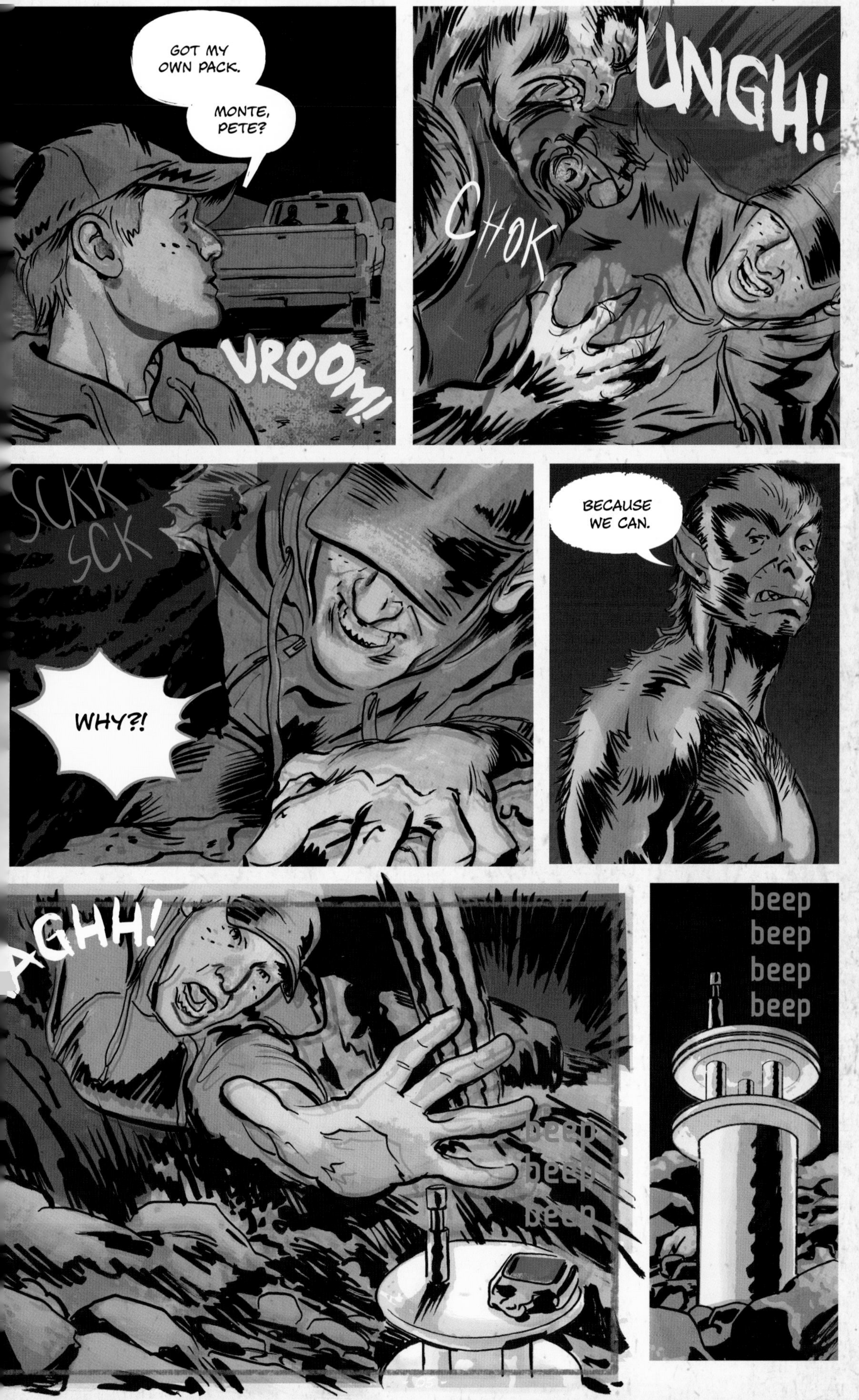
GOT MY OWN PACK.
MONTE, PETE?
VROOM!
UNGH!
CHOK
SCKK SCK
WHY?!
BECAUSE WE CAN.
AGHH!
beep
beep
beep
beep
beep
beep
beep

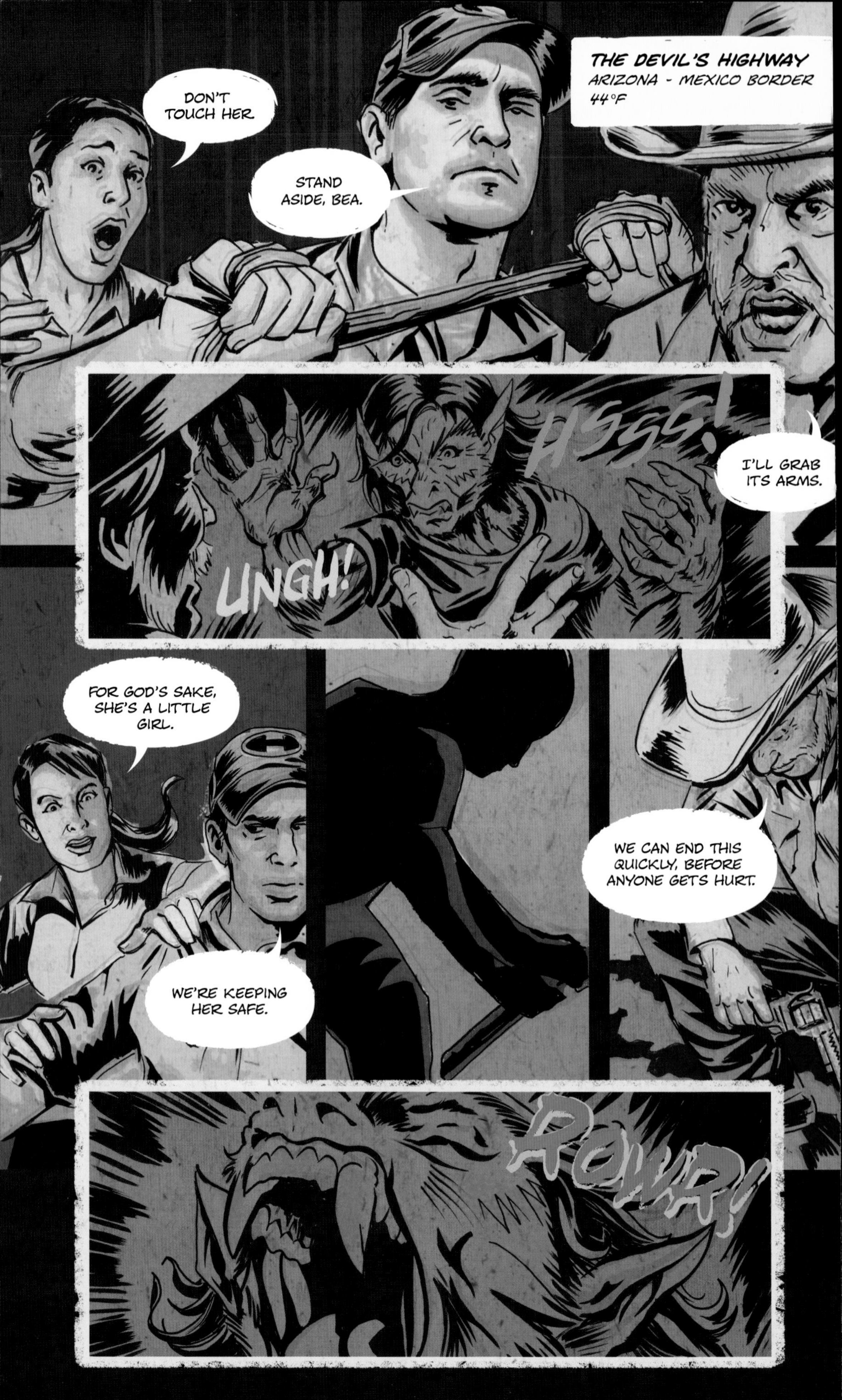
THE DEVIL'S HIGHWAY
ARIZONA - MEXICO BORDER
44°F
DON'T TOUCH HER.
STAND ASIDE, BEA.
HSSS!
UNGH!
I'LL GRAB ITS ARMS.
FOR GOD'S SAKE, SHE'S A LITTLE GIRL.
WE'RE KEEPING HER SAFE.
WE CAN END THIS QUICKLY, BEFORE ANYONE GETS HURT.
ROWR!

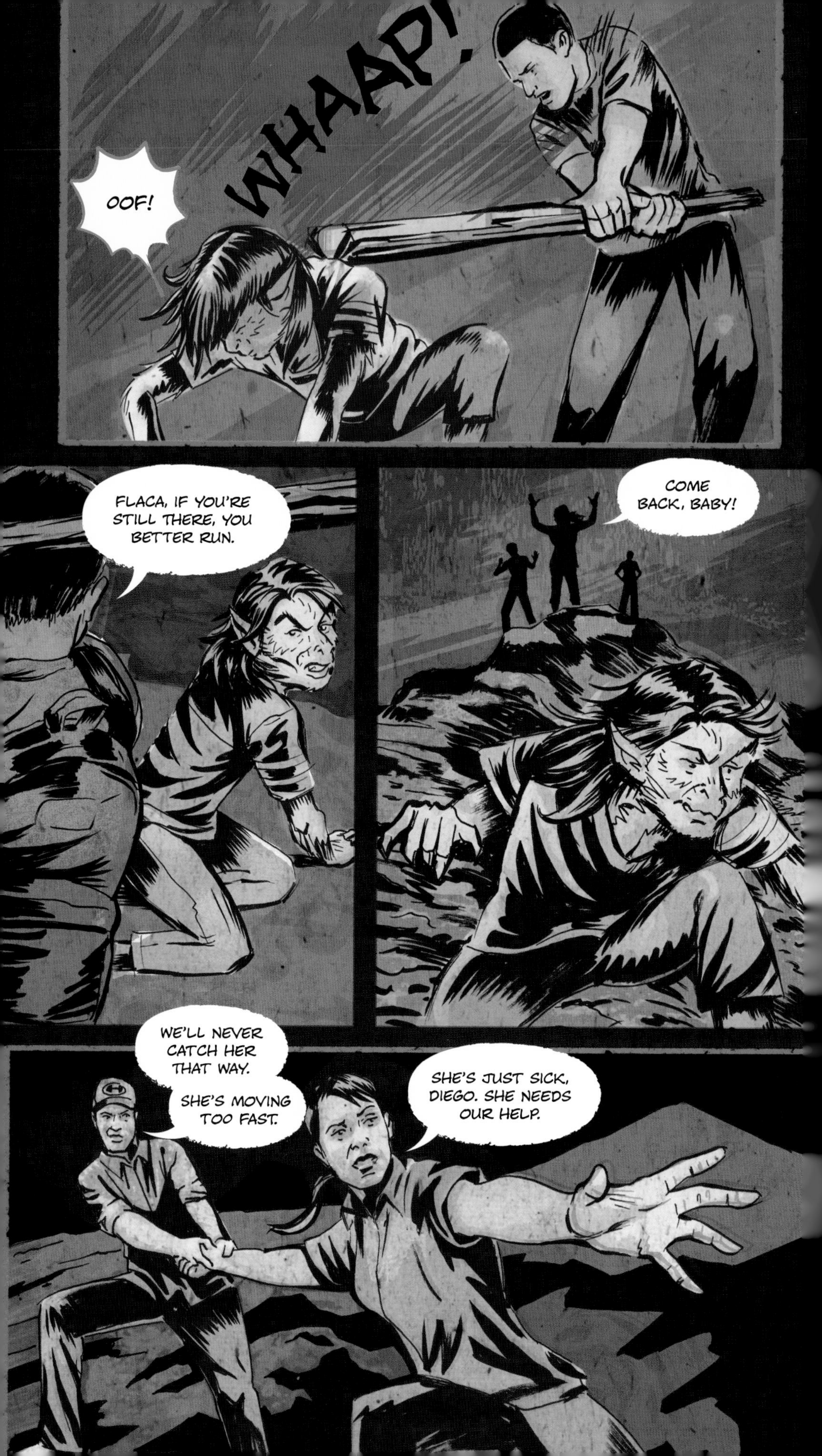
OOF!
WHAAP!
FLACA, IF YOU'RE STILL THERE, YOU BETTER RUN.
COME BACK, BABY!
WE'LL NEVER CATCH HER THAT WAY.
SHE'S MOVING TOO FAST.
SHE'S JUST SICK, DIEGO. SHE NEEDS OUR HELP.

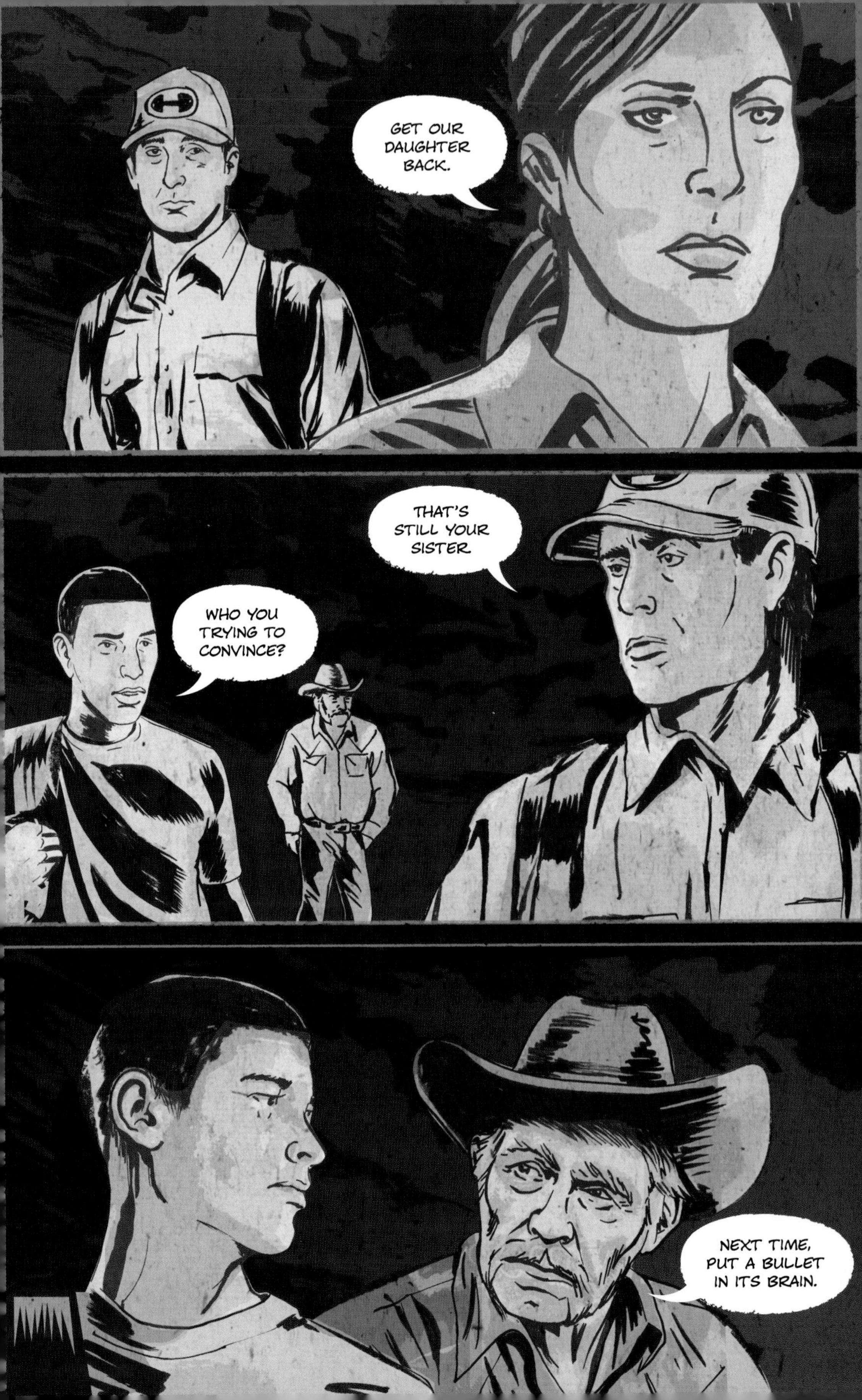
GET OUR DAUGHTER BACK.
THAT'S STILL YOUR SISTER
WHO YOU TRYING TO CONVINCE?
NEXT TIME, PUT A BULLET IN ITS BRAIN.

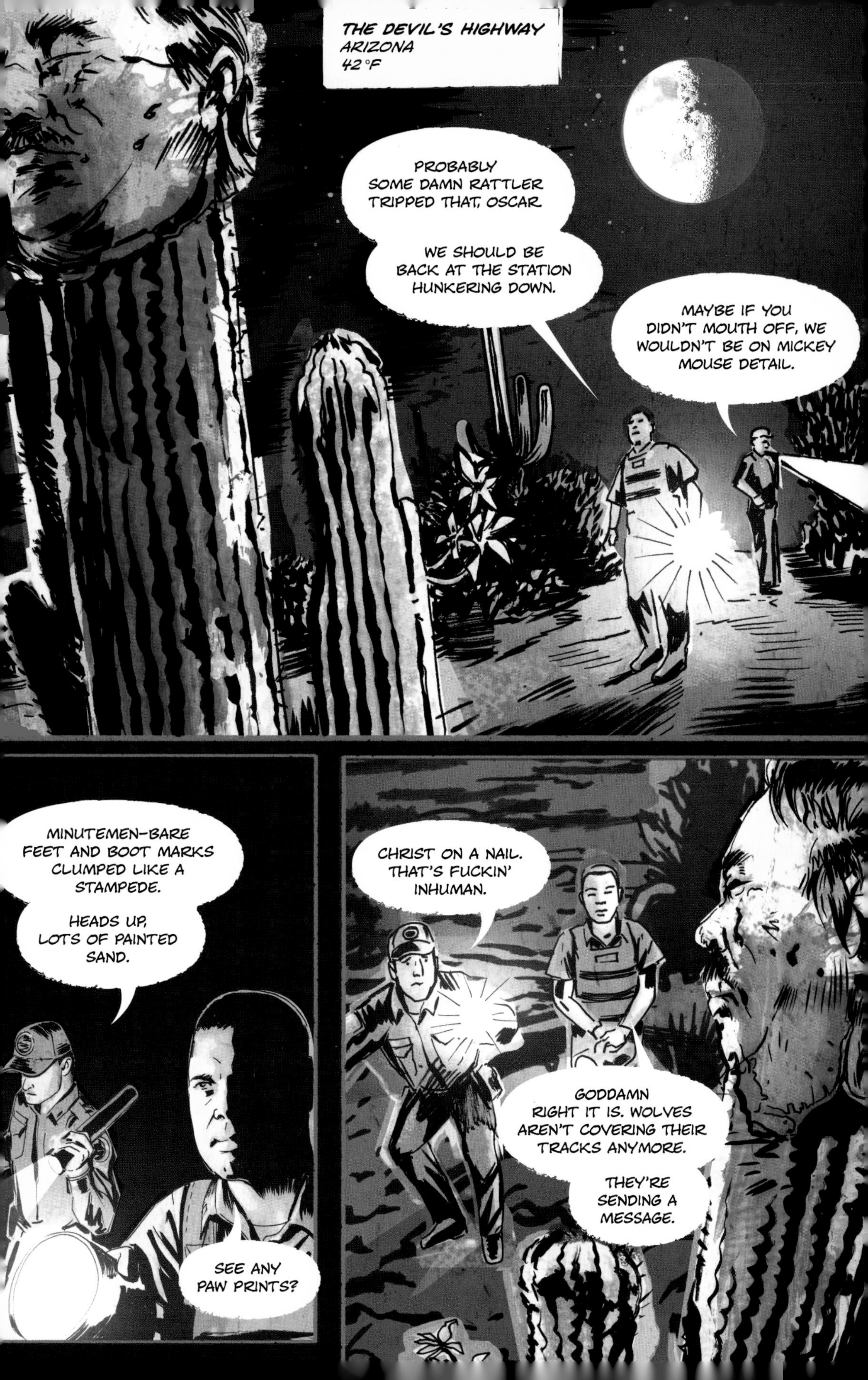
THE DEVIL'S HIGHWAY
ARIZONA
42°F
PROBABLY SOME DAMN RATTLER TRIPPED THAT, OSCAR.
WE SHOULD BE BACK AT THE STATION HUNKERING DOWN.
MAYBE IF YOU DIDN'T MOUTH OFF, WE WOULDN'T BE ON MICKEY MOUSE DETAIL.
MINUTEMEN—BARE FEET AND BOOT MARKS CLUMPED LIKE A STAMPEDE.
HEADS UP, LOTS OF PAINTED SAND.
SEE ANY PAW PRINTS?
CHRIST ON A NAIL. THAT'S FUCKIN' INHUMAN.
GODDAMN RIGHT IT IS. WOLVES AREN'T COVERING THEIR TRACKS ANYMORE.
THEY'RE SENDING A MESSAGE.

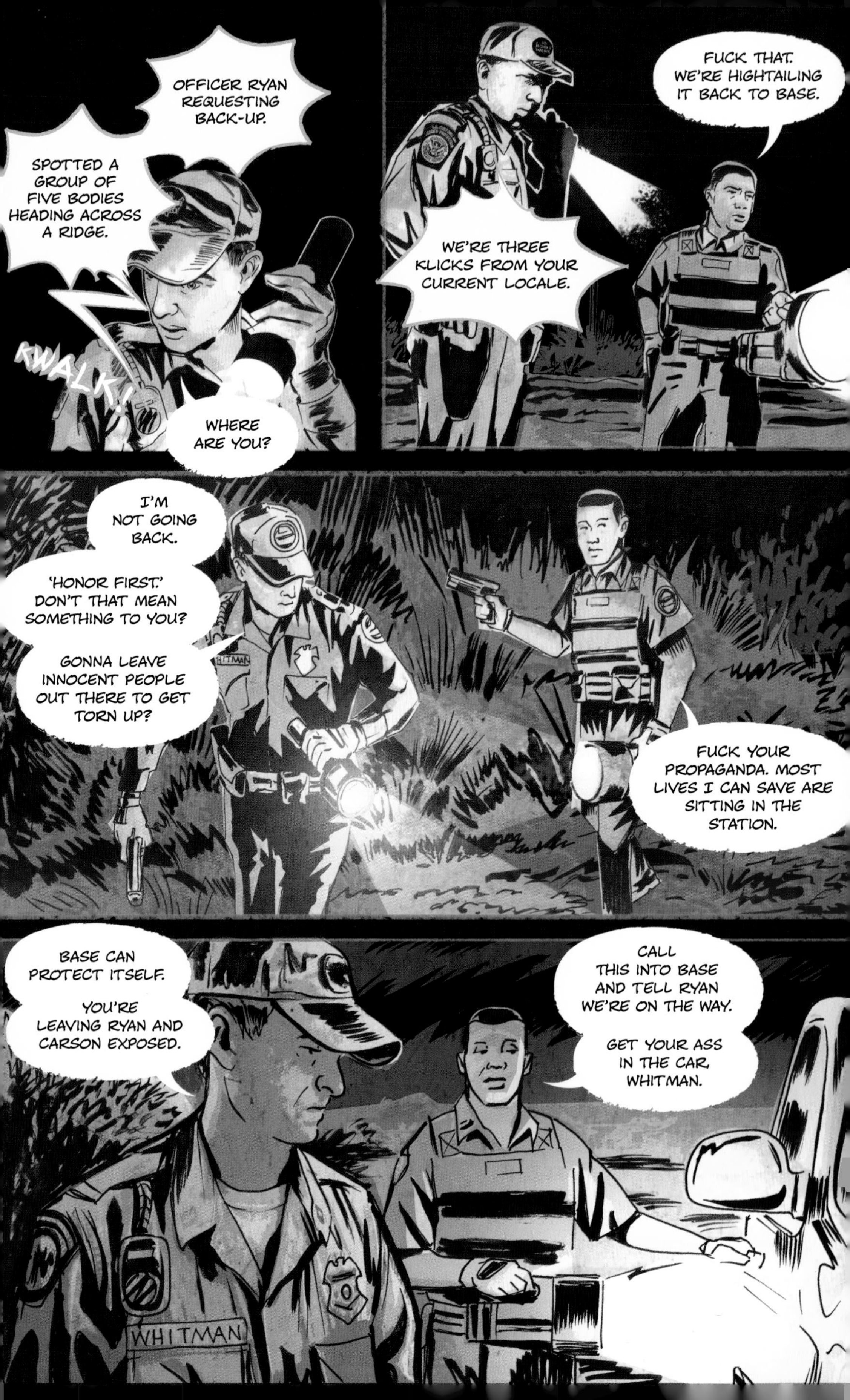
SPOTTED A GROUP OF FIVE BODIES HEADING ACROSS A RIDGE.
OFFICER RYAN REQUESTING BACK-UP.
KWALK!
WHERE ARE YOU?
WE'RE THREE KLICKS FROM YOUR CURRENT LOCALE.
FUCK THAT. WE'RE HIGHTAILING IT BACK TO BASE.
I'M NOT GOING BACK.
'HONOR FIRST.' DON'T THAT MEAN SOMETHING TO YOU?
GONNA LEAVE INNOCENT PEOPLE OUT THERE TO GET TORN UP?
WHITMAN
FUCK YOUR PROPAGANDA. MOST LIVES I CAN SAVE ARE SITTING IN THE STATION.
BASE CAN PROTECT ITSELF.
YOU'RE LEAVING RYAN AND CARSON EXPOSED.
CALL THIS INTO BASE AND TELL RYAN WE'RE ON THE WAY.
GET YOUR ASS IN THE CAR, WHITMAN.
WHITMAN

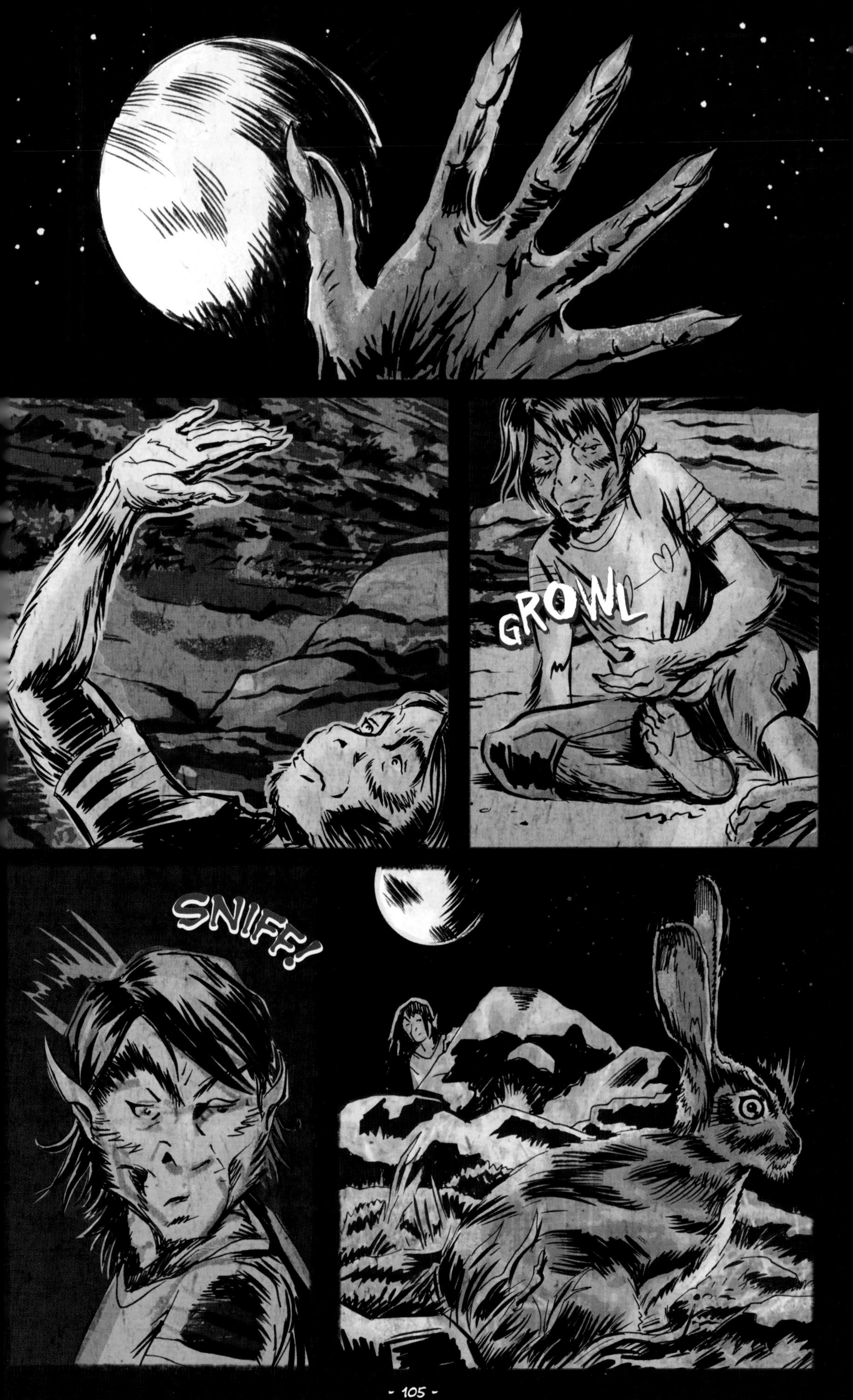
GROWL
SNIFF!

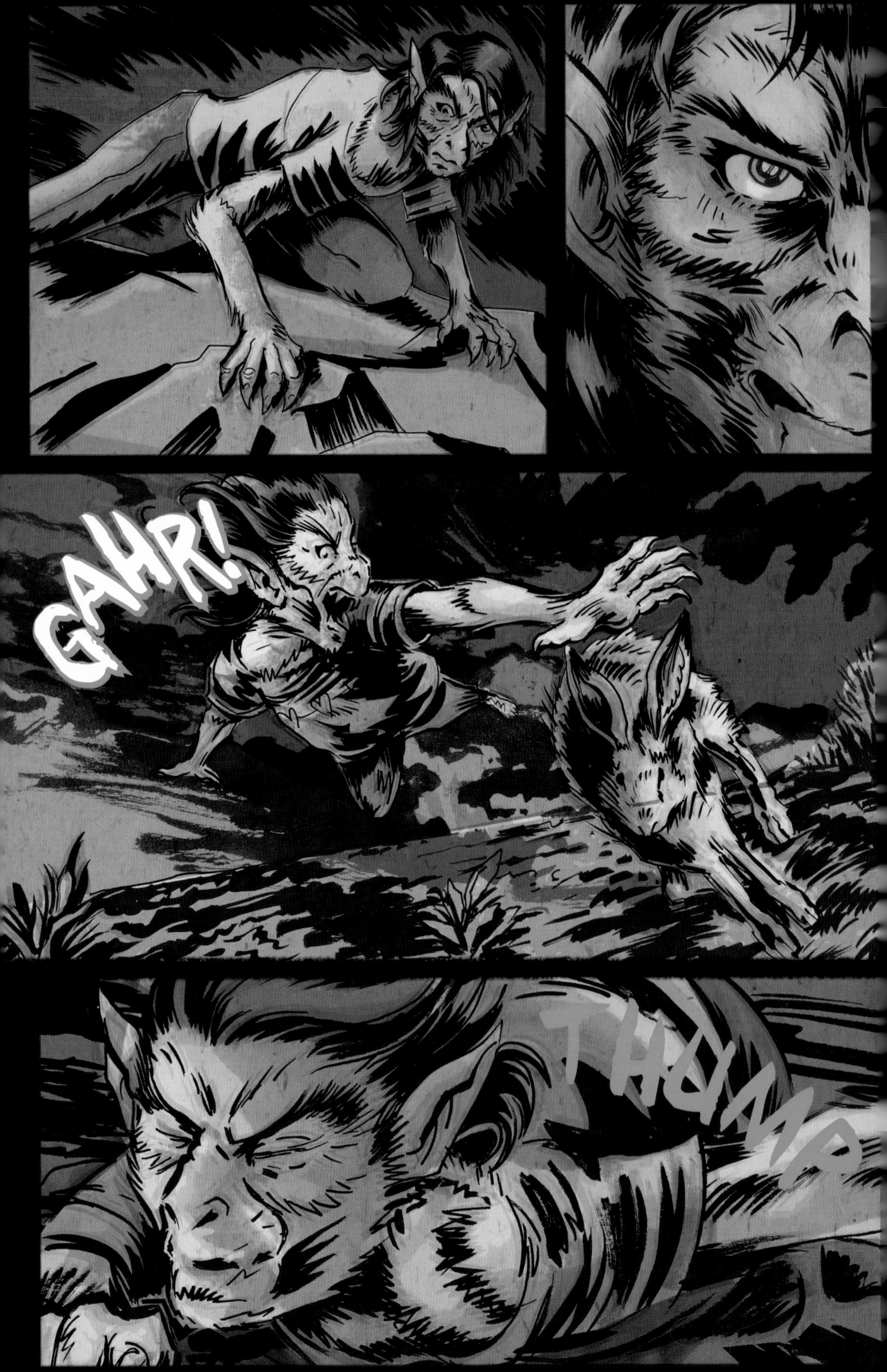
GAHR!
THUMP

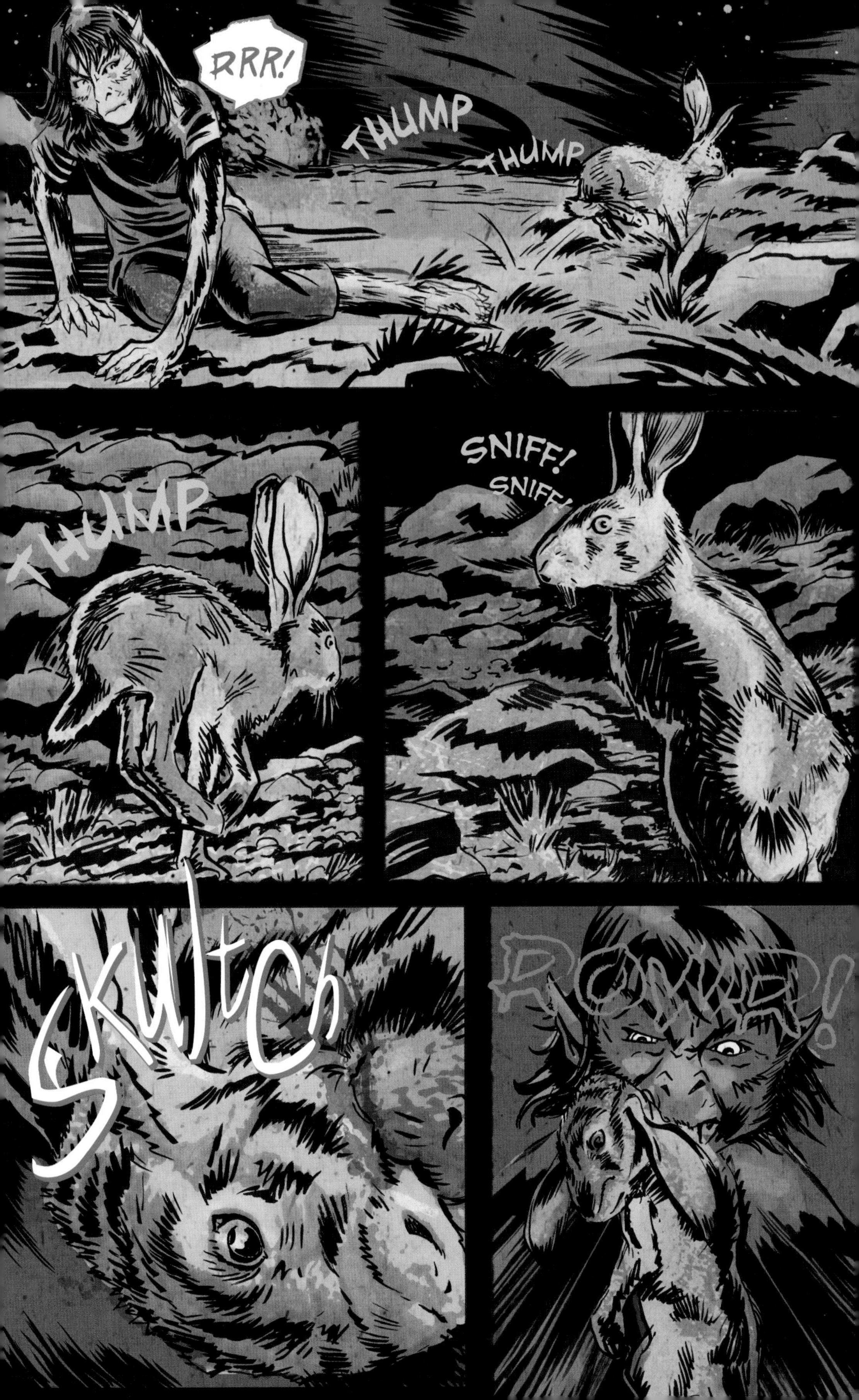
RRR!
THUMP
THUMP
THUMP
SNIFF!
SNIFF!
SKULTCH
ROWR!

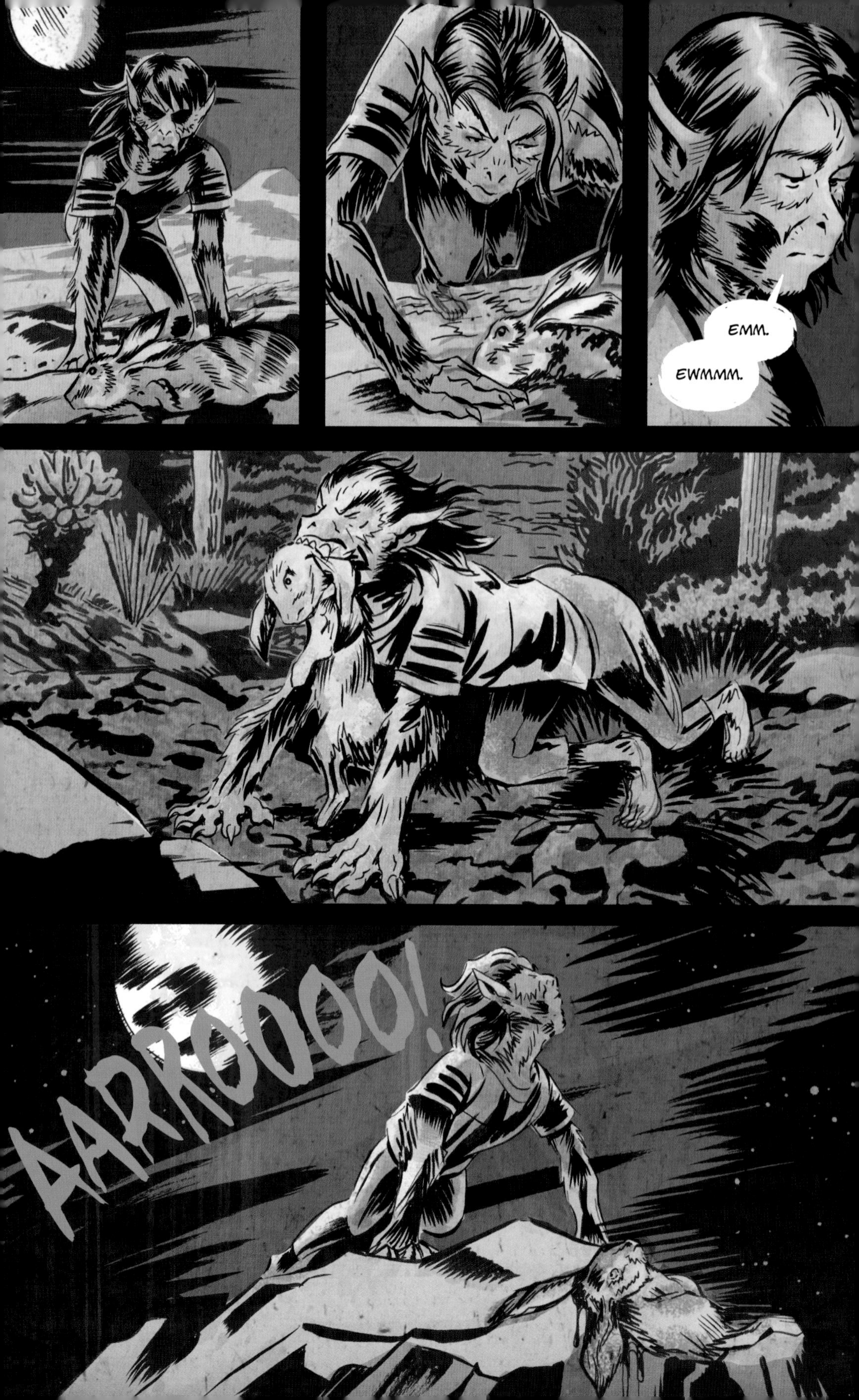
EMM.
EWMMM.
AARROOOO!

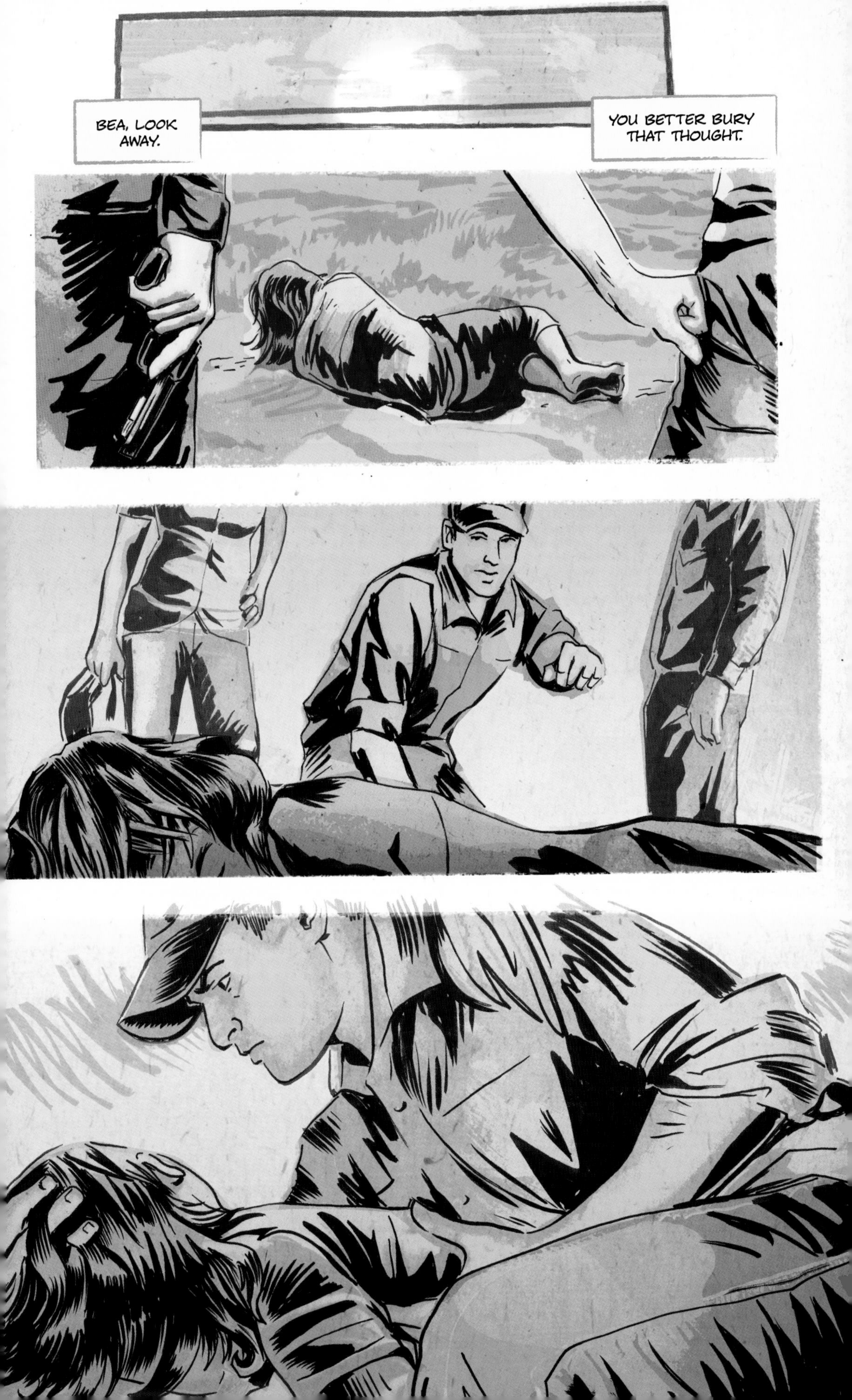
BEA, LOOK AWAY.
YOU BETTER BURY THAT THOUGHT.

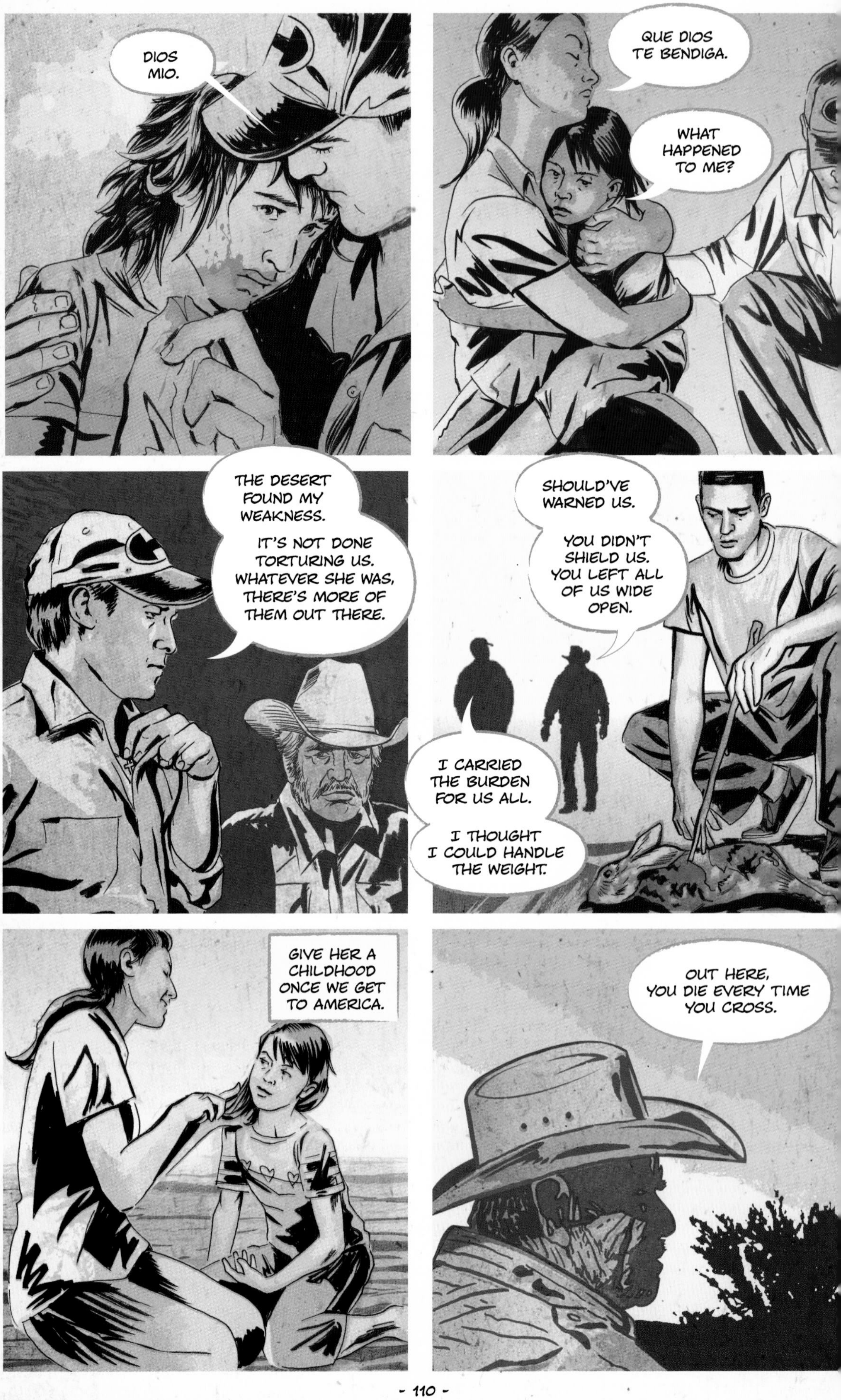
DIOS MIO.
QUE DIOS TE BENDIGA.
WHAT HAPPENED TO ME?
THE DESERT FOUND MY WEAKNESS.
IT'S NOT DONE TORTURING US. WHATEVER SHE WAS, THERE'S MORE OF THEM OUT THERE.
SHOULD'VE WARNED US.
YOU DIDN'T SHIELD US. YOU LEFT ALL OF US WIDE OPEN.
I CARRIED THE BURDEN FOR US ALL.
I THOUGHT I COULD HANDLE THE WEIGHT.
GIVE HER A CHILDHOOD ONCE WE GET TO AMERICA.
OUT HERE, YOU DIE EVERY TIME YOU CROSS.

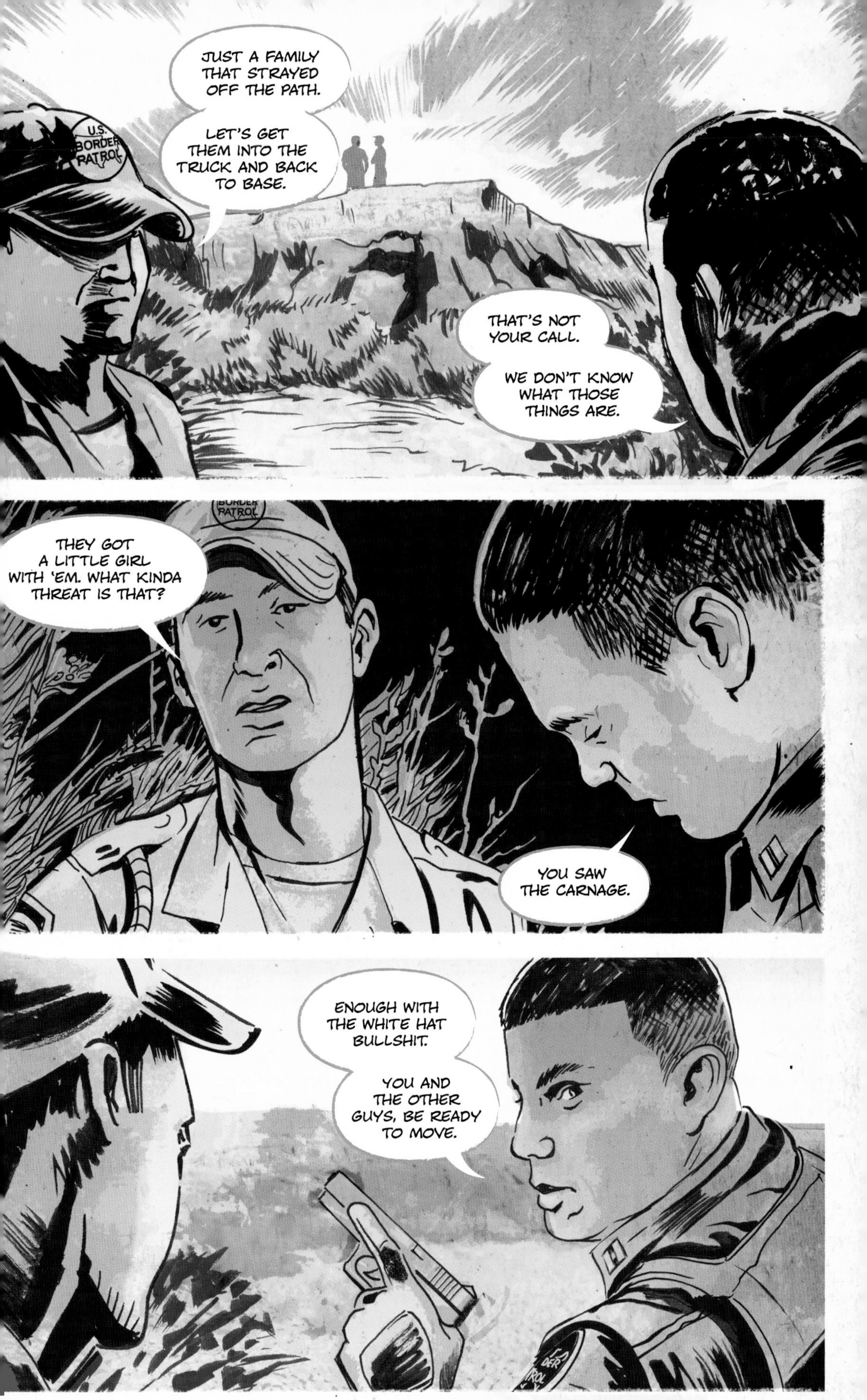
JUST A FAMILY THAT STRAYED OFF THE PATH.
LET'S GET THEM INTO THE TRUCK AND BACK TO BASE.
U.S. BORDER PATROL
THAT'S NOT YOUR CALL.
WE DON'T KNOW WHAT THOSE THINGS ARE.
BORDER PATROL
THEY GOT A LITTLE GIRL WITH 'EM. WHAT KINDA THREAT IS THAT?
YOU SAW THE CARNAGE.
ENOUGH WITH THE WHITE HAT BULLSHIT.
YOU AND THE OTHER GUYS, BE READY TO MOVE.

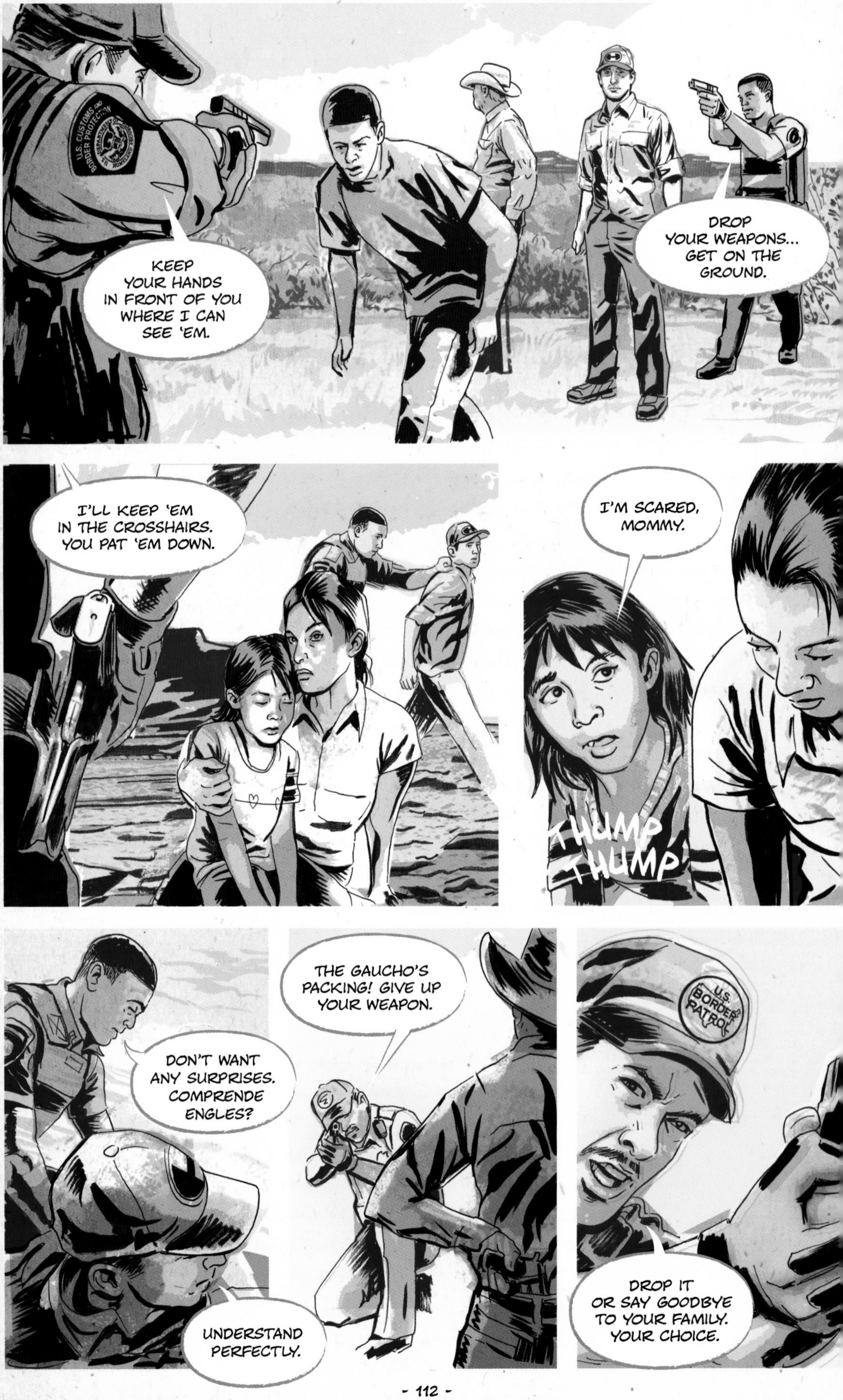
KEEP YOUR HANDS IN FRONT OF YOU WHERE I CAN SEE 'EM.
DROP YOUR WEAPONS... GET ON THE GROUND.
I'LL KEEP 'EM IN THE CROSSHAIRS. YOU PAT 'EM DOWN.
I'M SCARED, MOMMY.
THUMP THUMP
DON'T WANT ANY SURPRISES. COMPRENDE ENGLES?
UNDERSTAND PERFECTLY.
THE GAUCHO'S PACKING! GIVE UP YOUR WEAPON.
DROP IT OR SAY GOODBYE TO YOUR FAMILY. YOUR CHOICE.

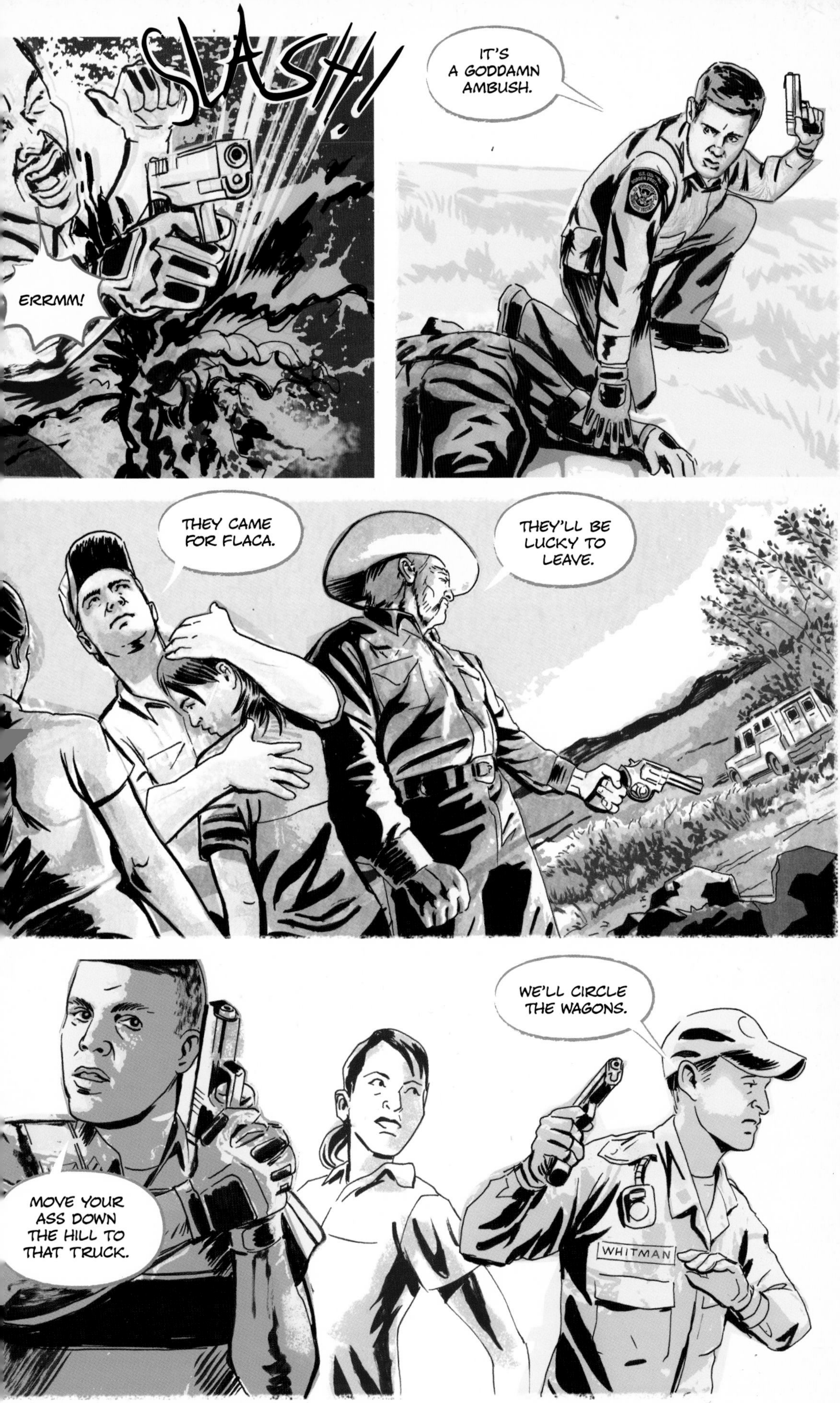
SLASH!
ERRMM!
IT'S A GODDAMN AMBUSH.
THEY CAME FOR FLACA.
THEY'LL BE LUCKY TO LEAVE.
MOVE YOUR ASS DOWN THE HILL TO THAT TRUCK.
WE'LL CIRCLE THE WAGONS.
WHITMAN

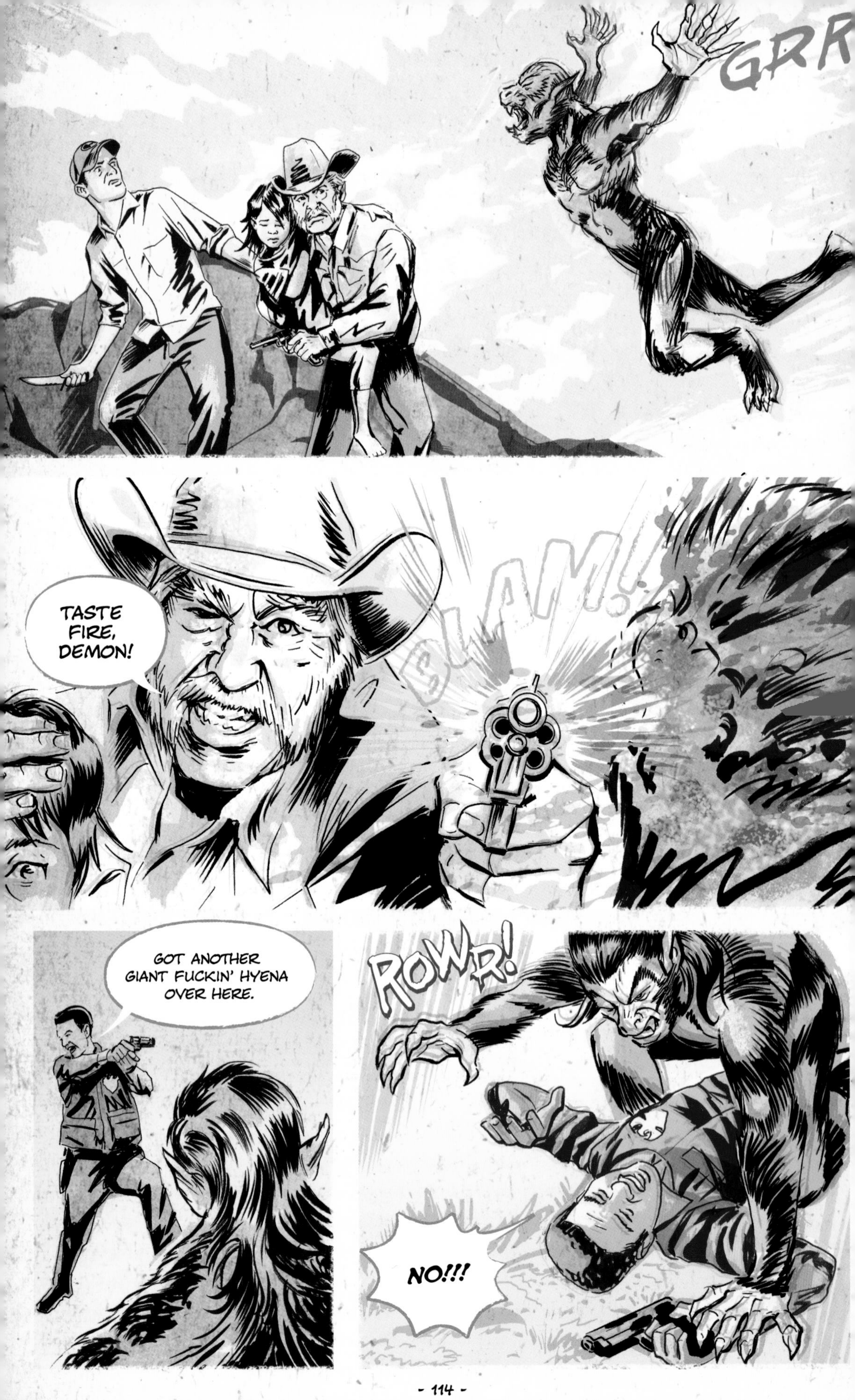
GRR
TASTE FIRE, DEMON!
BLAM!
GOT ANOTHER GIANT FUCKIN' HYENA OVER HERE.
ROWR!
NO!!!

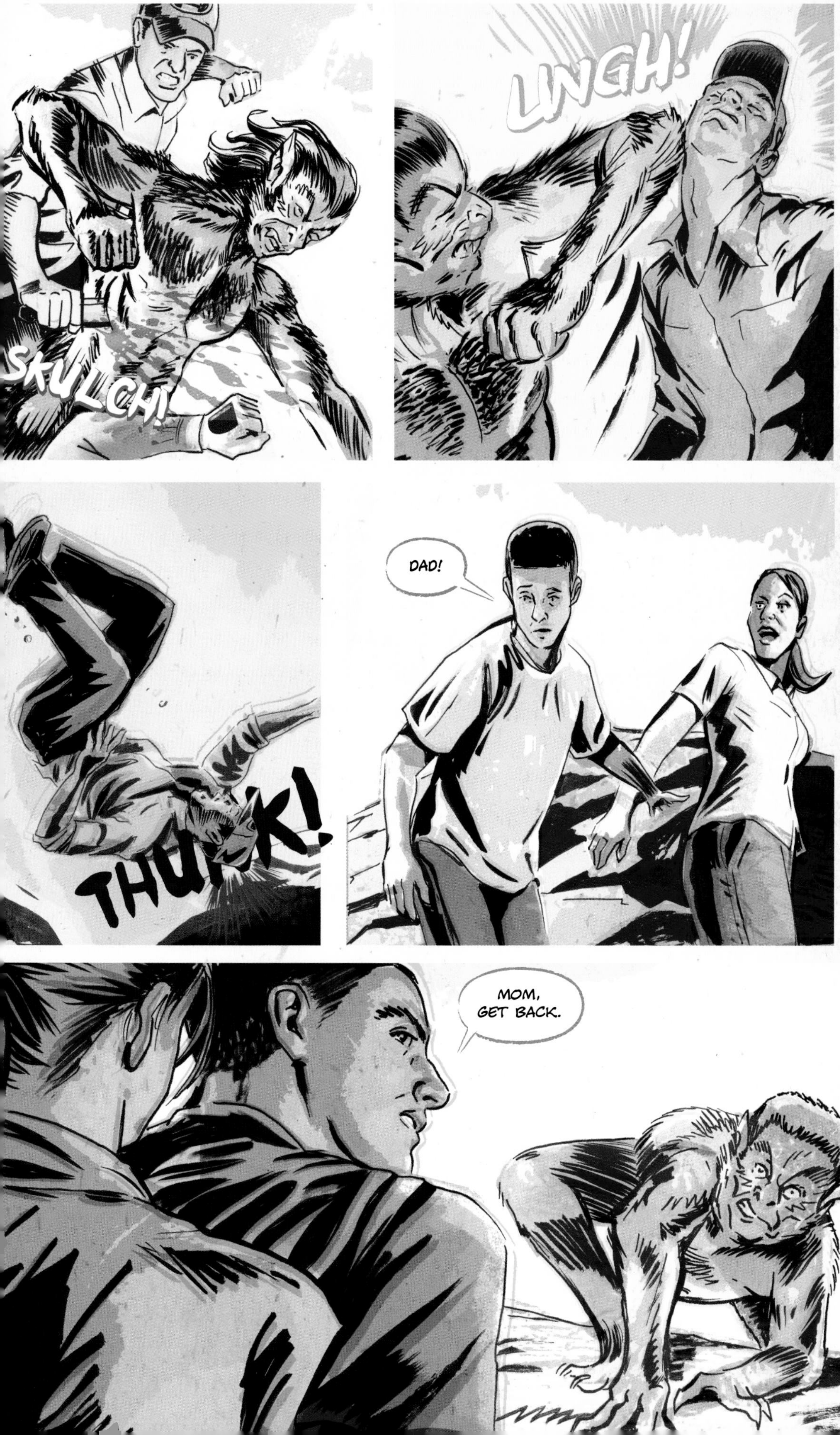
SKULCH!
UNGH!
THUNK!
DAD!
MOM,
GET BACK.

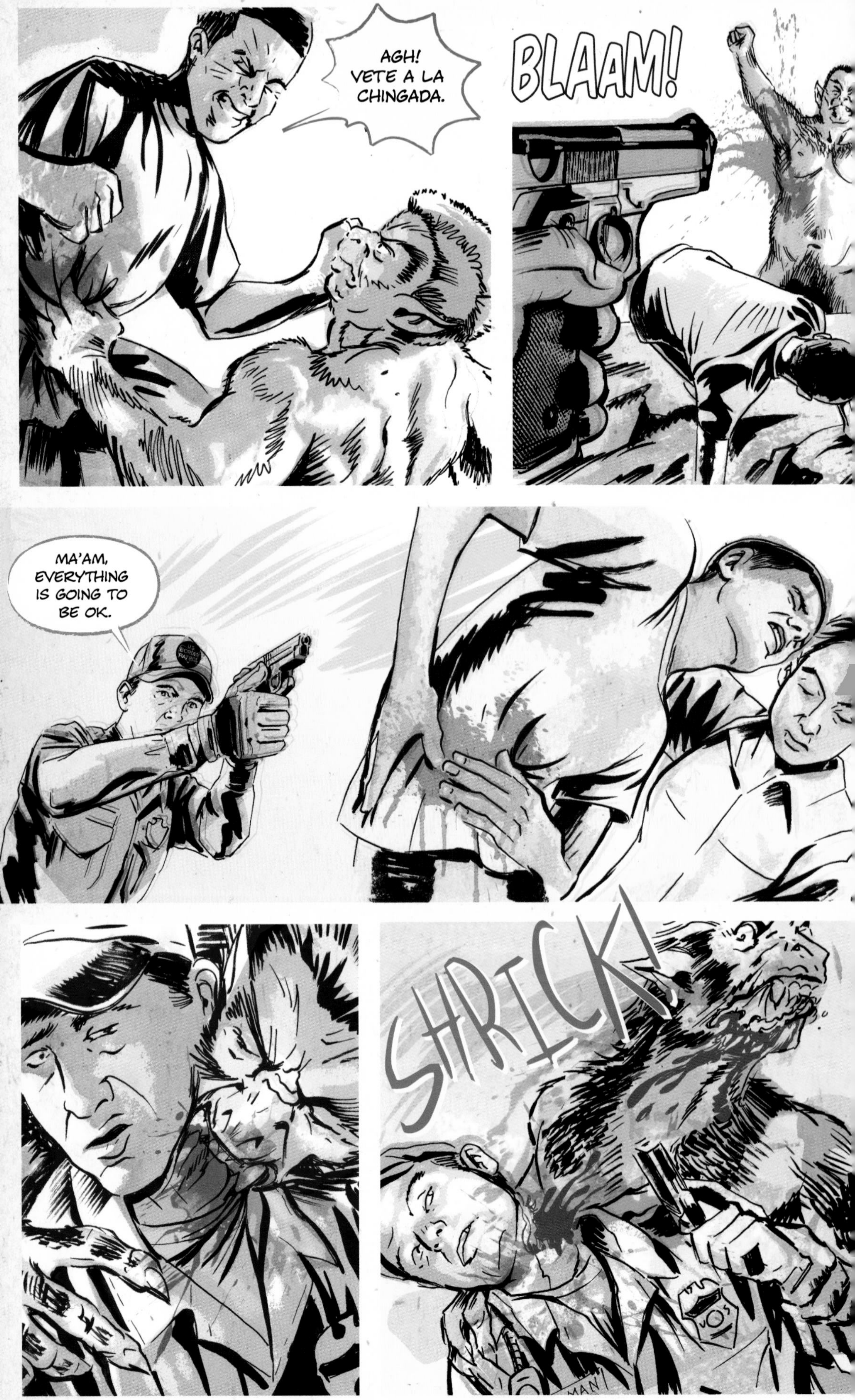
AGH! VETE A LA CHINGADA.
BLAAM!
MA'AM, EVERYTHING IS GOING TO BE OK.
SHRICK!

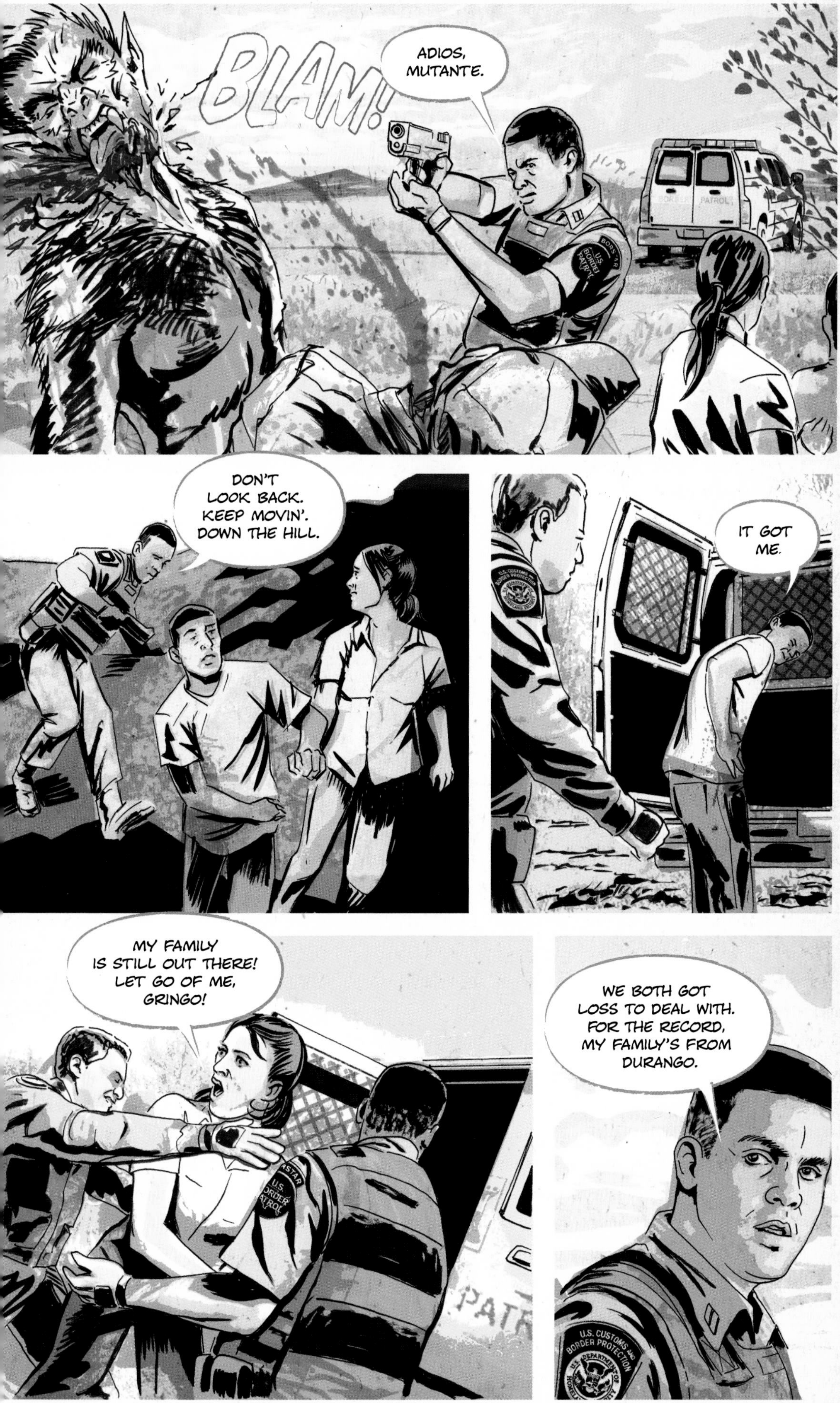
BLAM!
ADIOS, MUTANTE.
BORDER PATROL
DON'T LOOK BACK. KEEP MOVIN'. DOWN THE HILL.
IT GOT ME.
MY FAMILY IS STILL OUT THERE! LET GO OF ME, GRINGO!
WE BOTH GOT LOSS TO DEAL WITH. FOR THE RECORD, MY FAMILY'S FROM DURANGO.

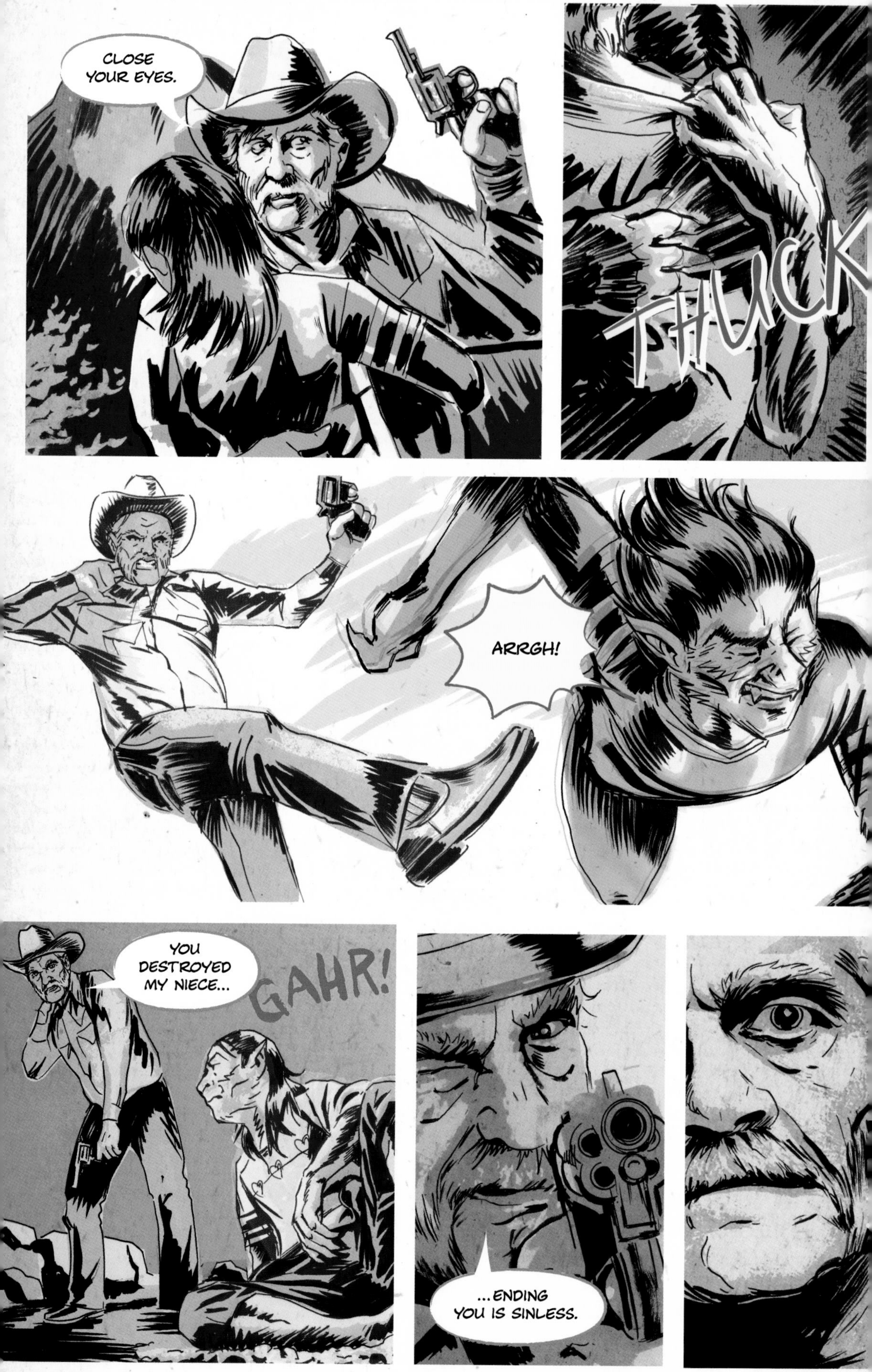
CLOSE YOUR EYES.
THUCK
ARRGH!
YOU DESTROYED MY NIECE...
GAHR!
...ENDING YOU IS SINLESS.

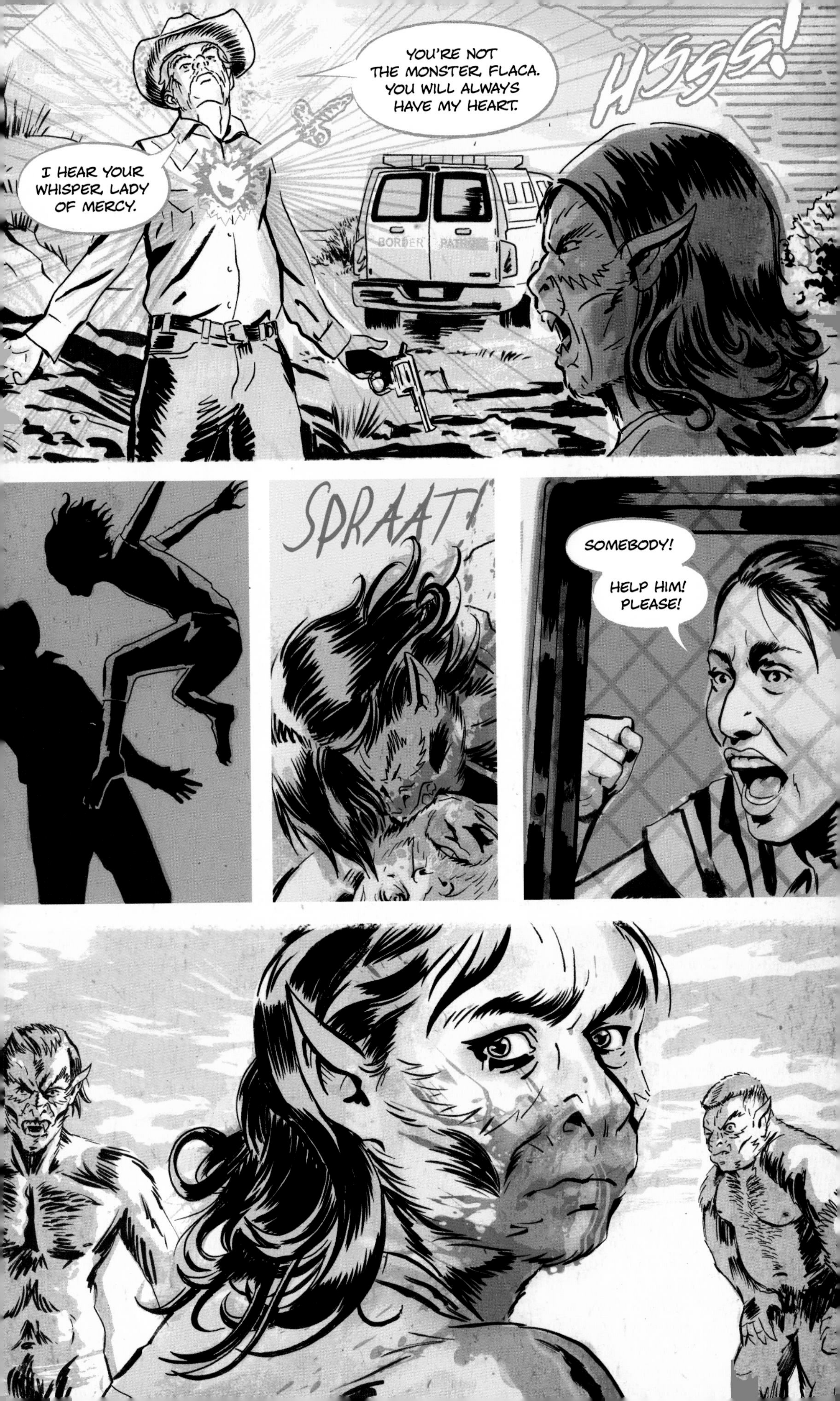
I HEAR YOUR WHISPER, LADY OF MERCY.
YOU'RE NOT THE MONSTER, FLACA. YOU WILL ALWAYS HAVE MY HEART.
HSSS!
BORDER PATROL
SPRAAT!
SOMEBODY!
HELP HIM! PLEASE!

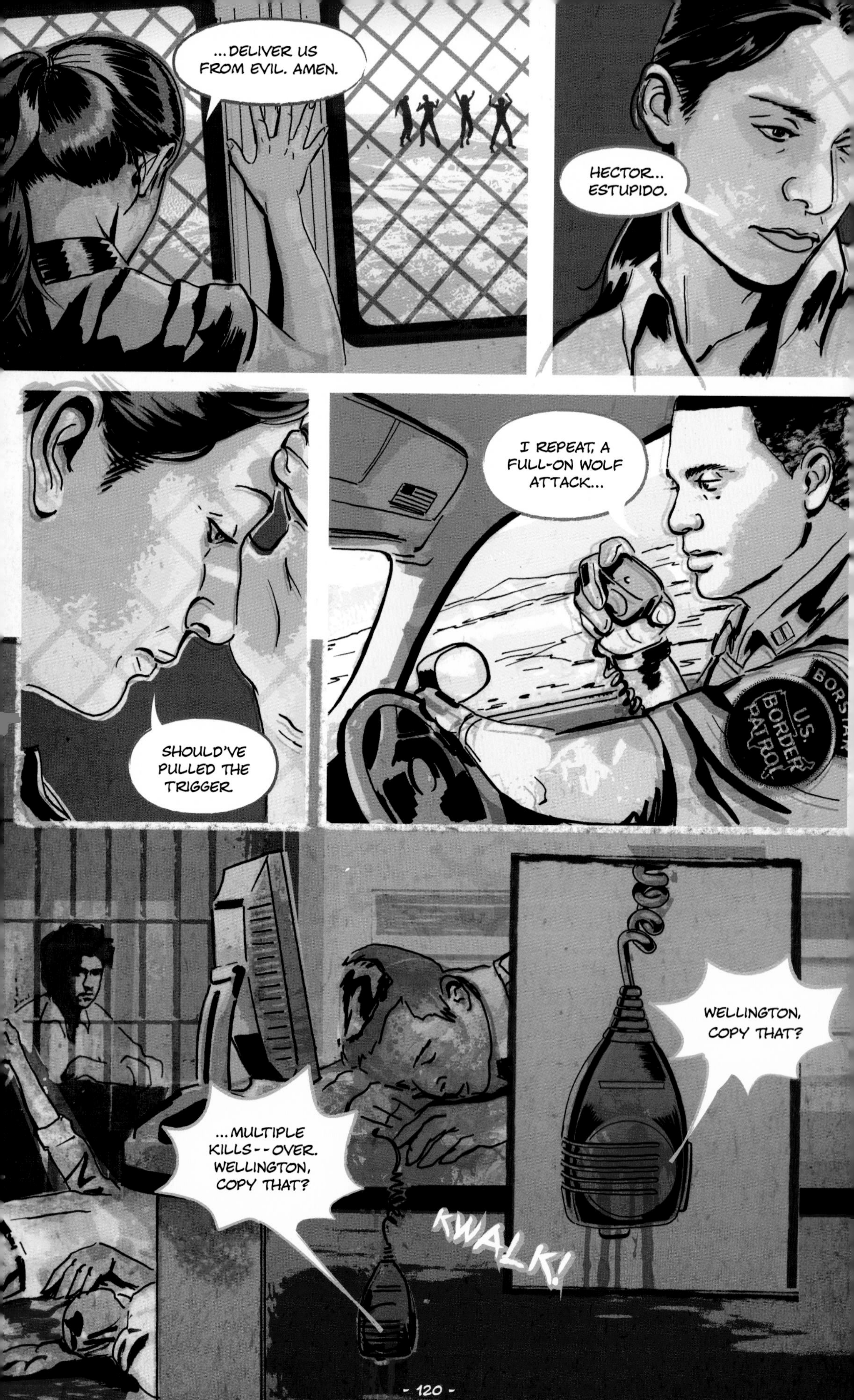
...DELIVER US FROM EVIL. AMEN.
HECTOR.. ESTUPIDO.
SHOULD'VE PULLED THE TRIGGER.
I REPEAT, A FULL-ON WOLF ATTACK...
BORSTAR
U.S. BORDER PATROL
...MULTIPLE KILLS--OVER. WELLINGTON, COPY THAT?
WELLINGTON, COPY THAT?
KWALK!

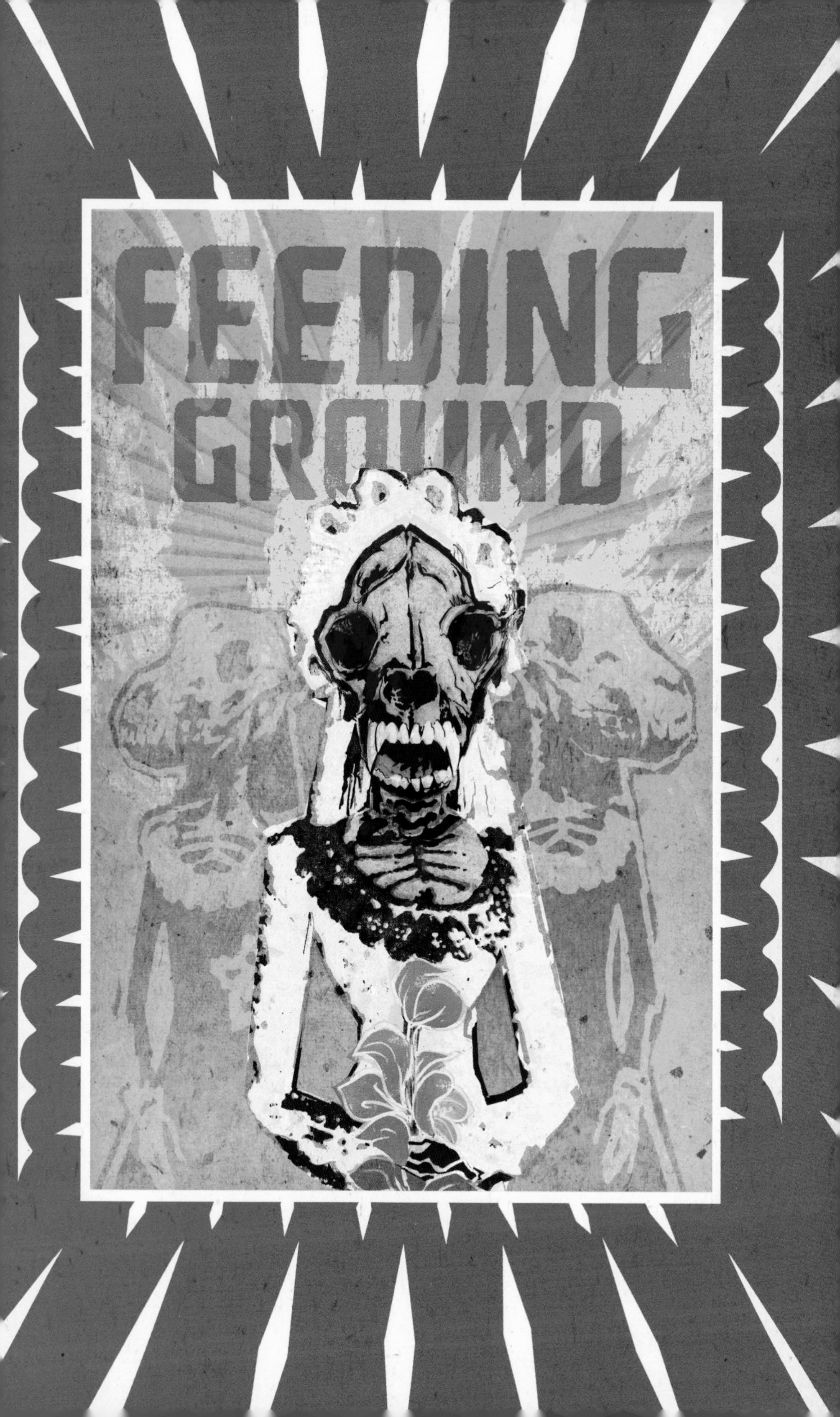
FEEDING
GROUND

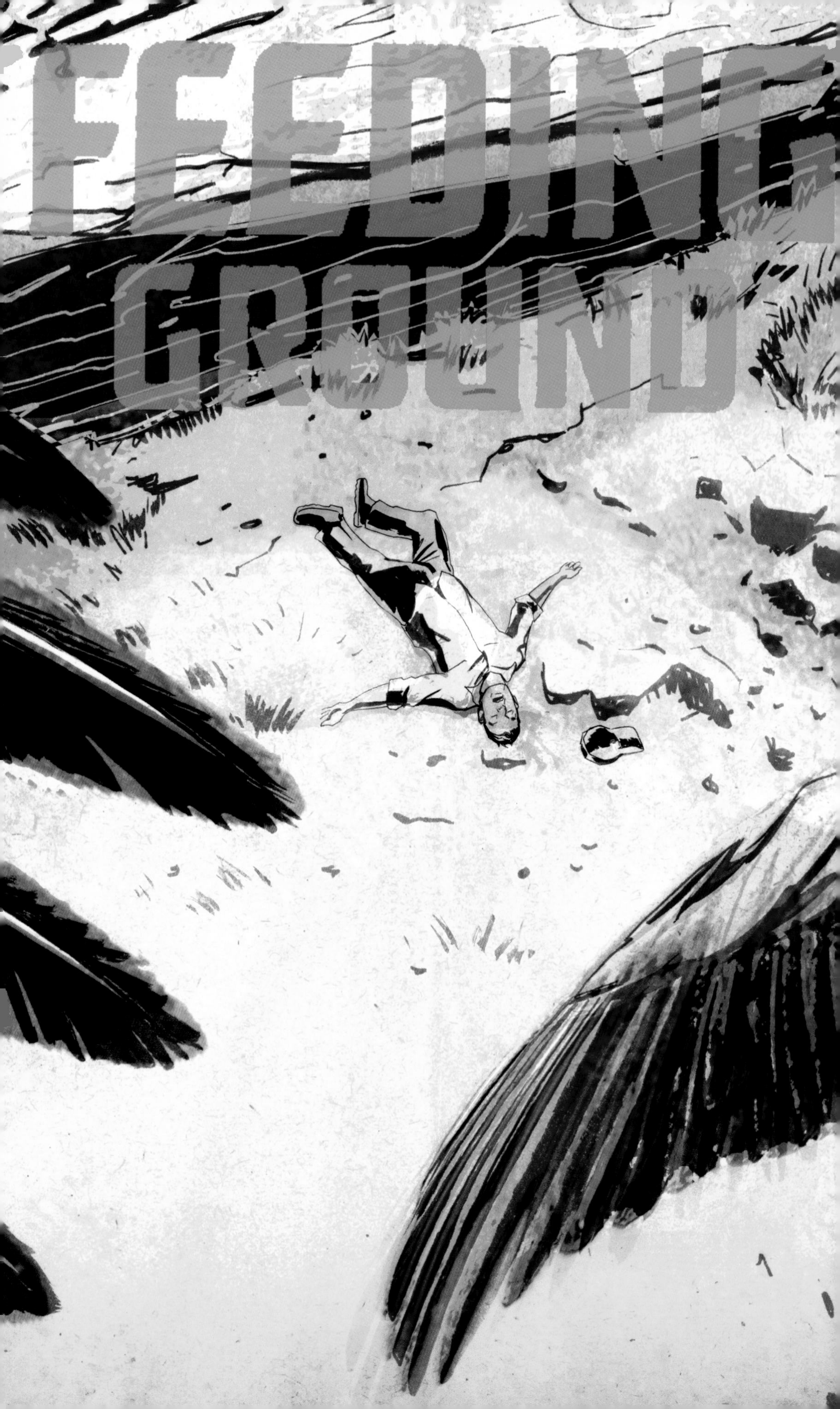
FEEDING
GROUND

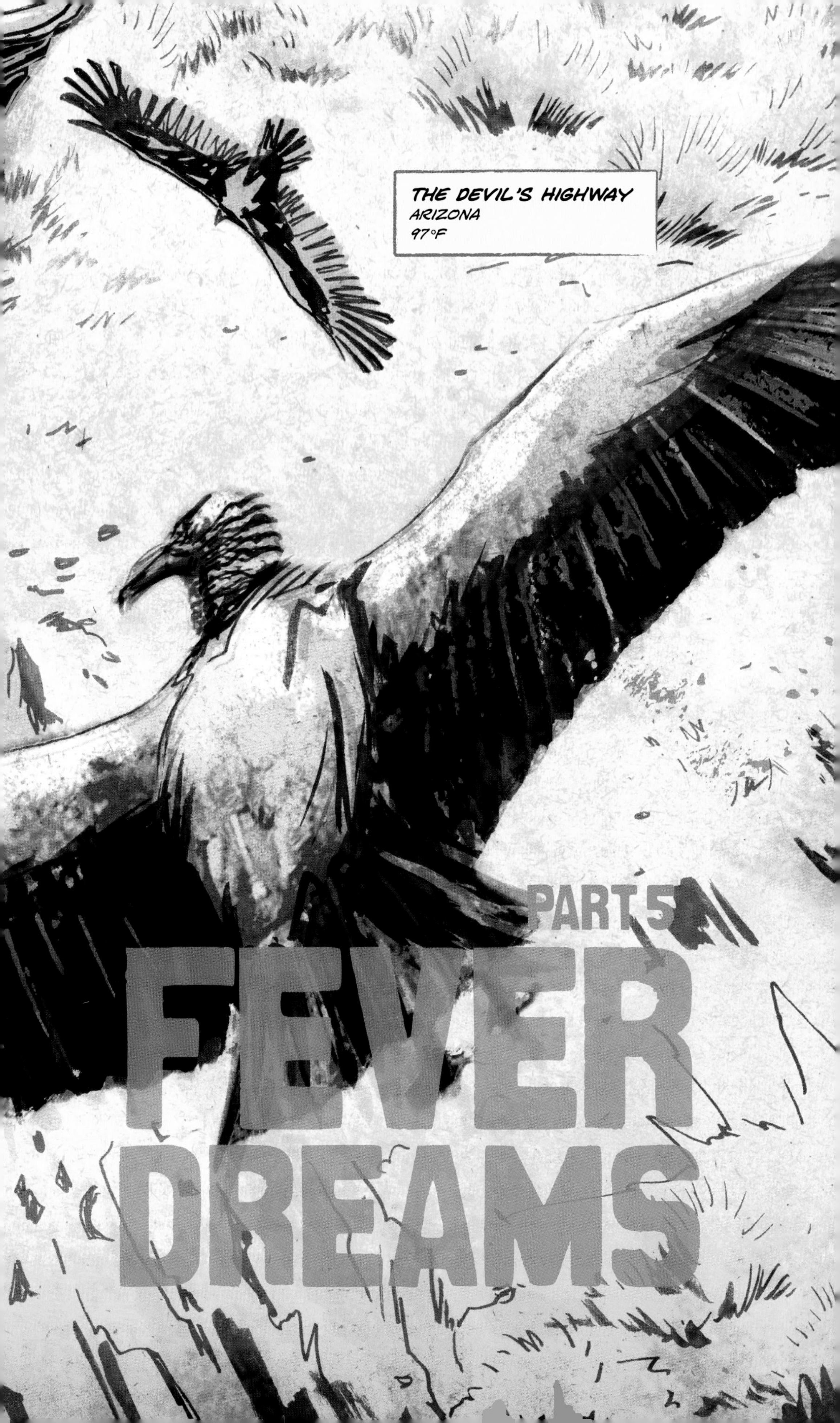
THE DEVIL'S HIGHWAY
ARIZONA
97°F
PART 5
FEVER DREAMS

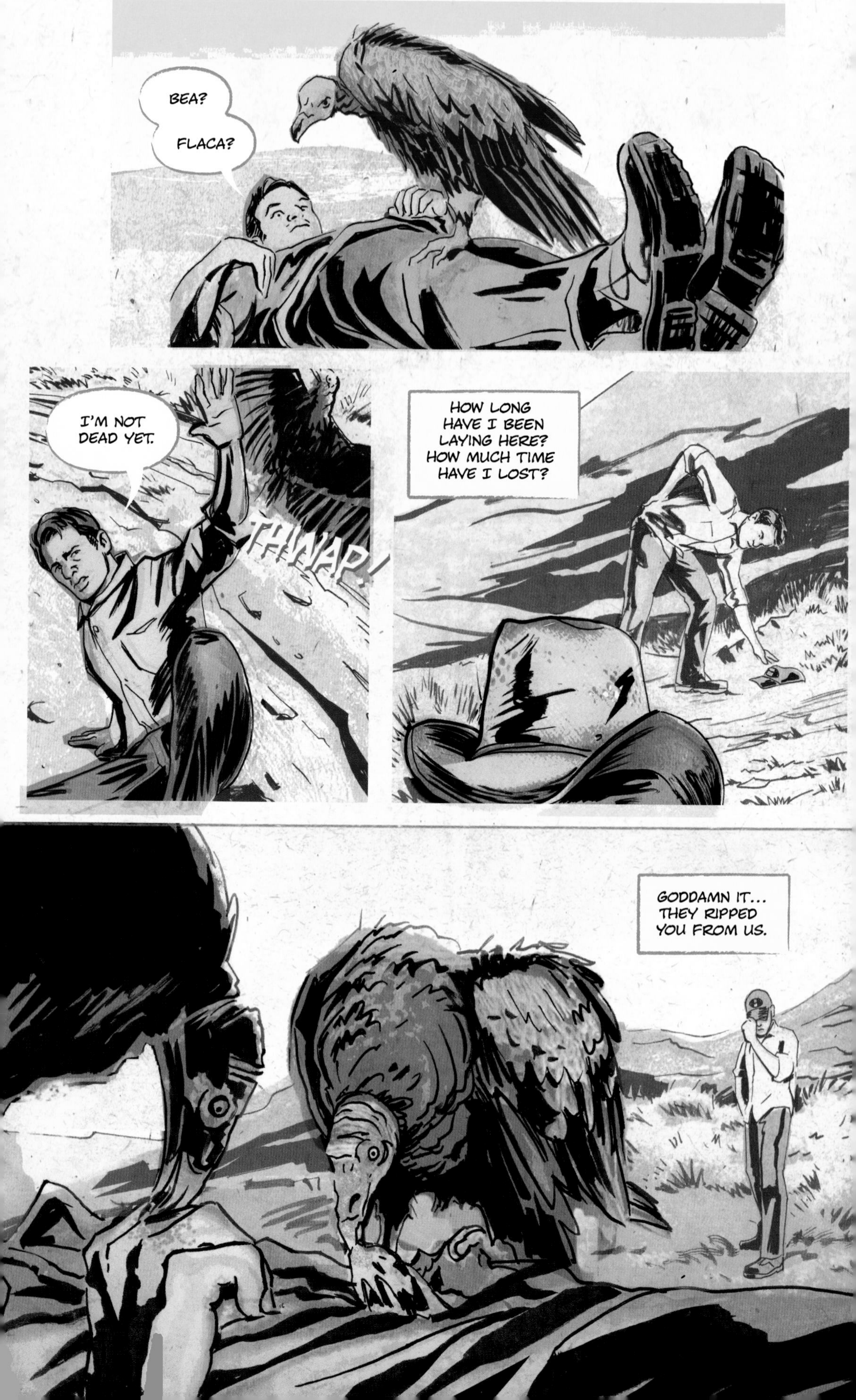
BEA?
FLACA?
I'M NOT DEAD YET.
THWAP!
HOW LONG HAVE I BEEN LAYING HERE? HOW MUCH TIME HAVE I LOST?
GODDAMN IT... THEY RIPPED YOU FROM US.

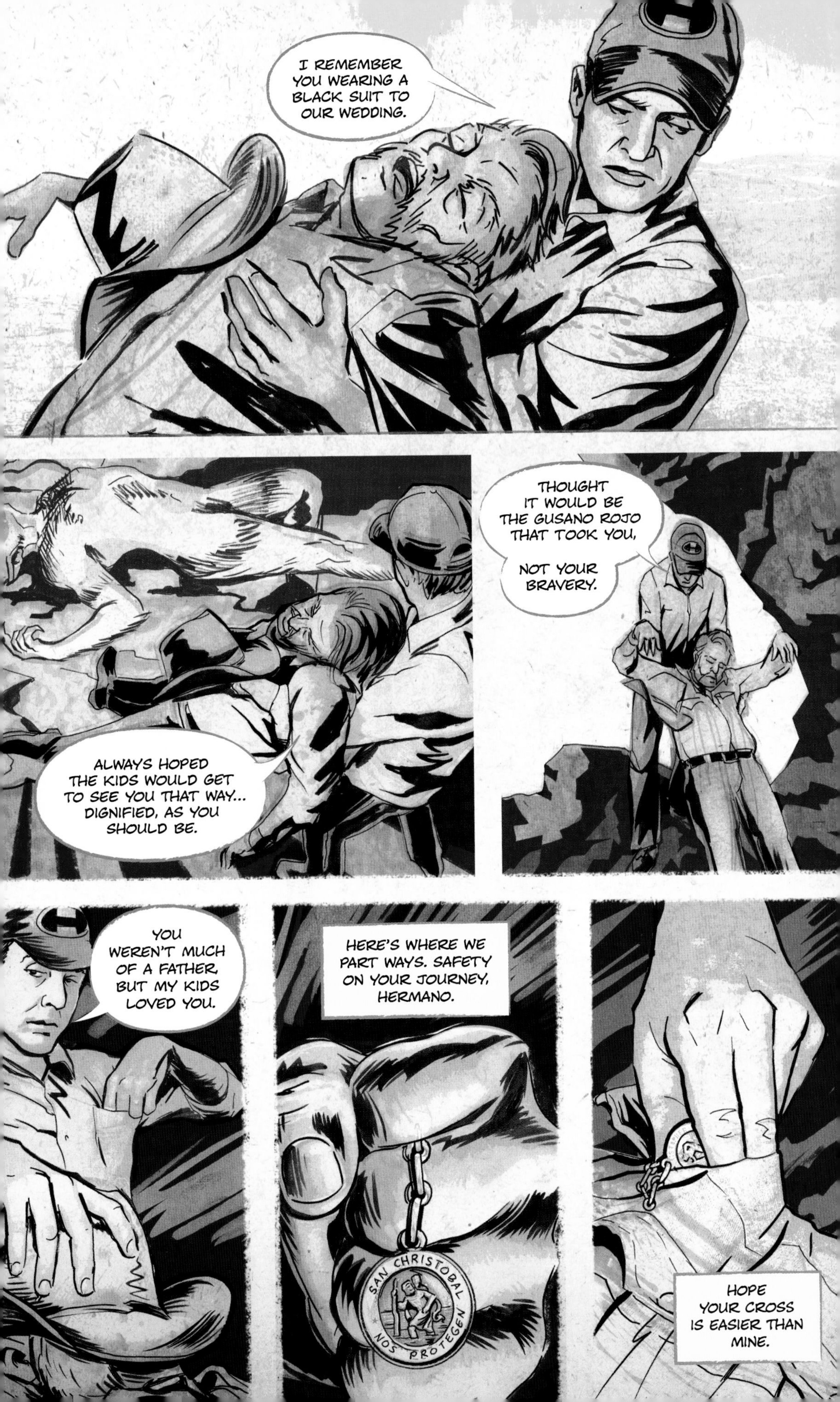
I REMEMBER YOU WEARING A BLACK SUIT TO OUR WEDDING.
ALWAYS HOPED THE KIDS WOULD GET TO SEE YOU THAT WAY... DIGNIFIED, AS YOU SHOULD BE.
THOUGHT IT WOULD BE THE GUSANO ROJO THAT TOOK YOU,
NOT YOUR BRAVERY.
YOU WEREN'T MUCH OF A FATHER, BUT MY KIDS LOVED YOU.
HERE'S WHERE WE PART WAYS. SAFETY ON YOUR JOURNEY, HERMANO.
SAN CHRISTOBAL NOS PROTEGEN
HOPE YOUR CROSS IS EASIER THAN MINE.

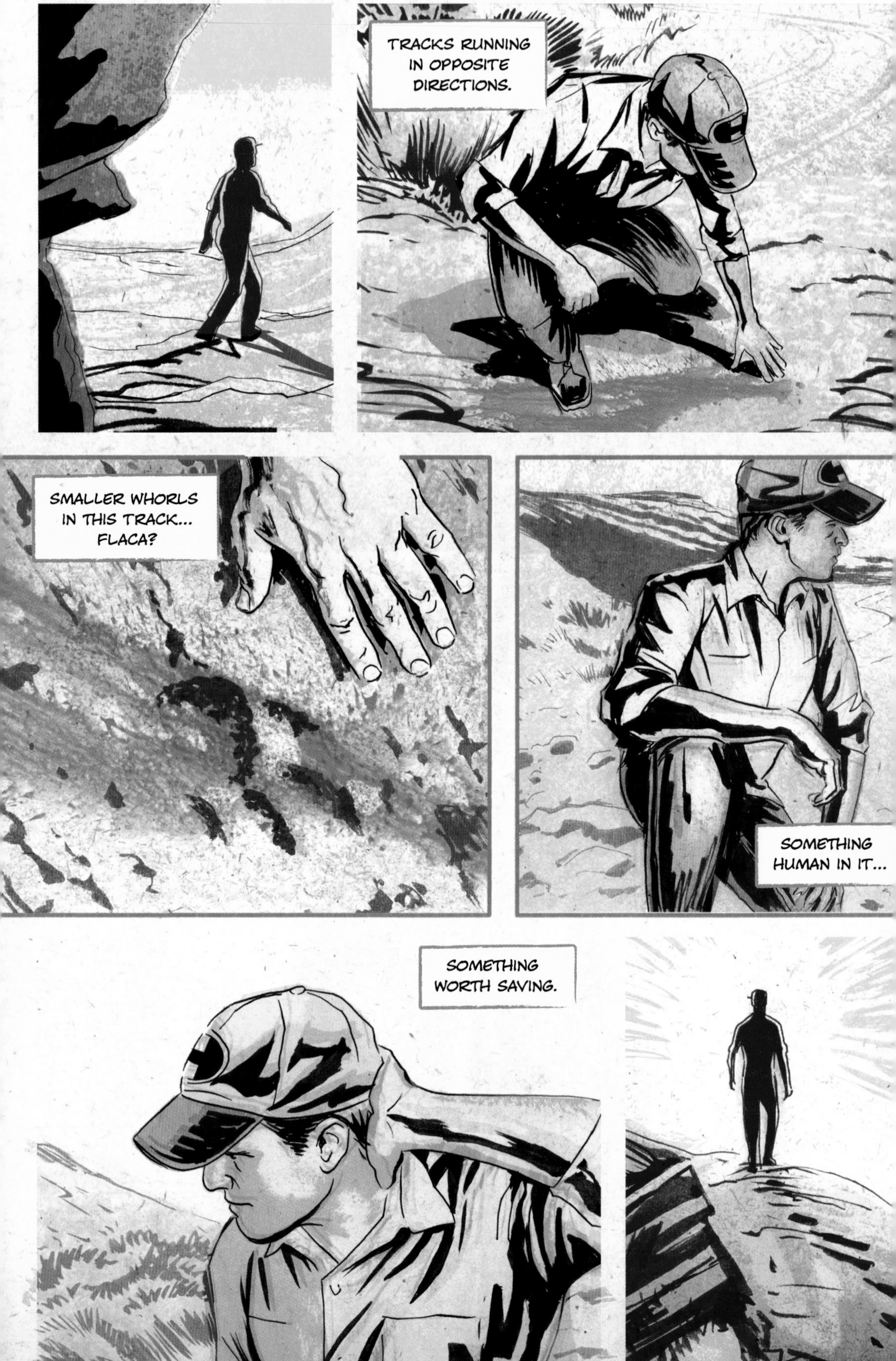
TRACKS RUNNING IN OPPOSITE DIRECTIONS.
SMALLER WHORLS IN THIS TRACK... FLACA?
SOMETHING HUMAN IN IT...
SOMETHING WORTH SAVING.

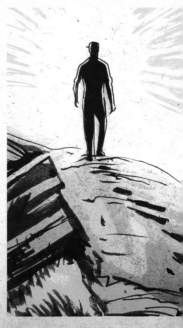

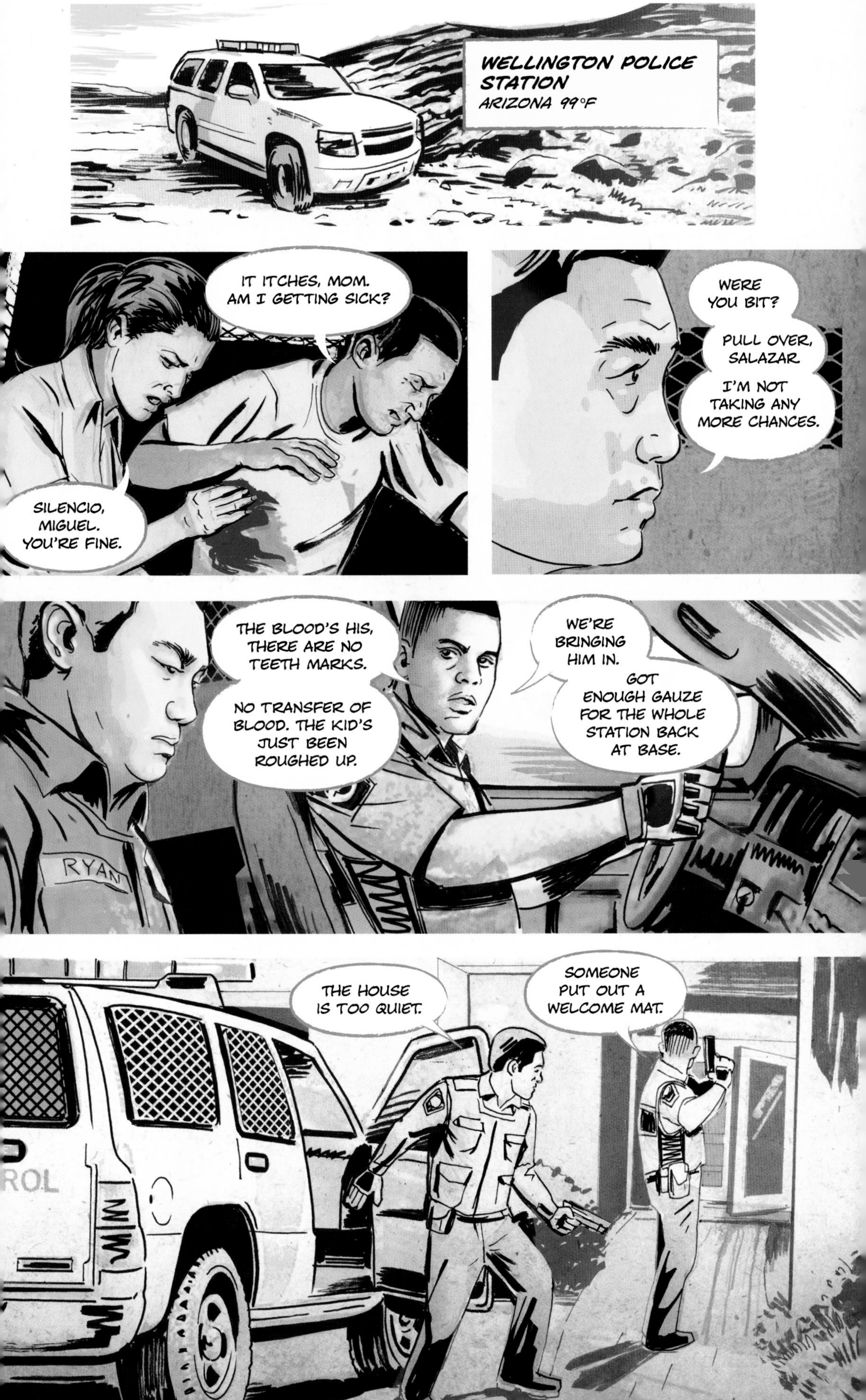
WELLINGTON POLICE STATION
ARIZONA 99°F
IT ITCHES, MOM. AM I GETTING SICK?
SILENCIO, MIGUEL. YOU'RE FINE.
WERE YOU BIT?
PULL OVER, SALAZAR
I'M NOT TAKING ANY MORE CHANCES.
THE BLOOD'S HIS, THERE ARE NO TEETH MARKS.
NO TRANSFER OF BLOOD. THE KID'S JUST BEEN ROUGHED UP.
RYAN
WE'RE BRINGING HIM IN.
GOT ENOUGH GAUZE FOR THE WHOLE STATION BACK AT BASE.
THE HOUSE IS TOO QUIET.
SOMEONE PUT OUT A WELCOME MAT.

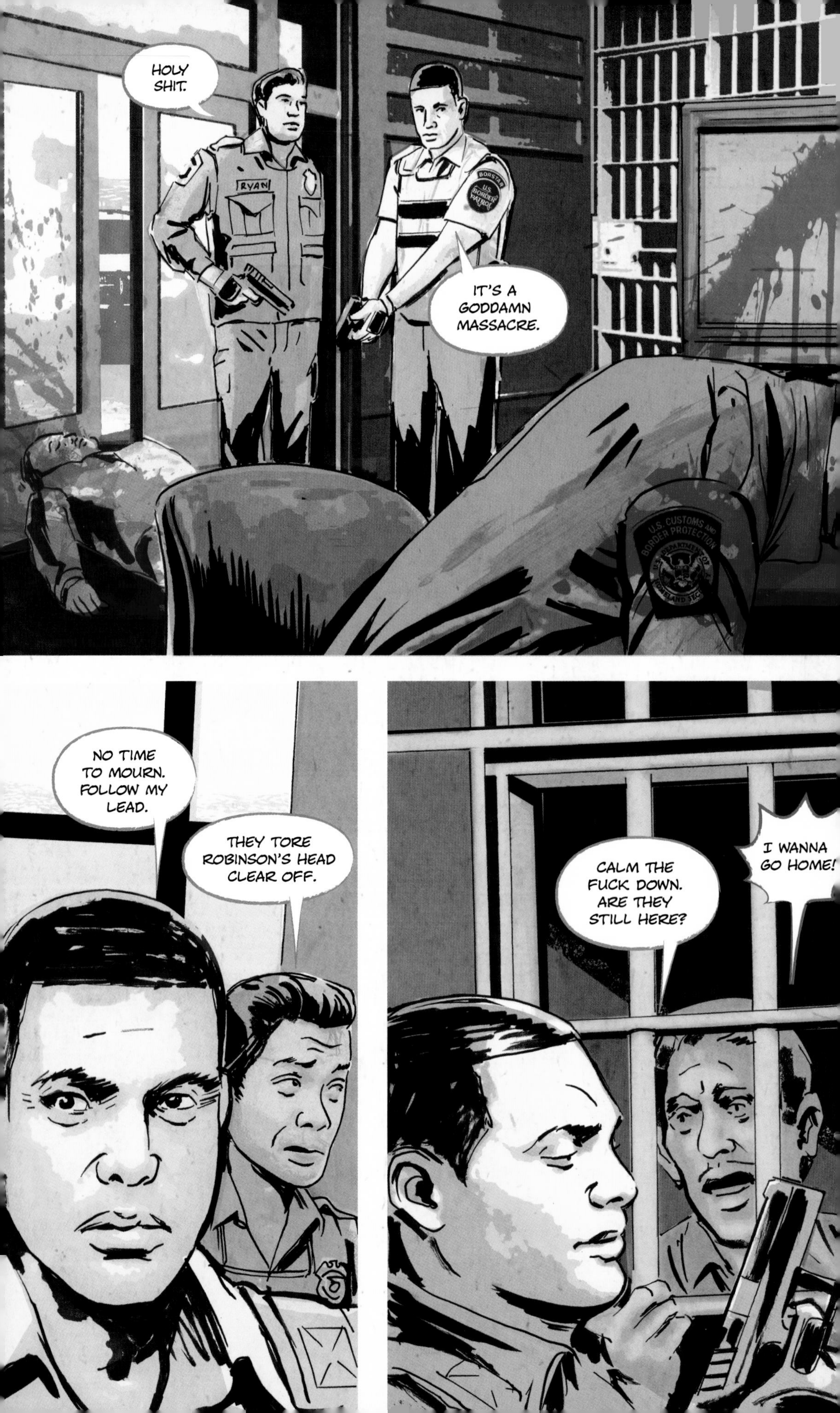
HOLY SHIT.
IT'S A GODDAMN MASSACRE.
RYAN
BORSTAR
U.S. BORDER PATROL
U.S. CUSTOMS AND BORDER PROTECTION
NO TIME TO MOURN. FOLLOW MY LEAD.
THEY TORE ROBINSON'S HEAD CLEAR OFF.
CALM THE FUCK DOWN. ARE THEY STILL HERE?
I WANNA GO HOME!

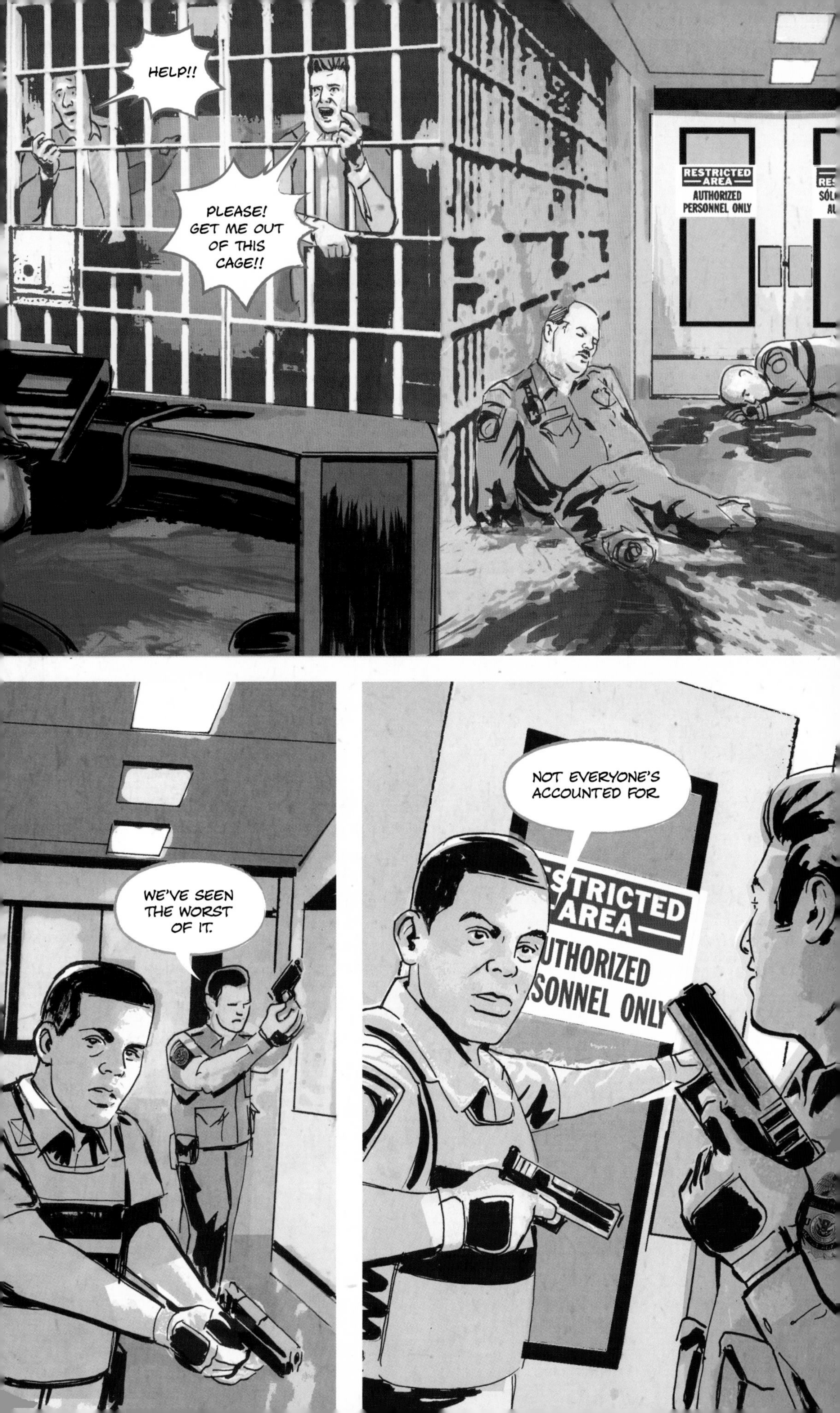
HELP!!
PLEASE! GET ME OUT OF THIS CAGE!!
RESTRICTED AREA AUTHORIZED PERSONNEL ONLY
WE'VE SEEN THE WORST OF IT.
NOT EVERYONE'S ACCOUNTED FOR

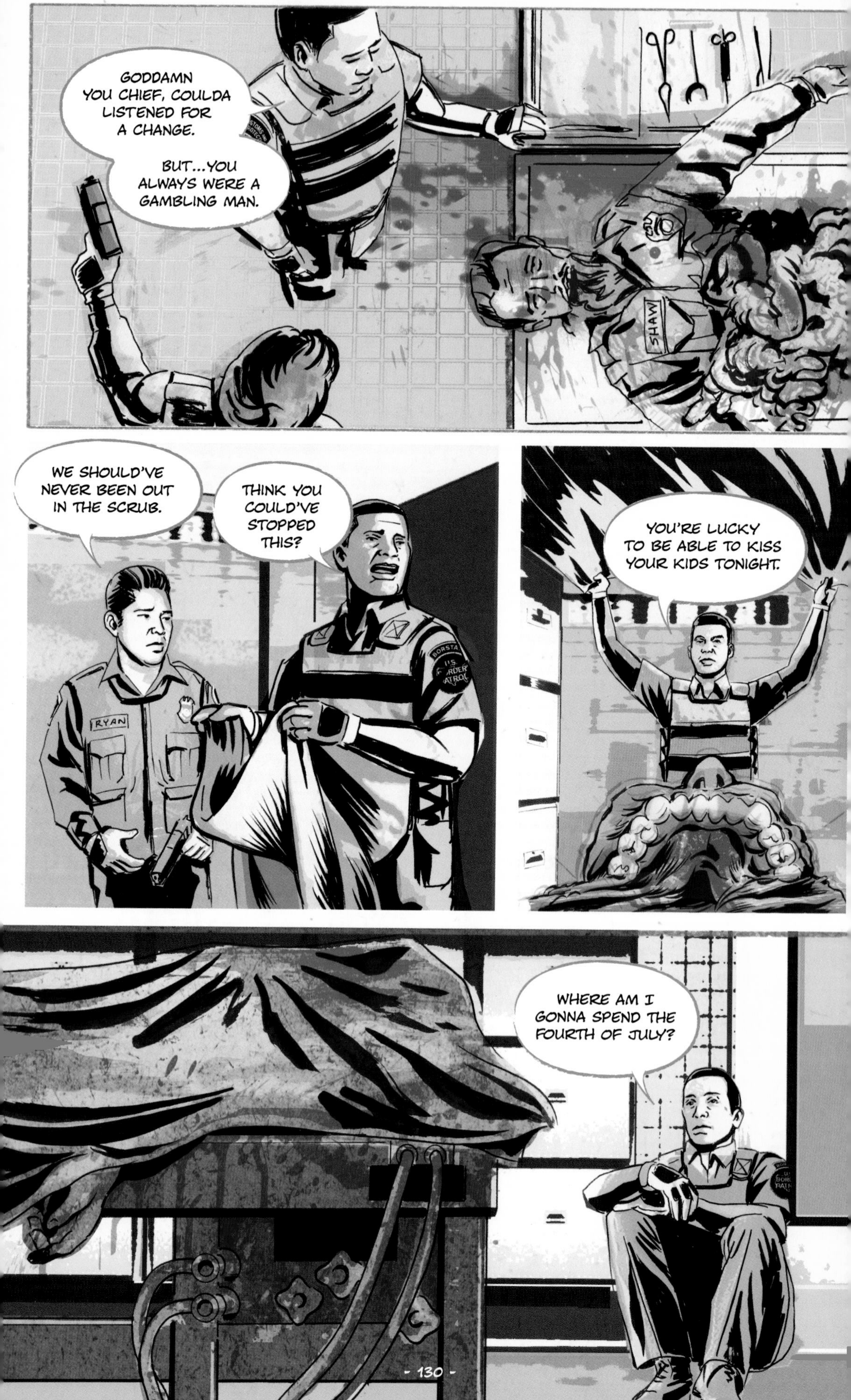
GODDAMN YOU CHIEF, COULDA LISTENED FOR A CHANGE.
BUT...YOU ALWAYS WERE A GAMBLING MAN.
SHAW
WE SHOULD'VE NEVER BEEN OUT IN THE SCRUB.
THINK YOU COULD'VE STOPPED THIS?
RYAN
YOU'RE LUCKY TO BE ABLE TO KISS YOUR KIDS TONIGHT.
WHERE AM I GONNA SPEND THE FOURTH OF JULY?

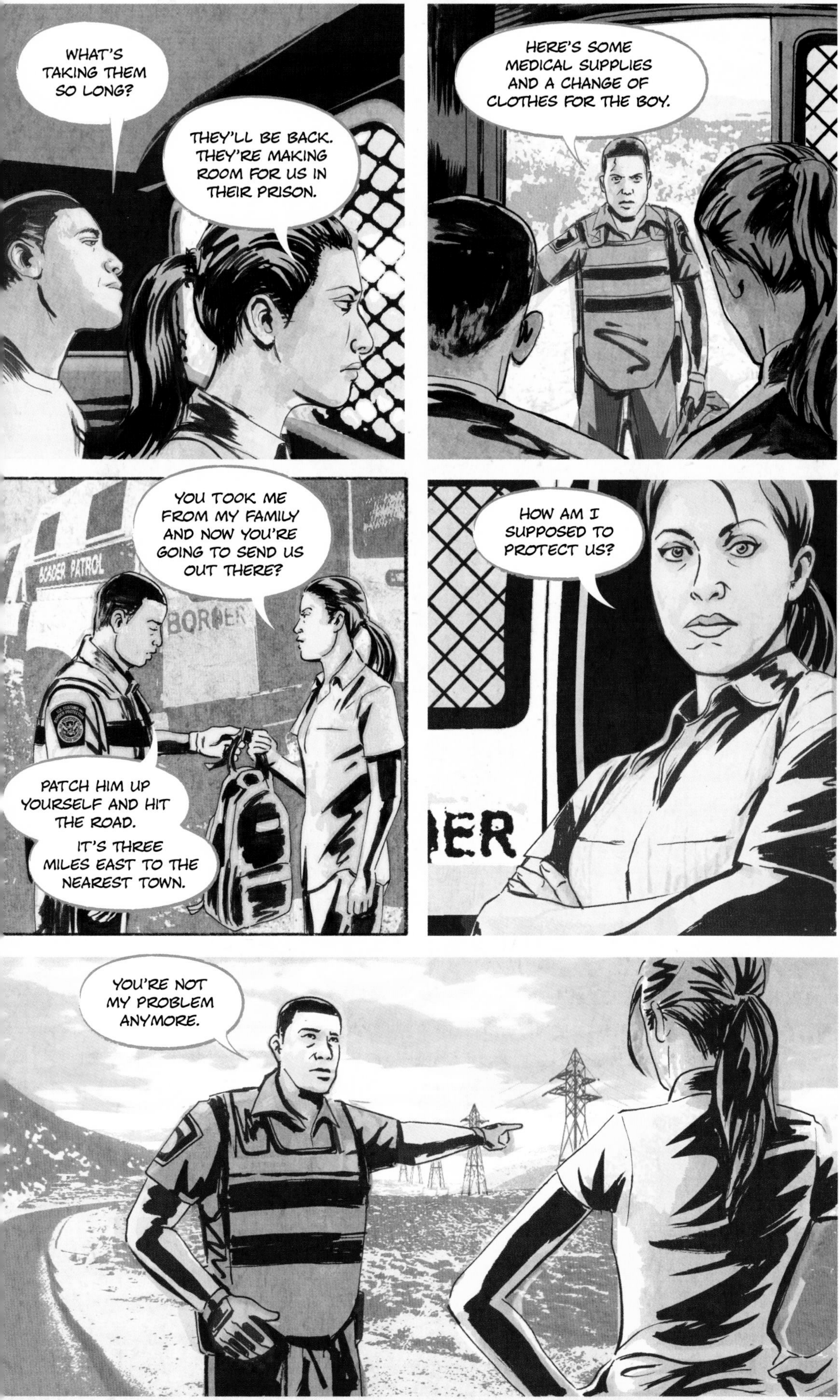
WHAT'S TAKING THEM SO LONG?
THEY'LL BE BACK. THEY'RE MAKING ROOM FOR US IN THEIR PRISON.
HERE'S SOME MEDICAL SUPPLIES AND A CHANGE OF CLOTHES FOR THE BOY.
YOU TOOK ME FROM MY FAMILY AND NOW YOU'RE GOING TO SEND US OUT THERE?
PATCH HIM UP YOURSELF AND HIT THE ROAD.
IT'S THREE MILES EAST TO THE NEAREST TOWN.
HOW AM I SUPPOSED TO PROTECT US?
YOU'RE NOT MY PROBLEM ANYMORE.

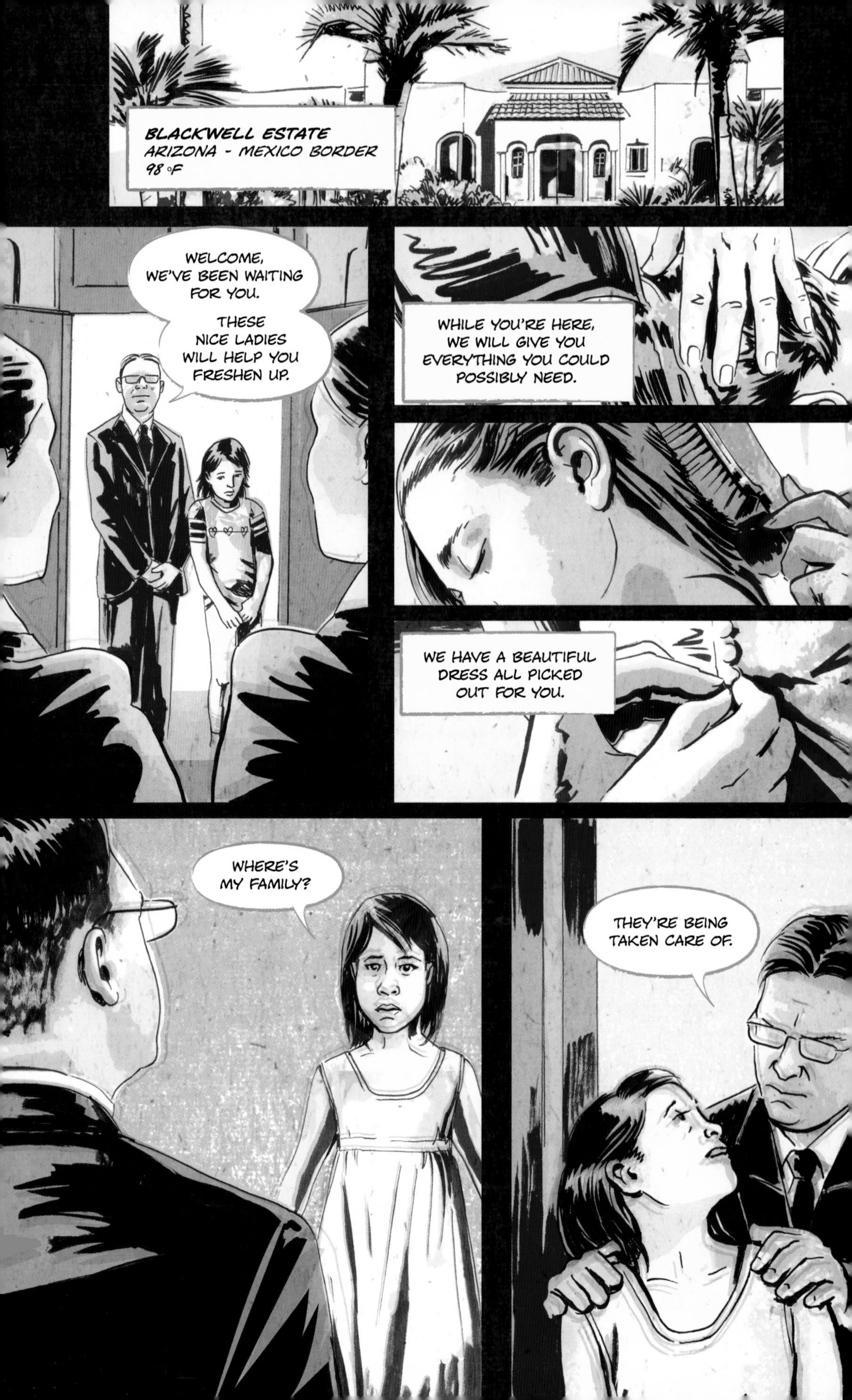
BLACKWELL ESTATE
ARIZONA - MEXICO BORDER
98 °F
WELCOME, WE'VE BEEN WAITING FOR YOU.
THESE NICE LADIES WILL HELP YOU FRESHEN UP.
WHILE YOU'RE HERE, WE WILL GIVE YOU EVERYTHING YOU COULD POSSIBLY NEED.
WE HAVE A BEAUTIFUL DRESS ALL PICKED OUT FOR YOU.
WHERE'S MY FAMILY?
THEY'RE BEING TAKEN CARE OF.

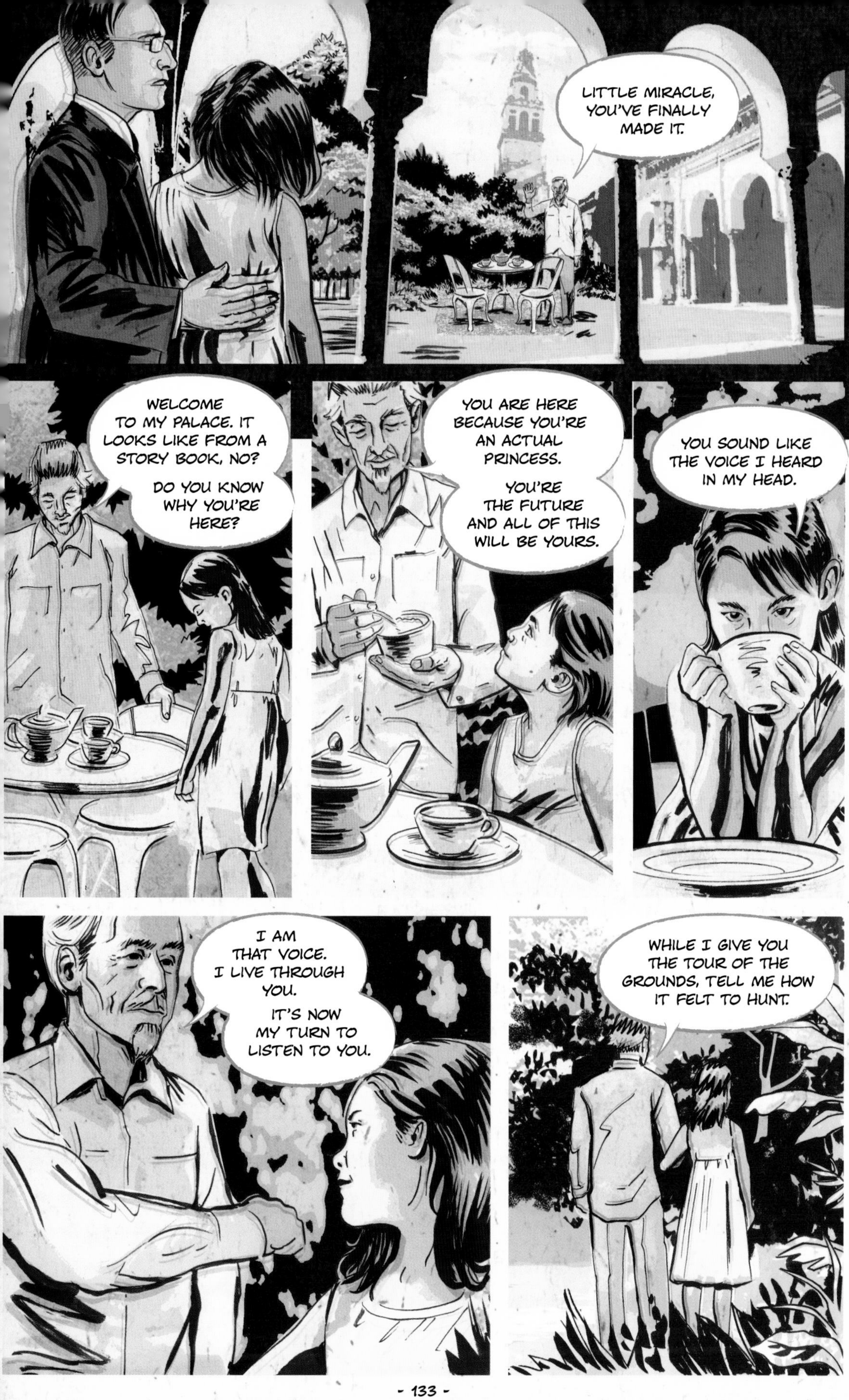
LITTLE MIRACLE, YOU'VE FINALLY MADE IT.
WELCOME TO MY PALACE. IT LOOKS LIKE FROM A STORY BOOK, NO?
DO YOU KNOW WHY YOU'RE HERE?
YOU ARE HERE BECAUSE YOU'RE AN ACTUAL PRINCESS.
YOU'RE THE FUTURE AND ALL OF THIS WILL BE YOURS.
YOU SOUND LIKE THE VOICE I HEARD IN MY HEAD.
I AM THAT VOICE. I LIVE THROUGH YOU.
IT'S NOW MY TURN TO LISTEN TO YOU.
WHILE I GIVE YOU THE TOUR OF THE GROUNDS, TELL ME HOW IT FELT TO HUNT.

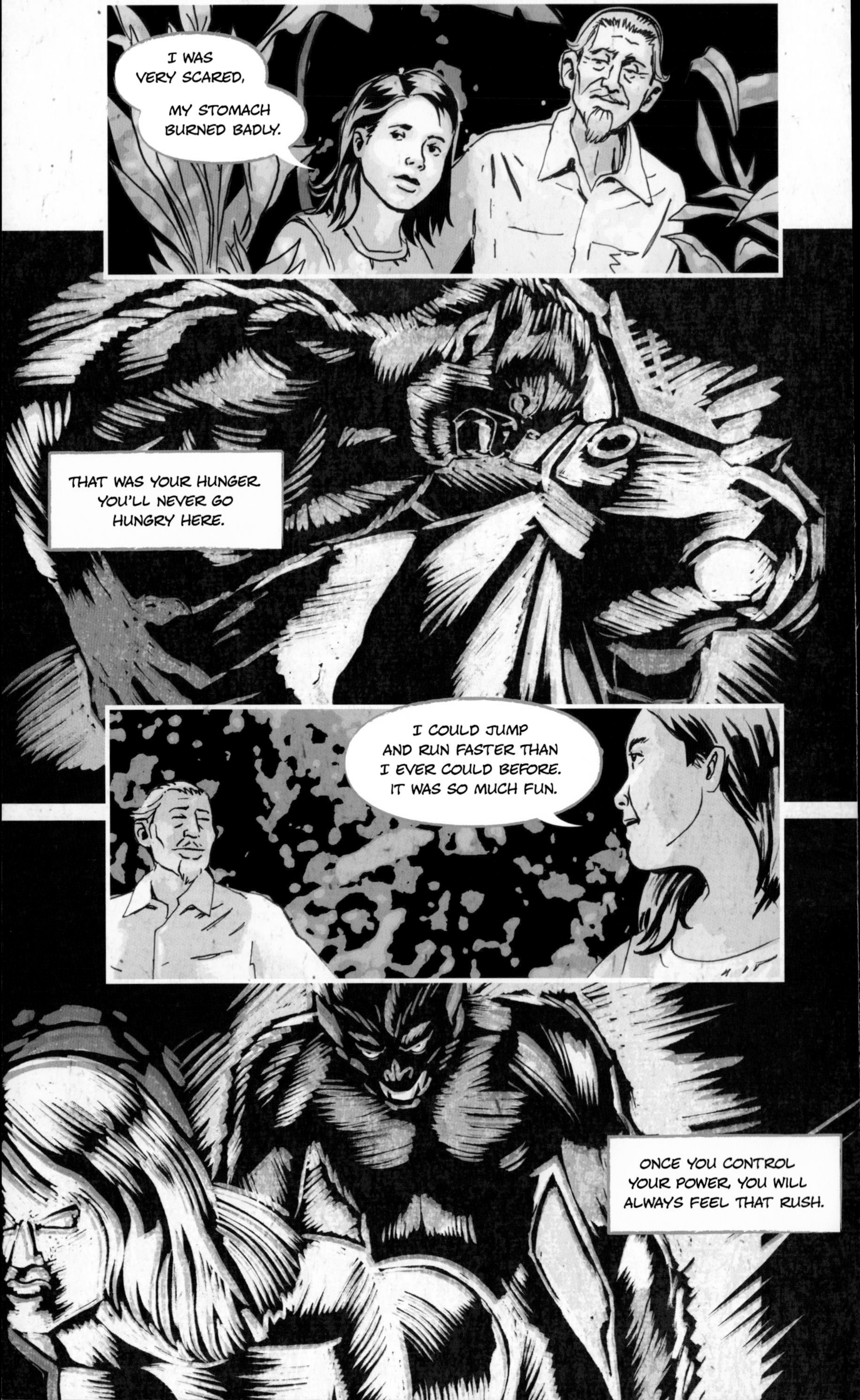
I WAS VERY SCARED,
MY STOMACH BURNED BADLY.
THAT WAS YOUR HUNGER YOU'LL NEVER GO HUNGRY HERE.
I COULD JUMP AND RUN FASTER THAN I EVER COULD BEFORE. IT WAS SO MUCH FUN.
ONCE YOU CONTROL YOUR POWER, YOU WILL ALWAYS FEEL THAT RUSH.

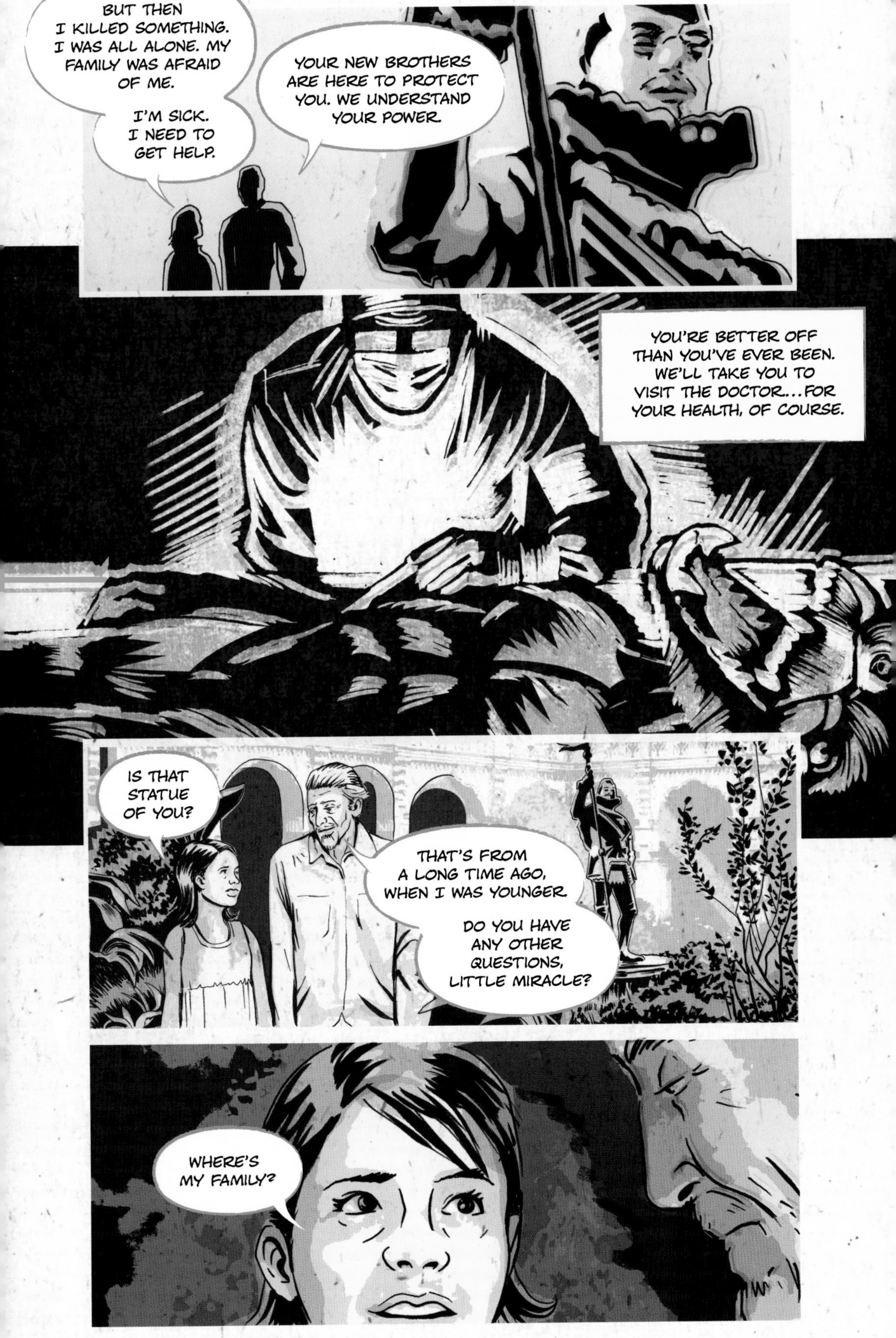
BUT THEN I KILLED SOMETHING. I WAS ALL ALONE. MY FAMILY WAS AFRAID OF ME.
I'M SICK. I NEED TO GET HELP.
YOUR NEW BROTHERS ARE HERE TO PROTECT YOU. WE UNDERSTAND YOUR POWER.
YOU'RE BETTER OFF THAN YOU'VE EVER BEEN. WE'LL TAKE YOU TO VISIT THE DOCTOR…FOR YOUR HEALTH, OF COURSE.
IS THAT STATUE OF YOU?
THAT'S FROM A LONG TIME AGO, WHEN I WAS YOUNGER.
DO YOU HAVE ANY OTHER QUESTIONS, LITTLE MIRACLE?
WHERE'S MY FAMILY?

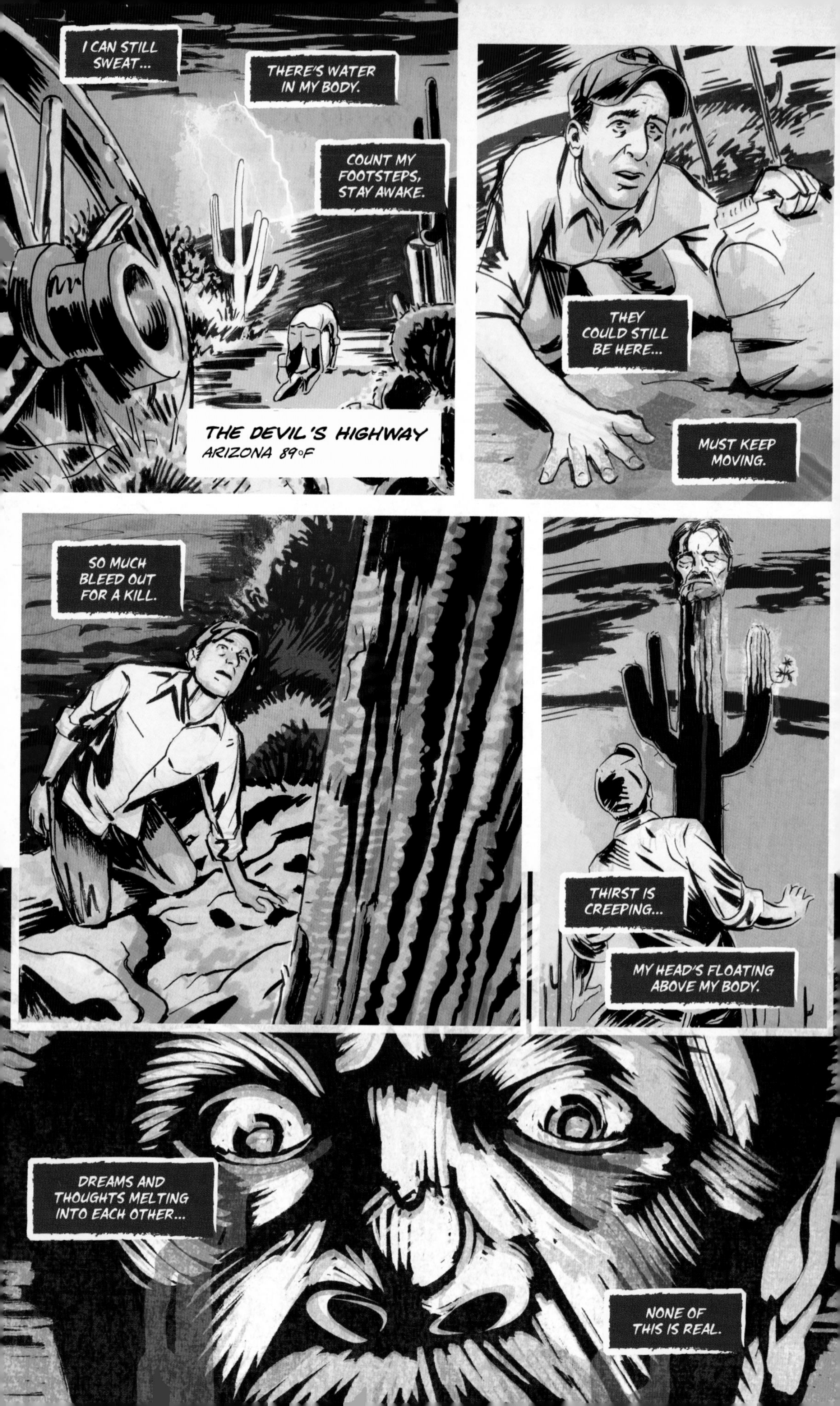
I CAN STILL SWEAT...
THERE'S WATER IN MY BODY.
COUNT MY FOOTSTEPS, STAY AWAKE.
THE DEVIL'S HIGHWAY
ARIZONA 89°F
THEY COULD STILL BE HERE...
MUST KEEP MOVING.
SO MUCH BLEED OUT FOR A KILL.
THIRST IS CREEPING...
MY HEAD'S FLOATING ABOVE MY BODY.
DREAMS AND THOUGHTS MELTING INTO EACH OTHER...
NONE OF THIS IS REAL.

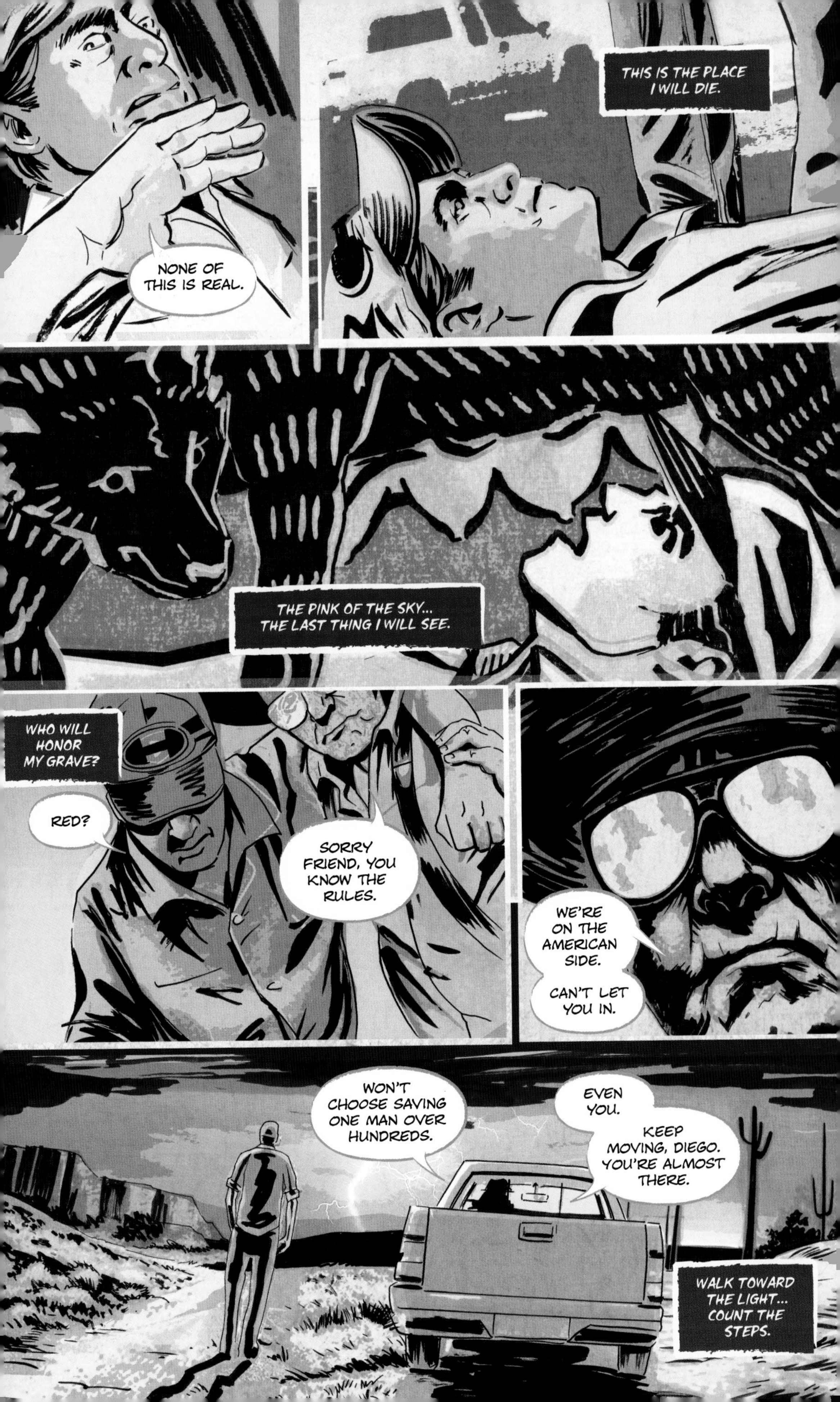
NONE OF THIS IS REAL.
THIS IS THE PLACE I WILL DIE.
THE PINK OF THE SKY... THE LAST THING I WILL SEE.
WHO WILL HONOR MY GRAVE?
RED?
SORRY FRIEND, YOU KNOW THE RULES.
WE'RE ON THE AMERICAN SIDE.
CAN'T LET YOU IN.
WON'T CHOOSE SAVING ONE MAN OVER HUNDREDS.
EVEN YOU.
KEEP MOVING, DIEGO. YOU'RE ALMOST THERE.
WALK TOWARD THE LIGHT... COUNT THE STEPS.

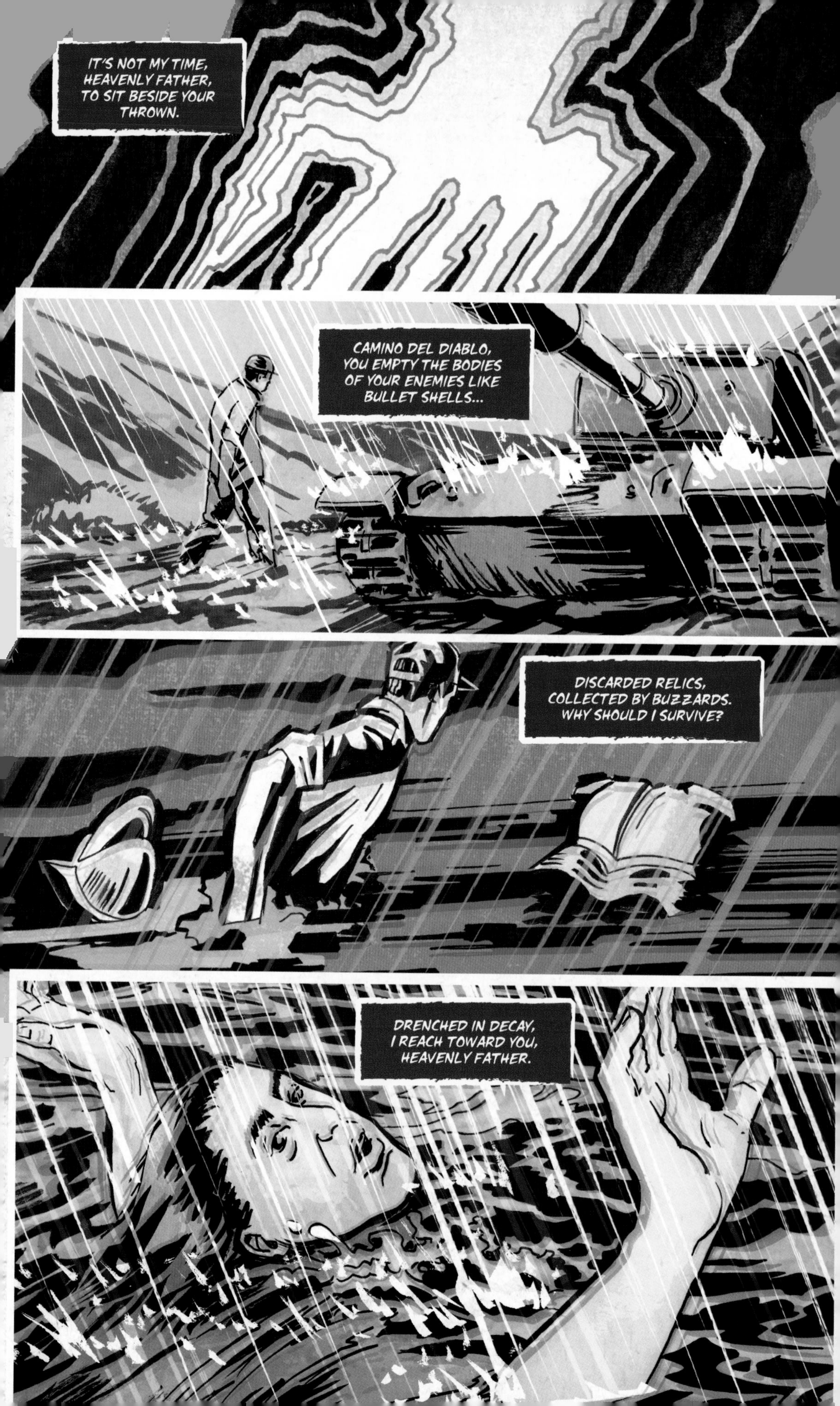
IT'S NOT MY TIME, HEAVENLY FATHER, TO SIT BESIDE YOUR THROWN.
CAMINO DEL DIABLO, YOU EMPTY THE BODIES OF YOUR ENEMIES LIKE BULLET SHELLS...
DISCARDED RELICS, COLLECTED BY BUZZARDS. WHY SHOULD I SURVIVE?
DRENCHED IN DECAY, I REACH TOWARD YOU, HEAVENLY FATHER.

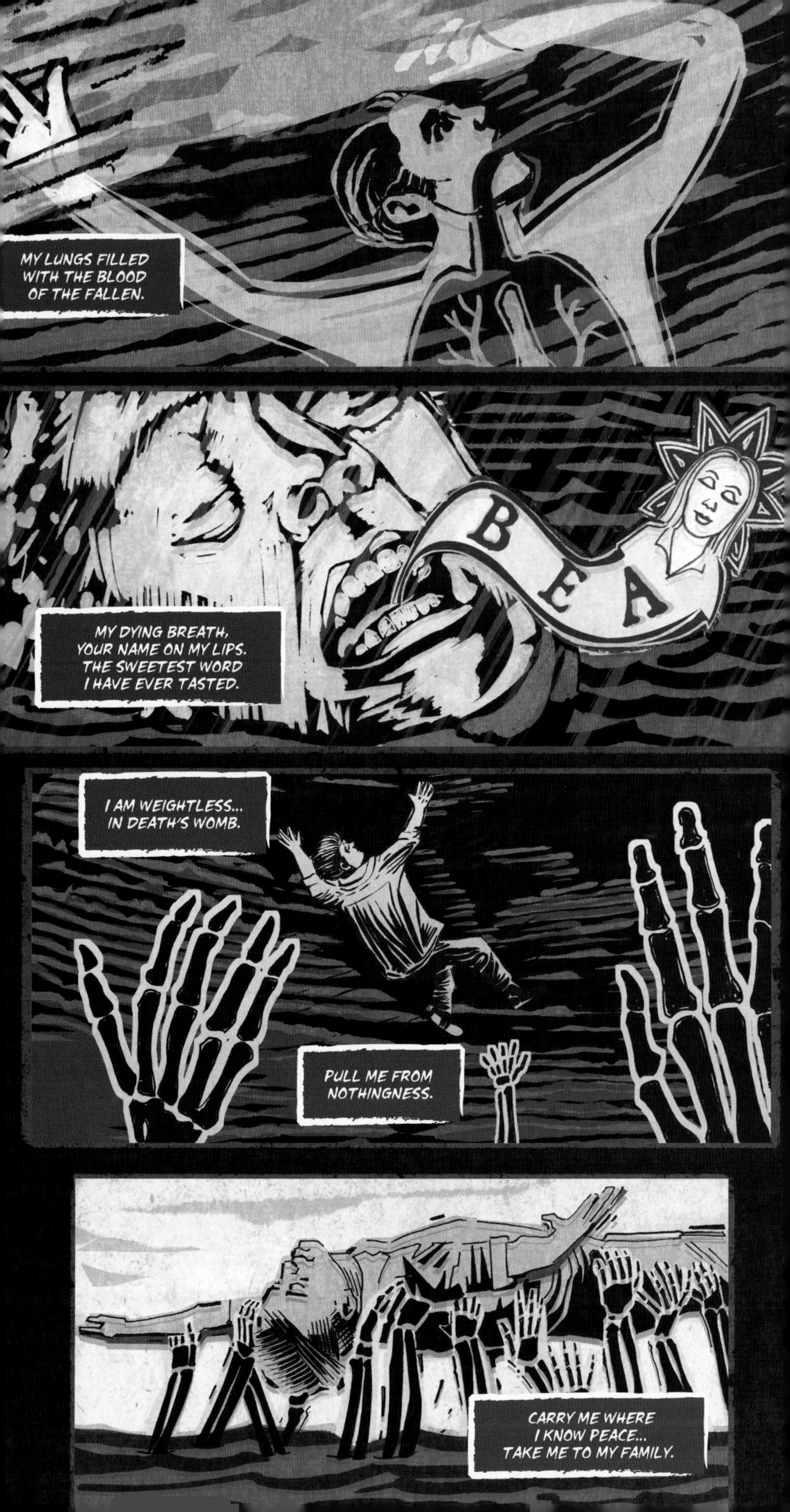
MY LUNGS FILLED WITH THE BLOOD OF THE FALLEN.
MY DYING BREATH, YOUR NAME ON MY LIPS. THE SWEETEST WORD I HAVE EVER TASTED.
BEA
I AM WEIGHTLESS... IN DEATH'S WOMB.
PULL ME FROM NOTHINGNESS.
CARRY ME WHERE I KNOW PEACE... TAKE ME TO MY FAMILY.

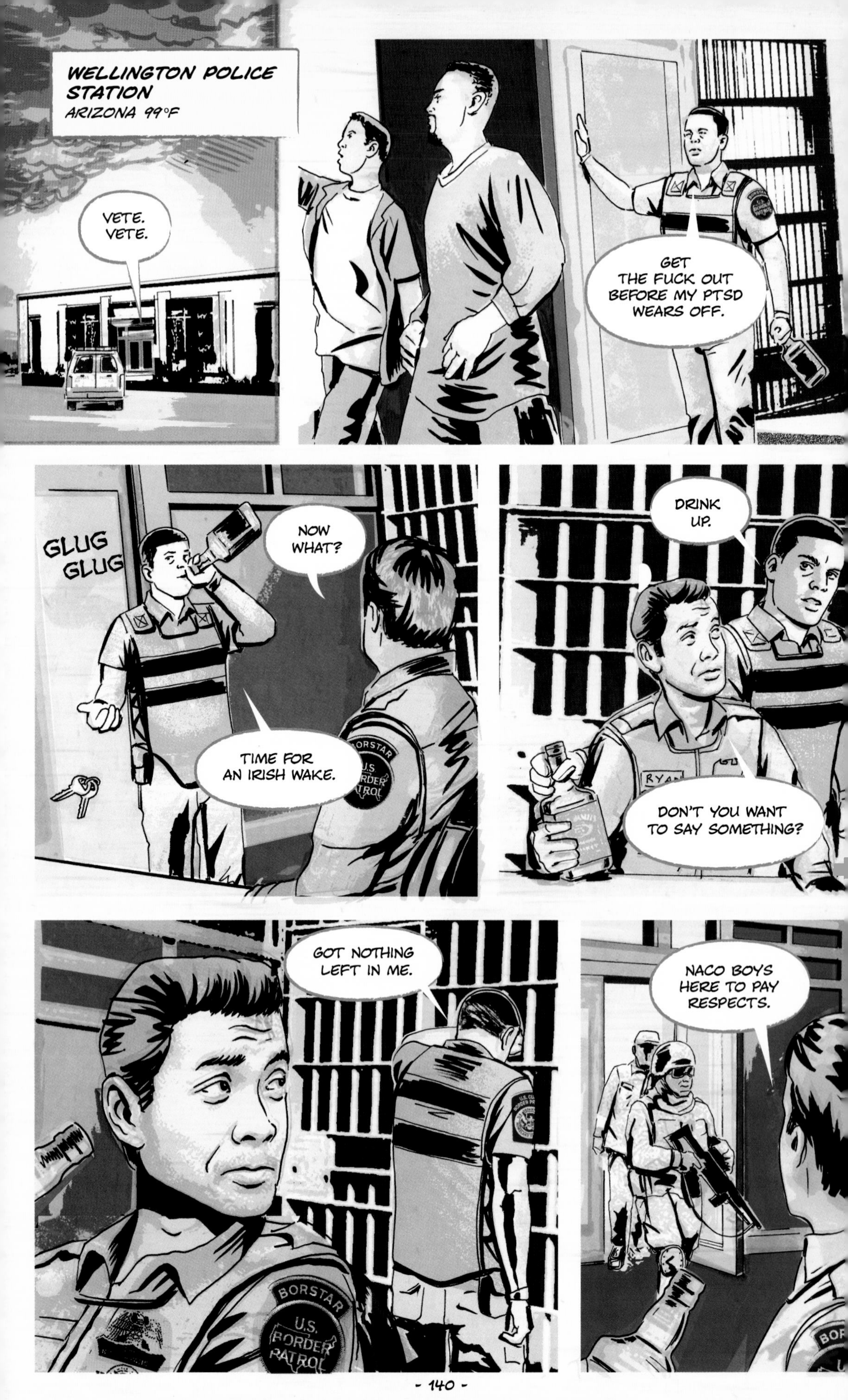
WELLINGTON POLICE STATION
ARIZONA 99°F
VETE. VETE.
GET THE FUCK OUT BEFORE MY PTSD WEARS OFF.
GLUG GLUG
NOW WHAT?
TIME FOR AN IRISH WAKE.
DRINK UP.
DON'T YOU WANT TO SAY SOMETHING?
GOT NOTHING LEFT IN ME.
NACO BOYS HERE TO PAY RESPECTS.

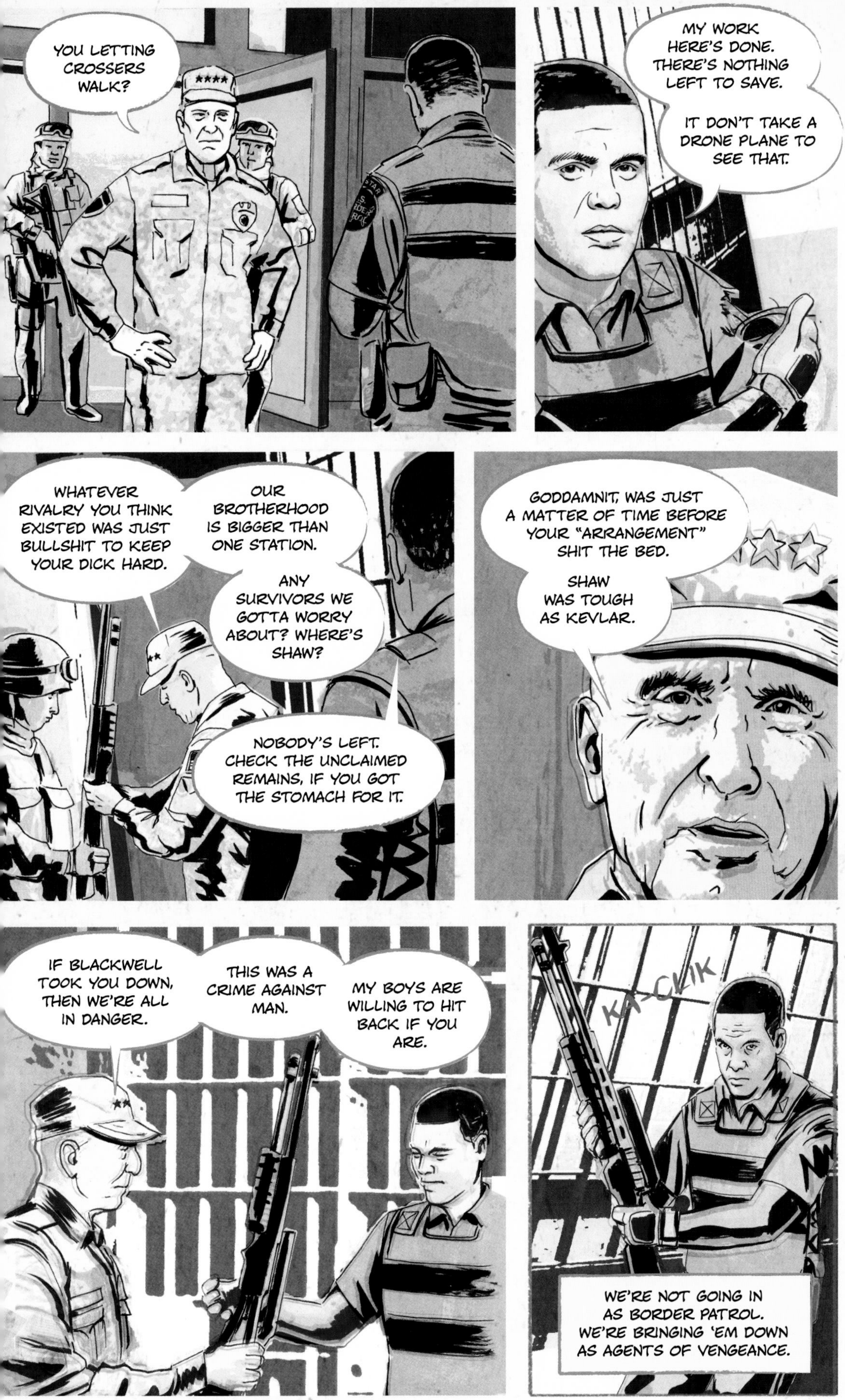
YOU LETTING CROSSERS WALK?
MY WORK HERE'S DONE. THERE'S NOTHING LEFT TO SAVE.
IT DON'T TAKE A DRONE PLANE TO SEE THAT.
WHATEVER RIVALRY YOU THINK EXISTED WAS JUST BULLSHIT TO KEEP YOUR DICK HARD.
OUR BROTHERHOOD IS BIGGER THAN ONE STATION.
ANY SURVIVORS WE GOTTA WORRY ABOUT? WHERE'S SHAW?
NOBODY'S LEFT. CHECK THE UNCLAIMED REMAINS, IF YOU GOT THE STOMACH FOR IT.
GODDAMNIT, WAS JUST A MATTER OF TIME BEFORE YOUR "ARRANGEMENT" SHIT THE BED.
SHAW WAS TOUGH AS KEVLAR.
IF BLACKWELL TOOK YOU DOWN, THEN WE'RE ALL IN DANGER.
THIS WAS A CRIME AGAINST MAN.
MY BOYS ARE WILLING TO HIT BACK IF YOU ARE.
KA-CLIK
WE'RE NOT GOING IN AS BORDER PATROL. WE'RE BRINGING 'EM DOWN AS AGENTS OF VENGEANCE.

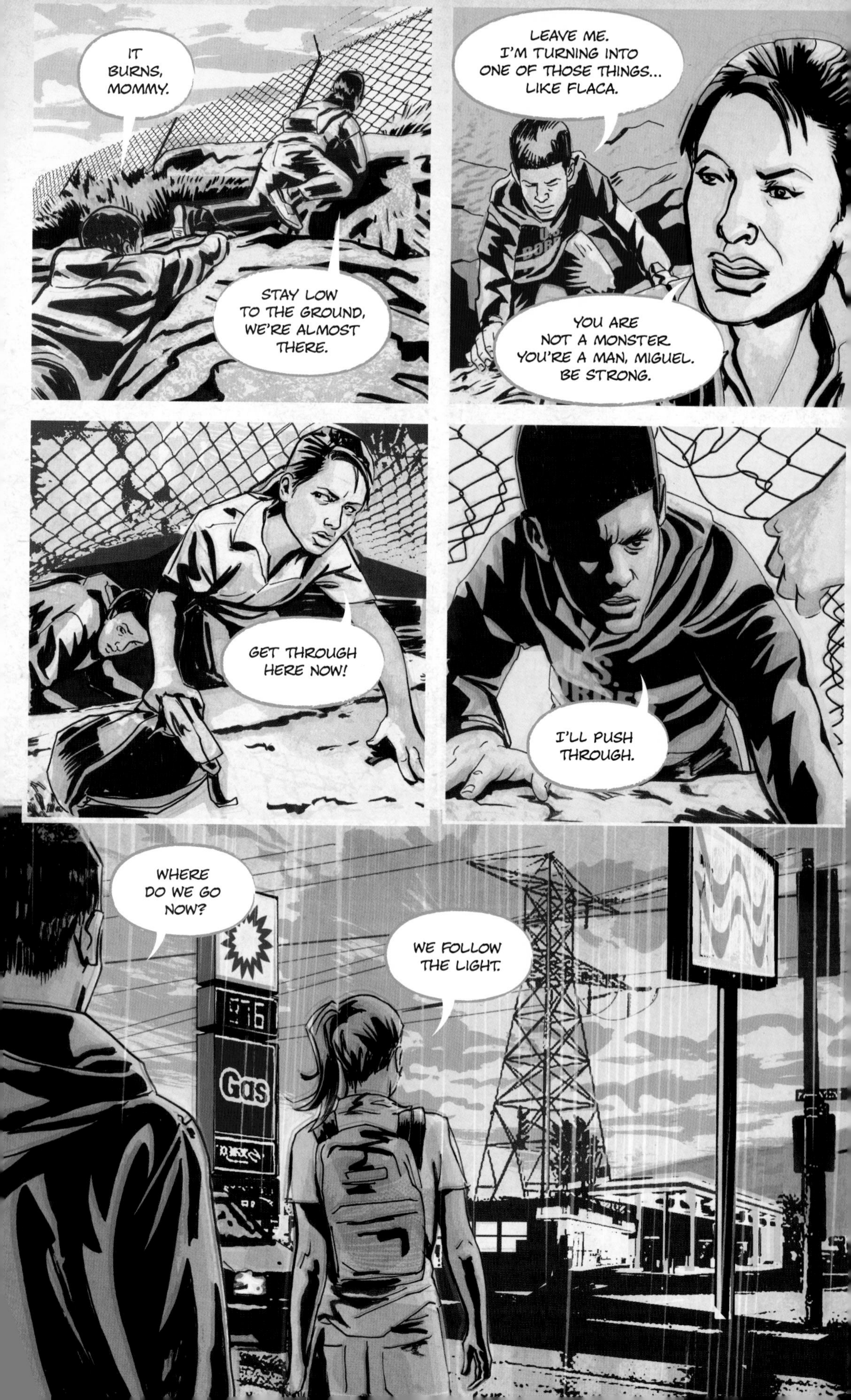
IT BURNS, MOMMY.
STAY LOW TO THE GROUND, WE'RE ALMOST THERE.
LEAVE ME. I'M TURNING INTO ONE OF THOSE THINGS... LIKE FLACA.
YOU ARE NOT A MONSTER. YOU'RE A MAN, MIGUEL. BE STRONG.
GET THROUGH HERE NOW!
I'LL PUSH THROUGH.
WHERE DO WE GO NOW?
WE FOLLOW THE LIGHT.
Gas

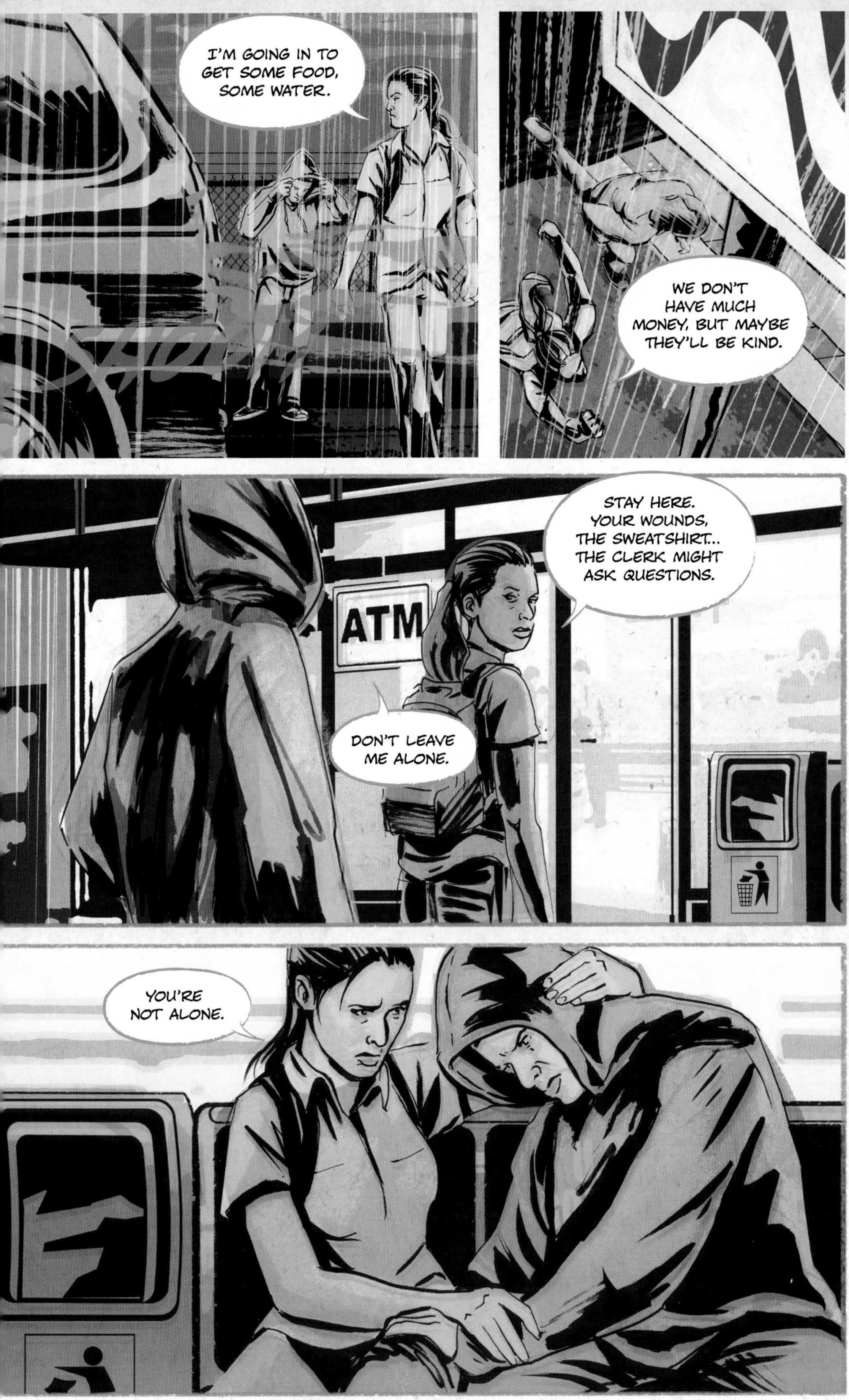
I'M GOING IN TO GET SOME FOOD, SOME WATER.
WE DON'T HAVE MUCH MONEY, BUT MAYBE THEY'LL BE KIND.
STAY HERE. YOUR WOUNDS, THE SWEATSHIRT... THE CLERK MIGHT ASK QUESTIONS.
ATM
DON'T LEAVE ME ALONE.
YOU'RE NOT ALONE.

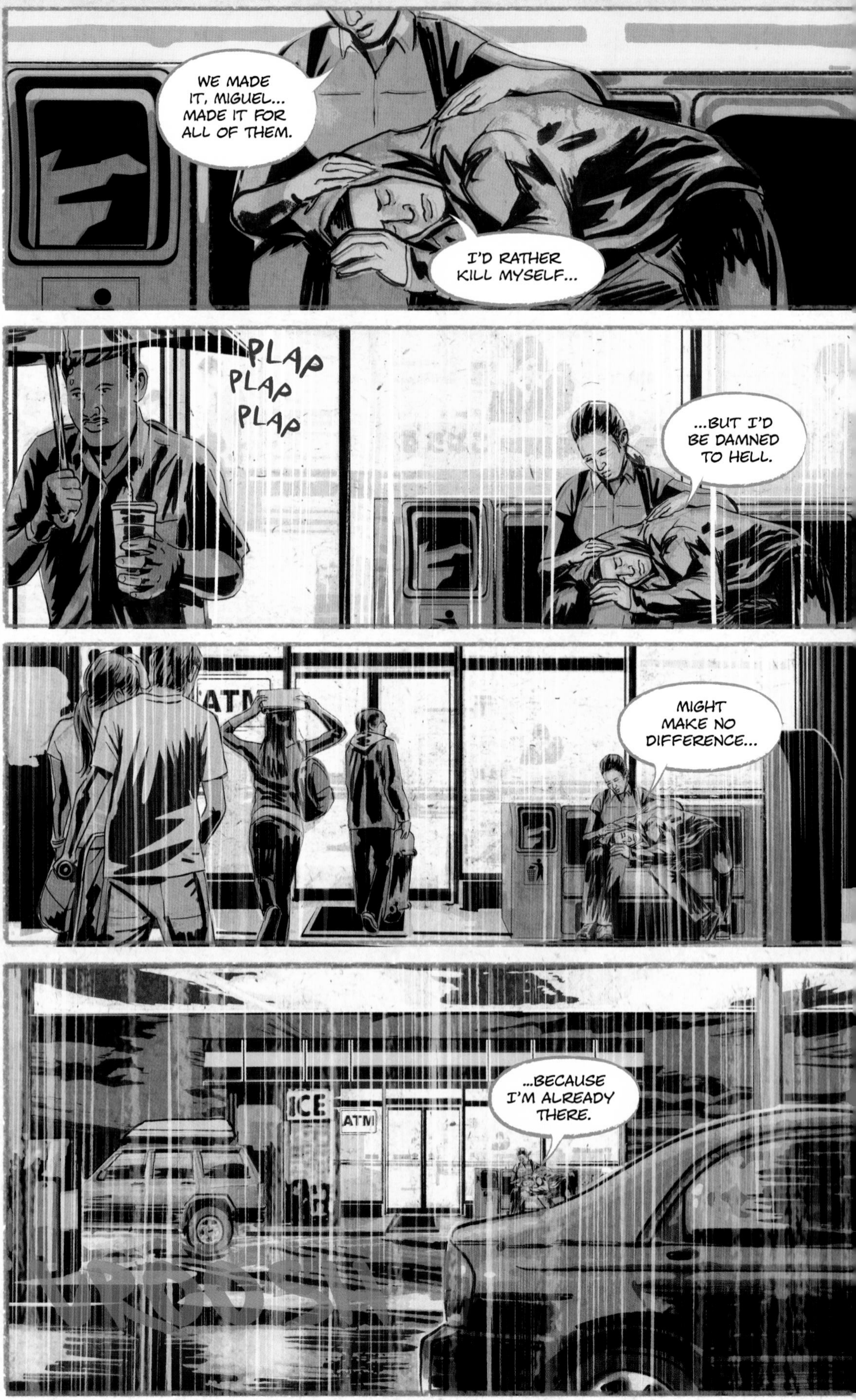
WE MADE IT, MIGUEL... MADE IT FOR ALL OF THEM.
I'D RATHER KILL MYSELF...
PLAP PLAP PLAP
...BUT I'D BE DAMNED TO HELL.
ATM
MIGHT MAKE NO DIFFERENCE...
ICE
ATM
...BECAUSE I'M ALREADY THERE.

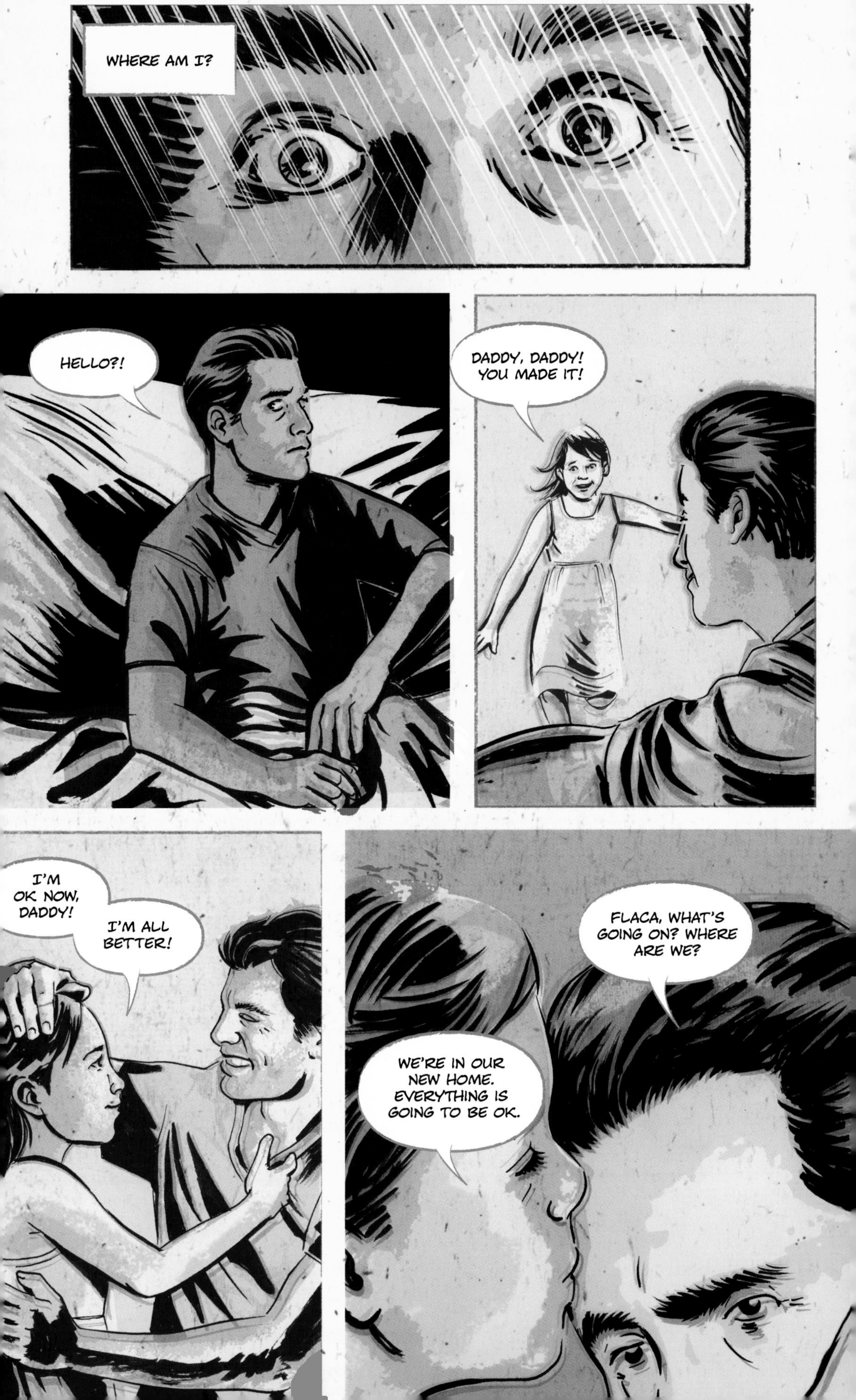
WHERE AM I?
HELLO?!
DADDY, DADDY! YOU MADE IT!
I'M OK NOW, DADDY!
I'M ALL BETTER!
FLACA, WHAT'S GOING ON? WHERE ARE WE?
WE'RE IN OUR NEW HOME. EVERYTHING IS GOING TO BE OK.

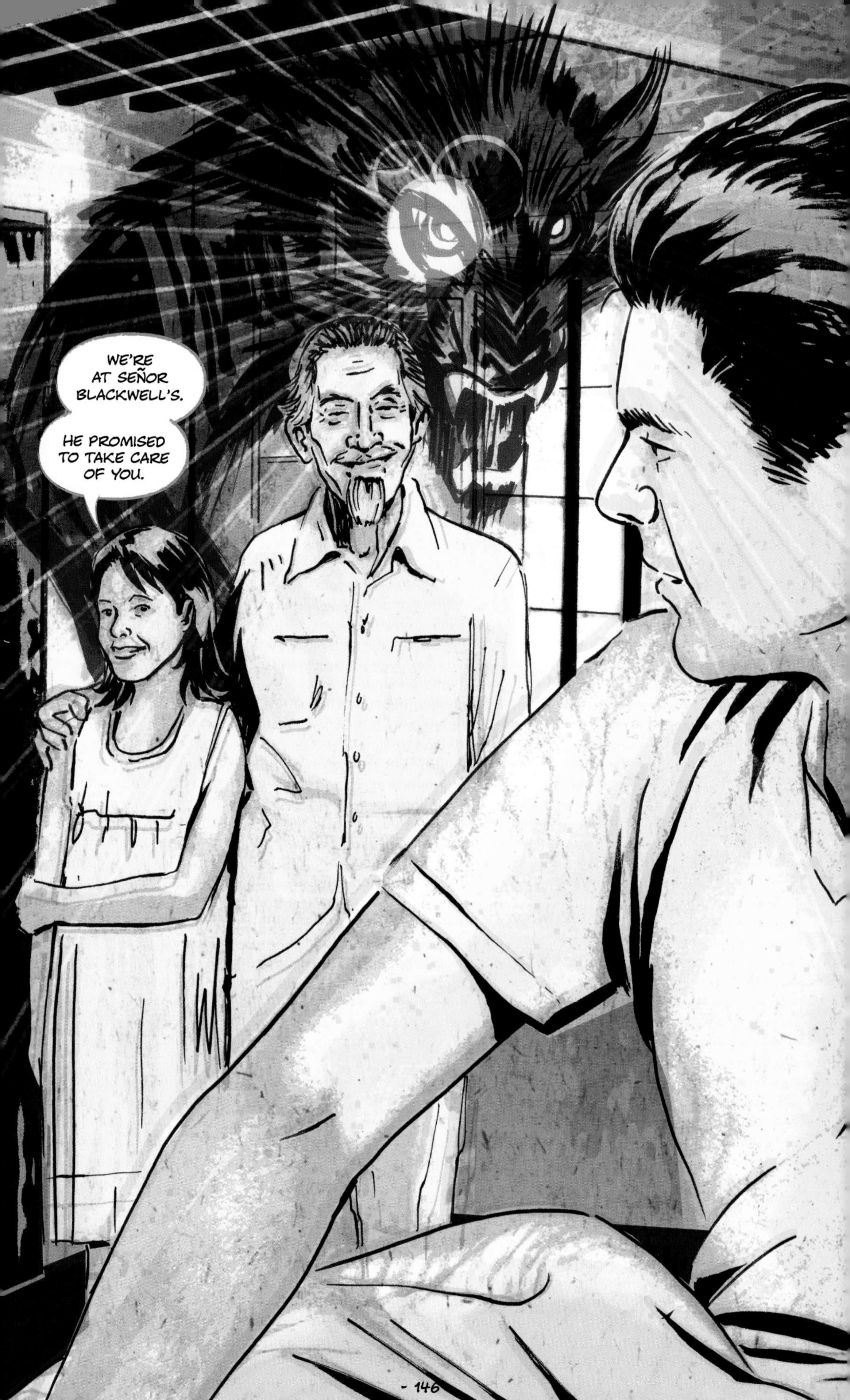
WE'RE AT SEÑOR BLACKWELL'S.
HE PROMISED TO TAKE CARE OF YOU.

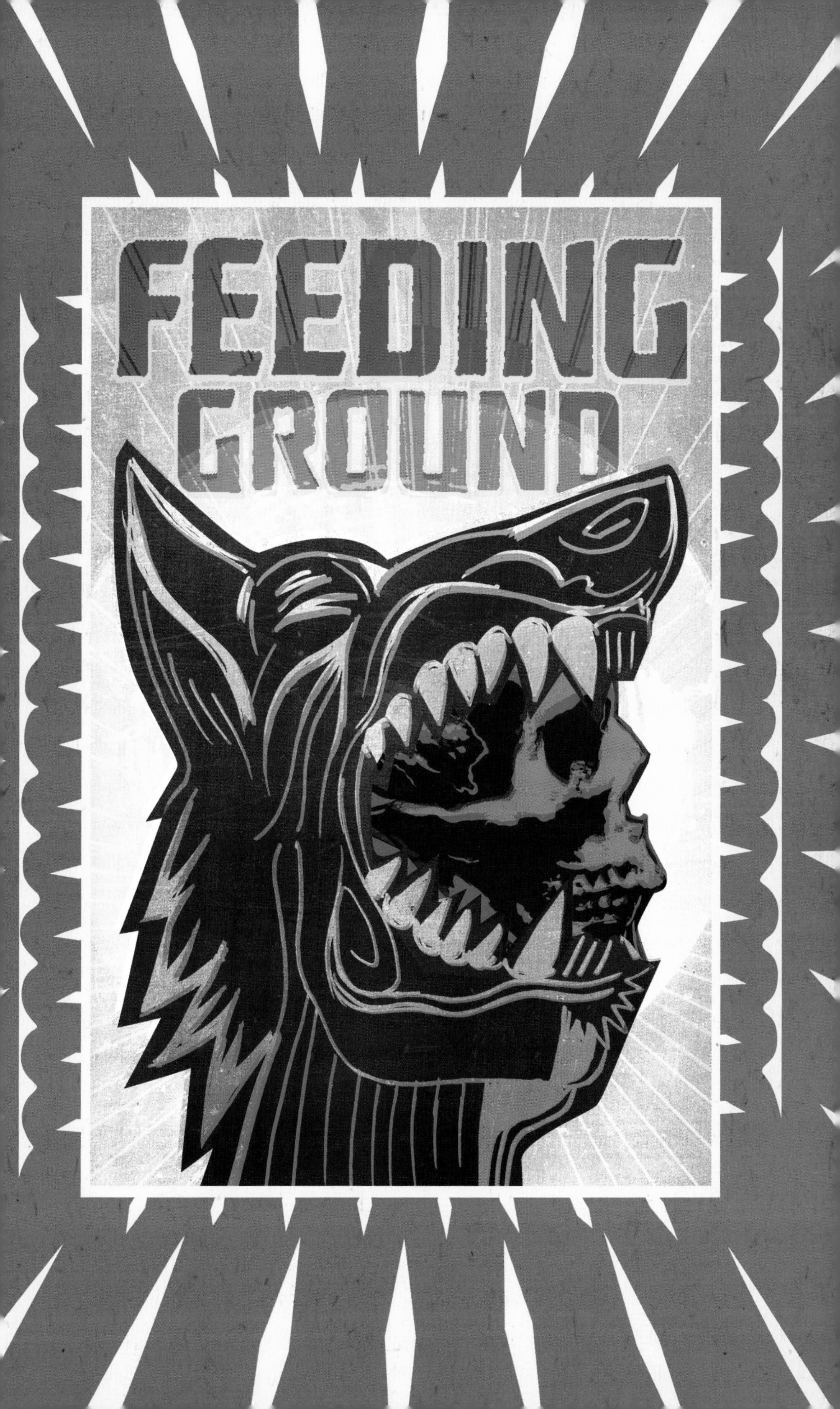
FEEDING
GROUND

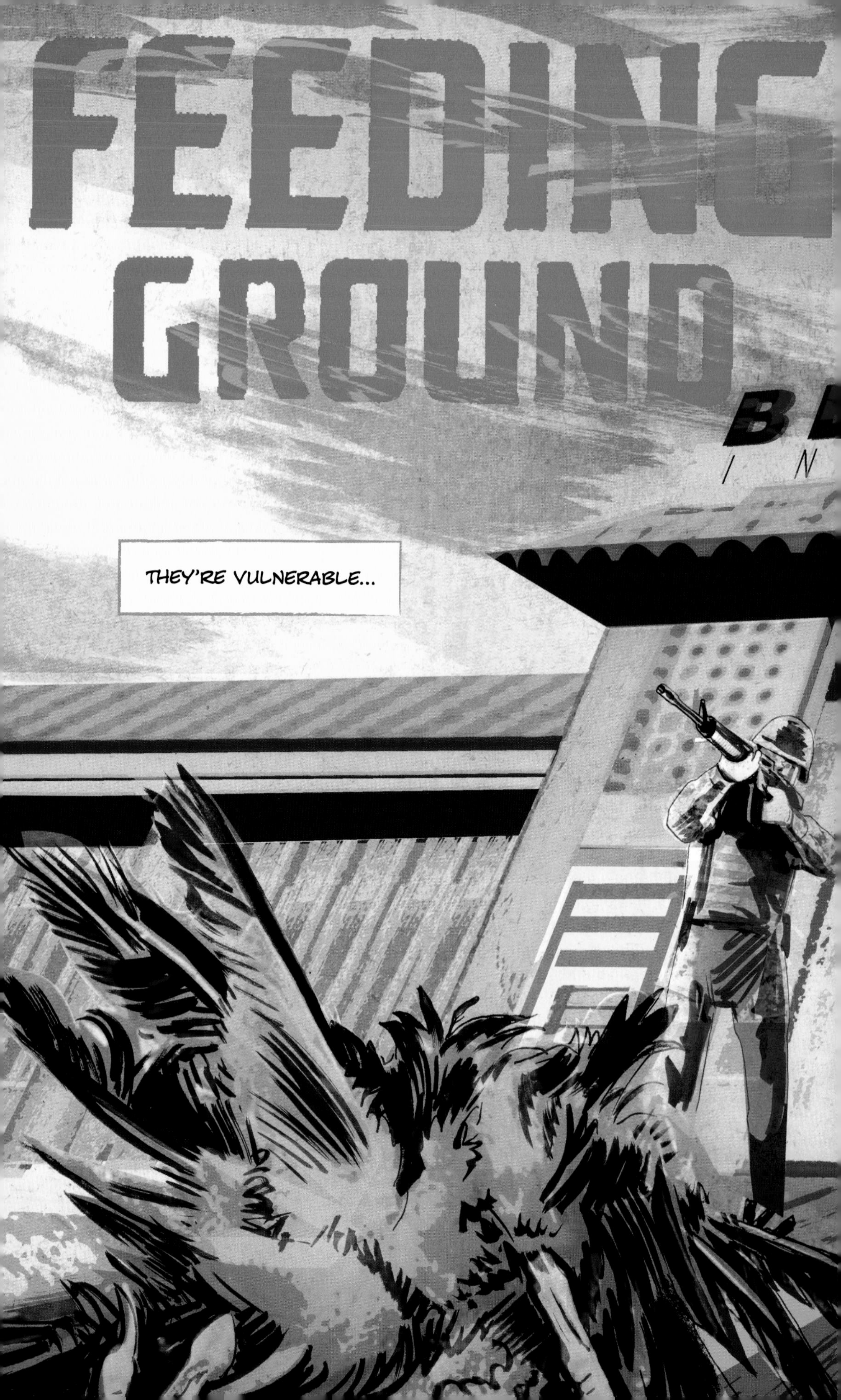
FEEDING GROUND
THEY'RE VULNERABLE...

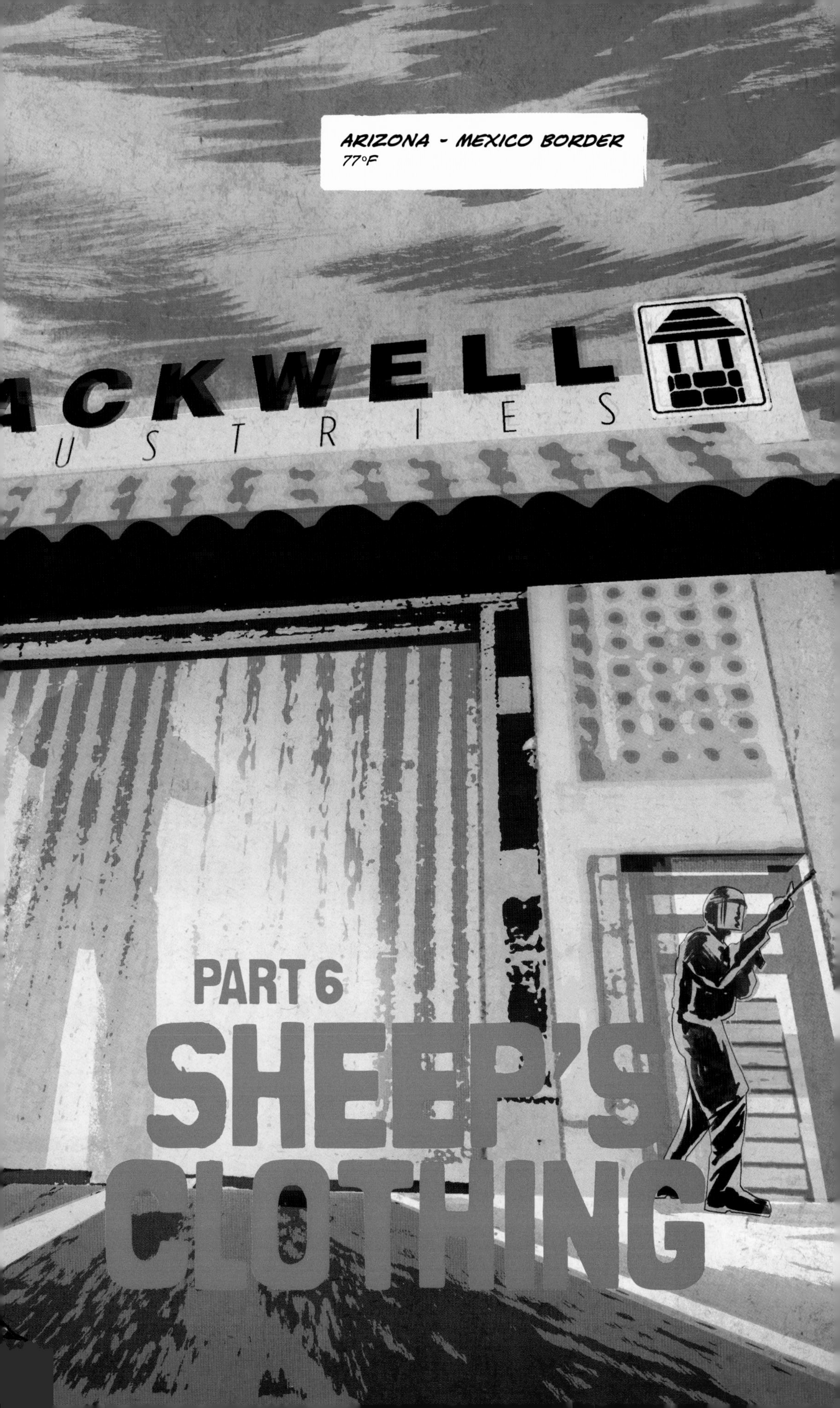

ARIZONA - MEXICO BORDER
77°F
ACKWELL
USTRIES
PART 6
SHEEP'S CLOTHING

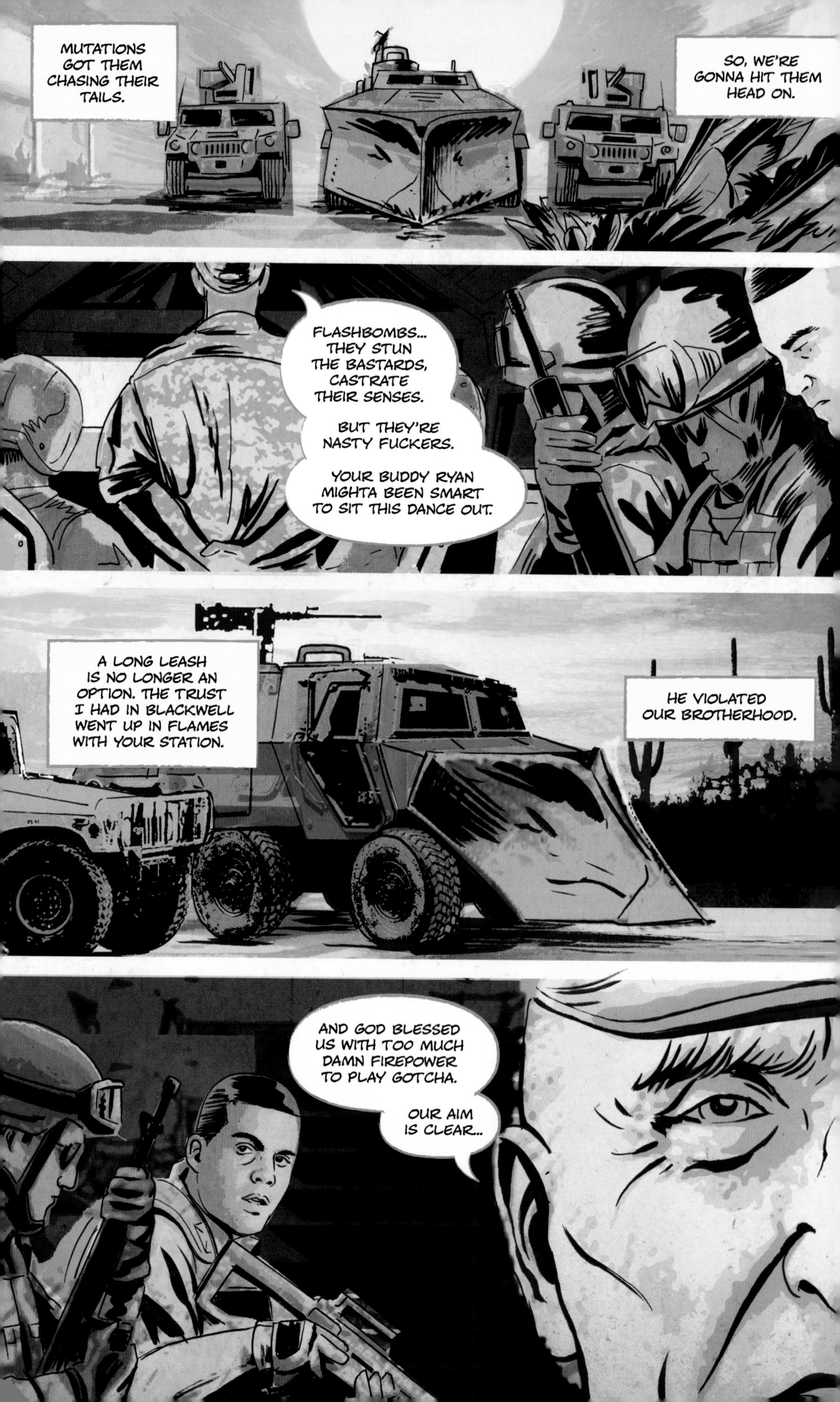
MUTATIONS GOT THEM CHASING THEIR TAILS.
SO, WE'RE GONNA HIT THEM HEAD ON.
FLASHBOMBS... THEY STUN THE BASTARDS, CASTRATE THEIR SENSES.
BUT THEY'RE NASTY FUCKERS.
YOUR BUDDY RYAN MIGHTA BEEN SMART TO SIT THIS DANCE OUT.
A LONG LEASH IS NO LONGER AN OPTION. THE TRUST I HAD IN BLACKWELL WENT UP IN FLAMES WITH YOUR STATION.
HE VIOLATED OUR BROTHERHOOD.
AND GOD BLESSED US WITH TOO MUCH DAMN FIREPOWER TO PLAY GOTCHA.
OUR AIM IS CLEAR...

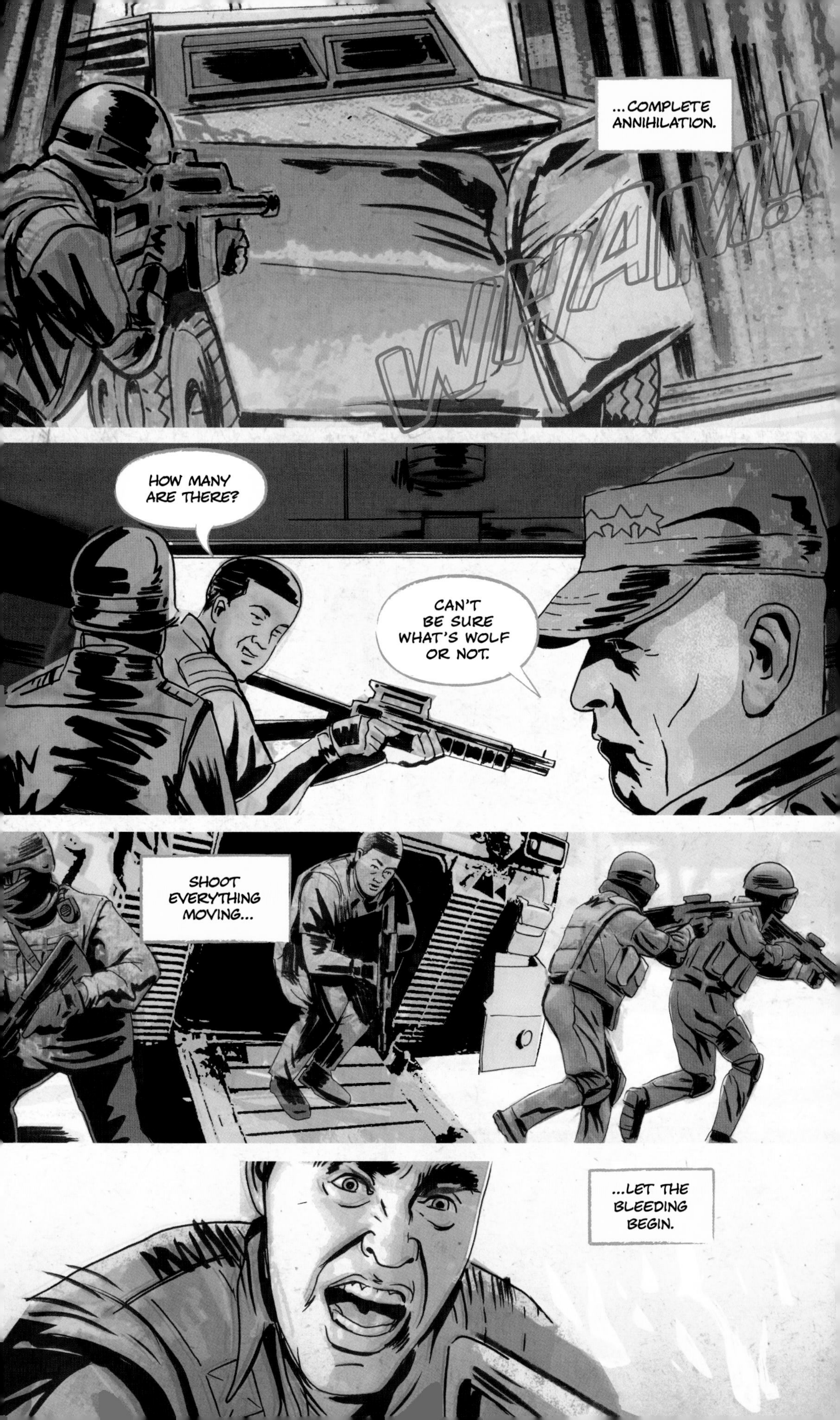
...COMPLETE ANNIHILATION.
WHAAM!!
HOW MANY ARE THERE?
CAN'T BE SURE WHAT'S WOLF OR NOT.
SHOOT EVERYTHING MOVING...
...LET THE BLEEDING BEGIN.

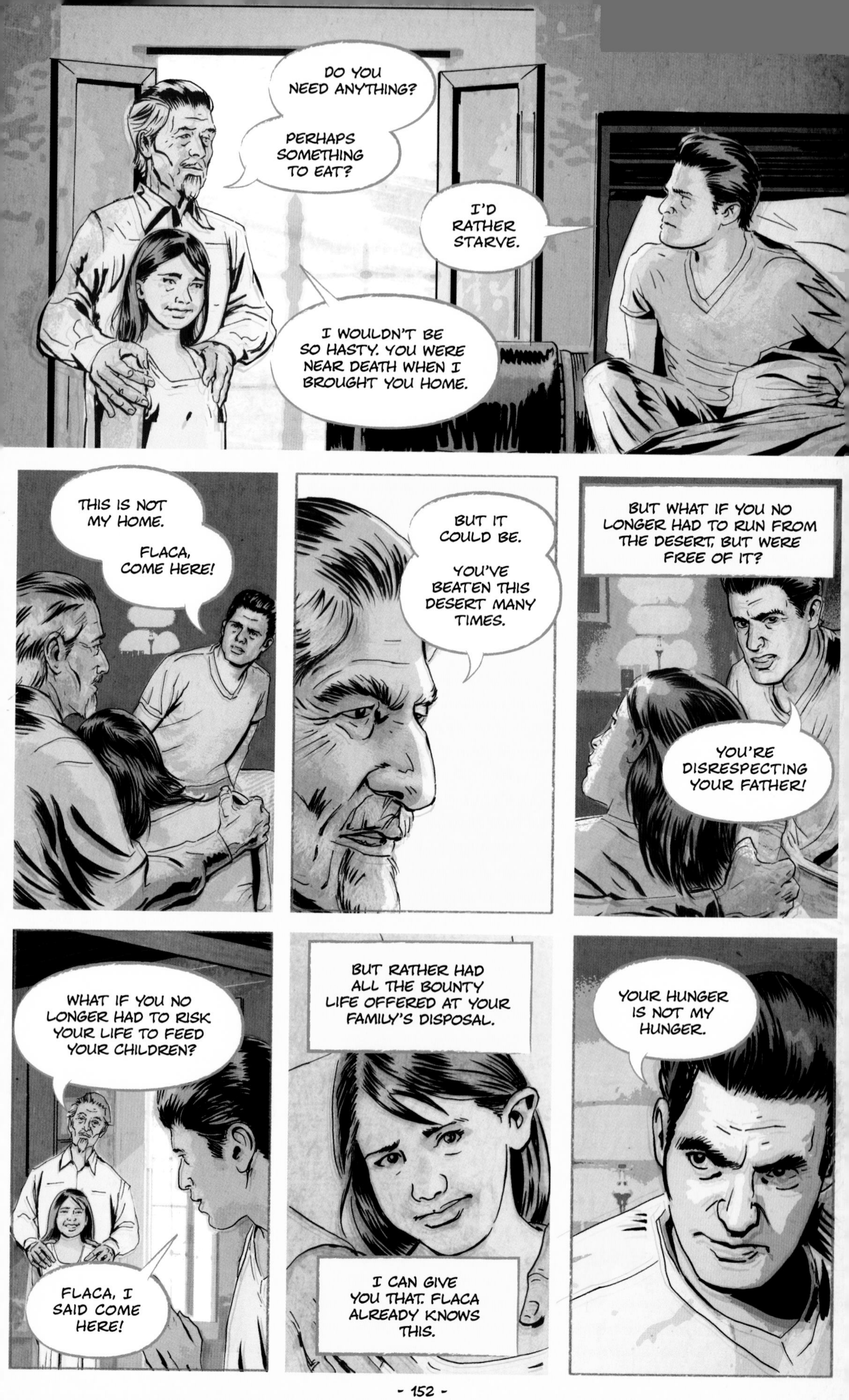
DO YOU NEED ANYTHING?
PERHAPS SOMETHING TO EAT?
I'D RATHER STARVE.
I WOULDN'T BE SO HASTY. YOU WERE NEAR DEATH WHEN I BROUGHT YOU HOME.
THIS IS NOT MY HOME.
FLACA, COME HERE!
BUT IT COULD BE.
YOU'VE BEATEN THIS DESERT MANY TIMES.
BUT WHAT IF YOU NO LONGER HAD TO RUN FROM THE DESERT, BUT WERE FREE OF IT?
YOU'RE DISRESPECTING YOUR FATHER!
WHAT IF YOU NO LONGER HAD TO RISK YOUR LIFE TO FEED YOUR CHILDREN?
FLACA, I SAID COME HERE!
BUT RATHER HAD ALL THE BOUNTY LIFE OFFERED AT YOUR FAMILY'S DISPOSAL.
I CAN GIVE YOU THAT. FLACA ALREADY KNOWS THIS.
YOUR HUNGER IS NOT MY HUNGER.

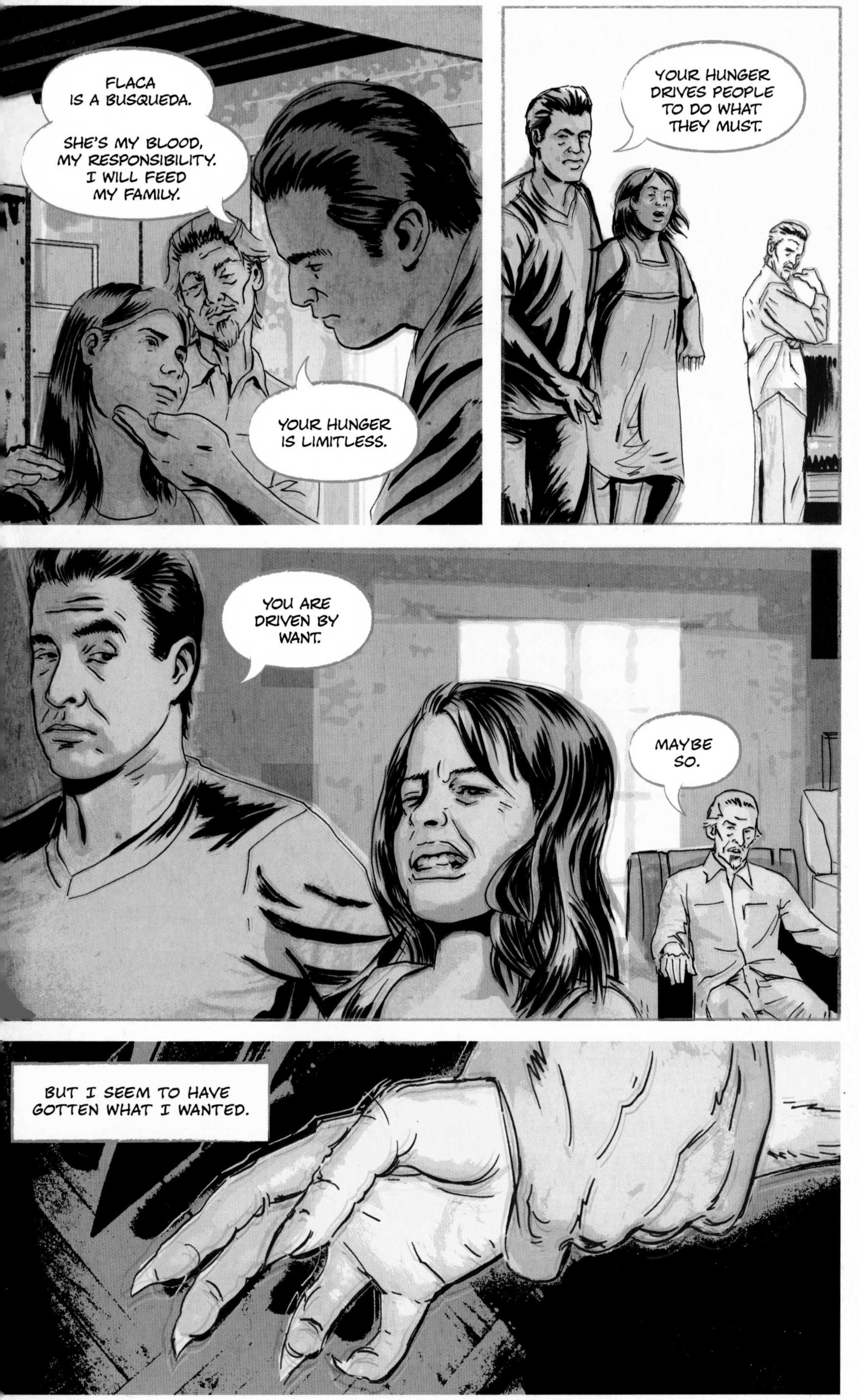
FLACA IS A BUSQUEDA.
SHE'S MY BLOOD, MY RESPONSIBILITY. I WILL FEED MY FAMILY.
YOUR HUNGER IS LIMITLESS.
YOUR HUNGER DRIVES PEOPLE TO DO WHAT THEY MUST.
YOU ARE DRIVEN BY WANT.
MAYBE SO.
BUT I SEEM TO HAVE GOTTEN WHAT I WANTED.

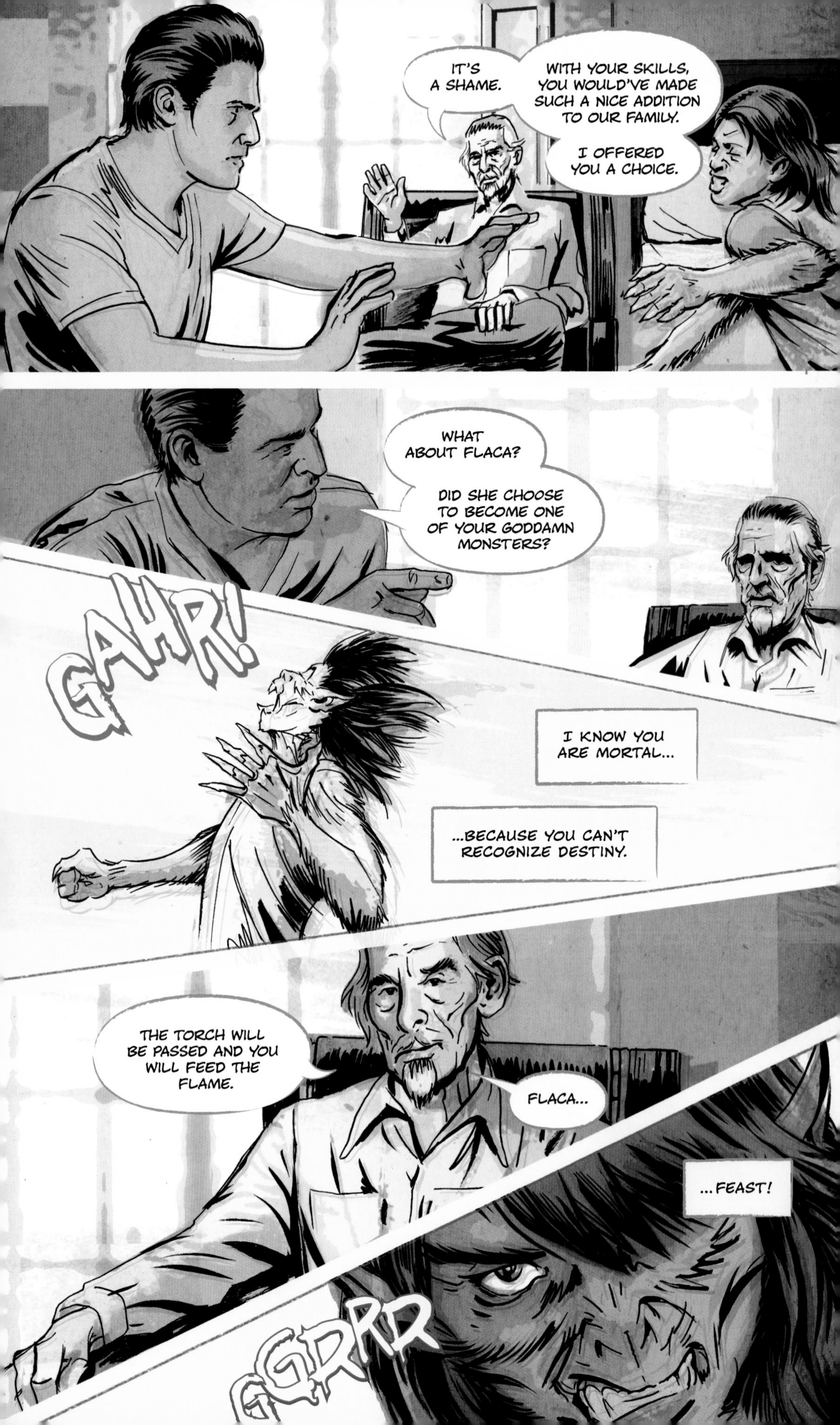
IT'S A SHAME.
WITH YOUR SKILLS, YOU WOULD'VE MADE SUCH A NICE ADDITION TO OUR FAMILY.
I OFFERED YOU A CHOICE.
WHAT ABOUT FLACA?
DID SHE CHOOSE TO BECOME ONE OF YOUR GODDAMN MONSTERS?
GAHR!
I KNOW YOU ARE MORTAL...
...BECAUSE YOU CAN'T RECOGNIZE DESTINY.
THE TORCH WILL BE PASSED AND YOU WILL FEED THE FLAME.
FLACA...
...FEAST!
GGRRR

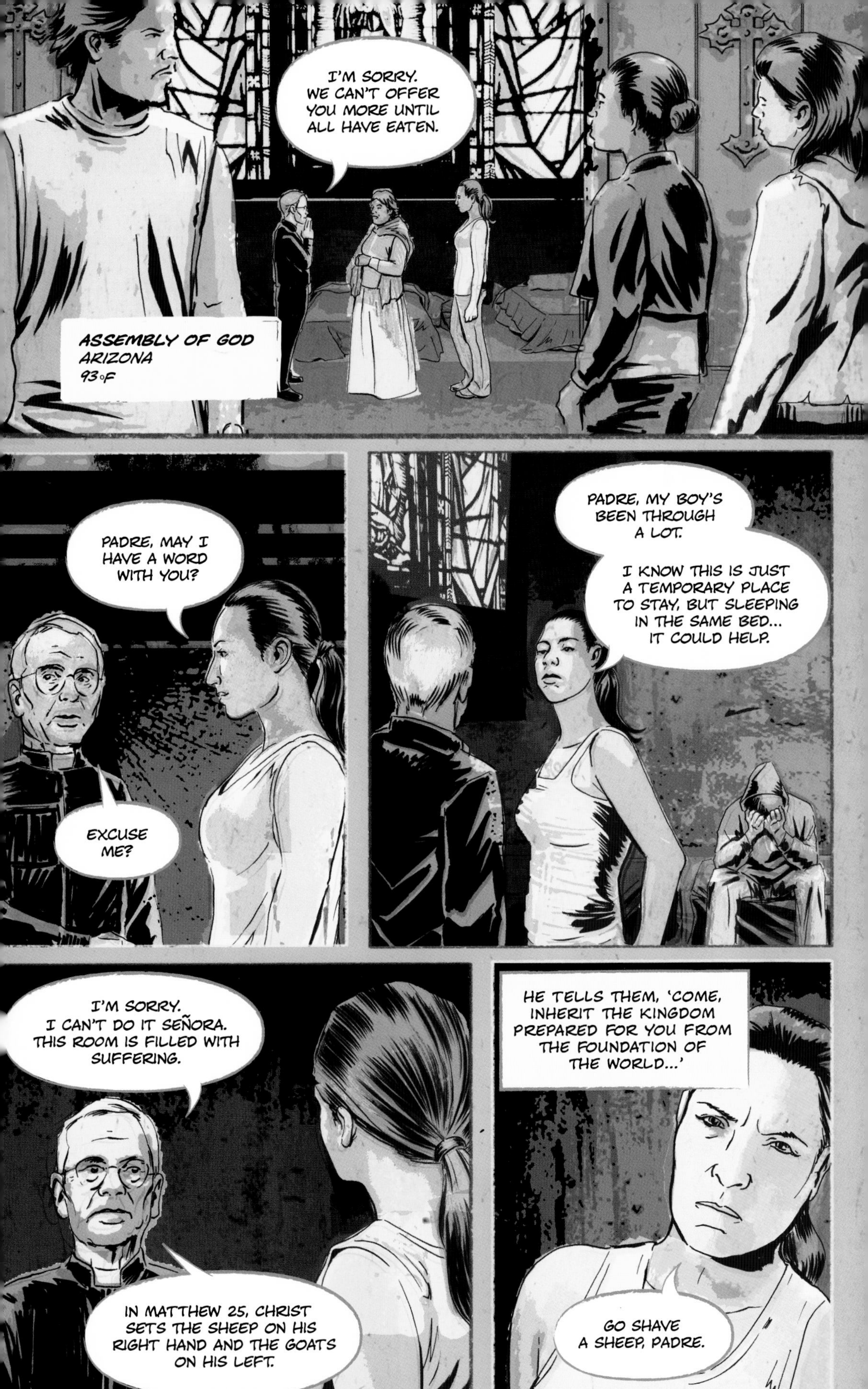
I'M SORRY. WE CAN'T OFFER YOU MORE UNTIL ALL HAVE EATEN.
ASSEMBLY OF GOD
ARIZONA
93°F
PADRE, MAY I HAVE A WORD WITH YOU?
EXCUSE ME?
PADRE, MY BOY'S BEEN THROUGH A LOT.
I KNOW THIS IS JUST A TEMPORARY PLACE TO STAY, BUT SLEEPING IN THE SAME BED... IT COULD HELP.
I'M SORRY. I CAN'T DO IT SEÑORA. THIS ROOM IS FILLED WITH SUFFERING.
IN MATTHEW 25, CHRIST SETS THE SHEEP ON HIS RIGHT HAND AND THE GOATS ON HIS LEFT.
HE TELLS THEM, 'COME, INHERIT THE KINGDOM PREPARED FOR YOU FROM THE FOUNDATION OF THE WORLD...'
GO SHAVE A SHEEP, PADRE.

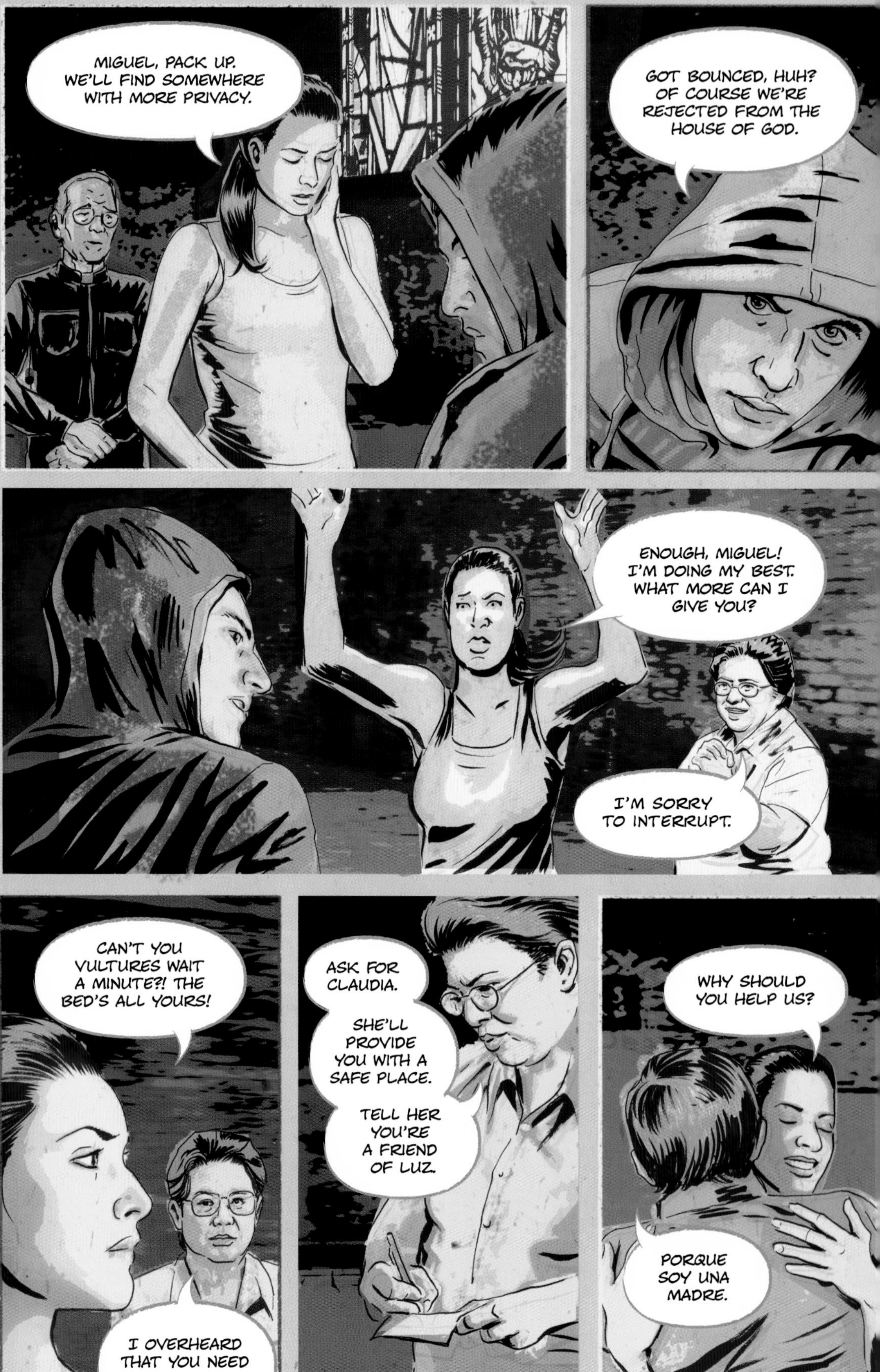
MIGUEL, PACK UP. WE'LL FIND SOMEWHERE WITH MORE PRIVACY.
GOT BOUNCED, HUH? OF COURSE WE'RE REJECTED FROM THE HOUSE OF GOD.
ENOUGH, MIGUEL! I'M DOING MY BEST. WHAT MORE CAN I GIVE YOU?
I'M SORRY TO INTERRUPT.
CAN'T YOU VULTURES WAIT A MINUTE?! THE BED'S ALL YOURS!
I OVERHEARD THAT YOU NEED SOMEWHERE TO STAY?
ASK FOR CLAUDIA.
SHE'LL PROVIDE YOU WITH A SAFE PLACE.
TELL HER YOU'RE A FRIEND OF LUZ.
WHY SHOULD YOU HELP US?
PORQUE SOY UNA MADRE.

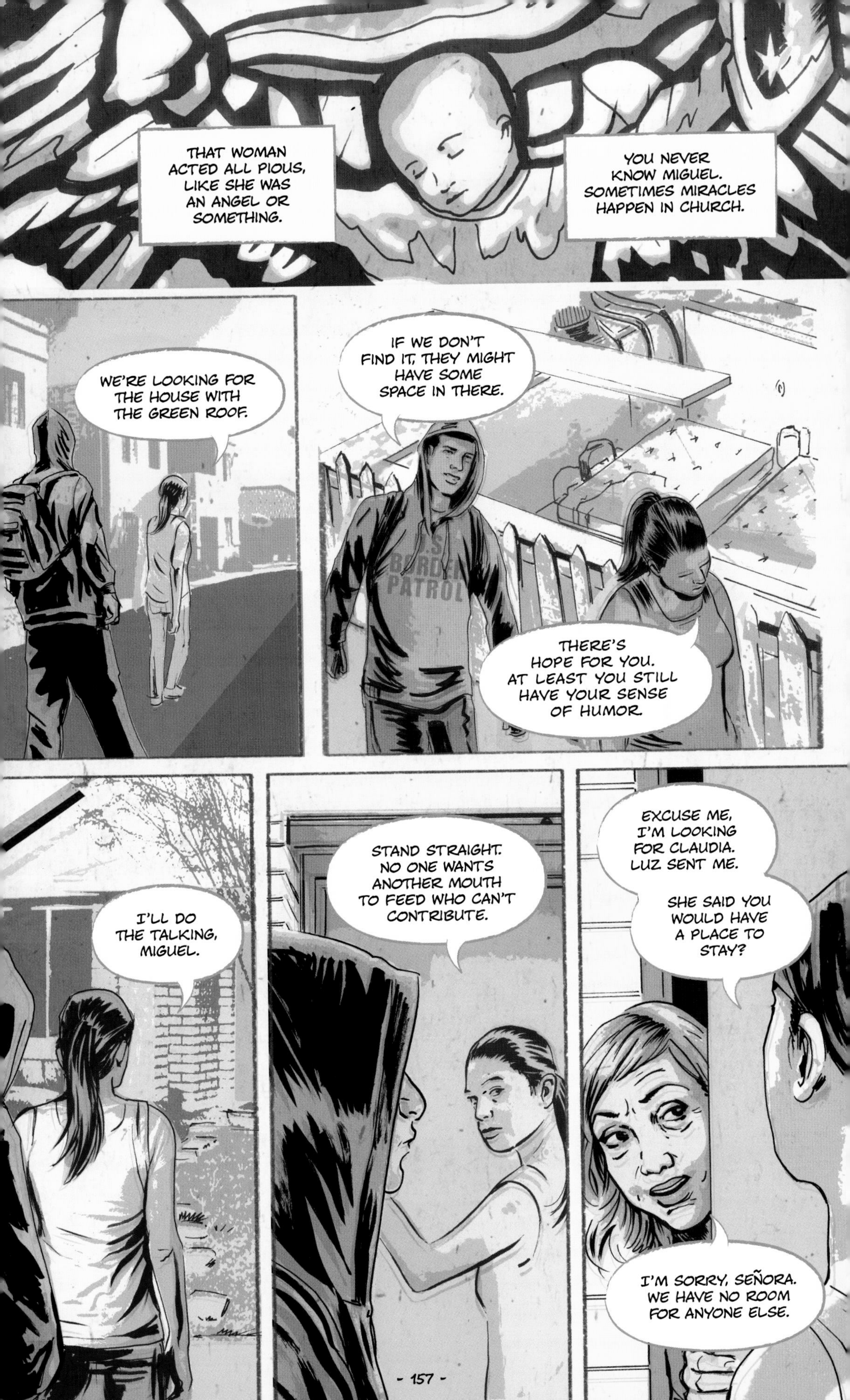
THAT WOMAN ACTED ALL PIOUS, LIKE SHE WAS AN ANGEL OR SOMETHING.
YOU NEVER KNOW MIGUEL. SOMETIMES MIRACLES HAPPEN IN CHURCH.
WE'RE LOOKING FOR THE HOUSE WITH THE GREEN ROOF.
IF WE DON'T FIND IT, THEY MIGHT HAVE SOME SPACE IN THERE.
U.S. BORDER PATROL
THERE'S HOPE FOR YOU. AT LEAST YOU STILL HAVE YOUR SENSE OF HUMOR.
I'LL DO THE TALKING, MIGUEL.
STAND STRAIGHT. NO ONE WANTS ANOTHER MOUTH TO FEED WHO CAN'T CONTRIBUTE.
EXCUSE ME, I'M LOOKING FOR CLAUDIA. LUZ SENT ME.
SHE SAID YOU WOULD HAVE A PLACE TO STAY?
I'M SORRY, SEÑORA. WE HAVE NO ROOM FOR ANYONE ELSE.

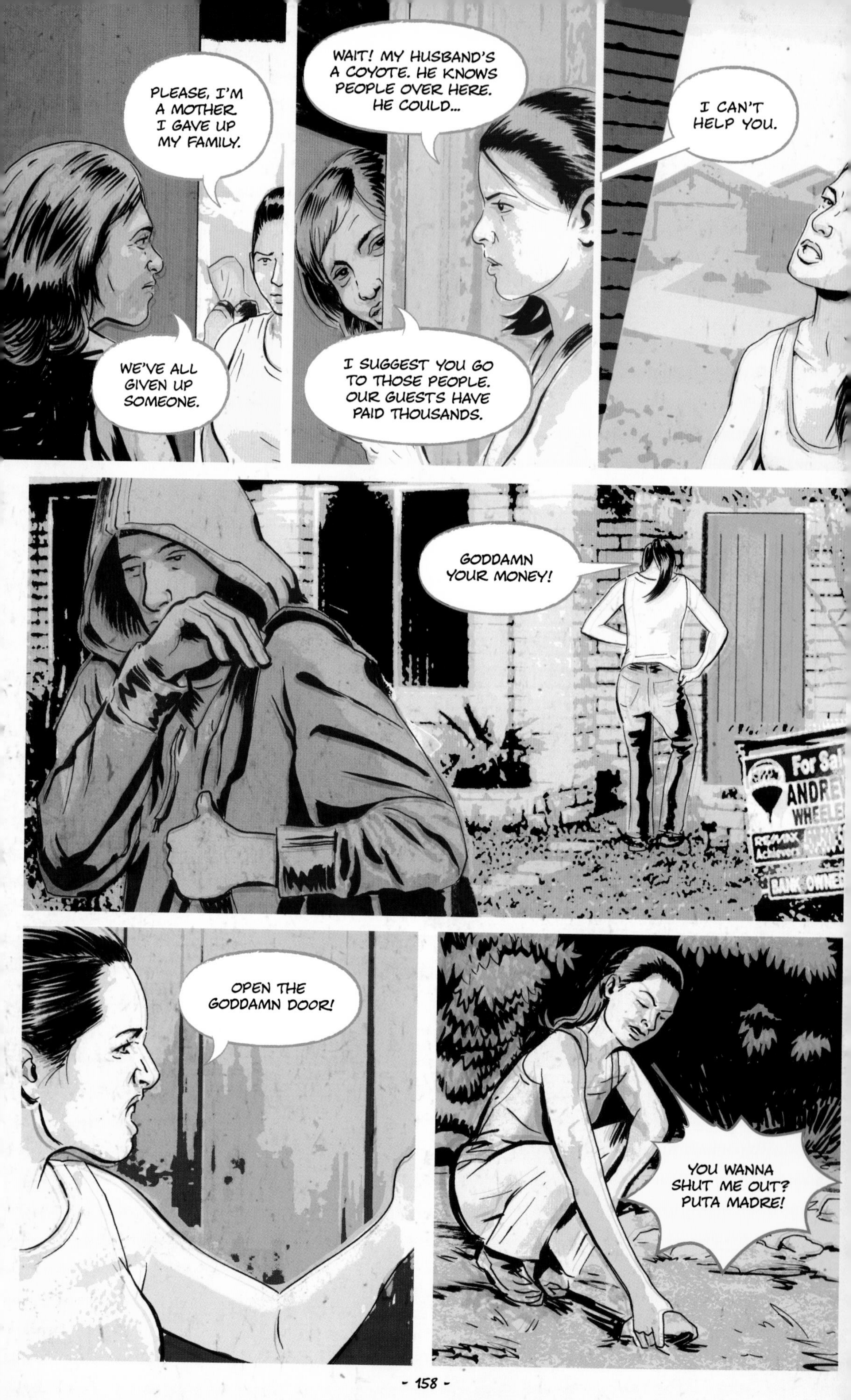
PLEASE, I'M A MOTHER. I GAVE UP MY FAMILY.
WE'VE ALL GIVEN UP SOMEONE.
WAIT! MY HUSBAND'S A COYOTE. HE KNOWS PEOPLE OVER HERE. HE COULD...
I SUGGEST YOU GO TO THOSE PEOPLE. OUR GUESTS HAVE PAID THOUSANDS.
I CAN'T HELP YOU.
GODDAMN YOUR MONEY!
For Sal
ANDRE
WHEELE
BANK OWNE
OPEN THE GODDAMN DOOR!
YOU WANNA SHUT ME OUT? PUTA MADRE!

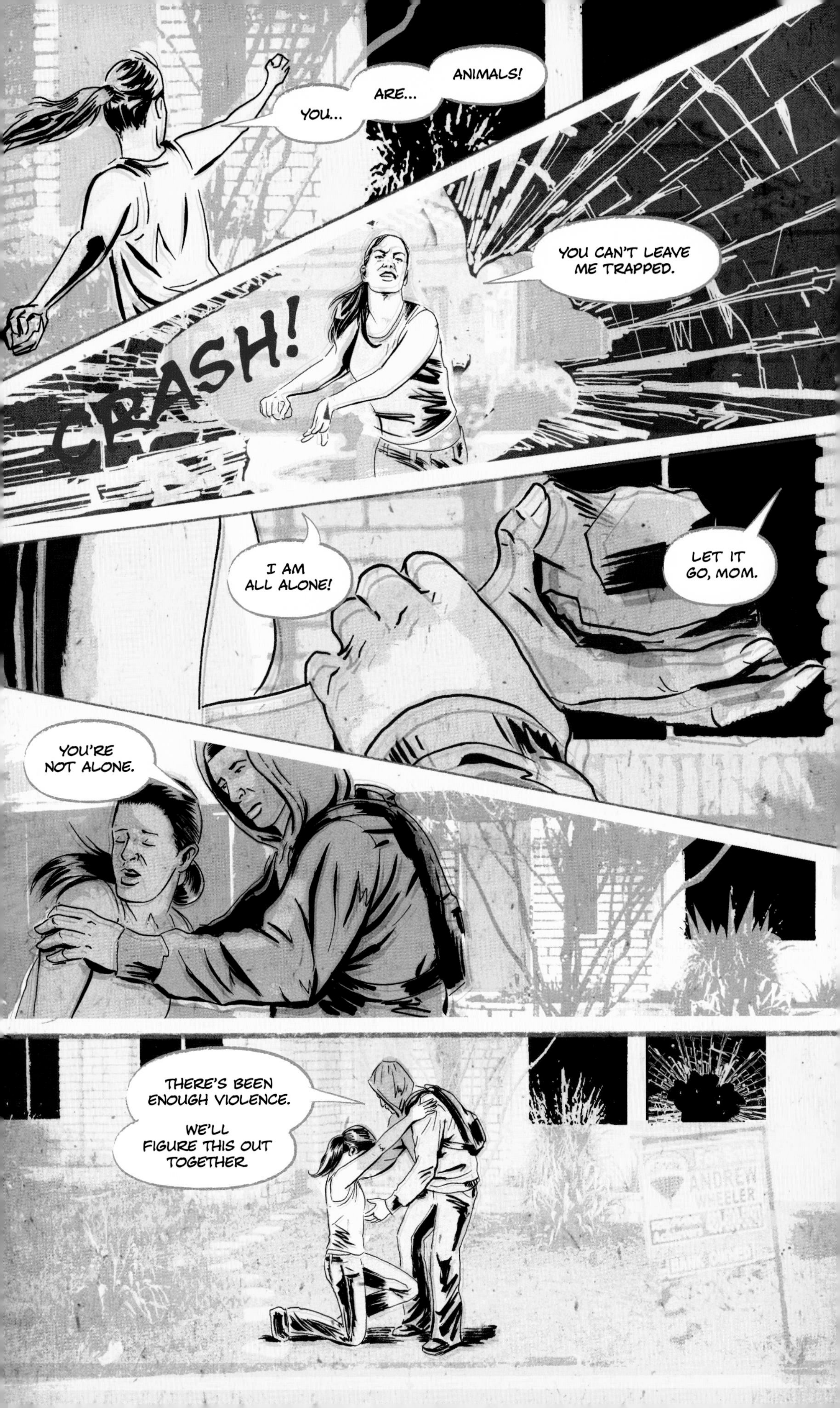
YOU...
ARE...
ANIMALS!
YOU CAN'T LEAVE ME TRAPPED.
CRASH!
I AM ALL ALONE!
LET IT GO, MOM.
YOU'RE NOT ALONE.
THERE'S BEEN ENOUGH VIOLENCE.
WE'LL FIGURE THIS OUT TOGETHER
ANDREW WHEELER
BANK OWNED

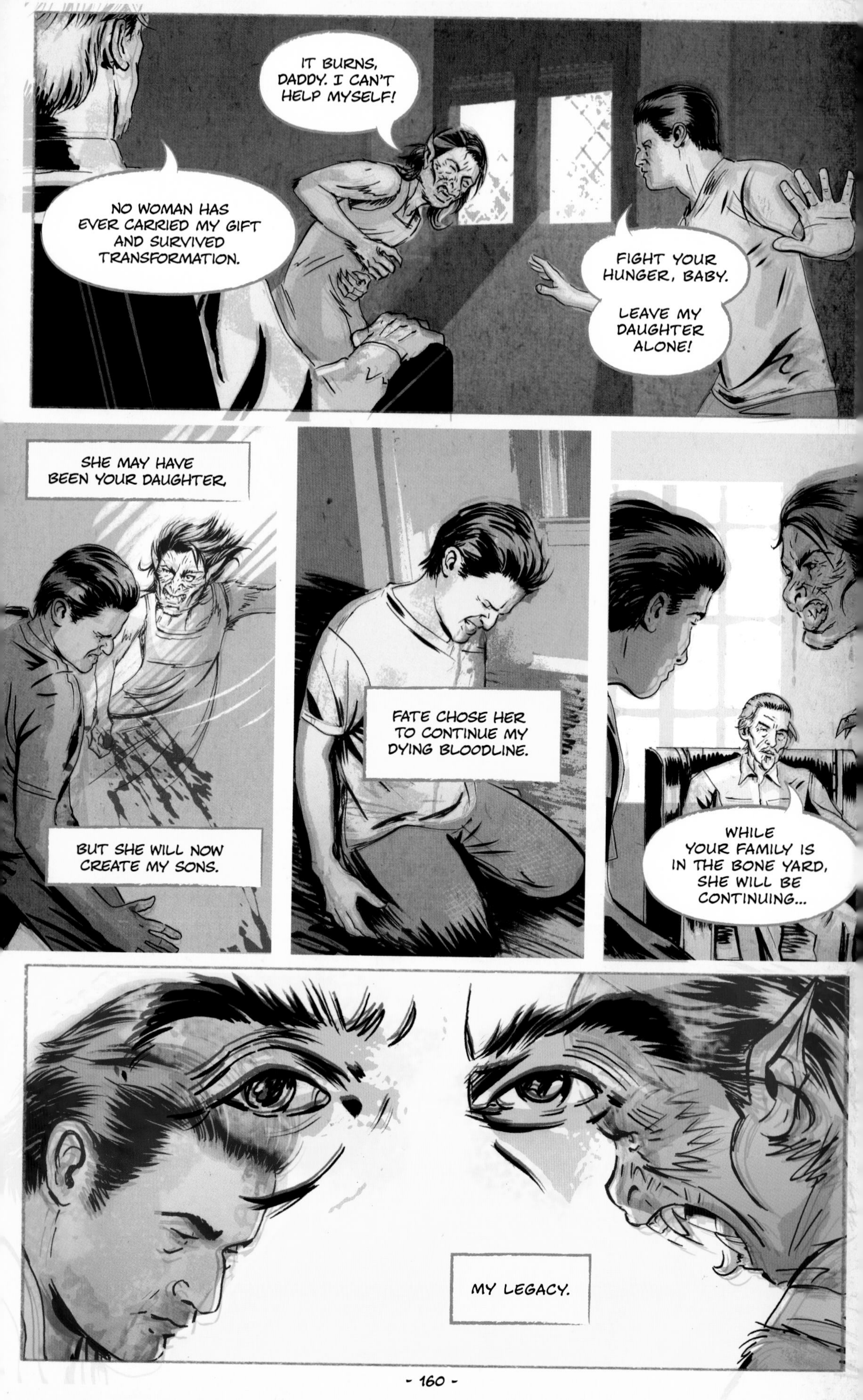

NO WOMAN HAS EVER CARRIED MY GIFT AND SURVIVED TRANSFORMATION.
IT BURNS, DADDY. I CAN'T HELP MYSELF!
FIGHT YOUR HUNGER, BABY.
LEAVE MY DAUGHTER ALONE!
SHE MAY HAVE BEEN YOUR DAUGHTER.
BUT SHE WILL NOW CREATE MY SONS.
FATE CHOSE HER TO CONTINUE MY DYING BLOODLINE.
WHILE YOUR FAMILY IS IN THE BONE YARD, SHE WILL BE CONTINUING...
MY LEGACY.

SO...

...THIS IS HOW YOU KILLED YOUR UNCLE.

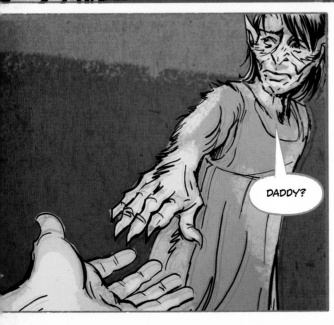

DADDY?

YOU'VE REFUSED MY OFFER THESE MEN, TOUGH IN LIFE...

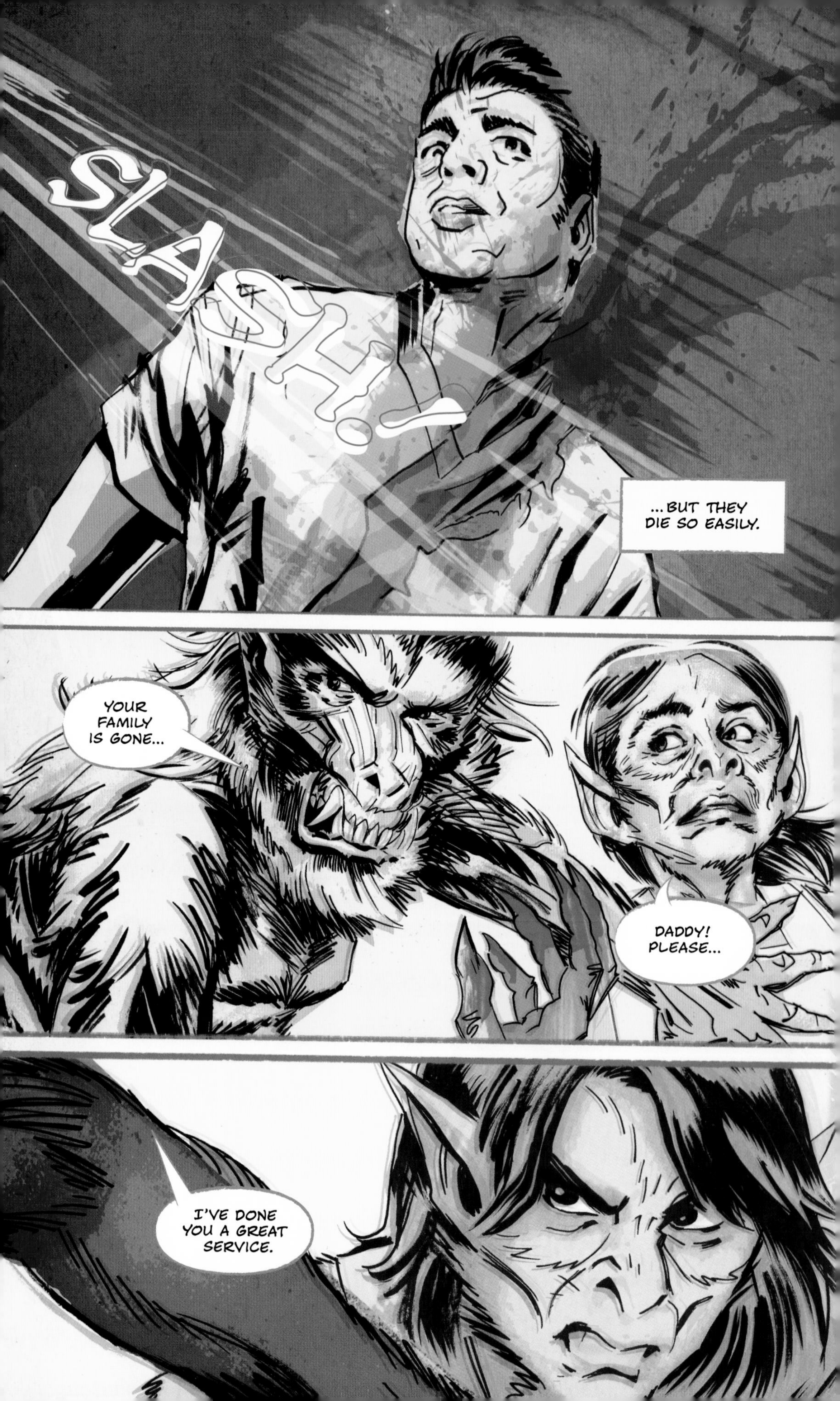
SLASH!
...BUT THEY DIE SO EASILY.
YOUR FAMILY IS GONE...
DADDY! PLEASE...
I'VE DONE YOU A GREAT SERVICE.

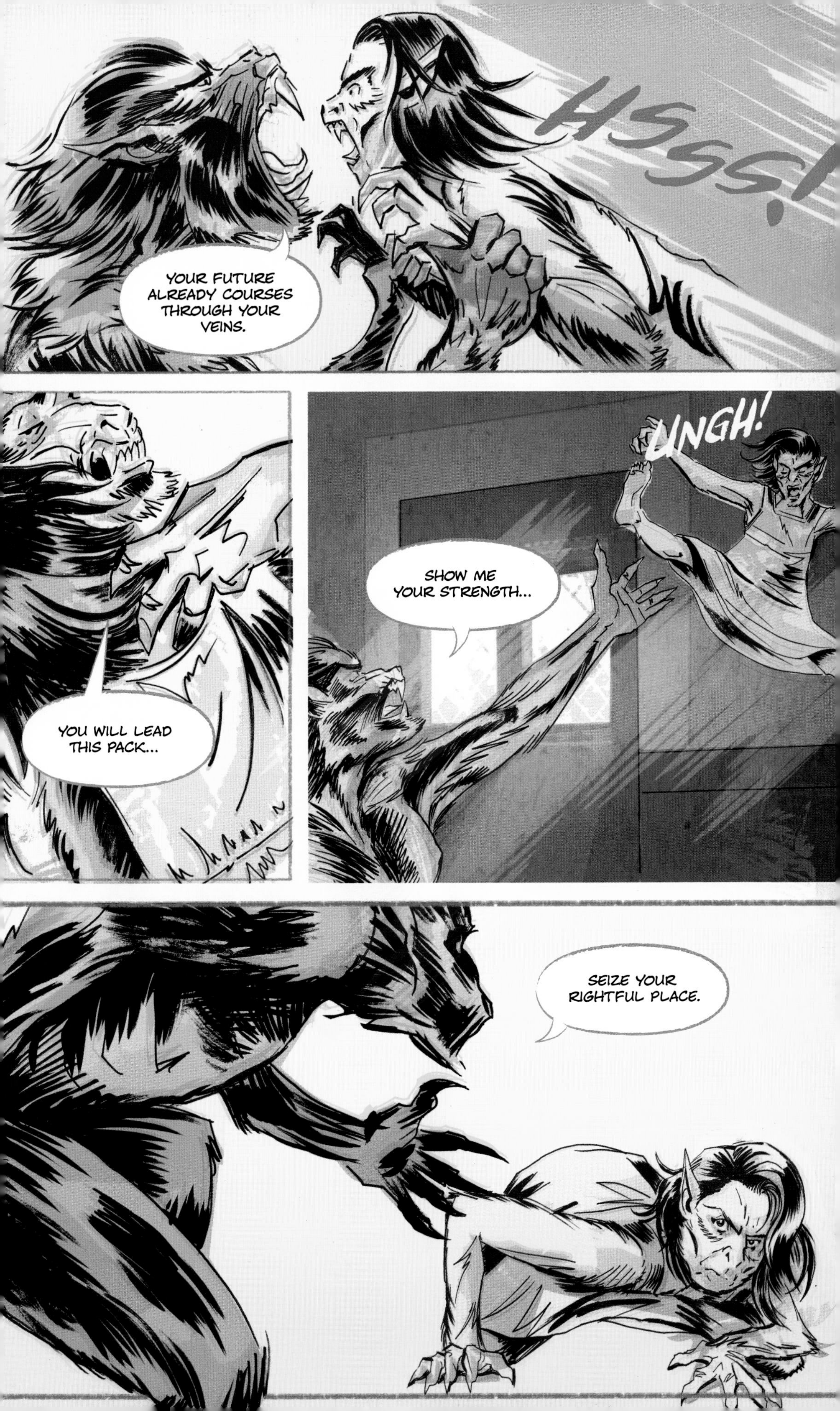
HSSS!
YOUR FUTURE ALREADY COURSES THROUGH YOUR VEINS.
YOU WILL LEAD THIS PACK...
SHOW ME YOUR STRENGTH...
UNGH!
SEIZE YOUR RIGHTFUL PLACE.

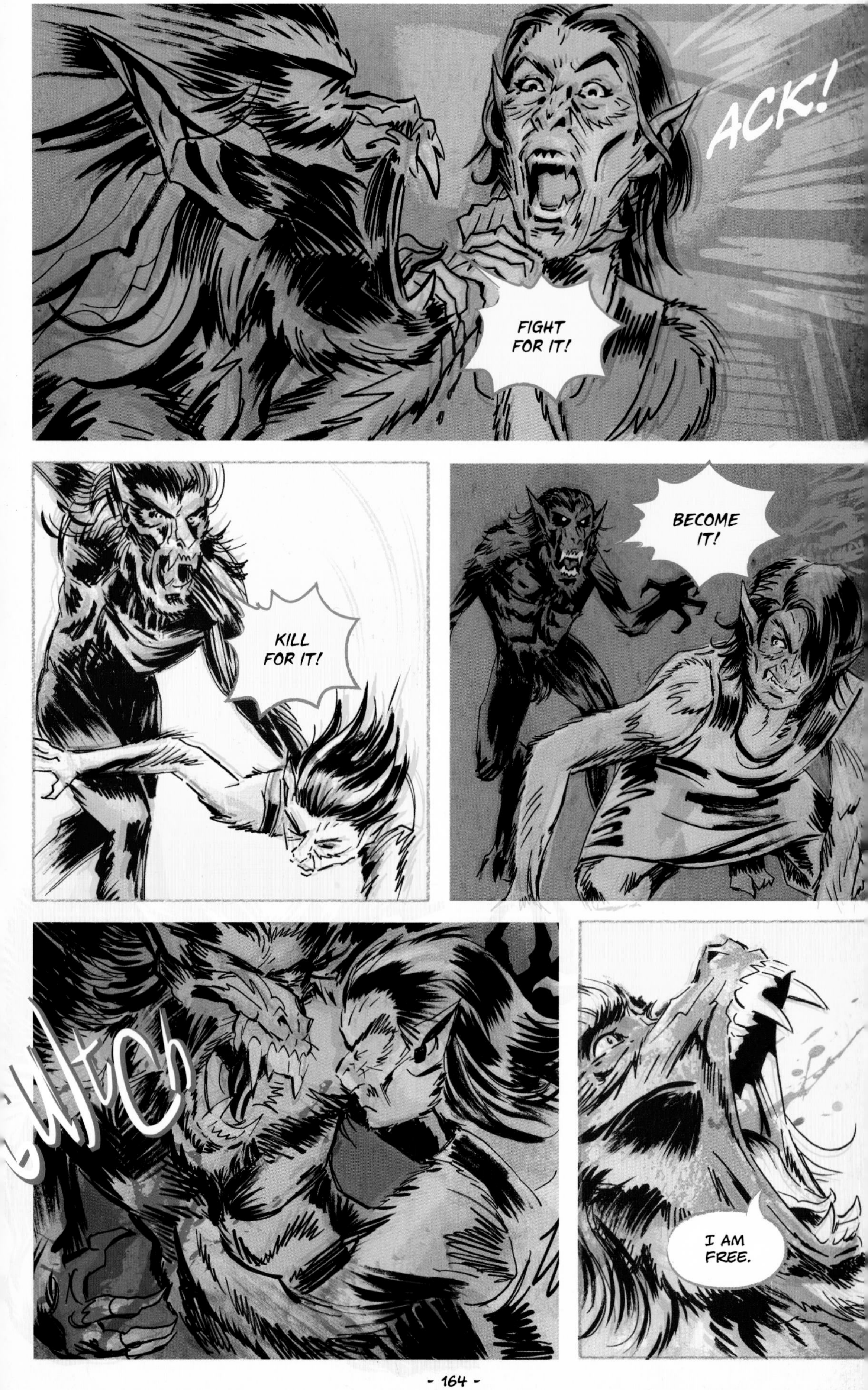
ACK!
FIGHT FOR IT!
KILL FOR IT!
BECOME IT!
I AM FREE.

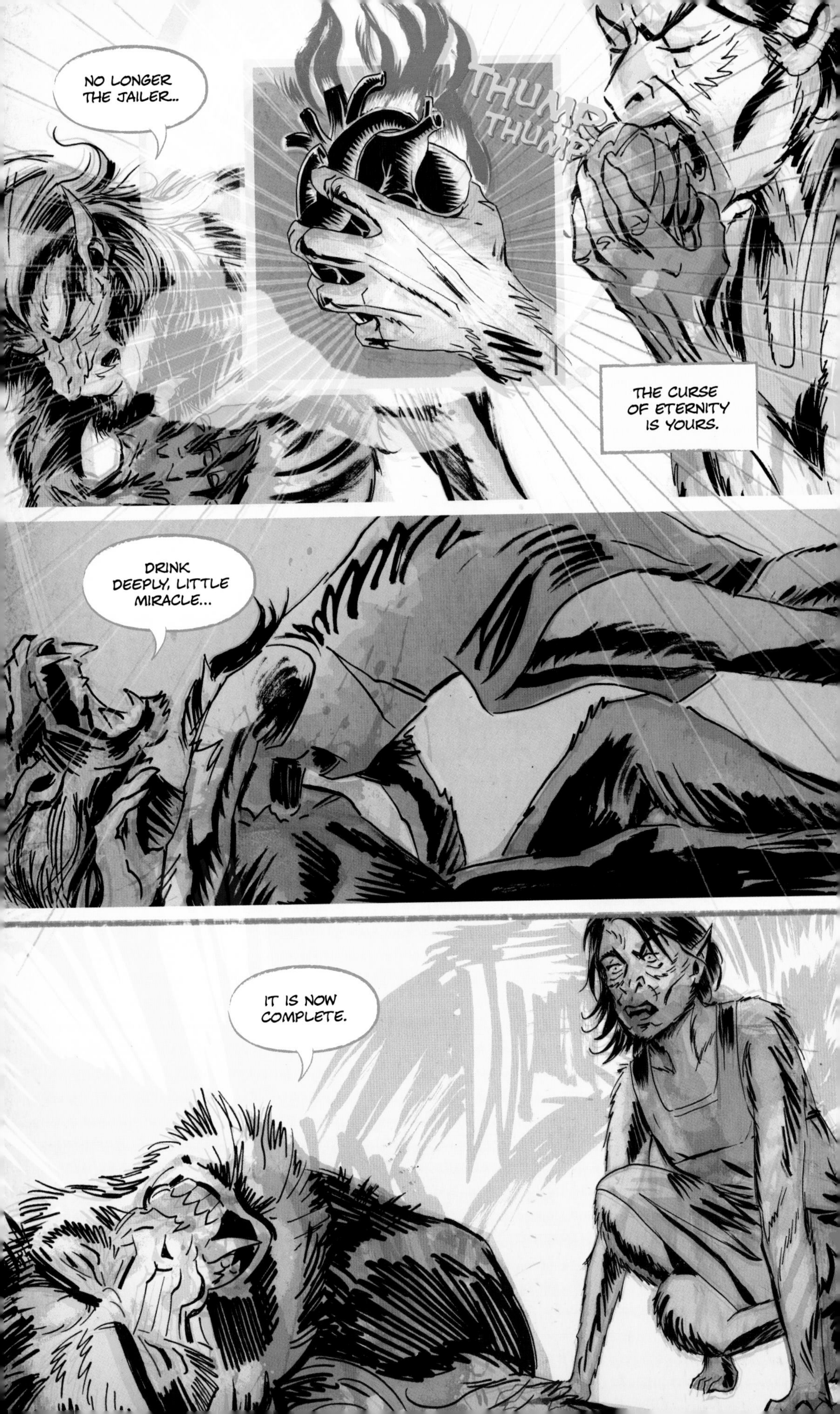
NO LONGER THE JAILER...
THUMP THUMP
THE CURSE OF ETERNITY IS YOURS.
DRINK DEEPLY, LITTLE MIRACLE...
IT IS NOW COMPLETE.

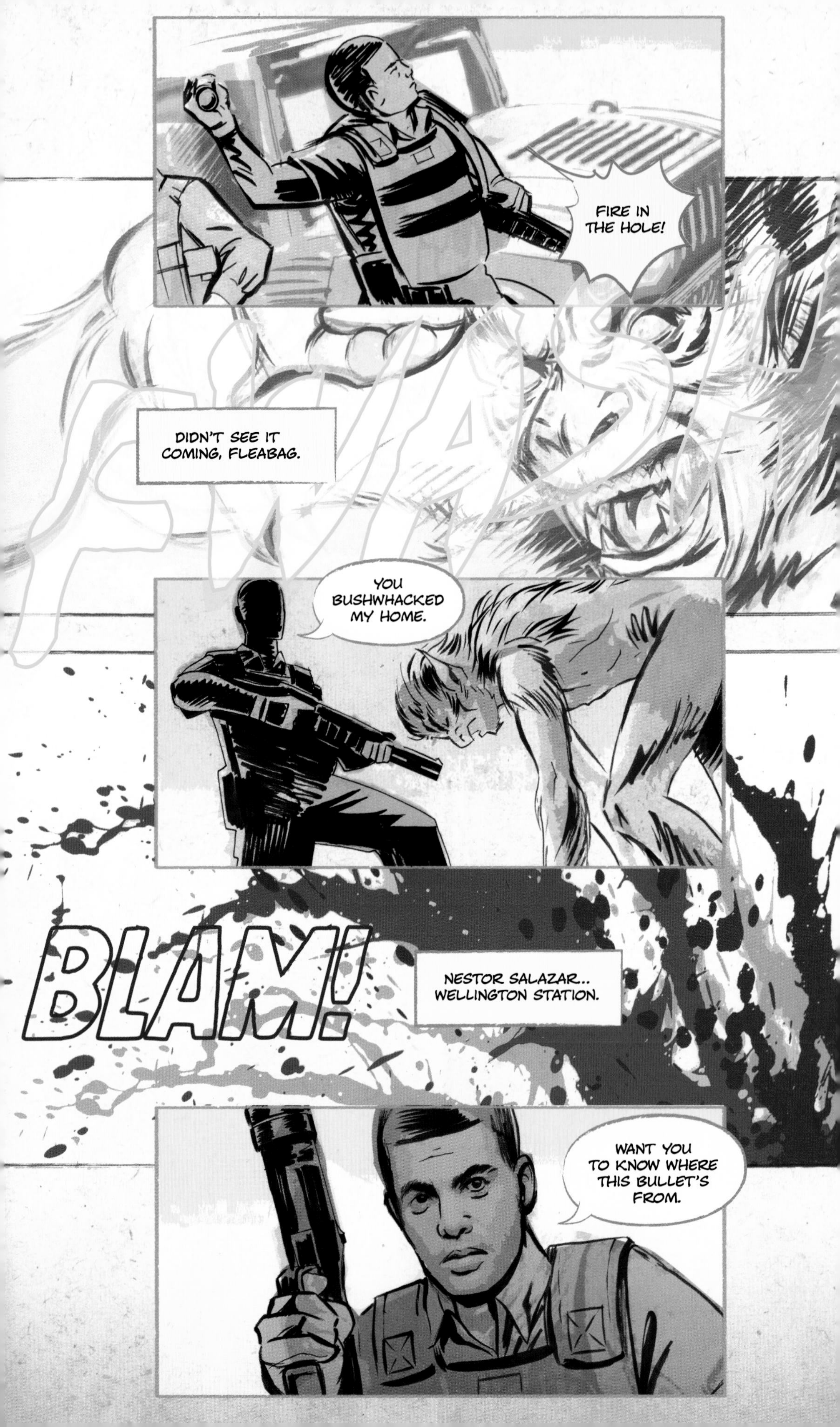

FIRE IN THE HOLE!
DIDN'T SEE IT COMING, FLEABAG.
YOU BUSHWHACKED MY HOME.
BLAM!
NESTOR SALAZAR... WELLINGTON STATION.
WANT YOU TO KNOW WHERE THIS BULLET'S FROM.

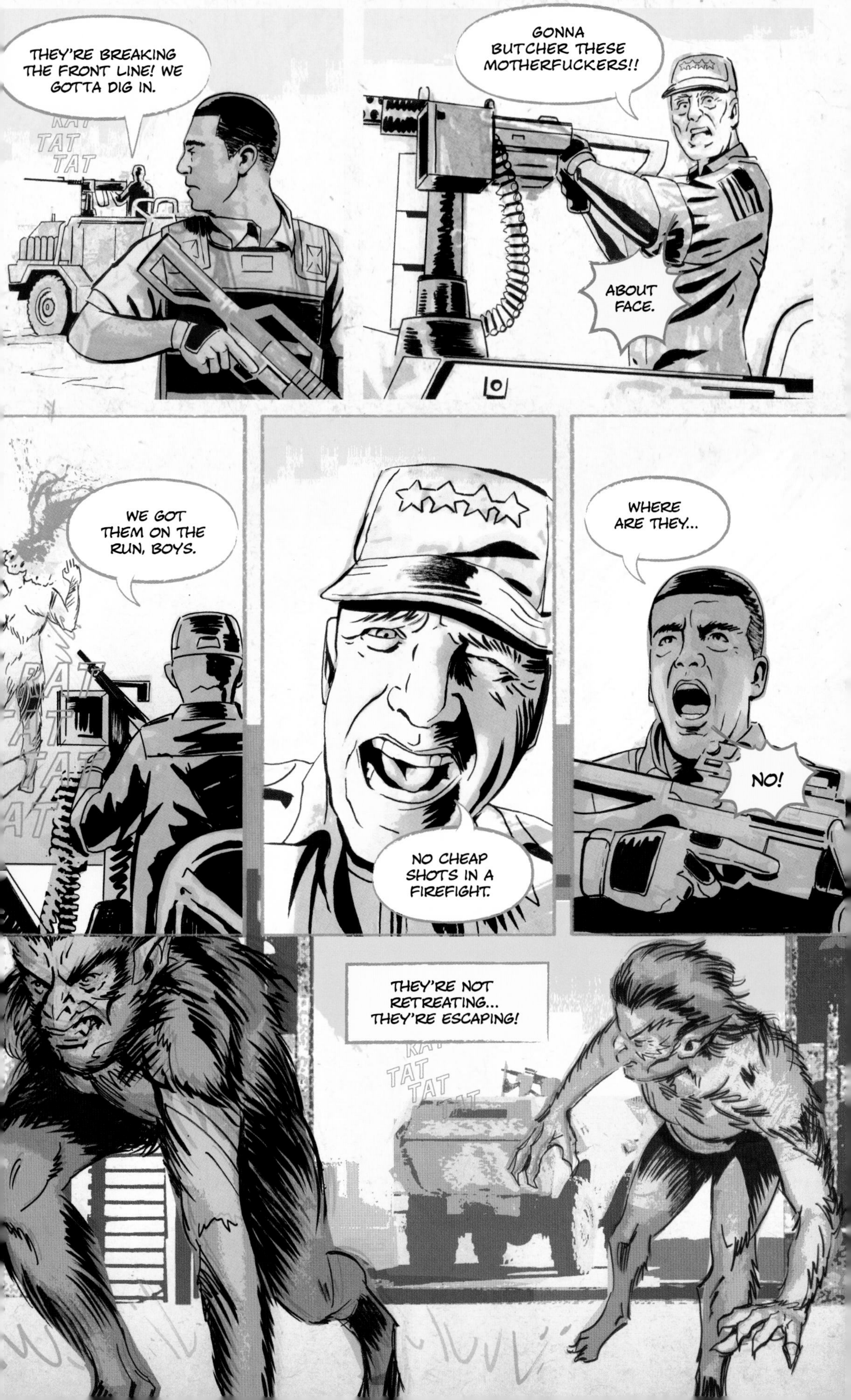
THEY'RE BREAKING THE FRONT LINE! WE GOTTA DIG IN.
RAT TAT TAT
GONNA BUTCHER THESE MOTHERFUCKERS!!
ABOUT FACE.
WE GOT THEM ON THE RUN, BOYS.
RAT TAT TAT TAT
NO CHEAP SHOTS IN A FIREFIGHT.
WHERE ARE THEY...
NO!
THEY'RE NOT RETREATING... THEY'RE ESCAPING!
RAT TAT TAT TAT

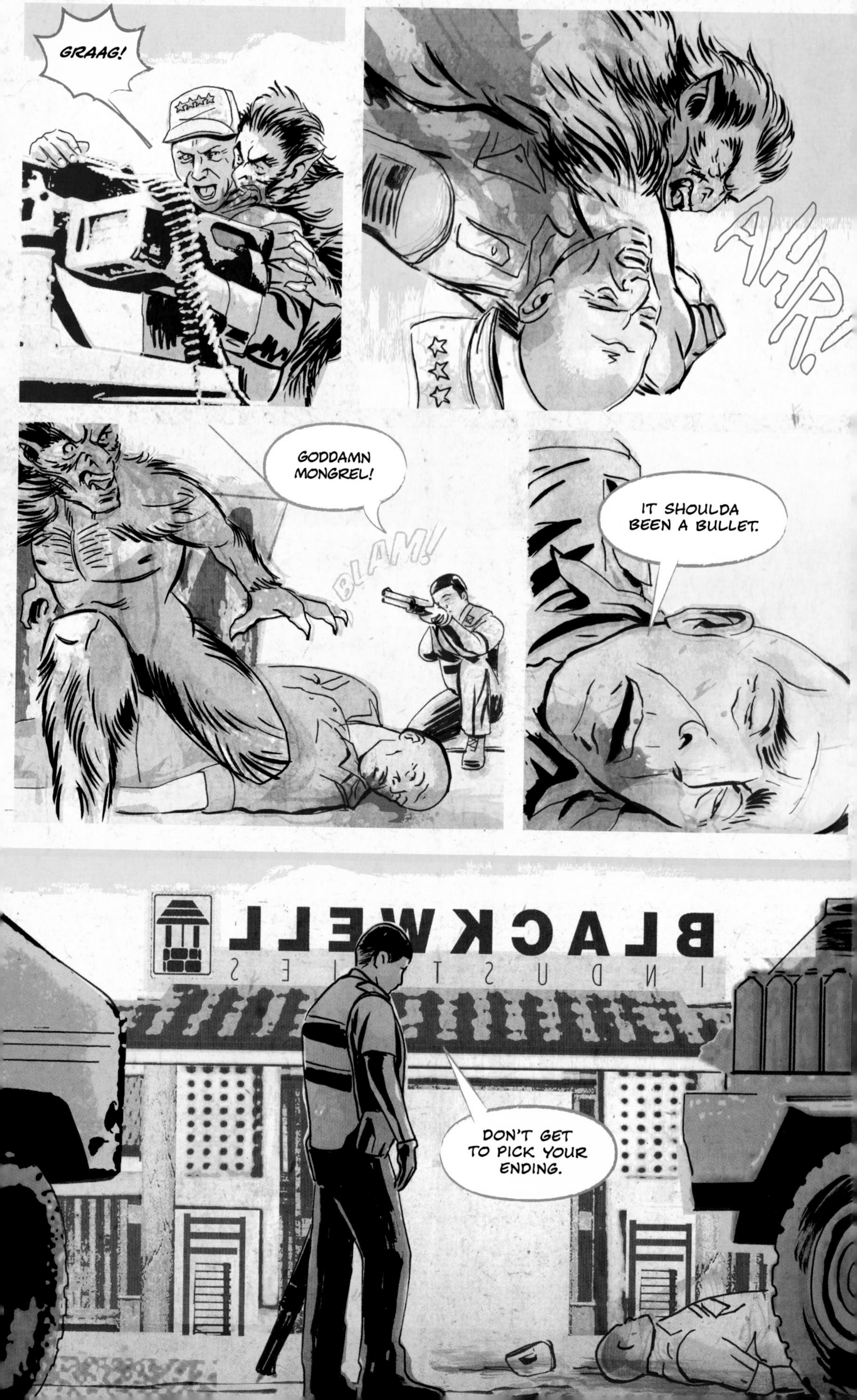
GRAAG!
AHR!
GODDAMN MONGREL!
BLAM!
IT SHOULDA BEEN A BULLET.
BLACKWELL
INDUSTRIES
DON'T GET TO PICK YOUR ENDING.

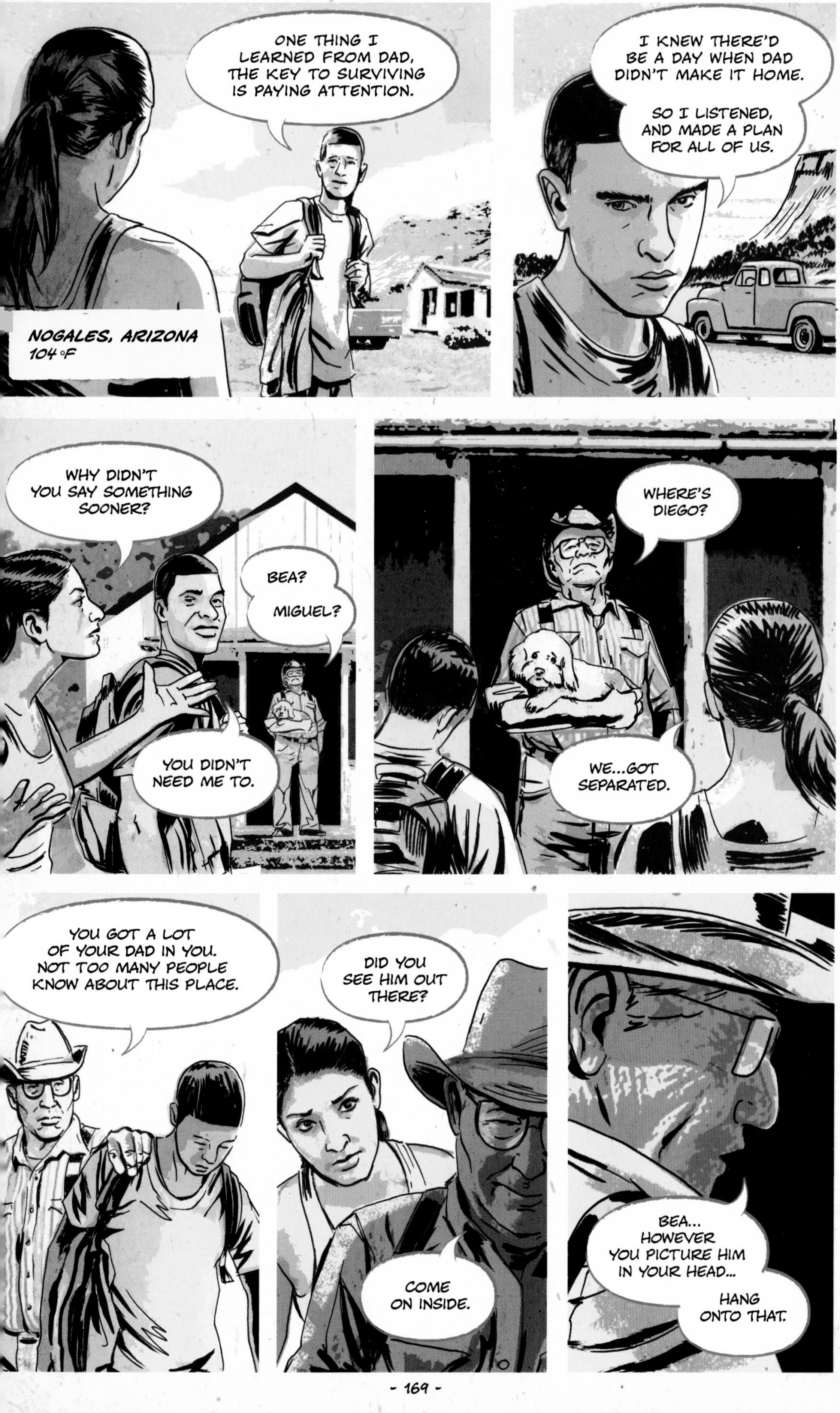
NOGALES, ARIZONA
104°F
ONE THING I LEARNED FROM DAD, THE KEY TO SURVIVING IS PAYING ATTENTION.
I KNEW THERE'D BE A DAY WHEN DAD DIDN'T MAKE IT HOME.
SO I LISTENED, AND MADE A PLAN FOR ALL OF US.
WHY DIDN'T YOU SAY SOMETHING SOONER?
BEA?
MIGUEL?
YOU DIDN'T NEED ME TO.
WHERE'S DIEGO?
WE...GOT SEPARATED.
YOU GOT A LOT OF YOUR DAD IN YOU. NOT TOO MANY PEOPLE KNOW ABOUT THIS PLACE.
DID YOU SEE HIM OUT THERE?
COME ON INSIDE.
BEA... HOWEVER YOU PICTURE HIM IN YOUR HEAD...
HANG ONTO THAT.

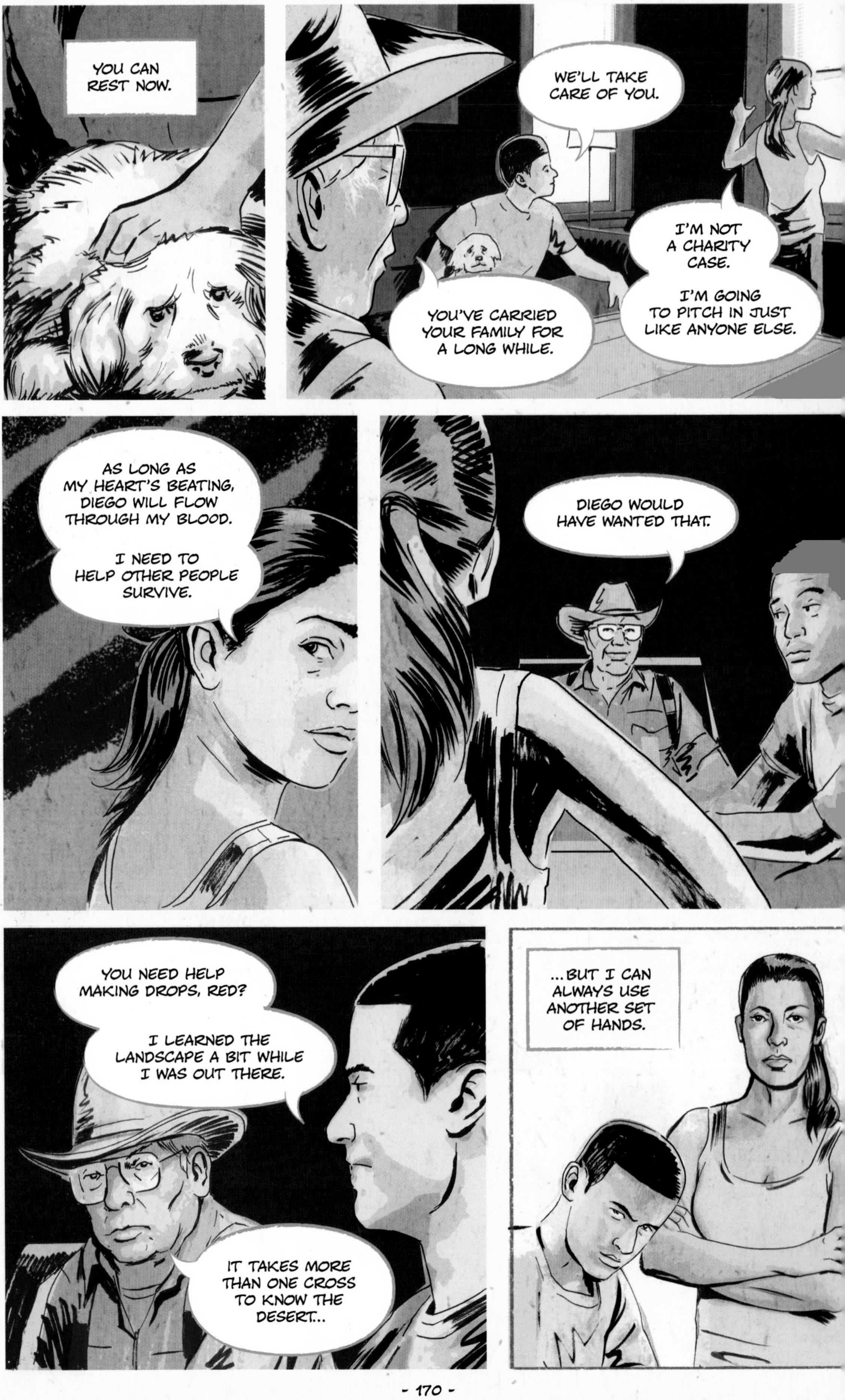
YOU CAN REST NOW.
WE'LL TAKE CARE OF YOU.
YOU'VE CARRIED YOUR FAMILY FOR A LONG WHILE.
I'M NOT A CHARITY CASE.
I'M GOING TO PITCH IN JUST LIKE ANYONE ELSE.
AS LONG AS MY HEART'S BEATING, DIEGO WILL FLOW THROUGH MY BLOOD.
I NEED TO HELP OTHER PEOPLE SURVIVE.
DIEGO WOULD HAVE WANTED THAT.
YOU NEED HELP MAKING DROPS, RED?
I LEARNED THE LANDSCAPE A BIT WHILE I WAS OUT THERE.
IT TAKES MORE THAN ONE CROSS TO KNOW THE DESERT...
...BUT I CAN ALWAYS USE ANOTHER SET OF HANDS.

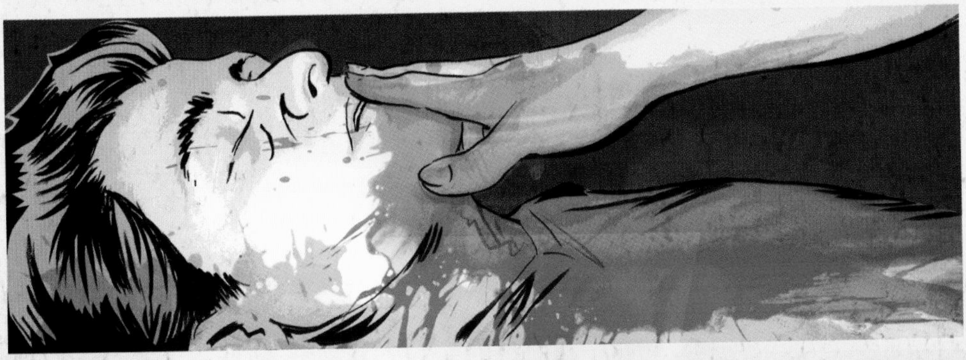

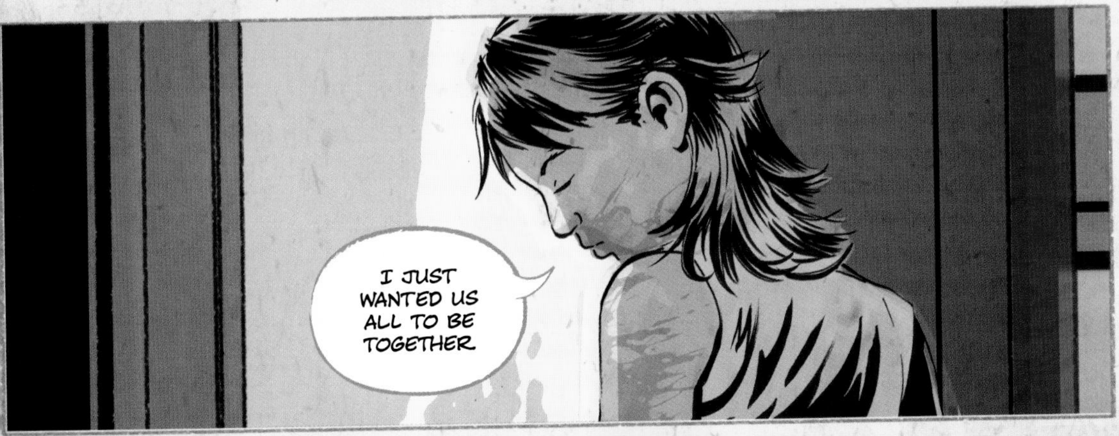
I JUST WANTED US ALL TO BE TOGETHER

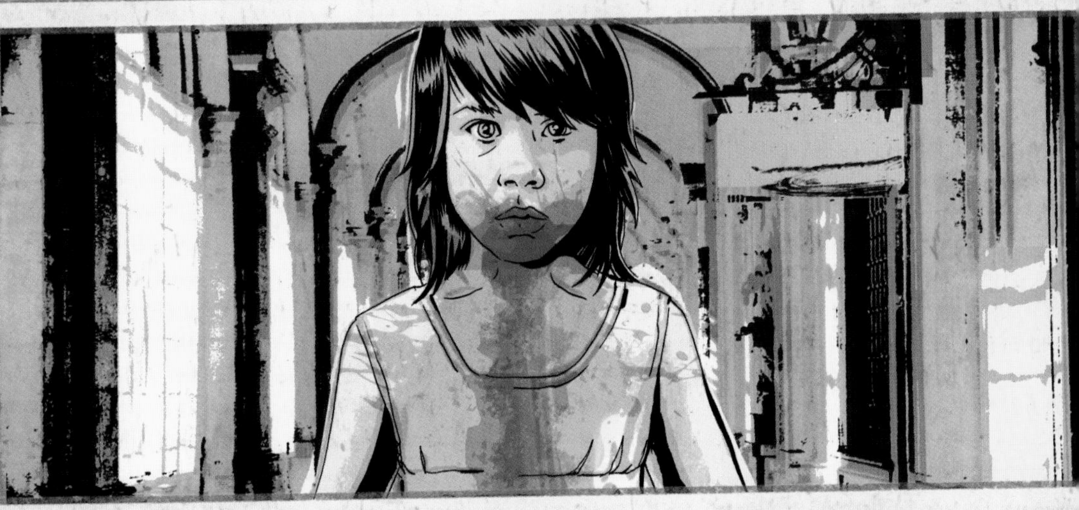

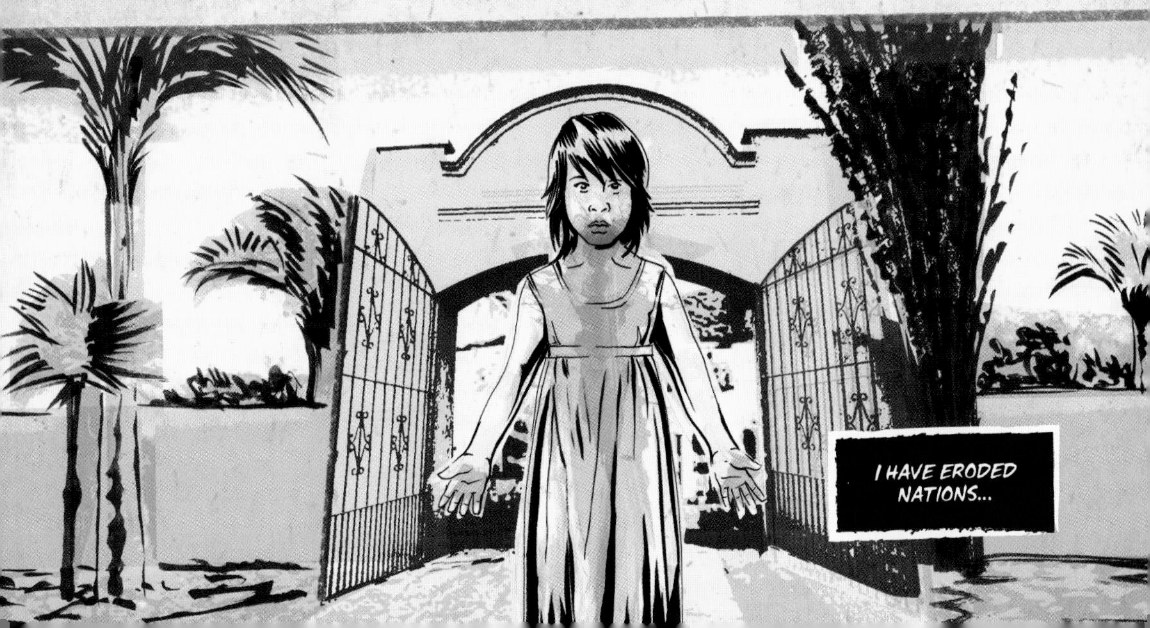
I HAVE ERODED NATIONS...

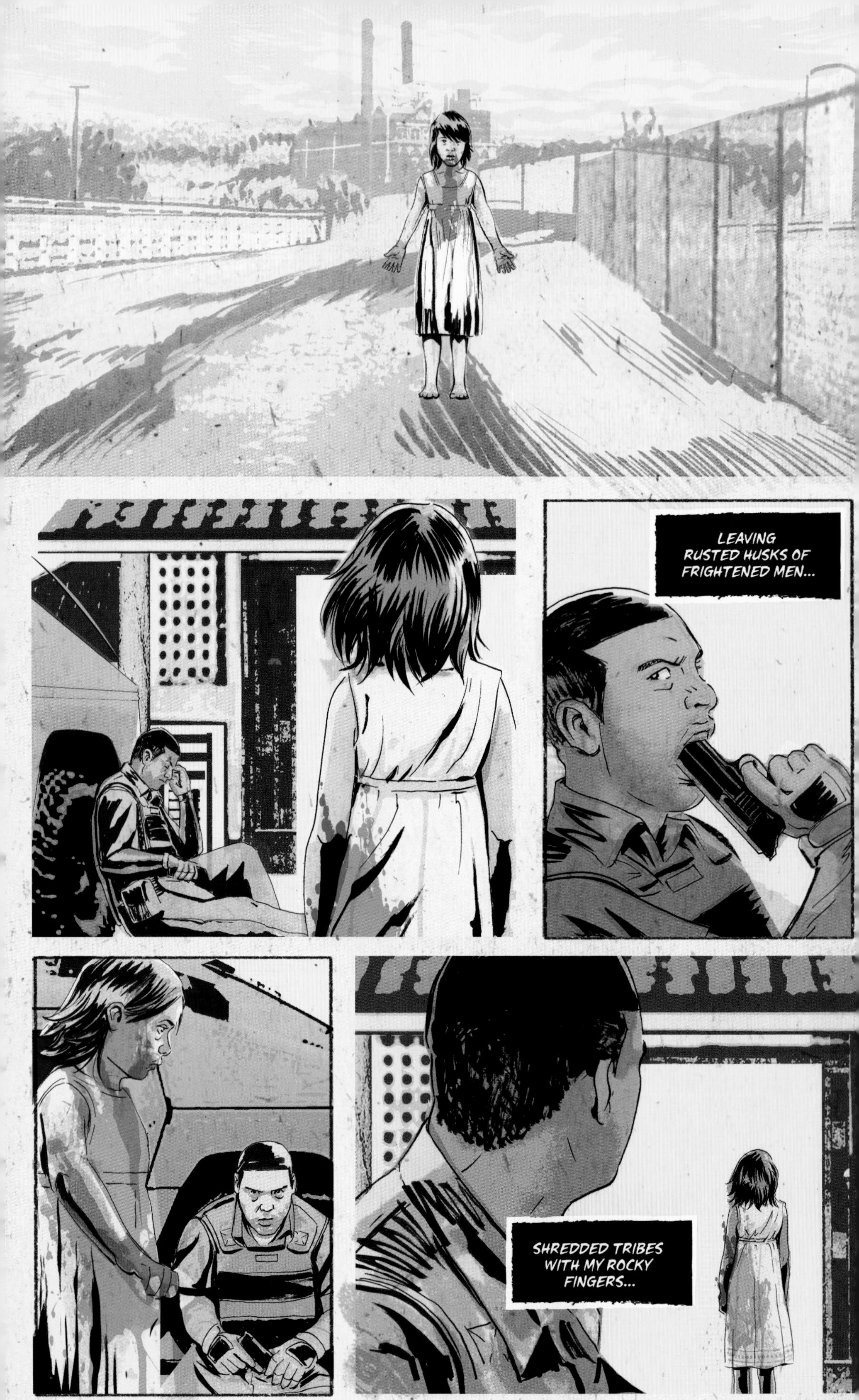
LEAVING RUSTED HUSKS OF FRIGHTENED MEN...
SHREDDED TRIBES WITH MY ROCKY FINGERS...

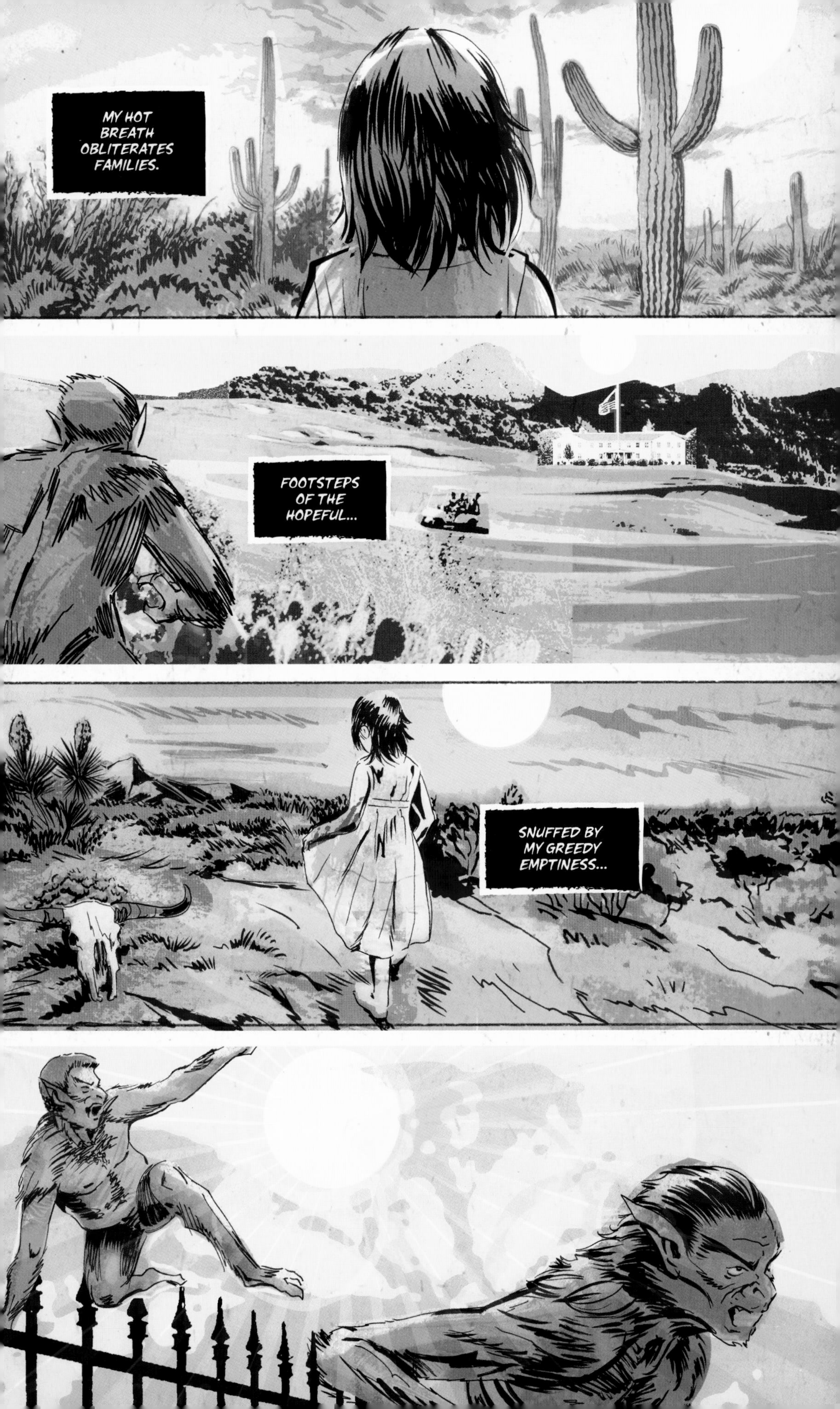
MY HOT BREATH OBLITERATES FAMILIES.
FOOTSTEPS OF THE HOPEFUL...
SNUFFED BY MY GREEDY EMPTINESS...

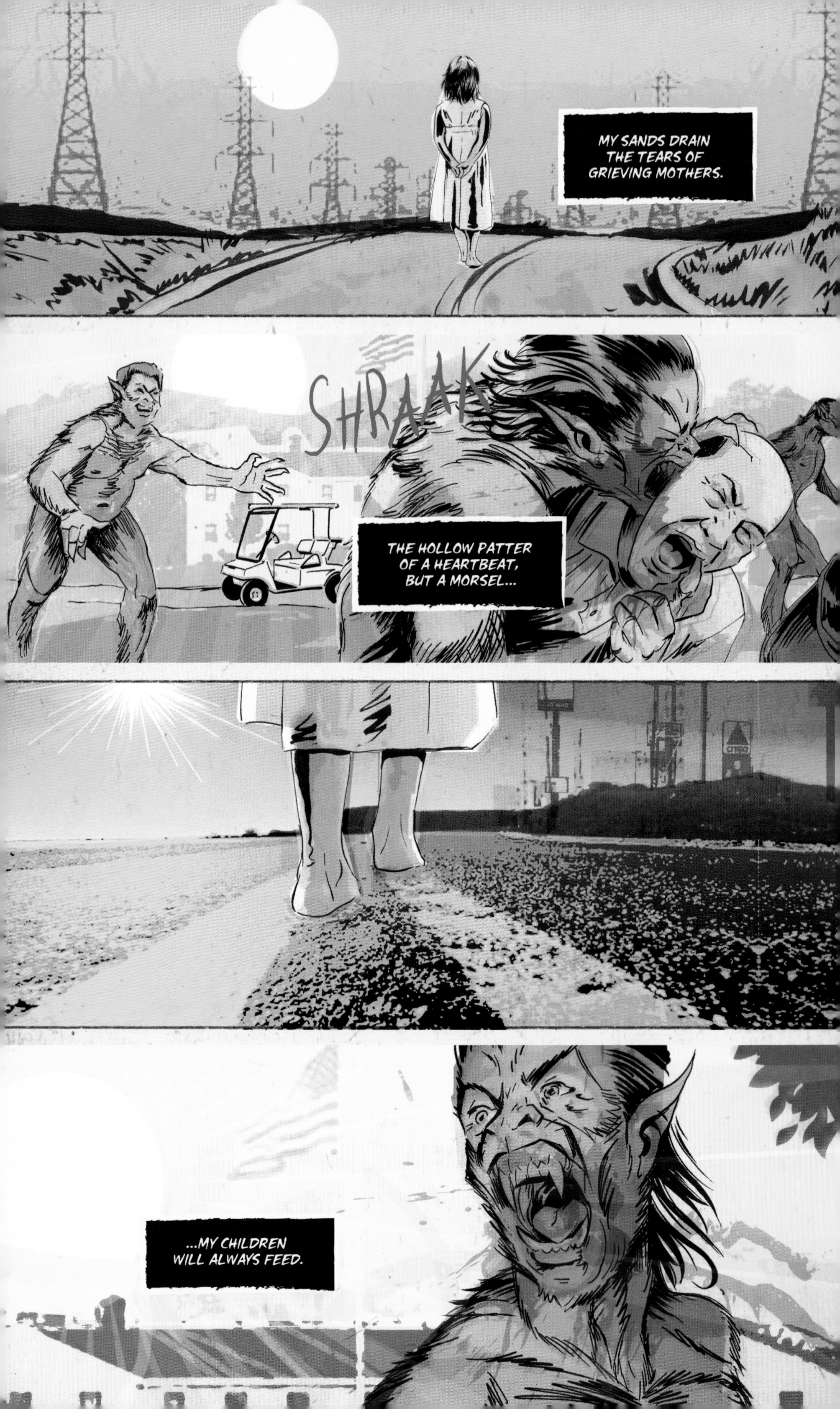
MY SANDS DRAIN THE TEARS OF GRIEVING MOTHERS.
SHRAAK
THE HOLLOW PATTER OF A HEARTBEAT, BUT A MORSEL...
...MY CHILDREN WILL ALWAYS FEED.

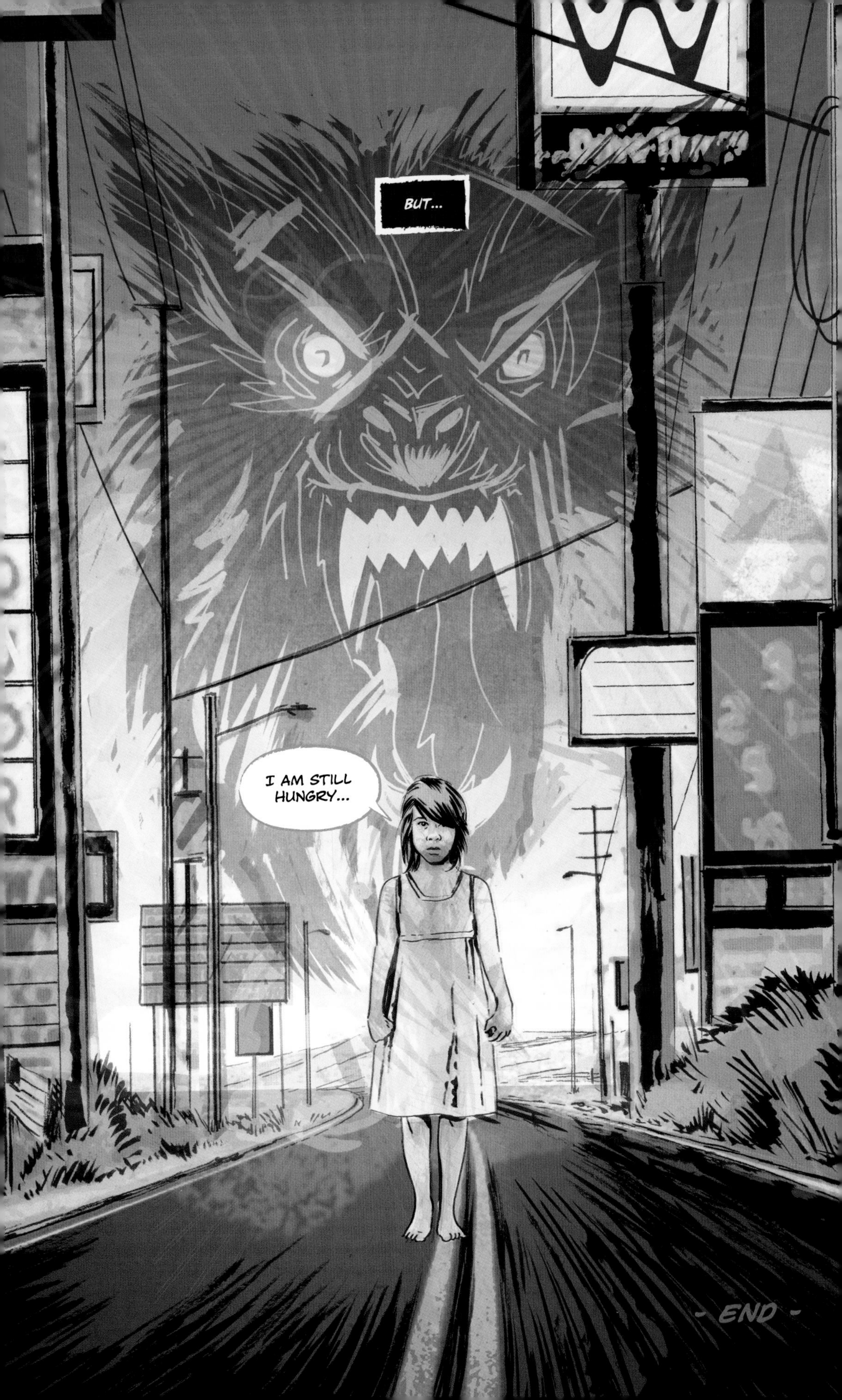
BUT...
I AM STILL HUNGRY...
- END -

MONSTERS
REAL AND IMAGINE

BY THOMAS PEYTON

FEEDING GROUND's mythology is inspired by true stories gathered along the Devil's Highway. To say I captured these firsthand would be disingenuous. Luckily, we know some truth tellers who brought the harsh reality of the Mexico/Arizona border into the sphere of our consciousness. Thomas Peyton, an extremely talented documentarian and horror fan, first planted the seed of what became FEEDING GROUND by relaying stories of his experience within the Devil's Highway. What follows are his thoughts about genre-horror's ability to convey the truly horrific.
~ Swifty Lang

A young boy's fear of monsters springs from his imagination. Unexplored, the world remains a land of shadows where boogey monsters lurk in dark closets or, as I used to fear, beneath the bed. Yet this fear is easily consoled. Turn on a light, illuminate the space, and the monster goes away.

A grown man fears monsters for a very different reason. He knows that every monster is a metaphor, a harrowing light cast upon his deepest shadows. He's aware of the horrors men commit. He's lost his innocence, and with it, the relative luxury of "imaginary monsters."

Real monsters are scarier than the imaginary ones. I've been documenting migrant deaths in Arizona for six years, and I know one thing for sure. The border is full of monsters. Real ones.

Before discussing those monsters, let's set the record straight about border crossing in 2011. There is a sadly persistent myth of the Mexican migrant hopping a fence, dashing past La Migra and starting their new life on "the other side". Nothing could be further from the truth, and this myth disregards the suffering people endure just to get here.

The Devil's Highway is a vast, barren stretch of the Sonora Desert. The road was given its ominous nickname by miners traveling the trail on their way to the 1849 California Gold Rush. Hundreds died, and those who survived would never forget traversing this unforgiving landscape, where "...frequent graves and bleaching skulls of animals are painful reminders of unfortunate travelers who died from thirst on the road."

Nowadays, crossing the border usually takes between two and five days, depending on the guide and the route. But two days is more than enough time to die, especially in the summer, when temperatures spike as high as 130 degrees and people require two gallons of water a day just to survive. Most migrants carry only one gallon of water, because their "guides" tell them it is all they will need.

Here are our "real monsters".

Many Americans are familiar with the term coyote, but the more common term used for migrants' guides is pollero,

which means someone who raises and sells chickens. Accordingly, the migrants are referred to as pollos, or chickens. Which is appropriate, because migrants are treated more like livestock than human beings.

Illegal immigration is a very lucrative business. Migrants pay anywhere from $1500 to $3000 each to cross. For polleros and their bosses this is almost always the only consideration. Say, for instance, a pollero is leading a group of ten migrants through the desert. A man twists his ankle and can't continue walking. The pollero leaves him behind to die because it's better to lose some of your profits than all of your profits. I've heard this story a hundred times.

Polleros also force migrants to pop pills, a cocktail of caffeine and pseudo-ephedrine, which can kill them, but keeps them moving. Life is cheap to the border's "real monsters".

For women, it's even worse. Stories of rape are so common that many migrant women either wait to travel with a male family member, or simply resign themselves to another "cost" of crossing the border.

If all this weren't enough, there are other monsters for migrants to contend with. Bandits often rob them along the way, which is why most migrants sew hidden pockets in their clothing for the trip across. Drug cartels sometimes hijack

entire groups of migrants, forcing them to cart 50lb burlap bundles of marijuana through remote mountain passes.

Those are the desert's "real" monsters. If there are "imaginary" monsters along the border, they aren't zombies or vampires or werewolves. They're ghosts. On average, about 200 migrant bodies are found in Arizona's desert every year. Many of these are skeletons that have laid in the desert so long, no one will ever know how long they've been there or who they are.

Last summer, while filming with a Border Patrol search and rescue team, we discovered two bodies. The first was a young mother, who took her final shelter beneath a mesquite tree. The second was her 11 year-old daughter, who had crawled about three hundred yards away once she finally realized her mother was gone. Her doll, a beautiful figure of a Mexican saint in a bright blue dress, lay on the ground next to her.

For several days, all I could think about was this young girl. She should've been worried about the boogie monster in her closet. Instead, she, like so many others, confronted "real monsters" crossing The Devil's Highway. And I, for the first time in many years, checked under my bed and slept with the lights on.

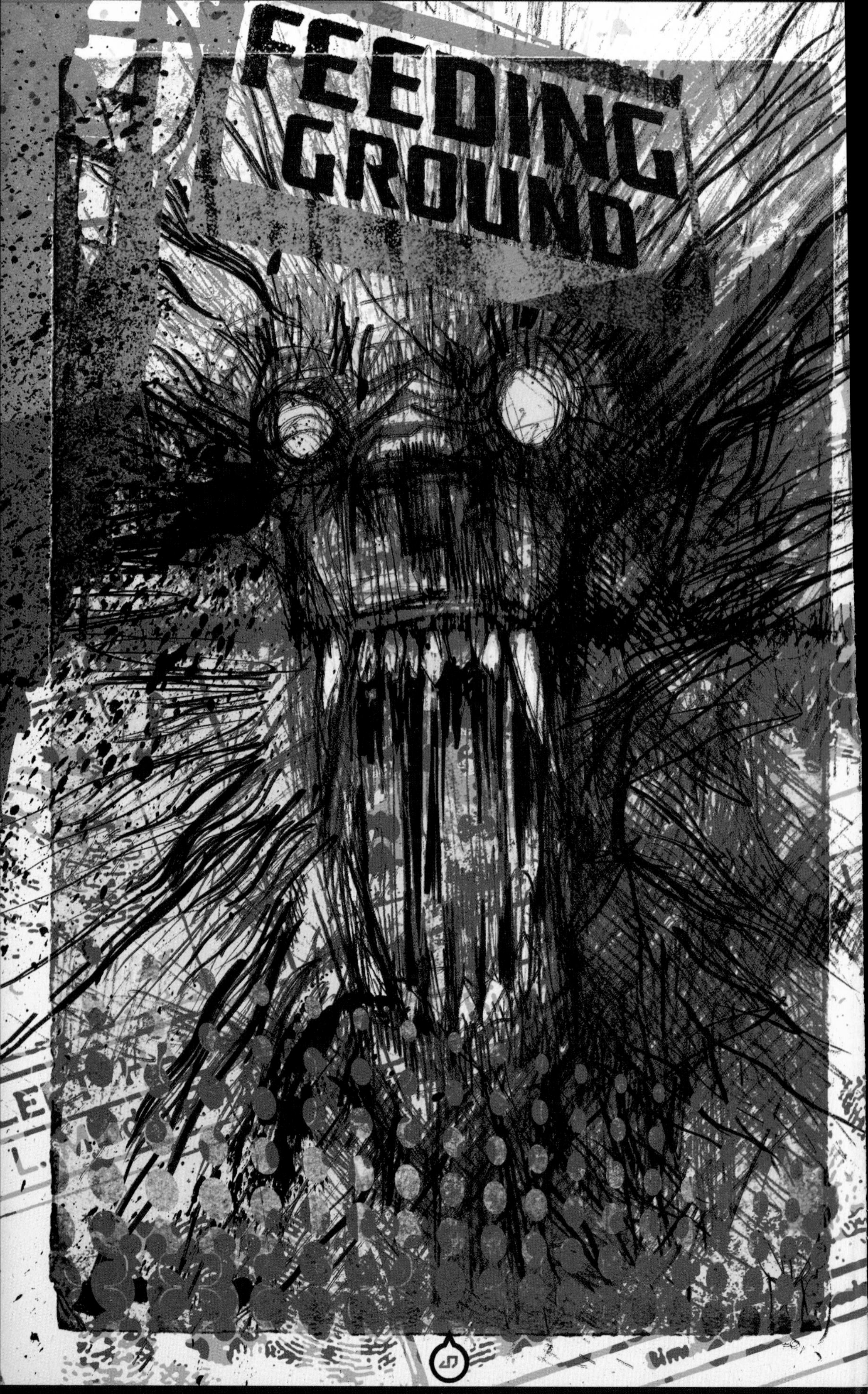
FEEDING
GROUND

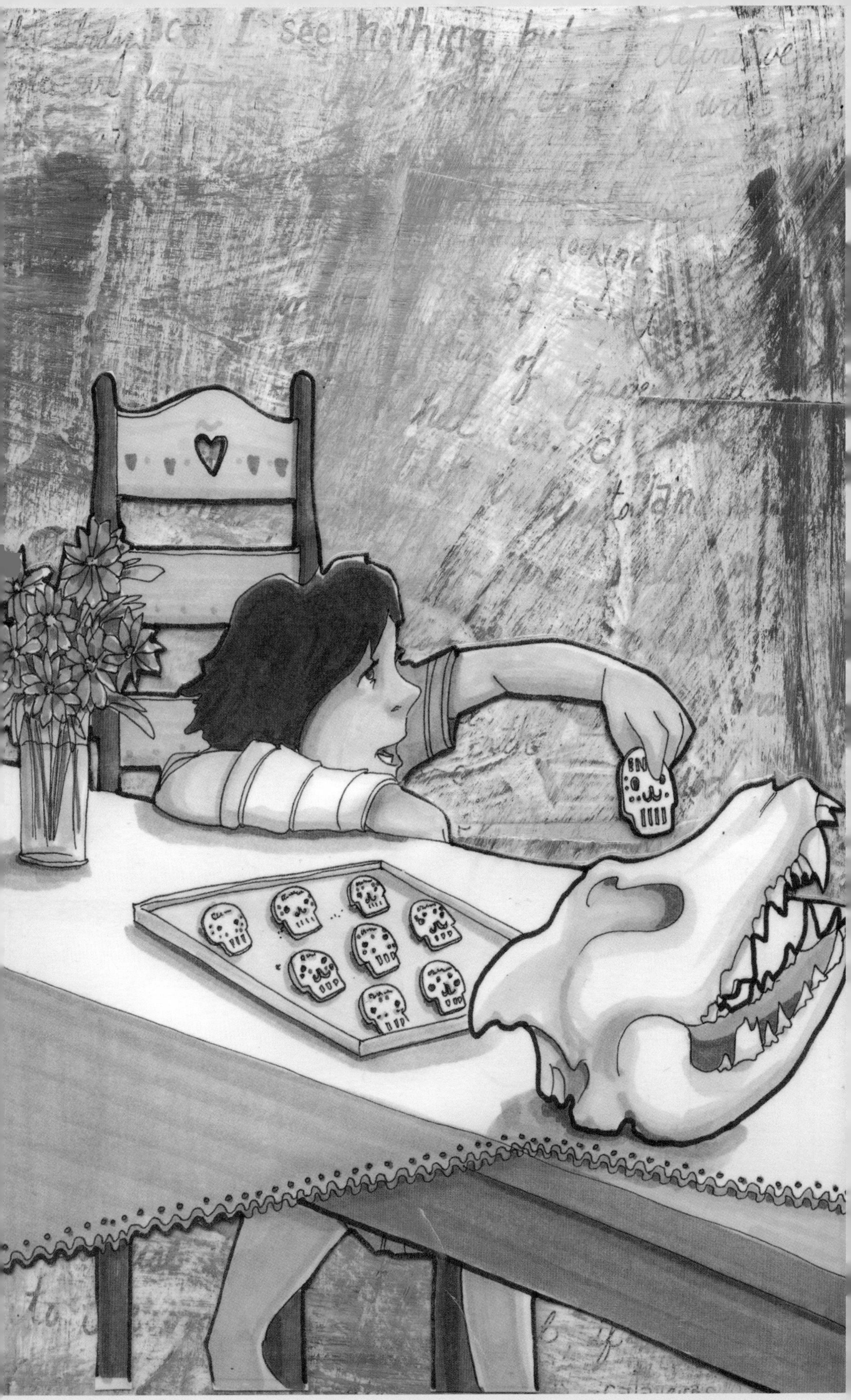

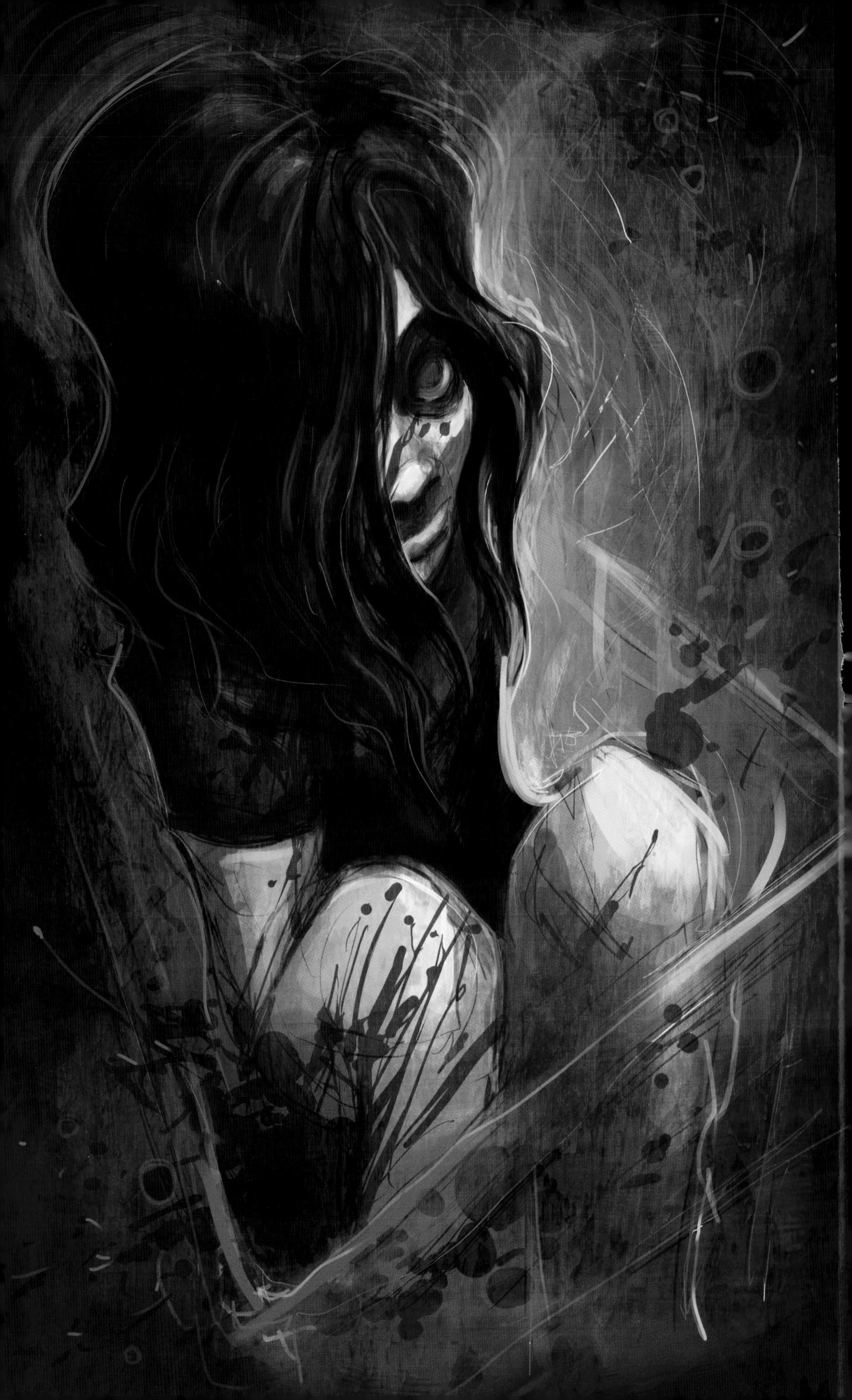

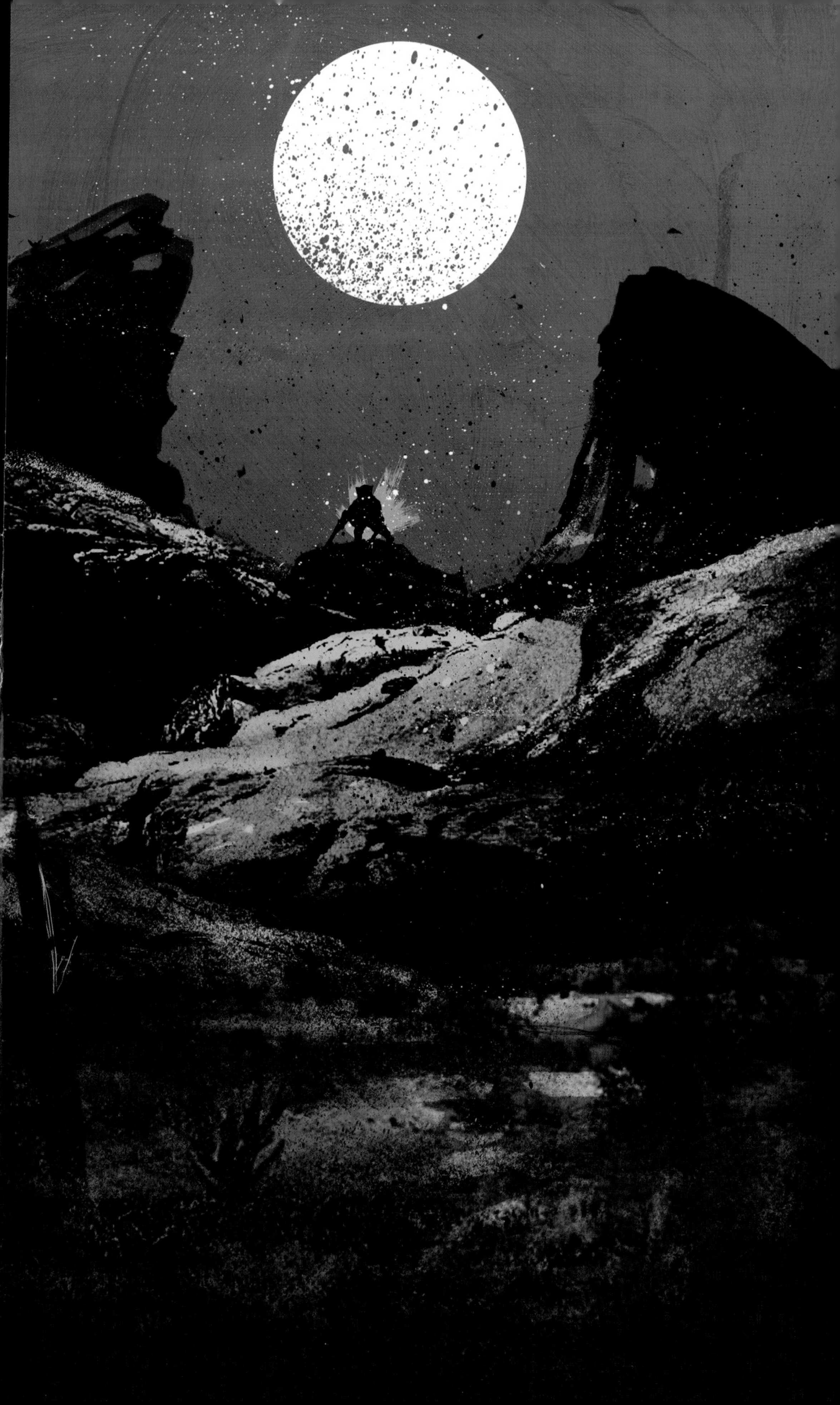

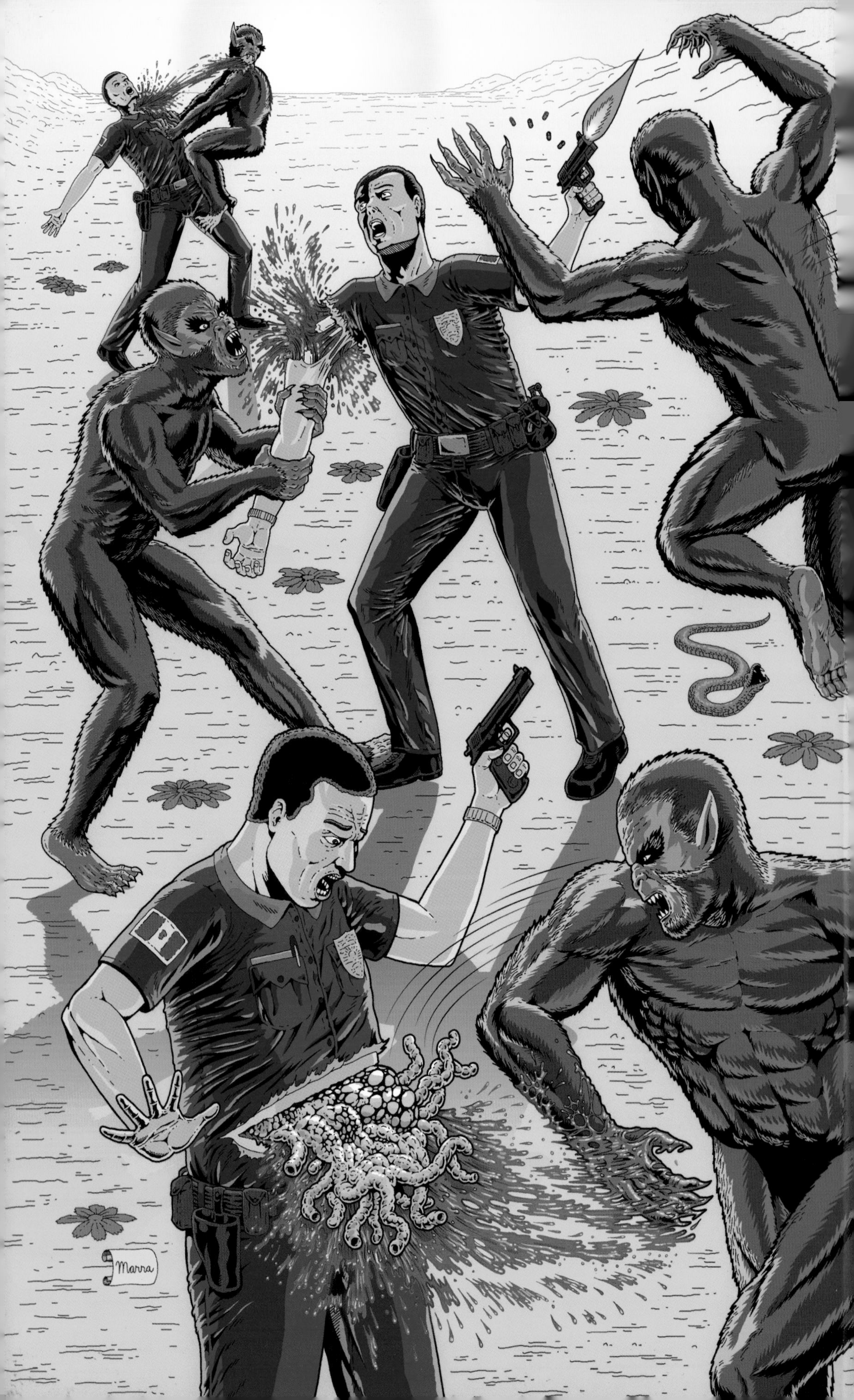
Marra

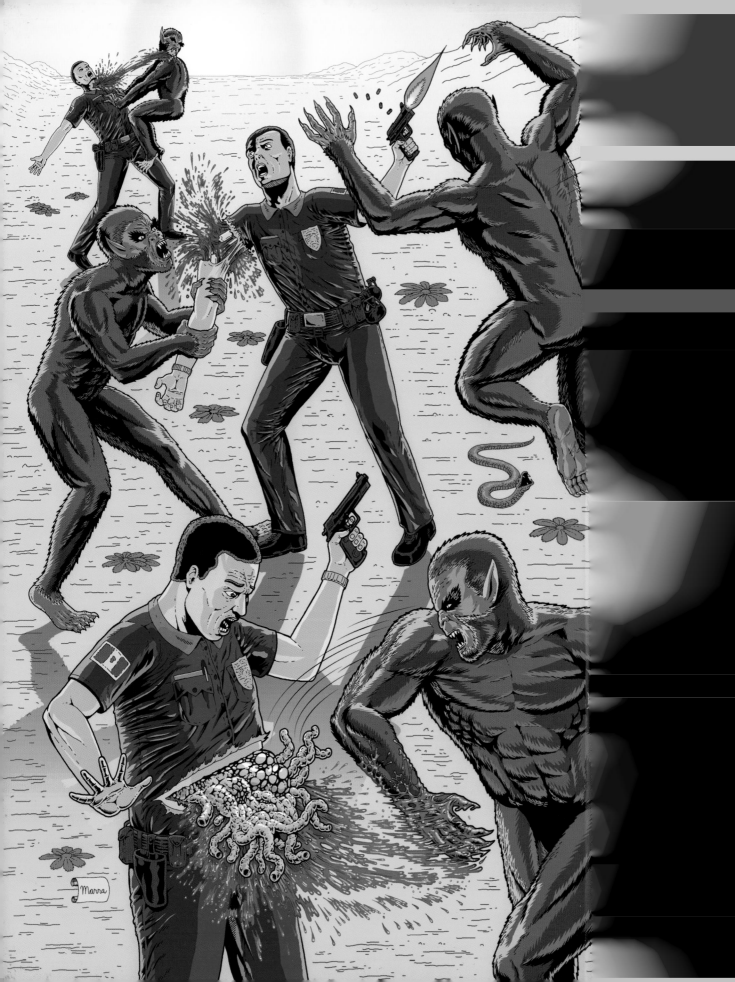

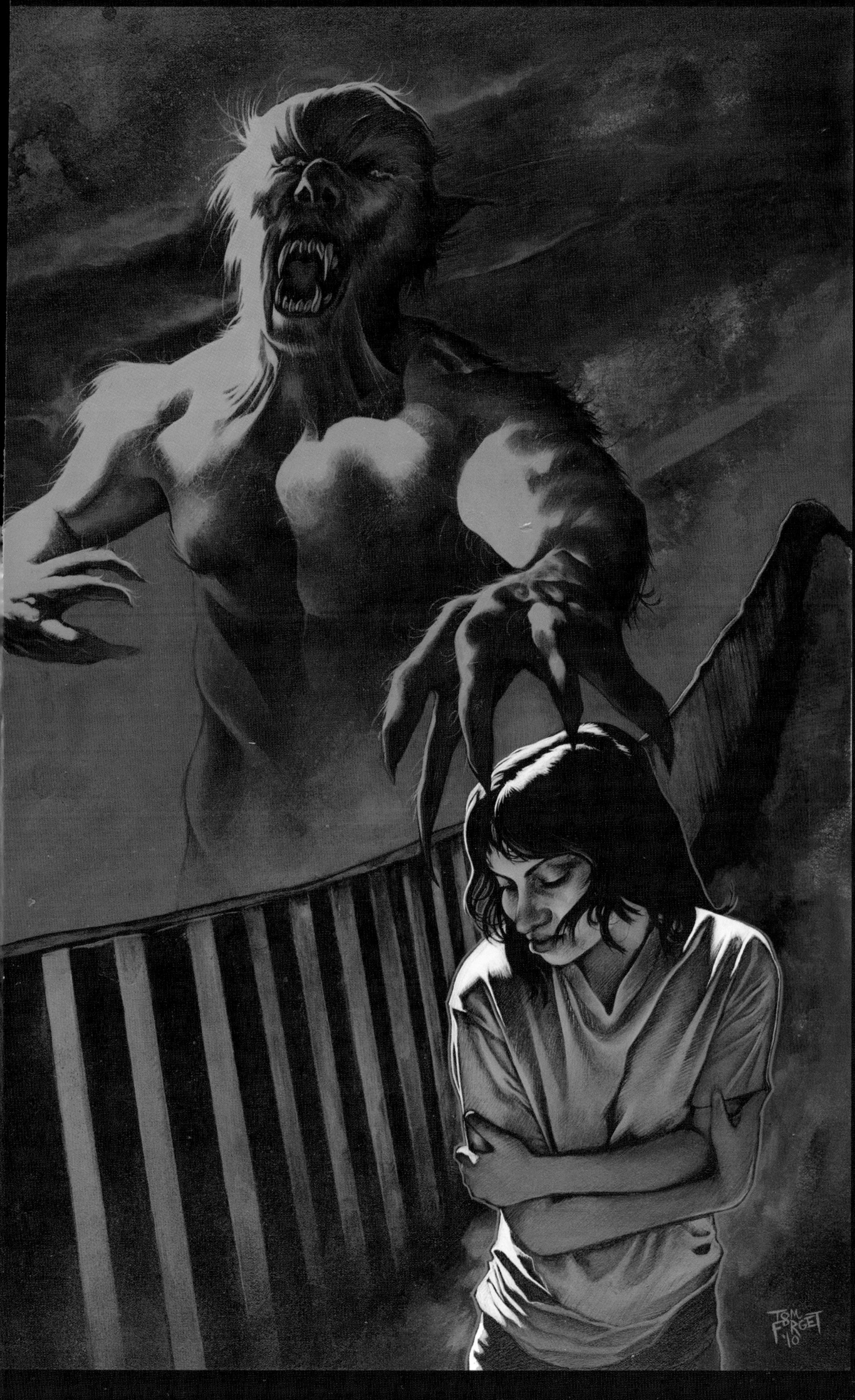
TOM FORGET '10

ABOUT THE AUTHORS

As a group, we benefited greatly from the insight and experiences of **Thomas Peyton** and **Luis Alberto Urrea**, the counsel of **Suzana Carlos**, the encouragement and camaraderie of artist **Juan Doe**, and the community of comic book creators surrounding **Bergen Street Comics** in Brooklyn, NY. Great thanks to everyone at **Archaia Entertainment** not only for recognizing our vision and taking a chance on FEEDING GROUND but also for the guidance and support to help make it stronger.

SWIFTY LANG   Follow him on Twitter - @SwiftyLang

Swifty Lang was born in Liege, Belgium and raised in South Florida. He received his M.A. in Film Studies from the University of Amsterdam. He is a reformed film critic whose writing has been featured in Sh'Ma and the Miami New Times. Swifty also went through a lot of paper writing screenplays and fiction. He began his horror fascination stealing glances into his father's medical oddity textbooks, and now has moved onto FEEDING GROUND, his first professional comic work. He calls Brooklyn, NY home.

Thanks to: My folks, Drs. Arnold & Gale, sibs, David and Samantha, Neal Mitnick, Moshe Pinchevsky, B.B., my people in South Florida, NYC, and worldwide. This is dedicated to my girl, Spooky, for listening without judgement, even about werewolves.

MICHAEL LAPINSKI   mlapinski.blogspot.com

Michael is an Art Director for the animation industry in NYC, starting as Cel Painter on *Disney's Doug*, to Lead Digital Designer on Nickelodeon's *Blue's Clues*, and then as Color Supervisor on *Teenage Mutant Ninja Turtles* with Dancing Diablo Studios. As co-founder of Uppercut Animation, he created the online boxing game *Batman Brawl!* for Warner Bros. He returned to Nick as the Art Director of *Chickiepoo & Fluff: Barnyard Detectives* and as Digital Designer on *Team Umizoomi*. FEEDING GROUND is his first professional comic work.

Thanks to Rick and Paul for the push to create my own book. Cheers to my family - to my cousin Ali for her assistance and to my parents whose generous affection has always allowed me to thrive. And, to Lindsay, thanks for adding sweetness to my life and for riding this wolf to Bayonne and beyond.

CHRIS MANGUN   www.chrismangun.com

Chris grew up in the Chicagoland area and graduated with BS in Education from Southern Illinois University in 2001. He now works as a Digital Design & Development Strategist for advertising agencies in New York where he currently lives. FEEDING GROUND is his first venture into published comics.

Chris would like to thank the following people: His father Rick, who taught him craftsmanship. His mother Kathie, who taught him how to listen to people. His sister Jenny, who opened his eyes to ideas and music at the right time. His brother Rob, the best reader he knows. His Uncle Tim, for evoking storytelling as an important part of sharing. And most of all, his best friend Mel, who believed in him through unbelievable weekends and continues to do so with kind support. Also, Pale Ale beer... that friendly spirit who sometimes helps grease the pleasant grind of so-called-life-events.

NATHALIA RUIZ MURRAY   venoozianmade.blogspot.com

Born in Caracas, Venezula, Nathalia was raised in the Big Apple. Ever fascinated by movement, she studies Kyudo, Belly Dance, Roller Derby, and Yoga. She then applies this knowledge by building puppets and making them come to life one frame at a time. This has been her first foray into translating comics.

Nathalia would like to thank Mike, Swifty and Chris for letting her be a part of this fascinating world of wolves. She is obliged to her husband Liam Murray for not complaining as she read the books aloud in Spanish (sometimes with telenovela emphasis). Mostly she'd like to thank her mother Ines Ruiz, for putting up with numerous questions on (hopefully not completely out of date) Mexicanisms and not yelling at her when she forgot an accent or two.

Thanks to Germán Ventriglia for the use of his font CAN CAN DE BOIS. And, lastly, mucho thanks to the artists who contributed their time and talents to realizing our story as the pin-up art included in the series and collected editions of FEEDING GROUND. You can find links to their work below:

Juan Doe *juandoe.com*   **Alex Eckman-Lawn** *alexeckmanlawn.com.com*   **Tom Forget** *tomforget.com*
Chandra Free *spookychan.com*   **Janet Lee** *j-k-lee.com*   **Benjamin Marra** *benjaminmarra.blogspot.com*